Architecture, Ambition, and Americans

Residence of Douglas Grant, Cedar Rapids, Ia., 1951 (Frank Lloyd Wright)

ARCHITECTURE, AMBITION, AND AMERICANS

A Social History of American Architecture

Revised Edition

WAYNE ANDREWS

ILLUSTRATED

THE FREE PRESS
A Division of Macmillan Publishing Co., Inc.
NEW YORK

Collier Macmillan Publishers
LONDON

copy (1)

The Free Press
A Division of Macmillan Publishing Co., Inc.
866 Third Avenue, New York, N.Y. 10022

Collier Macmillan Canada, Ltd.

Library of Congress Catalog Card Number: 78–50786

Printed in the United States of America

printing number

1 2 3 4 5 6 7 8 9 10

Library of Congress Cataloging in Publication Data

Andrews, Wayne.
    Architecture, ambition, and Americans.

    Bibliography: p.
    Includes index.
    1. Architecture--United States--History. I. Title.
NA705.A5 1978   720'.973   78-50786
ISBN 0-02-900770-4

Copyright Acknowledgments

Horizon Press Inc. for selections from *The Future of Architecture* by Frank Lloyd Wright.

Henry E. Huntington Library and Art Gallery for selections from *Letters of Robert Carter,* edited by L. B. Wright.

Institut Français de Washington for selections from *L'Enfant and Washington* by Elizabeth S. Kite.

Intercultural Publications Inc. for "Looking at the Latest of Frank Lloyd Wright," by the author, from *Perspectives USA 4.*

Alfred A. Knopf Inc. for selections from *Domestic Manners* by Mrs. Trollope and *North America* by Anthony Trollope.

The Macmillan Company for selections from *Robert Morris* by Ellis P. Oberholzer, copyright, 1903, by The Macmillan Company.

Maryland Historical Society for selections from issues of the *Maryland Historical Magazine,* March and September, 1934, March, 1941 and December, 1942.

Massachusetts Historical Society for selections from the *Diary of Josiah Quincy, Jr.*

The Museum of Modern Art for selections from *Mies van der Rohe* by Philip C. Johnson and *Bauhaus,* edited by Herbert Bayer *et al.*

Oxford University Press, Inc. for selections from *Survival through Design* by Richard Joseph Neutra.

Princeton University Press for selections from *Philip Vickers Fithian: Journal* by Philip Fithian.

Paul R. Reynolds & Son, 599 Fifth Avenue, New York 17, for selections from *Pragmatism* by William James published by Longmans, Green and Company.

Charles Scribner's Sons for selections from *American Scene* by Henry James and *Decoration of Houses* by Edith Wharton and Ogden Codman.

University of California Press for selections from *Greenough's Essays,* edited by Harold Small.

The University of North Carolina Press for selections from *Peter Harrison* by Carl Bridenbaugh and *Meeting House and Counting House* by Frederick Tolles.

The Viking Press Inc. for selections from *Theory of the Leisure Class* by Thorstein Veblen.

George Wittenborn, Inc., for selections from *Kindergarten Chats and Other Writings* by Louis H. Sullivan, published by Wittenborn, Schultz Inc., New York, 1947.

Frank Lloyd Wright for selections from *Genius and the Mobocracy.*

Yale University Press for selections from *Autobiography of Colonel John Trumbull* by Theodore Sizer.

For E. Λ. Λ.

CONTENTS

List of Illustrations

Preface to the Revised Edition

Where is now? This is the most embarrassing and therefore the best question that may be put to the author of any history extending down to the present. Although the argument may be made that the matter is best left in God's hands, with the understanding that He may change His mind at any moment, I have done my best to answer this question in the last chapter, displaying all the bias which I consider appropriate. Whether I am any wiser than I was a quarter of a century ago while at work on the first edition is yet another question.

However, something should be said on the very first page about *who* is dictating our now. I happen to believe that the dictator of the now of 1978 is the late John Maynard Keynes, the English economist to whom has been ascribed, at least by popular consent, the theory that government spending, undoing the damage done by the oversaving of the well-to-do, may be the best cure for a financial depression.

Keynes was a man of taste. He was also a man with a sense of humor. Whether he would be delighted with all the results of the application or misapplication of his theory is doubtful. He betrayed his sense of humor when he came, in his study of the economic consequences of the Treaty of Versailles, to consider the sin of saving.

"The immense accumulations of fixed capital which, to the great benefit of mankind, were built up during the half century before the war, could never have come about," he made plain, "in a society where wealth was divided equitably. The railways of the world, which the age built as a monument to prosperity, were not less than the Pyramids of Egypt, the work of labor which was not free to consume in immediate enjoyment the full equivalent of its efforts.

"Thus," he went on, "this remarkable deception depended for its growth on a double bluff or deception. On the one hand the laboring classes accepted from ignorance or powerlessness, or were compelled, persuaded, or cajoled by custom, convention, authority, and the well established order of society, into accepting a situation in which they could call their own very little of the cake that they and nature and the capitalists were co-operating to produce. And on the other hand the capitalist classes were allowed to call the best of the cake theirs and were theoretically free to consume it, on the tacit underlying condition that they consumed very little of it in practice. The duty of 'saving' became nine-tenths of virtue, and the growth of the cake the object of true religion. There grew round the non-consumption of the cake all those instincts of puritanism which in other ages has withdrawn itself from the world and has neglected the arts of production as well as those of enjoyment. And so the cake increased; but to what end was not clearly contemplated. Individuals would be exhorted not so much to abstain as to defer, and to cultivate the pleasures of security and anticipation. Saving was for old age or for your children; but this was only in theory— the virtue of the cake was that it was never to be consumed, neither by you, nor by your children after you." *

Here was an argument that might almost persuade a Morgan partner to dip deep into his capital. And here was an argument—Keynes might frown about this—for spending as the universal panacea. In any event, Keynes, understood or misunderstood, may have produced the world we live in, the world in which the Chase Manhattan Bank boasts a collection of modern art, a collection advertised not so long ago by David Rockefeller's reception, catered by the staff of Schrafft's Restaurants, for the artists Chase Manhattan has bought into. We are assuming that the collecting of art represents spending rather than saving, since the ultimate value of a work of art *may* not be as certain as other investments.

This should be a world of full employment—a goal no one in his right mind would scoff at—but it is also a world in which certain standards have vanished. Keynes might be amazed to learn that the latest offering by Tennessee Williams is given the serious attention our grandfathers' generation spent on a drama by Gerhart Hauptmann, or that a silk screen by Andy Warhol is treated with the reverence once paid a painting by Matisse.

And if Keynes were still with us, he might wonder about the anonymous spending of our giant foundations. The emphasis in our time is on collective judgments. The day has passed when a railroad car manufacturer like Charles Freer of Detroit took a personal interest in an artist like Whistler, or a banker like Otto Kahn listened to an appeal

* John Maynard Keynes, *Economic Consequences of the Peace* (New York: Harcourt, Brace, 1920) .

from the poet Hart Crane, or an attorney like John Quinn really cared about the survival of Eliot, Joyce, and Pound. We are familiar with the cowardly lion of the *Wizard of Oz*. We should be equally familiar with the cowardly millionaire, an art patron if you will, but so fearful of indulging his own preferences that he sets up a board of trustees. He thus avoids all personal contact with artists, but at a price. Naturally enough, the trustees are timid men, anxious to make no mistakes. Platitudes are appealing to them, originality in any form suspect. Mountains of cash are made available, now and then with admirable results. But standards have been sacrificed, even if income taxes have been slashed. All too often we regret the disappearance of the old-time individualist, whether his name be Freer, Kahn, or Quinn.

Spending for the sake of spending is certainly noticeable in the domain of architecture. We live in a time of real estate speculators, men who prey upon the cadavers of our great cities, pulling down one remarkable building after another in order to erect unwanted and unnecessary apartment houses, hotels, or skyscrapers. These buildings may not be feasible from an economic point of view, but once they go into bankruptcy, their promoters simply move on to richer game. The most that can be said is that cash has changed hands.

So Keynesian economics—how mortified he would be by all this—has been playing the very devil with the preservation movement in the United States. While we have every reason to be grateful to the National Trust for Historic Preservation, which has saved, among other buildings, A. J. Davis's "Lyndhurst" at Tarrytown, New York, and may be thankful that Louis Sullivan's Auditorium has been meticulously restored by Harry Weese and his Owatonna bank thoughtfully enlarged by Harwell Hamilton Harris, in the main our record has been lamentable.

In fact, if Paris were New York, Gabriel's Place de la Concorde would have been razed long ago to make way for a few more glass boxes by Skidmore, Owings, and Merrill. New York may be the best place to study the failure of the preservation movement. Since the last world war, the Pennsylvania Station has been demolished, Grand Central Station all but obliterated by the Pan-Am Tower, and now we are told that the Villard houses must be dismembered for the sake of another hotel.

Not that New York stands alone. In Chicago Sullivan's Stock Exchange was witlessly removed from LaSalle Street to please a speculator eager to build a nondescript pile in its place, a pile, incidentally, which could not pay its way. And in Bridgeport, Connecticut, where the kind owner of A. J. Davis's Harral house presented this Gothic treasure to the city in his will, a conceited mayor determined that a parking lot was essential on the site. Almost no one dared to stand in the mayor's way, and apparently no one in Bristol, Rhode Island, took the trouble to educate the new owner of McKim's Low house, who naïvely decided that this irreplaceable achievement was not "modern" enough for his family.

If we are to safeguard our heritage, we must rely, of course, on each and every subterfuge that the legal profession may offer us. But in the end we shall have to count on *personal* responsibility, the very element that was displayed in the last decade in the little town of Pittsford, New York. In this suburb of Rochester a certain Andrew D. Wolfe, editor-publisher of the Genesee Valley newspapers, masterminded the campaign to save the old Phoenix Hotel of 1812–14. It now serves as the head-quarters of the Wolfe newspapers besides giving Pittsford an ideal focal point. To be frank, the Phoenix Hotel is not one of the most important buildings in the United States, but it is all-important to Pittsford, re-minding its citizens of the charm that a careful student of Asher Benjamin's handbooks—we do not know the name of the architect—could impart to what was then a frontier.

But there must be an end to vituperation. What I most enjoy, when I contemplate this new edition of *Architecture, Ambition, and Americans,* is the chance to make new mistakes. The first edition was not altogether free of errors of fact or judgment. Neither is this, no matter how hard I have tried to eliminate them. Much as I admire, from time to time, the prose of John Ruskin, I have always been alarmed by that passage in *Modern Painters* in which he claims that *"there are laws of truth and right in painting as fixed as those of harmony in music. . . . These laws are perfectly ascertainable by labor and ascertainable no other way."* Dogmatic I may be in the pages to come, but I make no claim to the omniscience of Ruskin. Who knows, tomorrow may declare me wrong.

However, tomorrow cannot erase the debt I owe the late Allan Nevins, under whose auspices this book was accepted as a doctoral dissertation at Columbia University. Nor can I forget all the good advice I received from the late George Grant Elmslie, the late Talbot F. Hamlin, the late William Gray Purcell, the late Lawrence Grant White, the late William Wilson Wurster, and all the others who were of help with the first edition, including Russell Lynes and Mr. and Mrs. Harwell Hamilton Harris. This preface and the final chapter of this edition were also read with care by my friends Alan Burnham, Leonard K. Eaton, W. Hawkins Ferry, Roger G. Kennedy, G. Alden Smith, and Goldwin Smith. And finally a word of gratitude to my first editor, Simon Michael Bessie, and to my present editor, Charles E. Smith.

Almost all the photographs are my own. I must add that my negatives have been developed and my prints enlarged for over twenty years by Richard Schuler, now associated with Rasulo Graphic Service, New York. I owe him a lot.

Introduction

Though there is undoubtedly a need at the moment for an encyclopedic history of American architecture, *Architecture, Ambition, and Americans* does not pretend to tell the story of all the changes that have come over our buildings since Jamestown. For this there is a very good reason. This is a book with a theme, and themes, as you may be willing to admit, tend to become entangled with details in the best of treatises.

This is a book, not about building in America, but about architecture as a fine art. Or to put the matter more directly, this is a book about *taste*. Since the word taste means all things to all men, a definition may be in order. As I intend to use the word, taste is the record of the ambition which leads the architect to spend more time and energy than is reasonable, and the client, often but not always, to invest more money than common sense would dictate. If taste is to exercise this profound fascination, a certain prosperity must be assumed, and no misgivings entertained as to our right to enjoy the pleasures of this world. What is more, someone—either a patron like William Byrd in the early eighteenth century, a critic like Andrew Jackson Downing a hundred years later, or an architect like Stanford White or Frank Lloyd Wright—must convince a faithful audience that taste is worth while.

Much, then, will be left out that would ordinarily be included in a history of American architecture. The seventeenth century will be noticed, but not explored, since most settlers were too busy battling for survival to think of cultivating anything as esoteric as their taste buds. Folk art will be scarcely mentioned, since no one has ever accused the Pennsylvania Dutch, the Shakers, or any other group of folk artisans, of harboring worldly ambitions. There will be next to no talk of the home of the average citizen in any period, since this is a book not about average but about extraordinary buildings—those that were the last word in their time and place. No doubt the remains of Spanish civilization in the Southwest are extraordinary, but they, too, fall outside our scope, since we are primarily concerned with taste in an English-speaking environment.

Our emphasis is on *architectural* taste. The art of landscape gardening, therefore, will not always receive the attention it deserves. Nor will interior decoration be treated in detail. Finally, very little will be said about the feats of our engineers. Though our dams and bridges have unmistakably challenged the imagination of our greatest architects, anything resembling a technical discussion of stresses and strains would be out of place in a book of this kind.

Since so much has been omitted, it is only fair that something should be added. An honest effort has been made to find out *who* built what and *why*. I happen to believe that architectural history is only half told when the neatest analysis is made of the designs under consideration. I think that both client and architect are likely to be interesting individuals, and that how the client was persuaded is a story worth hearing.

Perhaps a word should be said about how I went about this book. I am a photographer, aware, as are all photographers, that the best photographs are often those that tell the best lies. So I have seen everything for myself, and the pictures, most of which I have taken, record a quest which has led me in the last thirty-eight years into forty-six of the fifty states.

The fact that I have seen everything I am describing does not mean that I have made no mistakes in judgment. Far from it. Nor does the fact that I have tried to sympathize with the last word in every era mean that I have succeeded. For instance, I might as well admit that I am not exactly an admirer of the financially successful architects of the 1920's. This may mean that I suffer from the blindness of many of the most distinguished critics. For if you will take the trouble to read over their indictment of the taste of their parents' generation, you will discover that taste was in a terrible predicament when the authors were in their teens. It only began to improve when they were able to correct the errors of their fathers and mothers. Later on, of course, it declined when the critics turned high priests found the next generation was unimpressed by their sermons.

In the United States, as in no other nation, standards of what we like to call good taste have fluctuated violently from decade to decade. This is something for which we must be all thankful. It proves that we are not easily satisfied, and then not for long. The French philosopher Henri Bergson could not avoid discussing this American characteristic when he came to comment on the work of William James. For James—and his French friend realized this—succeeded in expressing in his philosophy one of our gallant traditions. "We usually define truth by its conformity with what already exists," said Bergson. "James defines it by its relation to what does not yet exist." This meant, in spite of the natural tendency in all systems of thought for truth to look backward, that here was a man who insisted it must look forward.

Nothing, of course, could be more absurd than to claim that Americans in vast numbers have been eager to stare at the horizon discovered by William James. But it is true that our greatest statesmen have been haunted, all of them, by the notion of constant change, and it might be said that impatience was one of our native traits. Jefferson himself was restless. Writing to Madison from Paris in the fall of 1789, he argued that "no society can make a perpetual constitution, or even a perpetual law. The earth belongs always to the living generation." He went on to say that "every constitution, then, and every law, naturally expires at the end of 34 years. If it is enforced longer, it is an act of force, and not of right."

Our businessmen may have had more than a little to do with creating the sort of world in which the notion of perpetuity was greeted with less than respect. Though economic determinism may easily be overstressed, there is no denying the fact that one of the reasons for the acceptance and rejection of one architectural ideal after another in the nineteenth century was the almost uninterrupted economic advance of the nation. The masters of new fortunes naturally looked for new ways to impress their neighbors with their importance, and if we think over the results, we may agree that what has been drearily described as the battle of the styles was in reality the happy evidence of prosperity.

The more we understand the American past, the less likely we are to insist that there were periods of "good" and "bad" taste, or to condemn without a trial the strivings of architects who labored in what condescending critics have labeled "the dark ages." We may even discover— to the everlasting confusion of historians who claim that art must never be the slave of anything so mean as economics—that the most vital American architecture of any given time will usually be located in those communities where the most new money was being made and enjoyed. This is not the same thing as saying that the newly rich have always built the most interesting buildings. The newly rich in recent years, perhaps because they sense that the development of the corporation robs the individual businessman of much of his old glory, or perhaps because they feel that the income tax and other special legislation mark the end of the age of enterprise, have been less and less anxious to express their newly acquired social standing in vivid architecture.

But it must not be forgotten that the Chicago of the 1880's and '90's, surely one of the crudest of cities, is justly celebrated as the birthplace of much of what we call modern architecture. And if we look back at the Boston of Charles Bulfinch or the Salem of Samuel McIntire, we may have to acknowledge that these cities were swarming with aggressive business-men at the moment the buildings we cherish were going up. As for the Virginia of "Westover" and "Stratford," it was neither wistful nor serene, but one of the most enterprising colonies, in which alert real estate speculators, usually men of no antecedents, were bidding with undis-guised eagerness for bigger and bigger land grants.

Though it would be nonsense to pretend that the spending of a stupendous sum of money will of itself produce an architectural master-piece, it is nonetheless true that our architecture owes much to the initiative of business coming up in the world. These are the "American men of business with unspoiled instincts and untainted ideals" hailed by Frank Lloyd Wright. "A man of this type," Wright has told us, "usually has the faculty of judging for himself. . . . He errs on the side of charac-ter, at least, and when the test of time has tried his country's develop-ment architecturally, he will have contributed his quota, small enough in the final outcome though it be; he will be regarded as a true conservator."

Wright might have added that this type of businessman has often had a beneficial influence on his fellow citizens who were already established. As we shall see when we come to colonial Maryland, the exuberance in the air of an expanding—or lately expanded—economy may prompt even a family as old as the Lloyds of "Wye House" to show that they are capable of taste.

This emphasis on the role of the businessman in American archi-tecture may help us to understand one of the reasons for the premium paid on conservatism in the twenty years reaching from Woodrow Wil-son's inauguration to that of Franklin D. Roosevelt. As we all know, the individual businessman was the object of a veritable cult in the late nineteenth century; we forget, however, that this was an idolatry that died hard, surviving long after the growth of the corporation and the introduction of the income tax made it impossible for individualists of the stripe of Andrew Carnegie to attain their ends. Naturally, then, in the twenty years between the New Freedom and the New Deal many Americans were reluctant to admit that the age of elegance was over and that we were once again a middle-class nation in which an aristocracy of wealth could not be taken seriously. Was it any wonder, in the midst of this confusion, that our bolder architects were neglected in favor of their timid colleagues?

If neither the newly rich nor their immediate heirs may be said to offer the old opportunities to adventurous designers in the 1950's, their place may well have been taken by the countless Americans who have pulled up stakes and moved to the West Coast in recent years. These "displaced persons," bored by the environment of their native states, seem to be as willing to take a chance as the rising businessmen of the nineteenth century. At least that is one explanation for the phenomenal architectural development of California—certainly climate is not the only factor responsible for the experimentation rife in Los Angeles and San Francisco.

Any tourist could tell you that informality characterizes life in California. Any historian could prove that the longing for an informal existence has again and again struck foreign observers as typically American. The dream of an uncomplicated and untrammeled way of life has been denied often enough in our history, but it has been fulfilled just as frequently. It could not be suppressed even in colonial times. The Great Awakening of the early eighteenth century was certainly something more than a series of furious religious revivals; when it was all over, and the last preacher had given his last sermon, ritualism was at least momentarily so discredited that more than one God-fearing settler in the Back Parts little cared whether he listened on Sundays to a Presbyterian or a Methodist. All this was dreadful to a conscientious Calvinist like Jonathan Edwards. Tormented by the recollection of his own ecstasy on hearing that "exceedingly entertaining" thing, the "majestic and awful voice of God's thunder," he labored to restore the faith of his congregation in orthodox theology.

De Tocqueville, who met the great-grandchildren of those who harkened to the Great Awakening, noted that American society was so fluctuating as to be almost classless. Andrew Jackson Downing, who set the architectural standards for the Americans of De Tocqueville's generation, campaigned for Gothic cottages throughout the land, not merely because they were picturesque, but because their floor plans met the needs of an informal world.

"Informal," it must be admitted, was hardly the word that would have occurred to Anthony Trollope's mother. She was horror-struck by the anarchy of Cincinnati in the 1820's. "All the freedom in America, beyond what is enjoyed in England, is enjoyed solely by the disorderly at the expense of the orderly," she reported. "No one dreams of fastening a door in Western America," she complained on her return to England in 1832. "I was told that it would be considered an affront by the whole neighborhood. I was thus exposed to perpetual and most vexatious interruptions from people I had never seen and whose names were still oftener unknown to me."

As for Anthony Trollope himself, who was inclined to be a more benign critic, even he was puzzled to account for the behavior of little girls in the dining room of a Newport hotel of 1861. He was less than pleased by the gait of a child he watched escape from his presence. "Her father and mother, who are no more than her chief ministers, walk before her out of the saloon, and then she—swims after them. But swimming is not the proper word. . . . The peculiar step to which I allude is to be seen often on the Boulevards of Paris. . . . As a comedy at an hotel, it is very delightful, but in private life I should object to it."

This informal spirit that fascinated De Tocqueville and alarmed the Trollopes has not always, of course, been noticeable in our architecture. Our best buildings have been formal, impersonal, and anti-individualistic whenever the well-to-do have fancied that their world was unshakable. Such was the conviction of many of our first families in the eighteenth century, and since the American Revolution was after all a surprisingly orderly transfer of authority, the well-bred leaders of the revolt clung many of them to that belief long after the radical implications of the Jeffersonian program were evident. Later in the nineteenth century, when the children of our great capitalists came into their inheritance, they too imagined that our civilization was static and invested the money accumulated by their hyperindividualistic parents in anti-individualistic architecture.

On the other hand our best buildings have been informal, personal, and individualistic whenever our well-to-do have wondered what tomorrow would be like. Judging from the the monuments, businessmen did not think our society was sacrosanct in the forty years preceding the Civil War. Judging from the historical evidence, they were not mistaken. Those were the years in which Andrew Jackson curbed the Bank of the United States, and in which abolitionists were attacking the plantation system. As we all know, the business community has been expecting changes almost as momentous ever since the beginning of the New Deal, and again the businessman's state of mind has been reflected on the drafting boards of architects.

A backward glance will prove the truth of these statements. Leaving out of consideration the seventeenth century, in which taste, in our narrow sense of the word, was scarce, the eighteenth century has left the record of its impersonality in the plans of nearly all of its famous buildings. A house was then likely to be designed not so much for an individual as a representative of a certain social group, and the idiosyncrasies of the owner were certain to be slighted in the interest of decorum. Consider, for example, the noble outline of "Stratford," the home of the Lees in Westmoreland County, Virginia, dating from c. 1725. Nothing suggests that the Lees were gentlemen of this or that inclination; only the genuine grandeur of their pretentions is evident.

The Federal period, reaching from the 1790's to the 1820's, was equally impersonal. Thanks to the French influence in the early years of our independence, much use was made by advanced architects of such things as elliptical salons, but the plan, when all is said and done, remained as formal as in the preceding age. An excellent example is "Gore

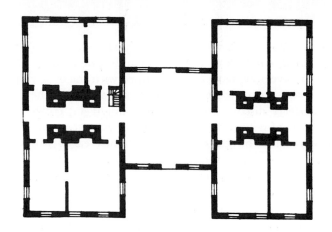

Plan of "Stratford," Westmoreland Co., Va., c. 1725

Plan of "Gore Place," Waltham, Mass., 1806

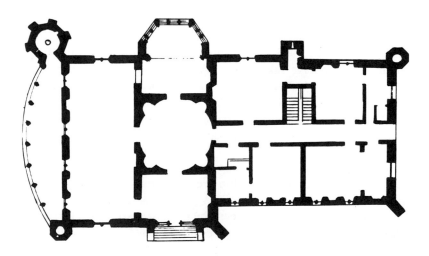

Plan of "Glen Ellen," Towson, Md., 1832 (Designer: Alexander Jackson Davis)

Place," the residence of Governor Christopher Gore at Waltham, Massachusetts, dating from 1806. In this era only Jefferson at "Monticello" may be said to have designed a house stamped with the owner's personality.

Not until the romantic decades—from the 1820's to the Civil War— did our architects discover that a house might be created for an individual instead of a symbolic businessman. Downing, who realized that this approach could be flattering to husbands eager to impress their wives, decreed that castles were just the thing for men of *imagination*. Typical of what he had in mind was "Glen Ellen," the Gothic seat of Robert Gilmor, Jr., near Baltimore, conceived by Alexander Jackson Davis in 1832. This certainly could not be mistaken for the dwelling of an average man. The irregular plan—highly informal compared with the conventional schemes of the colonial period—was obviously ideal for the entertainments the owner thought of staging. What was equally important, the crenelated towers, the gables enriched with crockets and finials, and the glorious oriel window—all these told that Mr. Gilmor was a connoisseur who had been received by Scott at "Abbotsford."

The informality of the Gilmor castle, minus the trappings of medieval romance, was recaptured by McKim, Mead and White in 1885 when they designed the country house at Mamaroneck, New York, of Jay Gould's confidential broker Charles J. Osborn. But the great patrons of the late nineteenth and early twentieth centuries on the Eastern seaboard, despite the individualism of the founders of our dynasties, ultimately demanded formal planning. One of the most beautiful examples of the formal, impersonal plan favored before the threat of the income tax is that of the James L. Breese residence at Southampton, Long Island, invented by McKim, Mead and White in 1906.

Today, when one effort after another has been made to level our world, we do not need to be reminded that the class distinctions so valiantly upheld in 1906 have vanished from American life. That personal distinctions have taken their place, that our best houses are once again designed by individuals for individuals, all this will be unmistakable to anyone who looks at the work of such modern architects as Frank Lloyd Wright or in more recent days Charles W. Moore.

Though no finials or crockets may be spotted at "Falling Water," the country house near Pittsburgh that Wright created in 1936 for Edgar J. Kaufmann, it has more in common than you might think with "Glen Ellen." Irregularity and informality are characteristic of the plans of both buildings—and both were built for very specific clients. The very same comparison might be made between the Gilmor castle and Harris' masterpiece, the Weston Havens house of 1941 at Berkeley, California.

Now that I have said something about what *Architecture, Ambition, and Americans* is supposed to contain, I should add that the only true test of the book's vitality will be the arguments it arouses. Matters of taste

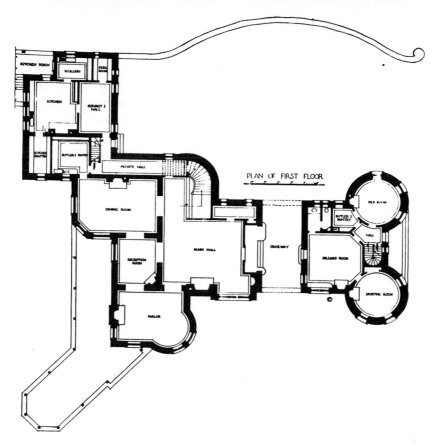

Plan of residence of C.J. Osborn, Mamaroneck, N.Y., 1885 (Designer: McKim, Mead & White)

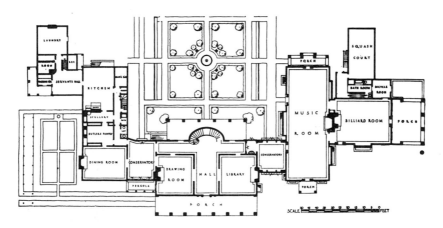

Plan of residence of James L. Breese, Southampton, N.Y., 1906 (Designer: McKim, Mead & White)

are not matters of morals, and the right or wrong of architectural trends must always be open to debate.

But I hope that no one who opens this book will greet this discussion of taste with a tantrum. A tantrum, no less, was what that estimable Whig Colonel Isaac Barré flew into, when young Josiah Quincy from Boston revealed in 1775 to his great friend in England that Harvard College Library possessed a book with pictures of the ruins of Herculaneum.

"Keep them there," Colonel Barré advised the visitor from America, "and they may be of some service as a matter of curiosity for the speculative, but let them get abroad, and you are ruined. They will infuse a taste for buildings and sculpture, and when a people get a taste for the fine arts, they are ruined. . . .

"I could not help weeping when I surveyed the ruins of Rome," Colonel Barré confessed. "All the remains of the Roman grandeur are works which were finished when Rome and the spirit of Romans was no more. . . . Let your countrymen beware of taste in their buildings, equipage, and dress, as a deadly poison. . . . 'Tis taste that ruins whole kingdoms; 'tis taste that depopulates whole nations."

It is just possible that the Colonel was guilty of exaggeration. For there has been a lot of taste in America since 1775, and no damage appears to have been done.

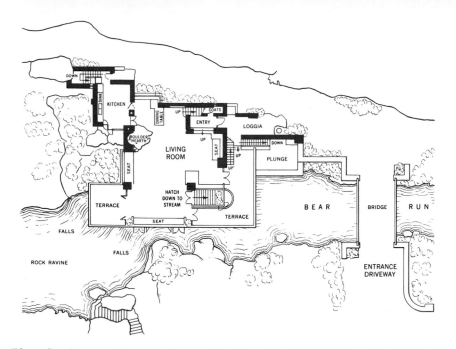

Plan of residence of E. J. Kaufmann, Bear Run, Pa., 1936 (Designer: Frank Lloyd Wright)

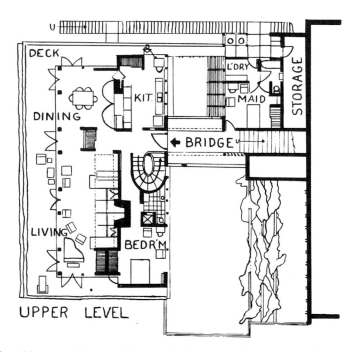

Plan of residence of Weston Havens, Berkeley, Calif., 1941 (Designer: Harwell Hamilton Harris)

*Architecture, Ambition,
and Americans*

"Le désordre est simplement l'ordre que nous ne cherchons pas."
Henri Bergson

CHAPTER ONE

The Southern Triumph: Architecture in the Southern Colonies

THE TASTE OF VIRGINIA

On that spring morning in 1607, when the *Sarah Constant,* the *Goodspeed,* and the *Discovery* touched at the site we know as Jamestown, and the first permanent colony of English settlers was established in the New World, the art of architecture in the Old World had just reached what we now consider to be one of the supreme heights. Though England was still slumbering in Gothic darkness—Inigo Jones's Banqueting Hall at Whitehall was a dozen years in the future—France was already aware of the glories of Italy, and in Italy itself the very soil of the peninsula was quick with inspiration for observant travelers. The Pazzi Chapel of Brunelleschi, the Palazzo Massimi of Peruzzi, the Villa Rotonda of Palladio, these and other buildings were as new and strange and wonderful as the tidings which Captain John Smith brought back from the bays and inlets penetrating the vast American wilderness.

It would be, however, a fatal error to suppose that any of the first colonists, even the young gentlemen whose dream of a life of ease in the New Continent dismayed Captain Smith, had any conception of or interest in the wonders of architecture. A certain Nathaniel Butler, who damned the Virginia experiment with a tract in 1622, probably told the truth when he declared that "their houses are generally the worst that ever I saw, the meanest cottages in England being every way equal (if not superior) with the most of the best, and besides so improvidently and scatteringly are they seated one from another, as partly by their distance but

1

especially by the interposition of creeks and swamps, as they call them, they offer all advantages to their savage enemies and are utterly deprived of all sudden recollection of themselves upon any terms whatsoever."

The promoters' reply was not altogether convincing. "The houses there," they protested, "were most built for use and not for ornament and are so far from being so mean as they are reported, that throughout His Majesty's Dominions here, all laboring men's houses (which we chiefly profess ourselves to be) are in no wise generally for goodness to be compared unto them. And for the houses of men of better rank and quality, there are so much better and convenient that no man of quality without blushing can make exception against them."

Though scholars acknowledge the possible survival of but one wooden house in Virginia dating from the seventeenth century, there is plenty of information respecting the homes of the earliest settlers—information so precise that it is astonishing that the myth still clouds many minds that the men of Jamestown and Plymouth Rock inhabited log cabins. As a matter of fact, the log cabin was imported no earlier than 1638 by the Scandinavians who descended the Delaware; the men and women of Virginia and Massachusetts, as soon as they were able, built in the as yet Gothic vernacular which was the tradition of the England they left behind.

At the very first, of course, the settlers of Virginia were the victims of their environment. Mere wigwams—lean-tos of poles matted with brush and earth—did for shelters, and as for the first house of God at Jamestown, John Smith has written that "in foul weather we shifted into an old rotten tent; for we had none better. . . . This was our first church, till we built a homely thing like a barn, set upon crotchets, covered with rafts, sedge, and earth, so also the walls." Crotchets, or posts with forked tops, formed the triangular ends of houses whose roofs were thatched with wattle and daub—or, to put the matter more clearly for twentieth-century readers, with a weave of hazel-bands stuffed with clay. These houses, Smith admitted, were of "far worse workmanship" than the church, which "could neither well defend wind nor rain."

Not until 1611 did the colonists think of erecting frame houses reminiscent of the half-timbered structures of rural Jacobean England. One Ralph Hamor, who published *A True Discourse of the Presente State of Virginia* in 1615, boasted that Jamestown "hath in it two fair rows of houses, all of framed timber, two stories, and an upper garret or corn-loft high, besides three large, and substantial storehouses, joined together in length some 120 feet, and in breadth 40." And in near-by Henrico, another attempt at a town, he noted "three streets of well-framed houses, a handsome church, and the foundations of a more stately one laid." Such row houses, better suited to the urban life of the Old

World than to the frontier of the New, were, of course, the exception rather than the rule.

If you remember that even glass windows were an oddity in the colonies at this time, you cannot help suspecting that Hamor was enthusiastic. More than forty years afterward, when John Hammond came to tell his version of the miracles of Virginia, glass windows were still scarce. Hammond found the cottages of the settlers "pleasant in their building . . . although for the most part, they are but one story besides the loft, and built of wood, yet contrived so delightful, that your ordinary houses in England are not so handsome, for usually the rooms are large, daubed, and whitelined . . . and if not glazed windows, shutters which are made very pretty and convenient."

Had Hammond talked with housewrights everywhere, he might have reported that the chimney was ever in the middle in the North, the better to conserve heat, while in the South, it was usually at one end. But such was the range of his travels that he did not glance beyond Maryland. The most interested, and surprisingly enough, the most candid commentator on the architecture of the region was the third Lord Baltimore, who declared that the houses were "very mean and little, and generally after the manner of the meanest farm houses in England."

If we are to see with our own eyes what has remained of the Southern seventeenth century, we must fix our attention on brick structures, since what was built of wood has largely vanished. Perhaps the most rewarding brick dwelling of the early seventeenth century still standing is that of Adam Thoroughgood in Princess Anne County, Virginia. Presumably dating from 1636, it may be not only the oldest house in the New World built by an Anglo-Saxon, but the very best evidence we possess of the highest standard of living at the time. The builder-owner was at least unmistakably ambitious. An indentured servant on reaching America in 1621, he rose to be a burgess in only seven years, and it was in his eighth year of freedom that he celebrated his standing in the community by erecting this four-room house of two rooms to a floor, the front wall in Flemish bond, the others in English. Incidentally, this may be the best moment to explain that by English bond, architects refer to courses of headers alternating with courses of stretchers, and by Flemish bond, headers and stretchers alternating in the same course.

Perhaps the first example of taste in the colonies is "Bacon's Castle" in near-by Surry County, said to have been begun in 1650 and completed in 1676. Originally of but four rooms, two to a floor, this house is extraordinary neither on account of its quasi-cruciform plan, with a porch in the front and a staircase in the rear to emphasize the pattern, nor on account of the excellence of its English bond, but because of the tremendous chimneys at either end. These are an exuberant expression of

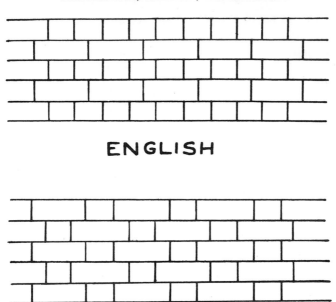

ENGLISH

FLEMISH

Flemish Bond and English Bond

the owner's yearning to brag in brick of his rise in the world, and such exuberance is the stuff of which the art of architecture has ever been made.

To rise high in the world of seventeenth-century Virginia was easier said than done. The very mention of "Bacon's Castle"—built by one Arthur Allen, it was afterward called Bacon's because overrun by his followers at the height of the Revolution of 1676—calls to mind Bacon's Rebellion and the misery which provoked the people to armed denial of the crown's rights. Galled by taxation, distressed by the damage done by the Dutch wars and the acts of trade to the all-important tobacco market, and infuriated by Governor Berkeley's indolence in the face of Indian outrages, Virginians were easily won to the leadership of Nathaniel Bacon. He marched on Jamestown crying, so an old chronicler insisted, "Come on, my hearts of gold, he who dies in the field of battle dies on the bed of honor."

Governor Berkeley himself admitted that most Virginians were so miserable they might even rally to the Dutch in time of war. "A large part of the people," he remarked on the eve of the rebellion, "are so desperately poor that they may reasonably be expected upon any small advantage of the enemy to revolt to them in hopes of bettering their condition by sharing the plunder of the colony with them."

In such a time, no wonder that mere frames with cross-slats did for beds, benches for chairs, and trestle boards for tables. Not until the end of the century did drop-leaf tables with swinging legs dignify the better homes. Whatever carving or ornamentation existed was so simple that housewives flaunted window curtains of the brightest colors against the as yet unpainted vertical boarding of their walls.

To talk of paneling, to hint the gradual use of paint, is to suggest the eighteenth century when, although trundles were still rolled under beds by day and rolled out at night to accommodate growing families, such luxuries as secretary desks with bookcases above were not uncommon, and the better American cabinetmakers were devising chests on chests worthy of mention in the history of English furniture.

Virginia itself in the eighteenth century bore little resemblance to the mean colony of the seventeenth. The most populous and the most extensive of His Majesty's dominions by the beginning of the American Revolution, it boasted an aristocracy as early as 1725. But first we must imagine the Tidewater area as it was prior to all modern communications—a lacy network of inlets and rivers which the historian John Fiske shrewdly likened to Venice. The planters dwelled close to the banks of the navigable streams down which they shipped their tobacco direct to the docks of London. Urban life was unthinkable in a land where there were almost as many harbors as plantations, and Williamsburg was never at any time a city in the sense of Charleston or Newport, but at best a seat of government that came to life only for the meetings of the House of Burgesses.

Tobacco was the crop on which the eminence of Williamsburg and the prosperity of the colony were founded. Despite the royal monopoly of the market, despite the restrictions of the Navigation Acts, despite frequent warnings that warehouses abroad were glutted, knowing settlers would grow little else.

The successful planting of tobacco required ever-virgin soil, which gave a fearful advantage to those ambitious Virginians who, early in the eighteenth century, began to lay hold of bigger and bigger stretches of the wilderness. Negro slavery, which had been nothing but a nuisance to the small farmer, was a boon to big landholders, and in the first thirty years of the new century, the number of slaves rose from six thousand to thirty thousand. This meant that over 26 per cent of the population was in bondage for life.

The big landholders who profited so splendidly from slavery, the Carters, the Lees, the Byrds, and the other founders of the first families of Virginia, were not, the truth can hardly be repeated too often, to the manner born. Modern scholarship has not only demolished the myth that Virginia was peopled by immigrants of gentler blood than other colonies, but succeeded in documenting the insinuation that the aristocrats who climbed to such heights in America stemmed as a rule from ancestors of no particular distinction in England. Though the adjective "self-made" is usually applied to the millionaires of the late nineteenth century, it might just as easily describe the barons of the Tidewater. Like their peers of 150 years later, they were not invariably scrupulous as to the means by which they acquired their property.

Since these big landholders were usually their own "architects," selecting plates out of English books to serve as models for builders and carpenters, the story of how they came to control their acres is well worth telling in a history of American architecture. If the system of headrights, under which planters were presented with fifty acres for every immigrant, free or indentured, who was transported or induced to remain in Virginia for three years, had been administered with exact impartiality, estates might not have stretched so soon to such a vast extent.

Land held under headrights was land held under absolute ownership, but this, however desirable, was only one of the available methods of appropriating tobacco lands. You might, without troubling yourself with questions of ultimate title, bid for and secure lands requiring the payment of modest quit-rents and yet be none the poorer. Now and then holders under headrights were faced, such was the uncertainty of the times, with the problem of quit-rents, too. When King Charles II presented a few of his faithful followers with the Northern Neck, a strip of five million acres lying between the Potomac and the Rappahannock, a considerable portion of which had already been acquired by headrights, the indignant settlers, once they came to appreciate the folly of questioning the royal pleasure, found it altogether to their interest to recognize facts and pay quit-rents to the Fairfaxes who inherited the domain from the King's favorites.

Much has been made of the taste of the big landholders who fared so handsomely under this economic system. No one can deny that they exercised nice judgment in building mansions in the Georgian style which Sir Christopher Wren, his senses stirred by Dutch craftsmen and his imagination fired by the French version of the Italian Renaissance, had so deeply influenced. More, perhaps, might be made of the big landholders' avarice, if the career of Robert "King" Carter, who died in 1732 worth 1,000 Negroes, 10,000 pounds, and over 300,000 acres, were examined for what it essentially represented, the rise of the first great real estate speculator in America.

Though the lines on "King" Carter's tomb tell us that he breathed his last "having discharged all the duties of an exemplary life," and remind us that "the wretched, the widowed, and the orphans, bereaved of their comforter, protector, and father," lamented his decease, the language of one of his letters to an agent in London suggests that he was not without the arrogance of one suddenly got rich. "Now, pray," Carter asked, "upon the whole, where was your prudence, or rather manners, to use with me the language that was hardly fit for your footman, if you keep one? . . . If you are so overgrown tumefied with the little success you have had in the world, I would have you vent your vanities upon those that are to be the gainers by you, and not upon your humble servant."

The son of one John Carter, who emigrated from no one knows where, possibly Middlesex, "King" Carter graced, as did his father, the Governor's Council, but was not one to sit meekly at the Governor's table. Rising to the dignity that was his as Acting Governor of Virginia in the Governor's absence, he let no one forget that he was the trusted representative of Lord Fairfax, owner under the royal grant of the Northern Neck. One of the governors was so sensitive as to be ruffled by "King" Carter's airs, murmuring that he used "several people haughtily, sometimes making the Justices of the Peace of the country wait two or three hours before they can speak to him."

"Corotoman," "King" Carter's own home, was burned to the ground in his lifetime and never rebuilt, but his architectural ambitions are superbly confessed in Christ Church, Lancaster County, in the shadow of which his ashes are entombed. Scholars have discovered what may be the inspiration of the doorways in the plates of *Palladio Londiniensis,* one of the British builders' guides of the period, but the name of the artisan who carried out the great landowner's wishes may never be known, and to single out the perfection of the Flemish bond is not to explain the mystery of a masterpiece. Here is one of the noble monuments of the American past.

No one in "King" Carter's family was the patron of a temple to compare with Christ Church, but his heirs demanded mansions that might have soothed even his temper. Typical of Carter grandeur is "Carter's Grove," begun by his grandson Carter Burwell in 1751 and finished in 1753, twenty-one years after the last brick was laid at the church. The plan of this residence fronting the James River is conventional but generous. Following the usual Georgian pattern, the great hall opens into four rooms, the latter two of which are here coupled with antechambers. Though the house has been somewhat altered for the present owner, the flankers for kitchens and services joined to the central block, the block itself deepened, and the roof pitched at a steeper angle, the exquisite paneling of the two rooms facing the James on the first floor has not been touched, and what remains is one of the great creations of colonial craftsmanship. In this instance we know the name of the builder, if not the architect. One David Minitree of Williamsburg was the workman under whose scrutiny the Flemish bond was so carefully set.

"Shirley" is simpler in plan than "Carter's Grove." Rebuilt in 1769 by yet another descendant of "King" Carter, the Charles Carter who was the grandfather of Robert E. Lee, this is in its essence merely a square brick block, four rooms to a floor, with a graceful stairwell rising in the room that does for a vestibule. North and south it is dignified by twin two-story porticoes which owe not a little to a design of Palladio, and which may or may not have been conceived by Thomas Jefferson.

The most magnificent house built by any of the descendants of "King" Carter, indeed the most magnificent house built by anyone in the colonial period, is "Rosewell," the seat of Mann Page on the bank of the York River. Now a ruin, its three stories of Flemish bond having been gutted by fire in the early twentieth century, this is still an almost perfect memorial to the poetry of extravagance. Were it not hidden from the highway by the thickest undergrowth, its survival might easily exasperate critics who praise the modesty of our colonial monuments.

A hundred years ago, honest Bishop Meade was so distressed by the sight of such splendor, even though already in decay, that when he came to the Pages in his chronicle of the Episcopal Church and its patrons in the Old Dominion, he broke into an all but Presbyterian sermon. "We do not admit," the Bishop made plain, "that anyone has the right thus to mis-spend the talent given him by God to be used for His glory, and God often punishes such misconduct by sending poverty on the persons thus acting, and on their posterity."

The Bishop was decidedly pleased to discover that "Rosewell" cost so much more than even the Pages could afford that their estate was embarrassed. "Would that this were the only example of this kind in ancient or modern Virginia!" he sighed. "How much wiser was it of the first William Randolph of Turkey Island to live in a house of moderate dimensions himself, though with every comfort, and to build during his lifetime good houses for his numerous children in various parts of the state! How much more becoming Christians, instead of building extravagant mansions for themselves, to see that the houses of worship are comely and comfortable, and that all God's ministers are provided with houses becoming their station, and [with] the means of living in them."

The Bishop might have wondered, not at the pomp and circumstance of Mann Page, but at his bravery in beginning the building of "Rosewell" in 1726, at a time when tobacco prices were depressed and cautious planters might be expected to defer all expenditures not immediately related to agriculture. However, Page was not alone in building a large house in bad times. Perhaps because the big planters enjoyed tremendous credits in London which saved them from the knowledge of economic realities, several other landholders contributed to the prestige of American architecture by erecting mansions in this depression. Both the "Stratford" of Thomas Lee and the "Westover" of William Byrd II date from this era.

Thomas Lee of "Stratford" was, as Virginia knew very well, a man whose ambition could not be curbed. The grandson of a Richard Lee whose English origins have so far baffled the genealogists, he succeeded for all that in following "King" Carter as resident manager for the Fairfaxes on the Northern Neck and as president of the Governor's Council.

"Carter's Grove," James City Co., Va. 1751-53

Staircase, "Carter's Grove," James City Co., Va., 1751-53

Finally, in 1748, he could no longer control his appetite for the unexploited lands of the Ohio Valley. Organizing the Ohio Company, he became its first president.

Only a monumental mansion could satisfy a land speculator of Lee's vision and determination. His "Stratford" evokes, on a colonial scale, the gigantic palaces conceived in early eighteenth century England by Sir John Vanbrugh. Fashioned in the form of an **H**, and fronting the Potomac on one of the choicest sites of the Northern Neck, the roof line of the seat of the Lees comes as close as any American residence to paralleling that of Vanbrugh's "Kings Weston."

Even though bricks cannot convey the solemn self-confidence of the stone and marble of which the English architect was so fond, the impersonal arrogance of the chimneys of "Stratford" suggests that no Lee would submit with indifference to what he considered an infringement of his natural rights. These natural rights were vast, as the British government learned to its cost before the American Revolution had run its course. Four of the six sons of Thomas Lee proved to be disrespectful subjects. There was William Lee, who settled down in London to do business, but found it far more exciting to court the radical John Wilkes. There was Francis Lightfoot Lee, who did not hesitate to sign the Declaration of Independence. There was Arthur Lee, who openly sided with the archrevolutionary Sam Adams. Lastly, there was Richard Henry Lee, who was proud of being Patrick Henry's accomplice.

"Westover," which William Byrd II began building in 1730, perhaps five years after the father of the disobedient Lees set his approval on the design of "Stratford," is undoubtedly more conventional in plan, for the hall, slightly off-center, divides the central block into the customary four rooms, two to each side. Nor is the brickwork exceptional. The traveler of today will stare, not at the Flemish bond, which suffers from having been painted, but at the extraordinary doorways of Portland stone, modeled possibly after the plates of *Palladio Londiniensis*. These set off the dignity of the composition to such an advantage, and tempt visitors to linger so long in admiration of the proportions of the steep roof, that the modern alterations which have reformed the layout of the interior and joined the flankers to the central block are easily forgotten and forgiven. Surveyed from the long lawn that skirts the James, "Westover" in its setting of ancient tulip poplars is more elegant, if less superb, than "Stratford." With this the Marquis de Chastellux, who passed by the estate during the Revolution, would have agreed. He was charmed by both house and garden.

No doubt because the odor of luxury still clung to "Westover" in the mid-nineteenth century, Bishop Meade was inclined to resent the high regard in which Virginians held the first owner of the estate. "Colonel Byrd," said the Bishop, "was a man of great enterprise, a classical scholar,

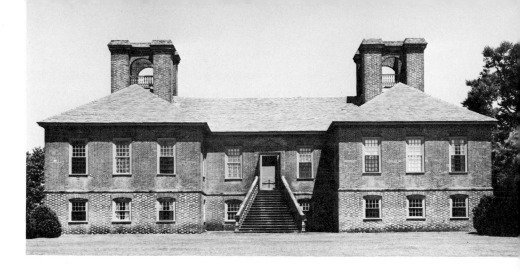

"Stratford," Westmoreland Co., Va., c. 1725

Ruins of "Rosewell," Gloucester Co., Va., 1726

and a very sprightly writer. The fault of his works is an abundance of humor and of jesting with serious things, which sometimes degenerates into that kind of wit which so disfigures and injures the writings of Shakespeare."

It was true that Byrd could be sharp when a factor in London failed to appreciate the importance of serving a gentleman of Virginia. "You will herewith receive the invoice for my family," he wrote one of his agents,

> and beg you will please to employ your interest with the tradesmen not to send all the refuse of their shops to Virginia. Desire them to keep them for the customers that never pay them. 'Tis hard we must take all the worst of their people and the worst of their goods, too. But now shopkeepers have left off their bands, and their frugality, and their spouses must be maintained in splendor, 'tis very fit the sweat of our brows should help support them in it. Luxury is bad enough amongst people of quality, but when it gets amongst that order of men that stand behind counters, they must turn cheats and pickpockets to get it, and then the Lord have mercy on those who are obliged to trust to their honesty.

As a cynical reader might suspect from the hauteur with which William Byrd II viewed shopkeepers, he was himself not too far removed from the world of trade. Though his father, William Byrd I, succeeded in the year of his death to the presidency of the Governor's Council, his grandfather was no more than a goldsmith in London, and the Byrds might never have become a dynasty if William Byrd I had not inherited the Virginia lands of a childless uncle. The Byrds were, of course, an established family by the time William Byrd II at the age of ten was sent to England for his education; no one to neglect such advantages, the future lord of "Westover" not only studied law at the Middle Temple but made friends of Sir Robert Walpole and noblemen of like consequence. Moreover, when he returned to America and the task of managing the 27,000 acres left by his father, he was never too busy to neglect his admirable library, no trifling accomplishment when you reflect that this bibliophile in the wilds ran his inheritance up to one hundred eighty thousand acres.

You could not, of course, sextuple your holdings without arousing the suspicions of conscientious public servants. It was Byrd's misfortune to raise the wrath of Governor Spotswood, who bravely but unsuccessfully strove to have him removed from the council, murmuring that the "interest and reputation of the King's Governor . . . be now reduced to a desperate gasp," and voicing the fear that "the haughtiness of a Carter . . . the malice of a Byrd . . . with about a score of base disloyalists and ungrateful Creolians for their adherents must for the future rule this province."

Fatigued by the struggle with Spotswood over the collection of quit-

"Westover," Charles City Co., Va., c. 1730

"Mount Airy," Richmond Co., Va., 1758

rents, the lord of "Westover," who came closer than any of his contemporaries to realizing the Southern ideal of English country life in the
New World, sought and found a delicate satisfaction in the quiet of his
estate. "We that are banished from those polite pleasures," he told a
friend caught up in the excitement of London, "are forced to take up
with rural entertainments. A library, a garden, a grove, and a purling
stream are the innocent scenes that divert our leisure." Unfortunately we
have no way of knowing how his taste in the art of architecture was
formed, or what building, if any, he was remembering when the time
came to lay the bricks of his Virginia estate.

We do know that Byrd was disappointed in Virginia's neighbors. "To
speak the truth," he wrote on his return from a survey beyond the southern border of the colony, " 'tis a thorough aversion to labor that makes
people file off to North Carolina, where plenty and a warm sun confirm
them in their disposition to laziness for their whole lives." The lack of
religion to the southward was equally discernible. "One thing may be
said for the inhabitants of that province," he remarked, "that they are
not troubled with any religious fumes, and have the least superstition of
any people living. They do not know Sunday from any other day, any
more than Robinson Crusoe did, which would give them a great advantage, were they given to be industrious."

Since Byrd entertained so low an opinion of the spirit of enterprise in
North Carolina, no one need be surprised to hear that there was next to
no taste in that unfortunate colony. A brilliant exception was the palace
of Governor Tryon. Completed in 1771 from designs by John Hawks, one
of the few builders who then aspired to the title of architect, this was
apparently modeled after "Newnham," the not undistinguished seat of
the Earl of Harcourt in Oxfordshire. The Governor was a really ambitious patron; his ambition was unfortunately not approved by his subjects, who fell to rioting when the necessary taxes were imposed to pay
for the fittings. The palace went up in flames in 1798 but has been
recently restored to its original dignity.

Happily for his peace of mind, no popular disorders threatened the
security of the last years of Byrd, who has left us a delightful casual
record of an expedition into the wilderness, in the course of which he
founded and laid out the present cities of Richmond and Petersburg.
"These two places being the uppermost landing of James and Appomattox Rivers are naturally intended for marts, where the traffic of the outer
inhabitants must center," he decided. "Thus we did not build castles
only, but also cities in the air."

To a Byrd, who founded cities at will, the presumption of the British
government in establishing Williamsburg in 1699 may have seemed in-
decently to interfere with the rights of a landholder. What he thought of
Governor Nicholson's ingenuity in laying out the town in the form of a
cipher made of the initials of William and Mary is not recorded. Nor do

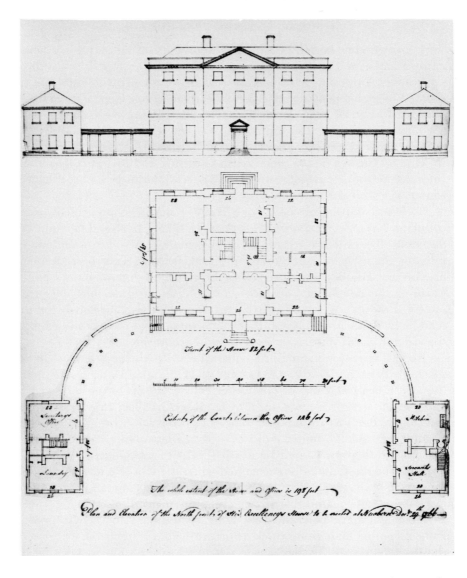

Elevation and Plan of "Tryon's Palace," New Bern, N.C., 1771 (Designer: John Hawks)

we know whether he relished the governor's insistence that every house enjoy a half-acre lot.

Possibly, however, Byrd was pleased. As Carl Bridenbaugh has reminded us in his penetrating essay on Williamsburg, eighteenth century Virginia was an orderly world. The symmetry of the great houses, with their flankers for kitchens and offices, was reflected in both the religious and the political spheres. The masters of the plantations were duty bound to serve on the vestries of their parish churches, and to watch over their interests in the House of Burgesses. So Williamsburg was the logical center of a formal society.

Such was the impression of one Hugh Jones, who published an account of *The Present State of Virginia* in 1724. "If New England," he declared, "be called a receptacle of dissenters, and an Amsterdam of religion, Pennsylvania the nursery of Quakers, Maryland the retirement of Roman Catholics, North Carolina the refuge of runaways, and South Carolina the delight of buccaneers and pirates, Virginia may be justly esteemed the happy retreat of true Britons and true churchmen for the most part, neither soaring too high nor dropping too low; consequently they should merit the greater esteem and encouragement."

According to Jones, Sir Christopher Wren was the architect of the respectable brick building of the College of William and Mary, still standing at the head of Duke of Gloucester Street. He may even have had a hand in the design of the Capitol. Completed in 1705, three years after the college, this was an imposing block of pink brick, with gracious semicircular bays on the south, crowned with a brave white cupola bearing Queen Anne's arms. Gutted by fire in 1747, it was rebuilt in 1751, but nothing but the foundations remained when the Rockefellers resurrected the original in 1928–1934. Jones found this "the best and most commodious pile of its kind that I have ever seen or heard of."

He might have paid the very same compliment to the Governor's Palace, another handsome brick structure whose restoration we owe to the Rockefellers. Its five-bay façade and five-dormered hip roof, set off by an elegant entrance of wrought iron, was completed in 1720, and again may have been designed by Wren.

But the most competent reconstructions lack what John Ruskin termed "the golden stain of time." "It is there," he felt, "that we are to look for the real light, and color, and preciousness of architecture; and it is not until a building has assumed this character, till it has been entrusted with the frame, and hallowed by the deeds of men, till its walls have been witnesses of suffering, and its pillars rise out of the shadows of death, that its existence, more lasting as it is than that of the natural objects of the world around it, can be gifted with even so much as these possess, of language and of life."

The stain that Ruskin cherished may be discovered in the countryside

surrounding the Rockefeller restoration. "Brandon," the James River seat
of Nathaniel Harrison, is an excellent example of a great house that has
weathered out the centuries. According to a charming, although unveri-
fied tradition, Jefferson himself was responsible for the subtle scheme
uniting the central block, wings, connections, and terminal buildings.
Surely this was only partly based on a plate from Robert Morris' *Select
Architecture*.

In 1758, seven years before Nathaniel Harrison thought of his retreat
on the James, John Tayloe II began "Mount Airy" on the Rappahannock.
Like "Brandon," its inspiration may have been drawn from a plate in a
book compiled by one of Palladio's English admirers, in this case James
Gibbs; less delicately balanced, it is far more formidable. Built, instead
of the brick preferred by Harrison, of a dark brown sandstone which
may have been originally plastered, its central pedimented pavilions of
rusticated Portland stone, facing north and south, recall the relentless
determination with which the first owner fought to realize his fastidious
hopes.

John Tayloe of "Mount Airy," who was rich enough to keep one of
the few private race tracks of colonial America, was not one to be content with mediocrity in either his stud or his children. In neither was he
disappointed. While American Eclipse and Henry won race after race
until they were the envy of all planters who followed the turf, the Tayloe
girls married one a Carter, another a Lee, and still another a Lloyd, who
presided over "Wye House" in Maryland, an estate whose merits no
history of American architecture may overlook.

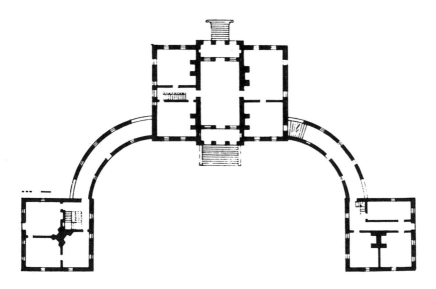

Plan of "Mount Airy," Richmond Co., Va., 1758

Philip Fithian, the Presbyterian from Princeton who tutored the children of one of Tayloe's Carter neighbors, was struck, despite his Calvinistic convictions, by the elegance in which the Tayloes were reared. No doubt he was worrying over the extravagance of "Mount Airy" and other Virginia estates when he set down in his diary that "the very slaves in some families here could not be bought under 30,000 pounds. Such amazing property, no matter how deep it is involved, blows up the owners to an imagination, which is visible in all, but in various degrees according to their respective virtue, that they are exalted as much above other men in worth and precedency, as blind stupid fortune has made a difference in their property."

No one could accuse George Washington of playing such a part, but then "Mount Vernon" was not half so ambitious as "Mount Airy." Perhaps the most candid of all descriptions of the President's seat is that of the brilliant British architect Benjamin Henry Latrobe, who removed to America not long after the Revolution. Unimpressed by Washington's prudence in remodeling an old house instead of building a new one, Latrobe was cool toward our national shrine. "Mount Vernon," he noted in his journal, "is a wooden building, painted to represent chamfered rustic, and sanded. The house is at the north end, and a study, etc. etc. at the south. The whole of this part of the building is in very indifferent taste. Along the other front is a portico supported by eight square pillars, of good proportions, and effect. There is a handsome statuary piece in the dining room. . . . This is the only piece of expensive decoration I have seen about the house, and is indeed remarkable in that respect. Everything else is extremely good and neat, but by no means above what would be expected in a plain English country gentleman's house of £500 or £600 a year."

Though the quadrant connections with the dependencies (a feature which may possibly have been copied from "Mount Airy") are not unpleasing, though this doorway may be traced to Batty Langley's *Ancient Masonry,* or that mantel to Abraham Swan's *British Architect,* neither the charm nor the scholarship of the craftsmen responsible for "Mount Vernon" are sufficiently astonishing to set any sensible visitor to quarreling with Latrobe's verdict. Yet it would be flippant to forget that our First President, who began altering his quarters in 1757, was not completely satisfied until thirty years later. Moreover, even if the proportions of many of the rooms are cramped, an occasional ceiling, like that of the dining room, is a minor triumph of the colonial plasterer's art. Perhaps Washington secretly envied the rich plaster ceilings of "Kenmore," the mansion at Fredericksburg of his brother-in-law Fielding Lewis. Perhaps he felt that Americans were entitled to recall, even if they could not equal, the ceilings invented by the Adam brothers in England.

The master of "Mount Vernon" may not have been a splendid architectural patron, but he was generous enough when it came to allowing the American public to inspect the premises. "I have," he announced, "no objection to any sober, or orderly persons gratifying their curiosity in viewing the buildings, gardens, etc." His wines, of course, he could not share with everyone. "My *particular* and intimate acquaintances . . . some of the *most* respectable foreigners . . . or . . . persons of some distinction . . . who may be traveling through the country from North to South"—these alone could sample his cellar.

At first glance "Gunston Hall," the brick home of George Mason in the neighborhood of "Mount Vernon," might seem even less architectural; merely one story high, with a gable roof pierced by dormers, its plan is unexceptional, with the customary central hall dividing the interior into four rooms, two on each side. But the lavishly carved Chippendale and Palladian rooms prove that Mason, who fought so gallantly for the first ten amendments to our Constitution, demanded a really sumptuous setting in which to rest after his struggle to guarantee our liberties.

THE TASTE OF MARYLAND

The "architect" of the interior of Gunston Hall"—if the term may be used to describe the very talented indentured servant whom Mason's brother brought over from England for this end in 1755—was William Buckland. Most of his work was done in Annapolis, Maryland, the respectable capital of the tobacco planters to the north of Virginia. Though nothing like so much money was apparently made on this side of Chesapeake Bay, taste could not be said to be neglected by the Lloyds, the Galloways, the Snowdens, the Kings, the Ridgelys, and the attorneys who solved their legal problems. Incidentally, the planters of Maryland could not be accused of stupid loyalty to the staple to which they owed their rise in the world. When tobacco turned unprofitable in the late eighteenth century, they risked their capital in grain, as did their Virginian rivals, and more than one of the aristocrats invested in iron foundries.

As for the center in which the planters gathered to watch over the legislature, it was—except for the government buildings—more pretentious than Williamsburg. For this much of the credit must go to Buckland. In 1771, when Edward Lloyd bought up the brick town house that the cantankerous attorney Samuel Chase had begun two years before, the designer of George Mason's seat was not forgotten. While one William Noke was allowed to work his will with the exterior, and the firm of Rawlings and Barnes given their chance with the ceilings, Buckland was let loose on the interior woodwork. He conceived of the quiet elegance of the deep reveals of the windows; he planned the deliberately rich carving of the dining and living rooms.

But this was not Buckland's greatest opportunity. From 1770 to 1774 he spent most of his time on the home of attorney Matthias Hammond, directly across the street. One story lower than the three-story Chase house, its proportions are far more delicate, its brickwork even less subject to reproach. Sensing that it was not only the architect's masterpiece, but one of the telling monuments of the colonial era, Charles Willson Peale painted Buckland's portrait with the plan and front elevation of this town house stretched out before him.

Covered passageways link the flankers with their octagonal bays to the central block of the Hammond house, calling to mind a Maryland plantation house in an urban setting, but no country home in the colony possesses a doorway whose delicacy so deftly relieves what would otherwise have been a simple symmetrical façade. Behind the engaged Ionic columns of the entrance, the plan is asymmetrical, and the woodwork even more superb than in the Chase-Lloyd residence.

Though the country houses of Maryland are far from insignificant, and though many of them may be compared with those of Virginia, one seat is the noblest of them all. This is "Wye House" on the Eastern Shore, the home of the Edward Lloyd who called on Buckland to distinguish his Annapolis town house.

To trace the origins of the Lloyds is impossible, for we know the dates neither of the birth nor of the death of Edward the Puritan, first of the name to inhabit Maryland, and we cannot even ascertain whether he sprung from England or Wales. An Indian trader, a planter, and a speculator in Maryland real estate, he made his home as early as 1648 on the site of "Wye House," and then, ten years afterward, sailed for England never to return. Of Edward the Puritan's grandson, styled Edward the President, we know somewhat more, for he climbed to the presidency of the council and became the father of Edward the Councilor, so named for his many years as one of the governor's advisers.

Edward the Councilor's son, Edward the Patriot—as the builder of the town house in Annapolis was titled for his services to the Revolution as a member both of the Maryland Council of Safety and of the Continental Congress—married Elizabeth Tayloe of "Mount Airy." But it would be illogical to attribute his love of luxury to his wife's family. The Lloyds, as the great baroque tombs in the family graveyard testify, had for long been inclined to elegance. Even in decay—and the urns which record the achievements of the Lloyds of the seventeenth century are near toppling—the graves confirm the legend that this was not only one of the ancient families in Maryland, but the most splendid.

The large frame house that Edward the Patriot may have erected between 1770 and 1792 is not half so commanding as the graveyard. But the orangery, which may date from 1779, and the name of whose architect we do not yet know, is in every respect worthy of the Lloyd whose sixty-ton pleasure boat mounted a battery and flew the family colors of azure and gold. Modeled after Sir William Chambers' arcade of glass and stone

Hammond-Harwood house,
Annapolis, Md., 1773-74
(Designer: William Buck-
land)

Dining room, Hammond-Harwood
house

Orangery, "Wye House,"
near Easton, Md., c. 1779

in Kew Gardens, this pavilion, with its rusticated façade and round-arched French windows, proves that Edward Lloyd was a truly difficult connoisseur.

THE TASTE OF SOUTH CAROLINA

Though no orangery fit to be considered a temple of luxury was ever erected, so far as we know, in the colony of South Carolina, the splendors of the Lloyds were not only equaled, but even, on occasion, surpassed by the town houses of Charleston and the villas on the banks of the Ashley and Cooper rivers.

In South Carolina, as in Maryland and Virginia, the art of architecture usually reflected the rise of those who rose from mediocrity in the Old World to opulence in the New, but it would be absurd to expect an exact parallel. While Maryland and Virginia were peopled almost exclusively with immigrants of British stock who came from the British Isles, South Carolina was settled not only by Britons from Britain, but by Britons who tarried first in the West Indies, and also by Huguenots driven from France by the revocation of the Edict of Nantes. And while tobacco was the staple on which the prosperity of Tidewater Maryland and Virginia was almost entirely based, South Carolina grew rich first on rice, then on indigo, and finally on cotton. The successful cultivation of these staples, like that of tobacco, invited the concentration of capital in fewer and fewer hands, but the beneficiaries of the system in South Carolina, unlike their rivals in Virginia, who surrendered the privilege of marketing their crops to factors in London, were so far from disdaining the art of bargaining that, often with the aid of members of their own families, they promoted the development of Charleston into a trading center quite beyond the imagination of Virginians. So Charleston, in whose breezes the planters sought safety in summer from the malaria of their rice and indigo fields, became, if not a metropolis, the only truly urban community of the South in colonial times.

Only 134 ships cleared Charleston harbor in 1724, but 248 docked in 1735, and the decade ending in 1739 witnessed the exportation of nearly 500,000 barrels or 100,000 tons of rice. Such was the evidence when the economy of South Carolina was centered on but one item. In 1741 Eliza Lucas demonstrated that indigo could be raised at a profit, in 1748 an act of parliament blessed her experiments with a bounty on the plant, and as early as 1749 Governor Glen shuddered at the fortunes accumulated by planters who concentrated on these two favored commodities.

"Plenty," Glen reminded the Board of Trade and Plantations in London, "is often the parent of luxury, and it will perhaps surprise your Lordships to be informed there is annually imported considerable quantities of fine laces of Flanders, the finest Dutch linens, and French cambrics, chintz, Hyson tea, and other East India goods, silks, gold, and silver lace, etc." All of which meant that Glen could not deplore in terms too earnest the habits of his subjects. "I have," he added, "always endeavored to correct and restrain the vices of luxury and extravagance by my example, and by my advice to inculcate the necessity of diligence, industry, and frugality, telling them that by pursuing these maxims, the Dutch from low beginnings climbed up to be high and mighty States, and by following contrary methods, the Commonwealth of Rome fell from being mistress of the world."

That the first families paid little or no attention to the advice of Governor Glen was eloquently advertised by the publication, not long after the Revolution, of John Drayton's *A View of South Carolina.* Drayton, who belonged to one of the local dynasties, saw no reason to apologize for the "many elegant and expensive country seats" of his peers. "At an early period," he recalled,

> gentlemen of fortune were invited to form these happy retreats from noise and bustle; the banks of the Ashley, as being near the metropolis of the state, was first the object of their attention. And here elegant buildings arose, which overlooked grounds, where art and nature happily combined. Gardeners were imported from Europe; and soon the stately laurel, and the soft spreading elm, shot up their heads in avenues and walks; while they were occasionally clasped by the yellow jasmine, or crimson woodbine. Soon the verdant lawn spread forth its carpet, contrasted with hedges, gravel walks, terraces, and wildernesses. And nature drawn from her recesses, presented landscapes, diversified and beautiful, where winds had not long before shook the trees of the forest; or savages had roamed, impatient of government and control.

Though no South Carolinian left us memories of this charmed existence to compare with the random remarks of William Byrd of "Westover," we may imagine that life on the Ashley and the Cooper was no less generous than on the James or the Potomac. No plantation worth mentioning was without its crew of carpenters, blacksmiths, coopers, tailors, and shoemakers, and the luckier Negroes might hope to become either butlers who guarded the cellars, coachmen who taught the coming generation to ride, or patroons who drilled the boat hands in the task of guiding the family barge down the river to Charleston.

A certain Charles Woodmason, who eventually turned into a frantic missionary for the Church of England in the Back Parts, was electrified by his first glimpse of the colony in 1753. Here are a few lines from a poem published by the future parson in the London *Gentleman's Magazine* of that year:

> *What! tho' a second Carthage here we raise,*
> *A late attempt, the work of modern days,*
> *Here Drayton's seat and Middleton's is found,*
> *Delightful villas! be they long renown'd.*

Swift fly the years when sciences retire,
From frigid climes to equinoctial fires
When Raphael's tints, and Titian's strokes shall faint,
As fair America shall deign to paint. . . .
Domes, temples, bridges, rise in distant views,
And sumptuous palaces the sight amuse.

Living in the larger sense was possible in South Carolina even earlier than in Virginia, and by 1714 one Thomas Broughton, one of the more ambitious Indian traders and rice planters, gloried in his exploitation of the frontier by building "Mulberry" on the Cooper River. Though this would not have been considered the last word in England, for it was Jacobean in inspiration, it was the most elaborate residence to be seen in the colonies at the time. The pavilions topped with pagoda-like roofs and cupolas, adding a picturesque accent to the corners of the square central block of English bond, may have been a reminiscence of the wings of "Hatfield House" in Hertfordshire, by then a hundred years old, but the composition is too sure and too charming for anyone except a pedant to dismiss the design as reactionary. Typically South Carolinian are the jerkin-head gables under the gambrel roof of the second story, the splaying-off of the peak of the gable with a third plane being one of the favorite devices of the carpenters who labored on the town houses of Charleston.

But it was on the banks of the Ashley, not the Cooper, that the greater number of plantation houses were erected. Perhaps the most imposing of these was "Drayton Hall," presumably built in 1738 by John Drayton, who cultivated not only rice but the good opinion of the best people and so gained admission into His Majesty's Council. Even though the gardens have vanished, and only the foundations are left of the supporting flankers, the great brick pile with its handsome two-story portico fronting the highway is still one of the superb American adaptations of the Georgian style. The plan is no less splendid than the façade, for the portico conceals an immense entrance hall, and the grand dining room on the second story is as richly paneled as the more intimate dining room on the first. It is now the property of the National Trust.

The Draytons who inherited the prestige of the builder of "Drayton Hall" faced the American Revolution with many more misgivings than the Lees of Virginia, but they were decently prominent, and William Drayton, Chief Justice of the colony, afterward served as the first judge of the United States Court of South Carolina. His cousin William Henry Drayton, who was suspended from the council for denying the right of parliament to legislate for the colonies, was also one of the first to insist that muskets alone could answer royal petulance. The president of the provincial congress, he was later chief justice under the state constitution.

The Draytons' neighbor, Henry Middleton, appeared in the first fine

"Drayton Hall," near Charleston, S.C., c. 1738

Mantel from Drayton Hall, near Charleston, S.C., c. 1738

hours to be a sincere friend of the patriotic cause, but once he realized that separation from Britain was imminent, he shrank, like many another planter, from the enormity of the deed. The grandson of one Edward Middleton who reached South Carolina after trying the climate and the opportunities of Barbados, he was the son of so rich a father and the husband of so rich an heiress that it was a surprise to no one when he became the biggest landowner of the colony, the master of fifty thousand acres and eight hundred slaves. As a member of the council he bridled when the assembly talked of offering a cash bonus to the British radical John Wilkes, yet consented, such was his amiable disposition, to assume the office of the second president of the Continental Congress. Afterward, when the British Army occupied Charleston, he swore loyalty to the British government, and possibly only the memory of his generosity to his fellow Americans in the early days of the revolutionary struggle—according to legend he equipped an entire regiment at his own expense—saved his lands from confiscation.

Of the twenty plantations owned by Henry Middleton by far the most sumptuous was "Middleton Place" on the Ashley whose gardens, even after the passing of two hundred years, are a magnificent evocation of the fever of extravagance which worked upon not only the *nouveaux riches* of South Carolina but also gentlemen of the mark of the Draytons and Middletons. The Jacobean mansion of Henry Middleton's father-in-law, John Williams, once the center of the estate, was burned to the ground in the Civil War, and so was the north flanker, but the south flanker is extant, though restored. A glance at its picturesque gables, and you may image the great brick plantation house very much as it was in 1755 when Henry Middleton remodeled and enlarged his father-in-law's far from insignificant essay in the art of architecture.

If you had the time to explore the crannies of the Charleston to which the Draytons, the Middletons, and their fellow planters repaired in summer, you might come upon an occasional trace of the Spanish concrete which was the traditional building material of South Carolina. But since no work of art was erected of this tabby—as the compound of seashells, part crushed, part burned to lime for binding, was locally named—it might be wiser in this brief summary to turn to the Charleston town house.

Built now and then of brick but more often of wood, these houses have been divided by historians into two types, the single and the double. Less pretentious than the double houses, the single houses were long and narrow, with their gable ends facing the street. Along the side was a lawn open to the southwest breeze, and usually there was a piazza as well.* As for the double houses, which were not so typical of Charles-

* The piazza, which may or may not have been an importation from the West Indies, has since become, as everyone knows, a standard characteristic of the American house in all parts of the country.

St. Michael's Church,
Charleston, S.C., 1761

Interior, St. James', Goose Creek,
near Charleston, S.C., c. 1711

ton—in fact, they could be found anywhere in the colonies—their front elevation looked on the street, and more often than not there was the customary entrance hall running through the middle.

The Charleston in which double houses were common—the Charleston of the superb and the rich—may be said to date from as early as 1725, when a company of players opened the first theatrical season with a performance of Otway's *Orphan*. Fond of the theater, Charlestonians were even fonder of the races, and by the eve of the Revolution, when the city numbered but twelve thousand inhabitants, half of them Negroes, the local race courses drew the largest crowds in the colonies. In such a world the collecting of paintings was not only tolerated but even envied, and Judge Egerton Leigh, ultimately knighted for his loyalty to Britain, is known to have created something like a sensation by displaying a supposedly genuine Veronese and Correggio.

According to one of the dustier legends of American history, the avenue to riches and elegance was barred to men of low birth in the Charleston of those days. Actually there is no evidence to support such a claim, and the career of Henry Laurens proves quite the contrary. The son of a Huguenot refugee turned sadler, Laurens married one of his daughters to a Pinckney and one of his sons to a Rutledge, neither family complaining. How could they, when he was one of the shrewdest merchants in the community, dealing with fantastic success in every conceivable commodity from rice and indigo to wine and marble mantels?

"Mepkin," the favorite of Laurens's many plantations, has been despoiled of its mansion, stopping critics from pondering his claims as a patron of architecture, but we may be sure that a man who traded so easily with Boston, New York, Philadelphia, London, Lisbon, Madrid, Rotterdam, and Bordeaux, not to mention every port of consequence in the West Indies, was worth cultivating by any builder in his right mind. Indeed Laurens was the very archetype of the aggressive American businessman whose piling up of profits, even if it has not called architecture into being, has at least spelled hope for architects willing to exploit the obvious opportunities.

Like nearly every successful American businessman before or since, Laurens looked with a cold eye on gentlemen of leisure. "I do not love to do business for a man who takes no care of his own affairs," he once remarked. "Such a man can never be a proper judge of the endeavors of his friends to serve him." Possibly he was thinking of the vagaries of his fellow Charlestonian, Ralph Izard.

Izard, who was a really elegant planter, may be forgiven for not having sacrificed his income on the altar of architecture—after all, he was the father-in-law of Gabriel Manigault, Charleston's distinguished amateur architect in the Federal period. Moreover, he was said to be the only American to keep a town house in London prior to the Revolution.

Residence of Miles Brewton, Charleston, S.C., 1769

Living room, residence of Miles Brewton, Charleston, S.C., 1769

The hatchment of Izard may be seen today in the ancient country church, presumably dating from 1711, of St. James, Goose Creek. His memorial in this opulent setting is a polite reminder that his Huguenot forebears lost no time in joining the Church of England. Educated in one of the British public schools, young Izard did not return to America until he was in his twenties; he then took a De Lancey of New York for his bride and in 1771 sailed for England with every intention of spending the rest of his life on the edge of the continent he so evidently adored. Yet he was occasionally disappointed in Europe, as when he observed, while sitting in Rome for his and his wife's portrait by Copley, that "the music in this country has not answered my expectation. . . . I am persuaded that, all Italy united, could not produce such a concert as Bach's." * As an ambassador—he was appointed our commissioner to the court of the Grand Duke of Tuscany in 1775—he was something less than successful, perhaps because he suffered so keenly from a fashionable ailment. "The anxiety of his mind at the then disastrous condition of his country," one of his admirers has written, "brought on a dreadful fit of the gout, which threatened his life, and confined him, in a state of helplessness, for several months to his bed." Recovering on the lawn of his plantation "The Elms" on the Cooper River, he dedicated the rest of his days to freeing his native land from what he fancied was the menace of an American nobility.

In Charleston Izard could not have been offended by the architecture of St. Michael's Church, even though he could never have mistaken its design, as did later Charlestonians, for the work of James Gibbs. Perhaps the only monumental church in America at the time of its completion in 1761, this was at once too provincial and too daring a building to resemble the creations of the author of St. Martin-in-the-Fields in London. Its steeple rising 182 feet above its stucco-covered brick walls, and its solemn Doric portico must remain, since we do not know the name of the architect, a tribute to the local builder Samuel Cardy.

One of the subtlest of the double houses in the neighborhood of St. Michael's is the three-story clapboarded residence of the merchant William Gibbes, allegedly completed in the first decade of our independence. The eave pediment is imposing without being earnest, and the double staircase leading to the elaborate pedimented doorway is generous without being prodigal. The owner of all this paid a penalty for his taste; his estates were sequestered by Cornwallis for his eagerness in arming the colony. Shortly after Gibbes' death in 1794, the house was remodeled, and the ballroom ceiling turned into an exquisite remembrance of the brothers Adam in England.

Even more splendid than William Gibbes was his fellow merchant

---

* This is probably a reference to Johann Christian, the Milan and London Bach, rather than to his father, Johann Sebastian Bach.

Miles Brewton, who fled revolutionary Charleston in 1775 for the apparent security of Philadelphia, only to lose his life at sea. His brick double house, which was appropriated by Sir Henry Clinton and Lord Rawdon during the British occupation, was, as you might expect from its military guests, the finest architectural achievement of the city. For that matter, its interior carving and its two-story portico set a standard of dignity unrivaled in the colonies.

Yet it would never do to sing too loud a hymn to Miles Brewton's taste. While a visitor in colonial times from Maryland or Virginia would have been both pleased and impressed by the sight of his residence, a traveler from England would in all likelihood have been merely pleased. And although many a Northerner would have been puzzled so many thousand pounds invested in a dwelling, only a New Englander would have been outraged.

Just such a New Englander was Josiah Quincy, Jr., a Bostonian of exemplary morals and unqualified devotion to the patriotic cause, who paid his respects to Brewton in the spring of 1773, four years after the local carver, Ezra Waite, had completed the last of his labors on the house. Though Quincy sipped at dinner of the richest wines he had ever tasted, exceeding "Mr. Hancock's, Vassall's, Phillips's, and others much in flavor, softness, and strength," he confided to his diary that he could not approve of such luxury. "Azure blue satin window curtains, rich blue paper with gilt, moshee borders, most elegant pictures, excessive grand and costly looking glasses—" these were no substitute for the correct political principles. Brewton, who boasted of the grandest hall that Quincy had ever seen, was so worldly as to tolerate a "flaming Tory" at his dinner table.

The art of architecture flourished in Charleston, Quincy conceded, but what of public morals? "State, magnificence, and ostentation, the natural attendants of riches, are conspicuous among this people: the number and subjection of their slaves tend this way. Cards, dice, the bottle, and horses engross prodigious portions of their time and attention: the gentlemen (planters and merchants) are mostly men of the turf and gamesters. Political inquiries and philosophical disquisitions are too laborious for them: they have no great passion for to shine and blaze in the forum or a senate."

And what of the church in a city where so many gentlemen cultivated the art of architecture? "The state of religion here," said Quincy, "is repugnant not only to the ordinances and institutions of Jesus Christ, but to every law of sound policy."

The state of religion in the Northern colonies is none of our business at the moment; as for the state of architecture in the region from which Quincy sprang, it differed as widely from that of the South, as Quincy's opinions from those of his dinner companions in Charleston.

CHAPTER TWO

The Northern Struggle: Architecture in the Northern Colonies

THE NORTHERN STATE OF MIND

Probably no American in colonial times was so easily embarrassed as John Adams in the presence of taste. In Paris itself he was in no danger of being seduced by the delights of civilization. "The richness, the magnificence, and splendor are beyond all description," he confided to his faithful Abigail. "But what is all this to me? I receive but little pleasure in beholding all these things, because I cannot but consider them as bagatelles, introduced by time and luxury in exchange for the great qualities, and hardy, manly virtues of the human heart. I cannot help suspecting that the more elegance, the less virtue, in all times and countries."

When he joined Jefferson on a tour of the great English estates, Adams was made positively unhappy by the sight of the gardens of Stowe. "The temples to Bacchus are quite unnecessary," he decided, "as mankind have no need of artificial incitement to such amusements. . . . It will be long, I hope, before ridings, parks, pleasure grounds, gardens, and ornamented farms grow so much in fashion in America."

The more Adams meditated on the problem of art and architecture, the more convinced he became that it would be wise to postpone to the distant future the development of the fine arts in the United States. "Another walk in the gardens of Versailles would be useful and agreeable," he admitted to Abigail. "But to observe these objects with taste, and to describe them so as to be understood, would require more time and thought than I can possibly spare. It is not indeed the fine arts which our country requires."

He went on to say that

> the useful, the mechanic arts are those which have occasion for in a young country as yet simple and not far advanced in luxury, although perhaps much too far for her age and character. I could fill volumes with descriptions to temples and palaces, paintings, sculptures, tapestry, porcelain, etc. etc. if I could have time; but I could not do this without neglecting my duty. . . . I must study politics and war, that my sons may have liberty to study mathematics and philosophy. My sons ought to study mathematics and philosophy, geography, natural history, and naval architecture, navigation, commerce, and agriculture, in order to give their children a right to study painting, poetry, music, architecture statuary, tapestry, and porcelain.

Even so, the fine arts might one day undermine American morals. "Is it possible," he asked, "to enlist the *fine arts* on the side of truth, of virtue or piety, or even of honor? . . . From the dawn of history, they have been prostituted to the service of superstition and despotism."

It would be easy to dismiss Adams as a typical Puritan, but it would not be accurate. What we in the twentieth century glibly refer to as Puritanism has less in common with the principles of the founders of New England than with the ideals of the revolutionaries in the Old World and the New in the late eighteenth century. They had their priggish moments, these revolutionaries who labored for the recognition of the middle class's contribution to society. Thomas Paine, who was no New Englander, was as much of a prig as Adams, for he declared that "government, like dress, is the badge of lost innocence; the palaces of kings are built upon the ruins of the bowers of paradise."

Not Cotton Mather but Jean-Jacques Rousseau may be responsible for much of what passes for Puritanism in our time. "Luxury and bad taste are inseparable," Rousseau made plain in *Emile*. "Those who set the styles," he sighed, "are the artists, the lords, and the very rich; and what sets their standard is their self-interest or their vanity. The latter, in order to show off their wealth, and the former, in order to take advantage of it, are constantly seeking for new ways to spend money. So luxury takes hold, and sets up the cult of the difficult and the expensive."

If we think of New England as the land where Rousseauistic Puritanism struck the surest foundation, it may be because the austerity practiced by the founding fathers in their quest for individual salvation produced the most congenial climate. Perry Miller has accented the grimness of this theocentric civilization by singling out as a radical utterance the advice in 1721 of the minister at Ipswich, John Wise. "For making wood, iron, brass, leather, etc. into fine coaches and chariots, and horses as fine and proud as they, suited to them—why were these made? . . . And turning glittering earth and glutinous matter of worms, into embroideries, etc.? But to furnish a generous people, that would banish sordidness, and live bright and civil, with fine accomplishments about them?"

With Wise reckoned a disturbing influence, taste could scarcely be cultivated in New England with Southern zeal. And since William Penn did his best to encourage the Quakers of Pennsylvania to hold to their frugal ideals, taste could not make too many converts in colonial Philadelphia. Yet it would be silly to suppose that the fine arts were neglected in the Northern colonies.

The South, after all, produced no painters to compare with West or Copley, no silversmiths to match Coney or Dummer, and no cabinet-makers to equal Savery or the Goddards. In fact, as Carl Bridenbaugh has pointed out, the crafts fared wretchedly in Southern latitudes. Artisans were naturally reluctant to compete with slave labor; even if they had desired to do so, they would have found almost no urban centers in which to ply their trades. What is more, gentlemen with the means to indulge themselves preferred to import their silverware and cabinetwork from England. This hankering after the latest from abroad distressed the Virginia historian Robert Beverley early in the eighteenth century. "They are," he scolded his fellow colonists, "such abominable ill-husbands that though their country be overrun with wood, yet they have all their wooden ware from England—their cabinets, chairs, tables, stools, chests, boxes, cart-wheels, and all other things, even so much as their bowls and birchen brooms, to the eternal reproach of their laziness."

So the artistic tradition of the Northern colonies is not to be despised, no matter if you argue that fine silver was approved of because it could be so easily melted down, or that portrait painting was respected because of the Calvinistic search for individual salvation, or that the very best tables and chairs did not cost anything like a great mansion. The crafts flourished, and with artisans so numerous to carry out an architect's commands, it was no wonder that the man we suppose to be the first architect in America happened to be a New Englander.

The North, then, made a contribution to taste in spite of the founders of Pennsylvania and New England.

TASTE IN NEW ENGLAND

Even if taste did not often tease the imagination of New Englanders, there were oases in the Bay Colony and its neighbors. These were the towns in which the Church of England gathered so many faithful worshipers that the severity of the founding fathers failed to inhibit men's joy in this world. Portsmouth was such a place, and so was Newport;

despite their inferior size, they were as significant as Boston in the architectural development of the area in colonial times.

But in the seventeenth century, New Englanders were too poor to indulge in taste, even if such a thing had been their heart's desire. It wasn't. According to the early chronicler Edward Johnson, one of the glories of the founders was their willingness to forsake "a fruitful land, stately buildings, goodly gardens, orchards, yea, dear friends and near relations, to go to a desert wilderness, thousands of leagues by sea, both turbulent and dangerous."

Once on American soil, the colonists, like their fellows in Virginia, had to make the best of living in the wilds. "They burrow themselves into the earth for their first shelter under some hillside," Johnson wrote. "Casting the earth aloft upon timber, they make a smoky fire against the earth at the highest side, and thus these poor servants of Christ provide shelter for themselves, their wives and little ones, keeping off the short showers from their lodgings, but the long rains penetrate through . . . yet in these poor wigwams they sing psalms, pray and praise their God, till they can provide them houses."

The angels of the several churches of Christ in New England had been sounding forth their silver trumpets for nearly a generation before anything like decent housing was available. "The Lord," Johnson proclaimed in 1653, "hath been pleased to turn all the wigwams, huts, and hovels the English dwelt in at their first coming into orderly, fair, and well-built houses, well-furnished many of them, together with orchards filled with goodly fruit trees and gardens with variety of flowers."

Johnson was speaking the truth. No one can deny that the seventeenth-century houses of New England are commendable examples of building, and no one has any reason to complain that so many of them have been preserved. They remind us that the earliest settlers not only preferred timber to brick or stone, but now and then expressed an unfeigned delight in the materials they had at hand.

Of course it is probably correct to say that no inspiration other than a wholesome respect for utility possessed the builders of most of these frame houses. To certain historians of an archaeological turn of mind any other incentive would have been unseemly, and they have chronicled the labor of these builders with a devotion it would be ungenerous to criticize. One of these specialists has succeeded in tracing the origin of the New England clapboarded house—clapboarding was early welcomed as a means of protecting half-timbered structures from the ravages of torrid summers and glacial winters—to the southeastern counties of England, the area from which most of the original population had streamed.

Until Anthony Garvan questioned the legend, it was commonly believed that the typical seventeenth-century house was built room-from-room, from a single-room end-chimney to a two-room plan with central chimney, plus a lean-to. But it now seems much more likely that every house, small or large, was modeled after a house type in Old England, and was full-grown the day the family moved in. This theory squares with the judgment of Hugh Morrison, the most thoughtful of all students of the architecture of the colonial period, who has found that "no single new building technique was invented, and no new architectural form evolved in the English colonies in the 17th century."

If this be true, a detailed study of house plans at this time obviously belongs in an archaeological manual rather than in a brief history of American architecture. So nothing will be said here as to the various methods of clustering rooms about the central chimney. Besides, it might be much more enjoyable to look twice at the most inviting of all these houses, that of Parson Capen at Topsfield, Massachusetts, dating from 1683. Its pilastered chimney, its deft overhangs, and its carved pendants reveal that there was a longing for taste even in seventeenth century New England.

As in the Southern colonies, however, there was no real sampling of taste until the eighteenth century. The very first example in Boston of the influence of the Renaissance was Christ Church—the old North of Paul Revere's time—contrived in brick in 1723 by William Price, a local print seller turned draftsman in his odd moments. Patiently patterned after Wren's St. James, Piccadilly, this Anglican house of worship was shortly rivaled by Old South, a brick meeting house planned between 1729 and 1733 by one Robert Twelves. Still another suggestion of grandeur was provided in 1740 by the itinerant painter, John Smibert, who conceived of the original Faneuil Hall, a brick structure of two stories, each with a row of Ionic pilasters. Later this was to be remodeled and enlarged by Bulfinch.

These were brave rather than commanding buildings, and the same thing might be said of the town and country houses in the vicinity of Boston. In these, nonetheless, the trend of the times may be followed. Before 1750, as Hugh Morrison has pointed out, the pitch of the roof was high, the façade usually unbroken, and more often then not a single arched window was set in the landing. As for the window panes, they were tiny. After 1750, the pitch was lower, the façade dignified now and then by an entrance portico, and a Palladian window fixed to light the stairway. Meantime the panes had grown larger.

Since very little is known of the original state of Governor Thomas Hutchinson's town house—and it is silly to argue from a nineteenth-century sketch of a building that vanished in 1833—it may be wiser to pay more attention to the residence of Thomas Hancock, the irrepressible uncle of the vainglorious patriot. This, too, was torn down in the last century, but there is general agreement that the house as portrayed in drawings remained unaltered up to the day of its demolition. Completed

Residence of Parson Capen, Topsfield, Mass., 1683

Wentworth-Gardner House, Portsmouth, N.H., 1760

in 1740, this was a solid structure of Braintree granite trimmed with sandstone. The gambrel roof was enhanced by a decorous, if not exactly graceful balustrade, and the doorway was rather fine for its time and place. The balcony window was even framed with a scroll pediment.

Thomas Hancock may not have built a mansion that a Charlestonian would have envied, but he was certainly eager to enjoy tasteful surroundings. Belligerently, this bookseller turned merchant and shipowner demanded what he believed to be the rarest of wallpapers. He also insisted on hangings of peacocks, squirrels, fruits, and flowers, and wrote his agent in London to take "particular care about my glass that it be the best and every square cut exactly to the size. It's for my own use and [I] would have it extraordinary."

"My gardens," Hancock wrote a London seedsman, "all lie on the south side of a hill with the most beautiful ascent to the top, and it's allowed on all hands the Kingdom of England don't afford so fine a prospect as I have both of land and water. Neither do I intend to spare any cost or pains in making my gardens beautiful or profitable."

Very likely Hancock's was the most distinguished house in Boston. However it was surpassed by two homes in the suburbs. One of these, the Usher-Royall house at Medford, begun by one John Usher in 1690 and totally rebuilt in the five years ending in 1737 to suit the Antigua trader Isaac Royall, is still intact. The clapboarded west facade of this three-story brick and frame dwelling, terminated by fluted Doric pilasters, is one of the genuine tributes to taste paid by a citizen of eighteenth-century Massachusetts.

In its day "Shirley Place," the retreat at Roxbury of Governor William Shirley, must have been much more impressive. Now altered almost beyond recognition, it once was famous for a commodious, even generous, first floor, with a grand salon for the Governor's guests. Moreover, the Doric pilasters that graced the imitation stone façade told, like the delicate balustrade and nice cupola atop the pitched roof, that the governor who boasted of plundering Louisburg in 1745 was also a gentleman of exquisite perceptions.

No drawing seems to have survived of Governor Hutchinson's country house at Milton. Sacrificed in the nineteenth century to a carpenter's whim, this was apparently remodeled in 1771 according to plans furnished by ex-Governor Francis Bernard. At least Bernard was so kind as to forward his successor a design for an arcaded porch with giant pilasters. This may, who knows, have been a work of art. While governor, Bernard had been so eager to advance the cause of taste that he laid out Harvard Hall in 1764. This, alas, was also made over in the nineteenth century.

Though the frame house at Marblehead of the merchant Jeremiah Lee, dating from 1768, has been admired, and rightly so, it is by no means so delicate an example of the fine art of architecture as many of the Portsmouth mansions. To tell the truth, the horizon of Portsmouth was broader than that of any town in Massachusetts. John Adams was well aware of this; by-passing the New Hampshire seaport on his way to Portland in 1770, he wrote in his diary that he would call on Governor John Wentworth on the return trip. "It is a duty—he is my friend and I am his. I should have seen enough of the pomps and vanities of that little world, Portsmouth, if I had gone there; but formalities and ceremonies are an abomination in my sight;—I hate them in religion, government, science, life."

For his part Governor Wentworth doubted that Portsmouth was the equal of Nineveh or Tyre. "This is a dull place for cards," he once noted. "I have not won enough lately to pay the postage of a letter."

Distressed by the pageantry of the governor's drawing room, Adams was probably equally perplexed by the quiet confidence of the ruling families who worshiped at Queen's Chapel, Portsmouth. As early as 1741, when this center of the Anglican Communion was only nine years old, as many as fifty or sixty of the six or seven hundred families of the town preferred to receive the sacraments as administered by the Reverend Arthur Browne. This was a minority that could not be overlooked. Included among the parishioners were the Wentworths and other names that have been remembered.

Minus the Wentworths, colonial New Hampshire would have been unthinkable. The founder of the dynasty, John by name, rose no higher than lieutenant governor before his death in 1730, but he laid the foundation for the greatest fortune in New England. His son Benning, governor of the colony for twenty-five years, made the most of the advantages that came to him from such a start. Never for a second was he absent-minded. Whenever he bestowed a grant of land—he did so over two hundred times—he prudently reserved for himself a tract of at least five hundred acres. Quite understandably, he was inclined to be short with men whose minds were not so clear as his own. "His passions were strong and his resentments lasting," commented one of his fellow colonists. "He was subject to frequent and long-continued visits of the gout, a distemper rather unfriendly to the virtue of patience. In his deportment there was an appearance of haughtiness, contracted by his residence in Spain, where he learned the manners of the people of rank." In 1766 he resigned—at the very moment when an unpleasant degree of curiosity had been aroused as to his right to hold 100,000 acres of New Hampshire soil.

Benning's successor was his nephew John Wentworth, who seems to have taken as deep an interest in governing the colony as in adding to his acreage. He sent out expert surveyors, improved the roads, and took the welfare of the militia to heart. Unfortunately no trace remains of "Wentworth House," the country home he planned with the assistance of the architect Peter Harrison. And in Portsmouth, although he insisted that his footmen play the French horn, he lived in what he called "a small hut with little, comfortable apartments."

But if no magnificence marks the spot where Governor John Wentworth lived, two of the great houses of Portsmouth are associated with the Wentworth family. One of these is the brick mansion of Captain Archibald McPhaedris, the Scottish-born ironmaster and merchant who married one of the daughters of the lieutenant governor. Begun in 1718 and finished in 1723, this may be the first example in New England of a town house touched with the spirit of the Renaissance. Though neither the gambrel roof, nor the balustrade, nor the cupola are original, there seems to be no doubt that the doorway was always there. Framed by two Corinthian pilasters, this is a subtle achievement.

The Wentworth-Gardner house is not quite so pretentious. A wedding gift in 1760 to young Thomas Wentworth, this is a two-story residence of wood blocks counterfeiting stone. Its charm is centered in the Corinthian pilasters and scrolled pediment of the paneled doorway. More splendid is Captain John Moffat's house of 1763—the Moffat-Ladd house opened by the Colonial Dames.

No eighteenth-century town house remaining in Newport is so exquisite. Of the country houses near the Rhode Island seaport the most elaborate may have been the now vanished seat of that Episcopalian trader Godfrey Malbone. In 1744 the perceptive tourist Hamilton termed this "the largest and most magnificent dwelling house I have seen in America . . . built entirely with hewn stone of a reddish color; the sides of the windows and corner stones . . . being painted like white marble."

The Trinity Church at which Malbone worshiped was much more of a monument than Portsmouth's Queen's Chapel. Designed in 1725 by the local builder Richard Munday,* it is still standing to evoke the pride of the Gibbses, the Cranstons, the Wantons, the Ayraults, and the Bowlers— an aristocracy that condoned if it did not exactly encourage the slave trade. Though the large frame building in which they said their prayers may have been inspired by Christ Church, Boston, it is far more impressive. Its fine spire is not unlike Wren's St. Lawrence Jewry. And its carved pulpit is simple but sufficient.

Trinity Church was not the only public building in Newport conceived by Munday. In 1739 he laid out the Old Colony House for the use of the provincial assembly. Surmounted by a cupola and a brave balustrade, this is a somewhat sumptuous brick building with a truncated gable. In the early twentieth century Henry James found it "an edifice ample, majestic, archaic, of the finest proportions and full of a certain Dutch dignity. . . . Here was the charming impression of a treasure of antiquity to the vague image of which, through the years, one hadn't done justice."

* Tradition hints that Munday planned Malbone's country home.

Trinity Church and the Old Colony House—these were the choicest tributes to taste in Newport when Peter Harrison, now claimed as the first American architect—meaning the first American to sketch buildings for others to build—made his appearance. No greater compliment could have been paid to the prosperity the seaport wrung from the triangular trade. With his coming, the columns in the ledgers dedicated to rum and molasses added up to something more fanciful than profit or loss. He was to immortalize the credit balances.

A native of York in Old England, Harrison was by birth a Quaker, yet sufficiently aware of the advantages, spiritual and temporal, of the Anglican Communion to prefer to worship his Maker in Trinity Church. He did not reach Newport until 1739. Seven years later, at twenty-three, having toiled quite long enough over the account books of a local merchant, he made the conquest of an heiress. She happened to be the sister-in-law of the master of the countinghouse, who was not one to approve of ambitious clerks. "When I came home," Harrison's employer complained, "I found everything in the utmost confusion. Goods in the store wrong marked, no cash entered in the books since July . . . which I partly attribute to a scandalous affair of Peter Harrison, who finally got Betty Pelham with child, and was so foolish as to bring up a doctor from Boston twice, at the expense of £100, to cure Mistress Betty, as he said, of the hysterics."

Whereupon Harrison married the heiress, and set up as a merchant on his own account, with his older brother to help him. The Harrisons were evidently successful enough in business, for Peter and his wife had their portraits painted by Smibert, and once, when the architect was badgering customers in Charleston, he was so fortunate as to be wined and dined by the fastidious Manigaults. And all the while, putting his training as a shipbuilder in York to an unexpected test, he was devoting his evenings and whatever time he could spare from his ledgers to the designing of a number of buildings which made Newport the center of the art of architecture in colonial New England.

A certain Abraham Redwood, an Antigua planter who was so charmed with the climate of Newport that he donated five hundred pounds for a library, may be said to have started the architect on his career, although Peter's older brother Joseph, a member of the committee that went about raising funds for the library building, was the one who saw to it that he submitted the plans that were finally accepted. Meantime Ezra Stiles, the relentless minister of the Second Congregational Church, was not exactly pleased to find that the Anglicans were managing the enterprise. "This set out as a Quaker affair," noted Stiles in his diary. "Through the blindness of Mr. Redwood . . . the Episcopalians slyly got into it and obtained a majority which they are careful to keep."

Whether we owe the design of the Redwood Library to the cunning of the Church of England, or whether Harrison, who was never paid a

shilling for the trouble he took, might have been prevailed upon to contribute the drawings, no matter what his religion, the building that tells
the beginning of Bellevue Avenue today is one of the refined accomplishments of our colonial architecture. Merely to point out that the façade
derives from an English edition of Palladio's works, the doorway from
Kent's *Designs of Inigo Jones,* and the panels on the bookcases from
Batty Langley's *Treasure of Design* is to forget the secret of the architect's
charm. No one in the colonies was so well acquainted with the British
version of the Renaissance; no one was so skilled in adapting this tradition to American use as the contriver of this pedimented portico of four
Doric columns set in the center of a frame of pine planks imitating stone.

The library was scarcely begun when Harrison was honored by a
request from the Anglicans of King's Chapel, Boston. "As the chief
beauty and strength of building depends upon a due proportion of the
several members to each other," wrote the Reverend Henry Caner, "the
gentlemen of the committee are encouraged to make this application to
you, whom they have often heard mentioned with advantage for a particular judgment and taste in things of this kind, and for the knowledge
you have acquired by traveling and observation. We do not require any
great expense of ornament, but chiefly aim at symmetry and proportion,
which we entirely submit to your judgment."

Though the Episcopalians of Boston, despite the promise implicit in
their flattering approach, had no intention of rewarding him for his
labors, the architect of the Redwood Library prepared a generous set of
drawings. Included was a sketch for a steeple, which was never built.
King's Chapel was never really completed, even if the portico—in wood,
instead of stone, as intended—was added in 1785. Nevertheless this is, as
it now stands, one of the most thoughtfully conceived of all our colonial
churches. Harrison was never surer of himself than when he relied, as he
did in this instance, on James Gibbs's *Book of Architecture.* Here he
found the inspiration for the fenestration—especially for the Palladian
window in the apse. Lighting up the double Corinthian columns that
support the vaulted ceiling, this cleverly relieves the austerity of the exterior of Quincy granite.

In 1761, seven years after King's Chapel was opened for services, Harrison again set the example for Bostonians, this time by fashioning Christ
Church for the Episcopalians of Cambridge. Though this frame structure
was never surfaced with plaster as he hoped, nor adorned with the steeple
he considered appropriate, it again handsomely reflects the architect's
study of the works of Gibbs. And for once the designer was congratulated
in the currency of the realm. From the Vassalls, the Olivers, and the
other gentlemen of means on the vestry he got forty-five pounds for his
pains.

In Newport Harrison was, of course, far more appreciated. A summer-

Interior, Congregation Jeshuat Israel, Newport, R.I., 1763 (Designer: Peter Harrison)

Redwood Library, Newport, R.I., 1750 (Peter Harrison)

house invented for Abraham Redwood—a delightful garden temple in the Gibbs manner—may be seen today on the lawn of the Redwood Library. A more ambitious building was the brick Market House still standing on Thames Street, created in 1761. Here he was unmistakably encouraged by a plate of Somerset House in Colin Campbell's *Vitruvius Britannicus.*

Not far from the Market House is Harrison's masterpiece, the Synagogue of the Congregation Jeshuat Israel, commissioned by the Sephardic community in 1759, eleven years after the beginning of the Redwood Library, but not completed, such was the expense, until 1763. An unprepossessing brick pile on the exterior, the synagogue conceals, if not the most beautiful interior of any church in America, at least the only miraculous ecclesiastical interior of colonial times.

Reminded by Rabbi Isaac Touro of the requirements of the Portuguese-Spanish services in Holland, Harrison solved the problem at hand by turning to the pages of William Kent's *Designs of Inigo Jones,* where he came upon a plate of the arched, two-storied, galleried Hall of Whitehall Palace, whose Corinthian columns superimposed on Ionic he lovingly remembered in the midst of his sketches. For the ark, he relied on a Tuscan altarpiece to be found in Batty Langley's *Treasury of Designs,* whose paneling discreetly echoed the elegance of the colonnade.

The Jews who worshiped in this setting were not forgotten by George Washington. "It is now no more that toleration is spoken of, as if it was by the indulgence of one class of people, that another enjoyed the exercise of their inherent natural rights," Washington addressed Touro's congregation in the summer of 1790. "For happily the Government of the United States, which gives to bigotry no sanction, to persecution no assistance, requires only that they who live under its protection should demean themselves as good citizens, in giving it on all occasions their effectual support."

Fifteen years before Washington's pronouncement, Harrison dropped dead of an apoplectic fit. Bewildered by the radicals promoting the cause of American independence, the aging architect had accepted what he belived to be the snug office of collector of the port of New Haven, only to be appalled in his last hours by the news of Lexington and Concord.

Had Harrison spent all of his life in the New Haven to which he retired, he could scarcely have acquired the notoriety which was his in Newport. Despite the elegant carving of many a doorway in the Connecticut River Valley—the entrance to the home of Ebenezer Grant in South Windsor, dating from 1757, is only one of many charming examples—the colony was not sufficiently prosperous for anyone to gamble a considerable sum on anything as intangible as taste.

An admittedly unfriendly correspondent of a Connecticut Anglican reported on the eve of the Revolution that "he would not give £800 for

Residence of Julius Deming, Litchfield, Conn., c. 1790 (William Sprats)

Residence of Zenas Cowles, Farmington, Conn., c. 1780 (William Sprats)

the whole province," and swore that "they are all mortgaged to the full to the Bostonians and New Yorkers . . . they have all their goods from those two places, and import very little; very few merchants, chiefly farmers, all upon a level . . . very great rogues, no money amongst them, and nobody would live amongst them that could possibly live anywhere else."

This comment could hardly have been made in the decade following the peace with Britain. With the opening of the French West Indies to American shipping, sizable fortunes were accumulated in the hamlets of Connecticut, and the Cowleses of Farmington, who set up country stores in the neighboring villages to market the products of the Caribbean, were soon rich enough to build a row of houses that were all of them works of art.

By far the loveliest of the Cowles houses—and perhaps the most beautiful house of the eighteenth century in all New England—is that of Zenas Cowles. Attributed to the master builder William Sprats, who served with the Royal Artillery in the Revolution, it was doubtless completed in the 1780's. To say that this is a frame structure, gambrel-roofed, with quoins—blocks terminating the façade in imitation of the stone which not even a Cowles could afford—is to give a most inadequate idea of its distinction. The correct pediment of the central block crowns an enchanting Palladian window in the second story, framed with Ionic pilasters, and the doorway, sunk in the shadow of four fluted Ionic columns, would have forced the admiration even of a Charlestonian.

Like Farmington, near-by Litchfield comes close to satisfying the American dream of the idyllic New England village, and like Farmington, Litchfield owes its architectural glories to the prosperity that followed the Revolution. One Julius Deming, who took to importing from England and from China too, eventually founding the Litchfield China Trading Company, grew so splendid that, so the tradition declares, in 1790 he asked William Sprats to design his town house. Very like the Zenas Cowles mansion, with a hip instead of gambrel roof, Julius Deming's residence, with its Palladian window above the Ionic doorway, fastidiously recalls the beauties of Georgian England.

Across the street from the Deming house stands yet another building attributed to William Sprats, the one-time Sheldon's Tavern. This is said to have been remodeled by the master builder in 1790 into a home for the Federalist senator, Uriah Tracy. As is true of the Deming and Cowles houses, its most remarkable feature is the Palladian window above the Ionic doorway.

Close at hand is the Litchfield village green, which must be counted among the most handsome in all New England. But the white frame Congregational church dates from the early nineteenth century, and any examination of the late-eighteenth-century notions which the local builder admired and incorporated would be out of place in this chapter. This may be the time, however, to point out that the meeting houses in whose honor the most ink has been spilled are those whose steeples and whose plans reflect the influence of the Episcopal Church. A typical meeting house of the seventeenth century is that at Hingham in Massachusetts, a square thing of interest to archaeologists. Somewhat more interesting is that at Farmington, planned by the local builder Judah Woodruff in 1771. Though the principal entrance is on the side—as if to prove that no Congregationalist could imitate the Anglicans—the steeple indicates that Christ Church, Boston, set an irresistible example.

TASTE IN PENNSYLVANIA AND ELSEWHERE

Writing to one of his children in the spring of 1785, Robert Livingston, Third Lord of the Manor, could not conceal his disappointment in the trend of the times in New York City. He was, he admitted, "sorry to hear that living in our capital is become so very expensive, and what is worse, that it is become fashionable." One of the great landholders of New York in the eighteenth century, Livingston was a typical representative of an aristocracy that would rather be prudent than elegant. He and his peers may be accused of nipping taste in the bud on the banks of the Hudson.

Even if Sir William Johnson at "Johnson Hall" dared to remember in the wilderness of the Mohawk Valley the splendors of Georgian England, and even if one James McBean made an unusually competent translation of James Gibbs's St. Martin-in-the-Fields when he came to build St. Paul's Chapel, New York prior to the Revolution offered so few opportunities for artists catering to taste that it could not pretend to compare with Pennsylvania. Although the "Jumel Mansion," the house built by Roger Morris of the British Army at the northern end of Manhattan, displays a two-story portico, this was a later addition. This is not to deny that the buildings of the colonial carpenters and stonemasons are without a certain stubborn charm—they are simply outside of the scope of this book.

There was, after all, no New Yorker in the eighteenth century with anything like the trained perception of Dr. John Morgan. Said to be the first Philadelphian to sport an umbrella, Morgan deserves to be remembered for more than his contribution to either haberdashery or medicine. In 1764 he and his friend Samuel Powel enjoyed a Grand Tour of the Continent which even so particular a traveler as Ralph Izard of Charleston would have envied. The two young Philadelphians, who made a point of paying their respects to Voltaire at Ferney, returned familiar with the wonders of Paris and Rome and Venice and Vicenza. Most important, Morgan brought back a volume of Vignola's works and a drawing by one of the Mansarts. This meant that there was at least one critic of the monuments of the Quaker City.

That a critic would one day walk the streets of Philadelphia, was, of course, the last thing that would have occurred to William Penn. The benevolent founder of the city set his sights on such things as public parks. "Let every house be placed," he recommended, "if the person pleases, in the middle of its plat, as to the breadth way of it, so there may be ground on each side for gardens or orchards or fields, that it may be a green country town, which will never be burnt and always wholesome."

The inhabitants of this "green country town" were warned that Penn had not gone to the trouble of preparing a paradise in the wilderness for hedonists. "It is," he said, "a most inexcusable superfluity to bestow an estate to line walls, dress cabinets, embroider beds, with a hundred other unprofitable pieces of state, such as many plate, rich china, costly pictures, sculpture, fret work, inlayings, and painted windows."

In later years Penn's fellow Quakers who piled up fortunes were tempted to waste their substance on such things, but frivolity was unflinchingly condemned by earnest members of the sect. Early in the eighteenth century the Philadelphia Yearly Meeting ruled that "no Friends suffer romances, playbooks, and other vain and idle pamphlets in their homes and families, which tend to corrupt the minds of youth."

For every Quaker who spent his income, another Quaker was certain to blast the sin of extravagance. In the midst of the Revolution soberminded Anthony Benezet was grieved to find that many Friends had strayed from the path laid out by the shepherds of the fold. "Has not our conformity to the world . . . in order to please ourselves and gain wealth . . . been productive to all the evils pointed out in the Gospel?" he asked. "Has it not naturally led us and begot a desire in our children to live in conformity with other people; hence the sumptuousness of our dwellings, our equipages, our dress; furniture and the luxury of our tables have become a snare to us and a matter of offence to the thinking part of mankind."

Morgan and his friend Powel moved with the ease of Episcopalians, and they naturally failed to heed Benezet's advice. They could have told us, however, that Philadelphia was not half so extravagant as the earnest Quaker presumed. Though it had become a respectable city of the New World by 1776, with a population of forty thousand, its architecture was no more remarkable than that of Charleston, which claimed only twelve thousand inhabitants, half of them Negroes. Philadelphia might have been far more splendid had it not been for the Friends. Whether it would have become the intellectual center of America without their sober counsel is another matter.

Typical of Quaker austerity was "Stenton," the country seat (in what is now Germantown) of William Penn's secretary, James Logan. Though Logan was one of the most influential gentlemen in the province, eventually rising to be president of the council, the brick house he built in 1728 was as modest as the homes of the Byrds, the Lees, and the Carters were pretentious, and only in the paneling of the drawing rooms, opening off the front hall did he reveal that he had once glanced— probably without a sign of envy—at an elegant mansion.

"Graeme Park," the retreat of Governor William Keith at Horsham, was no more magnificent than Stenton, but while Logan's estate was at best an anemic recollection of Georgian England, Keith's country home was an inspired creation of the carpenters and stonemasons (presumably Swedish) whom he hired in 1722. The floor plan, as a recent historian has advanced, might be traced to a Swedish source, and the narrow windows and high gambrel roof could be assigned to the same homely origin, but no merely racial explanation can account for the rough stone walls. Here is one occasion when artisans were as eager as artists to stress the beauty of the materials with which they worked.

In Philadelphia itself at the time "Graeme Park" was completed no public building was its equal, and Gloria Dei, the Old Swedes' Church of 1700 or thereabouts was so crude that no visitor could have guessed that within a few years intelligent amateurs would be striving to raise the architectural standards of the city. Yet in the 1730's Andrew Hamilton, the attorney best remembered for his defense of the journalist John Peter Zenger, would be superintending the construction of the Old State House or Independence Hall. And even if Dr. John Kearsley, a physician honored in those days for his campaign to check yellow fever and malaria, was the presumed rather than the authenticated creator of Christ Church in 1754, he was at least the sponsor of that adaptation of Wren's St. Andrew-by-the-Wardrobe.

There were plenty of expert builders whose zeal matched that of the amateurs. One of the best of these builders was one Samuel Rhoads. A director of the Pennsylvania Hospital, he planned the present handsome edifice in 1751. Still another prominent contractor was Robert Smith, the Scottish-born member of the conservative, clannish Carpenters' Company who was responsible for Nassau Hall at Princeton and eventually, in 1770, superintended the Carpenters' Hall in which the first sessions of the Continental Congress were held.

Andrew Hamilton, John Kearsley, Samuel Rhoads, and Robert Smith—these names have been mentioned in nearly every survey of colonial architecture, but it would be an error to believe that only their work was of significance in the Philadelphia area, or that all of the best buildings in the locality were in Philadelphia itself. In Cantwell's Bridge in the Lower Counties—as the now stagnant town of Odessa, Delaware, was known in colonial times—the prosperity of the farmers was reflected in a church and two town houses worthy of the talents of the best artisans and amateurs in the capital. Here David Wilson, who married into the town's cleverest family, the Corbits, amazed his neighbors in 1769 with a tasteful two-story brick house in the Georgian manner which quite possibly inspired the Presbyterians to put up the Old Drawyers' Church four years later. The pride of Cantwell's Bridge, however, was the home of the tanner William Corbit. Built of brick in 1773, its Georgian façade overlooked Appoquinimink Creek. The unusually elaborate interiors of the Corbit mansion have been credited to one Robert May, a craftsman about whose other achievements historians are as yet uninformed.

More willful, less academic than the glories of Cantwell's Bridge was the rough stone home in Philadelphia of John Bartram, the pioneer botanist, whose son William was to become even more famous for his account of the flora and fauna of the Southern United States. Begun in 1731, and probably completed in 1770, the Bartram house is exceptional for its three-columned Ionic portico in the local stone, and for fanciful, nearly baroque stone frames on the windows overlooking the gardens.

"Cliveden," the house of Chief Justice Benjamin Chew in Germantown, dating from 1761, is far more magnificent, in keeping with the pretentions of the Tory judge whose daughter was courted by Major André during the British occupation. It is indeed a fortunate thing that this fastidious Georgian façade, built of the same local stone that Bartram preferred, survived the Battle of Germantown. Such elegance was not frequent in colonial Pennsylvania. The house has now been opened by the National Trust.

The only Philadelphia house still standing that could be compared with "Cliveden" is "Mount Pleasant," begun in the same year by John MacPherson, a privateer who lost his right arm beating off a Frenchman from his decks, but whose winnings were so inspiring that he was entitled to live in a higher style than Justice Chew. Set off by twin dependencies in the manner of the great country homes of Virginia, "Mount Pleasant" might have been approved by the most difficult Southerner. Its scale alone is threatening for its time and place. Of yellow stucco, framed by rustic blocks of red brick, with twin chimneys rising above a hipped roof and balustraded deck, this memorial to MacPherson's plundering cannot be overlooked. The composition of the central projecting block is especially distinguished. Here is a delicate pediment, beneath which is a Palladian window; here is also a pedimented doorway caught between engaged columns of the Tuscan order.

Benedict Arnold acquired "Mount Pleasant" during the Revolution with the hope that his treachery would one day be either excused or forgotten, and that in this setting he and Peggy Shippen could stage their dinner parties. The layout is spacious, and the mantels and doorways richly carved.

"Cliveden," Germantown, Pa., 1763-64

"Mount Pleasant," Philadelphia, Pa., 1761-62

Living room, "Mount Pleasant"

Unfortunately, the very finest country house of Philadelphia in the eighteenth century has been demolished, as has the finest town house. Both belonged to William Bingham, the superb banker who married lovely Ann Willing. Before she died of consumption at thirty-seven, he had the satisfaction of knowing that she had enjoyed the most brilliant social career of any woman in the New World. In the country the Binghams leased "Lansdown," the seat John Penn, the grandson of the founder of Pennsylvania, had erected toward 1773 in defiance of William Penn's homilies. Its two-story portico, as engraved by William Birch, tells of an extravagance undreamed of by John MacPherson. In town the Binghams were even more confident. The brick house they built in 1789 on Third Street just below Spruce, though said to be a replica of the Duke of Manchester's residence on Manchester Square in London—a thing they had admired during the five years they spent abroad—was really bolder than the original, as well as ingeniously simplified for American use.

Mrs. Bingham was clever, as Thomas Jefferson discovered when he suggested she was an uncritical admirer of the great ladies of France. "We are," she replied, "irresistibly pleased with them, because they possess the happy art of making us pleased with ourselves." And even Abigail Adams, who made her acquaintance at Auteuil, admitted there were extenuating circumstances in her case. "Mrs. Bingham," she wrote, "is a fine figure and a beautiful person; her manners are easy and affable, but she was too young to go abroad without a pilot, given too much into the follies of this country, has money enough and knows how to lavish it with an unsparing hand. Less money and more years may make her wiser, but she is so handsome she must be pardoned."

Henry Wansey, a Wiltshire clothier who toured the United States not long after our independence, was far less critical than Mrs. Adams. "I found," he wrote after calling on the Binghams in town, "a magnificent house and gardens in the best English style, with elegant and even superb furniture. The chairs of the drawing room were from Seddons' in London, of the newest taste; the back in the form of a lyre, with festoons of crimson and yellow silk. The curtains of the room a festoon of the same. The carpet was one of Moore's most expensive patterns." He added that "the room was papered in the French taste, after the style of the Vatican in Rome. In the garden was a profusion of lemon, orange, and citron trees; and many aloes and other exotics."

Not every visitor was so favorably impressed. Brissot de Warville, a French revolutionary who fancied that he was also a financial genius, was displeased to find such splendor in America. "A very ingenious woman," he reported, "is reproached with having contributed more than all others to introduce this taste for luxury. I really regret to see her husband, who appears to be well informed, and of an amiable character, affect, in his

Town house of William Bingham, Philadelphia, Pa., 1789

"Lansdown," country house of William Bingham, Philadelphia, Pa., 1773

buildings and furniture, a pomp which ought for ever to have been a stranger to Philadelphia; and why? To draw around him the gaudy prigs and parasites of Europe. And what does he gain by it? jealousy, the reproach of his fellow citizens, and the ridicule of strangers."

The stern American patriot Samuel Breck was equally offended by the "showy style" of the Binghams. "The forms at his house," Breck decided, "were not suited to our manners. I was often at his parties, at which each guest was announced; first at the entrance door his name was called aloud, and taken up by a servant on the stairs, who passed it on to the men in waiting at the drawing room door. In this drawing room the furniture was superb Gobelin [sic], and the folding doors were covered with mirrors, which reflected the figures of the company, so as to deceive an untravelled countryman, who, having paraded up the marble stairway amid the echoes of his name—oftimes made very ridiculous by the queer manner in which the servants pronounced it—would enter the brilliant apartment and salute the looking glasses instead of the master and mistress of the house and their guests. . . . There is," warned Breck, "too much sobriety in our American common sense to tolerate such pageantry, or indeed any outlandish fashion contrary to the plain unvarnished manners of the people."

Benjamin Franklin, who could not take himself so seriously, was not half so perturbed as Breck by the thought of luxury in the New World. "The arts have always traveled westward," he said, "and there is no doubt of their flourishing hereafter on our side of the Atlantic, as the number of wealthy inhabitants shall increase, who may be able and willing to reward them; since, from several instances, it appears that our people are not deficient in genius."

Of course in Franklin's time as in ours there were Americans who felt that elegance, no matter how ingratiating its charms, threatened the very foundations of public morality. No one expressed this point of view in the eighteenth century with quite the gentle persuasion of St. John Crèvecoeur. "Never having seen the beauties which Europe contains," his poetic American farmer declared, "I . . . cheerfully satisfy myself with attentively examining what my native country exhibits: if we have neither ancient amphitheaters, gilded palaces, nor elevated spires, we enjoy in our woods a substantial happiness which the wonders of art cannot communicate." In his mind no architect could compare with the untutored carpenters who labored over the sheds in our countryside. "For my part," he said, "I had rather admire the ample barn of one of our opulent farmers . . . than study the dimensions of the Temple of Ceres."

The fate of taste in America, from the Revolution down to our own time, has hung on the outcome of the battle between the Puritans—few of whom have been as benevolent as Crèvecoeur—and the hedonists— few of whom have been as shrewd as Franklin.

CHAPTER THREE

The Federal Period, or the Birth of the Nation, 1790–1820

THE FEDERAL PATTERN

Since American architecture in the early years of the republic could without exaggeration be considered the equal of that of any nation in the world, it would be pleasant to sum up the achievements of the Federal period in a single sentence. But that is impossible. Architectural history is, after all, no less complicated than political history, and just as no one catchword can express the significance of our presidents from George Washington to John Quincy Adams, so no single formula will increase our understanding of the architecture of those years.

But if catchwords and formulas are of no use, we cannot escape discussing what appear to be the trends of the times. Of these by far the most novel was the reverence for the grandeur of Rome, whose shadow fell on revolutionary Europe as well. Thomas Jefferson is known to have sighed over the Roman remains in France, and the Roman influence on the character of Washington, D.C., must not be underestimated.

Hardly less influential than the Roman revival was the vogue in Salem and other cities of the Adam style, the delicate classical ornamentation with which the brothers Adam had wrought such miracles in the England of the 1760's and 1770's. Though America had already witnessed charming ceilings in the Adam style at "Kenmore," the Fielding Lewis house in Fredericksburg, Virginia, it remained for Samuel McIntire of Salem to exploit the inventions of the Adam brothers to the fullest. His town houses and those of his followers along the New England seacoast might well be termed typically Federal. Easily distinguished from colonial houses by flat roofs, or by low-pitched roofs concealed behind omnipresent balustrades, these boxlike structures of brick or timber reveal Adamite influence not only in their precise interiors, but occasionally in their exteriors as well. Yankee carpenters were not averse to front doors of an intricacy usually reserved abroad for the intimacy of a drawing room.

Meantime American architecture was rejoicing not only in the inheritance of England but in the direct inspiration of the Continent itself, and Charles Bulfinch thoughtfully visited France and Italy after casting a shrewd glance at London. Most stimulating of all was the presence of a number of foreign-born architects, not a few of whom were driven to seek shelter in the United States from the disorders of the revolutionary and Napoleonic wars. Indeed, had not Thornton found his way from the Virgin Islands, Hoban from Ireland, Hallet, Godefroy, Mangin, Ramée, and L'Enfant from France, as well as Hadfield, Jay, and Latrobe from England, our native artists would not have been dared to the full expression of their own powers.

Though there was no such thing as a "Federal" type of plan, and Americans were reluctant to abandon the colonial layout of four rooms to a floor, our leading architects altered the colonial ideal beyond recognition, flouting the tradition of a century by compressing the familiar grand staircase and robbing it of its central position in the floor plan. Proving they were bored by the traditional rectangular rooms, they daringly introduced elliptical shapes; weary of the usual brick, stone, or timber façades, they even coated the exteriors with stucco.

That there was, for the first time in American history, a group of professional architects at work, was, of course, the most startling development of all in the Federal period. But this group was naturally limited in its numbers, and not a little of the general excellence of contemporary building must be attributed to the influence of Asher Benjamin, the first American to publish handbooks for the guidance of carpenters.

THE WORLD OF THOMAS JEFFERSON

In another world from Benjamin lived Thomas Jefferson, who dreamed not of teaching carpenters the rudiments, but of charting the course of American civil architecture. He was not altogether successful; he did not begin to wield over architects the power he possessed over statesmen and politicians alike, but at least he spoke with an authority few presumed to question.

Though Jefferson the political philosopher is correctly remembered as one of the serene prophets, Jefferson the architectural critic, like nearly all architects before or since, was supremely intolerant of what passed for the last word in the generation preceding his own. "The genius of architecture seems to have shed its maledictions over this land," he remarked in his *Notes on Virginia* in 1784. "Buildings are often erected, by individuals, of considerable expense. To give these symmetry and taste, would not increase their cost. It would only change the arrangement of the materials, the form and combination of the members. This would often cost less than the burthen of barbarous ornament with which these buildings are sometimes charged. But the first principles of the art are unknown, and there exists scarcely a model among us sufficiently chaste to give an idea of them."

In Jefferson's eyes even the public buildings at Williamsburg were worth no more than a glance. "The capitol," he admitted, "is a light and airy structure, with a portico in front of two orders, the lower of which, being Doric, is tolerably just in its proportions and ornaments, save only that the intercolonations are too large. The upper is Ionic, much too small for that on which it is mounted, its ornaments not proper to the order, nor proportioned within themselves. It is crowned with a pediment, which is too high for its span. Yet, on the whole, it is the most pleasing piece of architecture we have.*

"The palace," he continued, "is not handsome without, but it is spacious and commodious within, is prettily situated, and with the grounds annexed to it, is capable of being made an elegant seat." All other edifices were beneath contempt. "The college and hospital are rude, misshapen piles, which, but that they have roofs, would be taken for brick-kilns. There are no other public buildings but churches and court-houses, in which no attempts are made at elegance. Indeed, it would not be easy to execute such an attempt, as a workman could scarcely be found capable of drawing an order."

Suffering as he was from divine discontent, Jefferson was in no danger of repeating the Virginia formula when he began building "Monticello" in 1769. Disdaining his first few sketches in the style of his neighbors, he sensed that "Mount Airy" was the only mansion in the colony on which he might model his own; faintly Palladian in style, it was a denial of the universal application in Virginia of Wren's principles. Incidentally, although Jefferson has occasionally been cited as an Anglophobe in his architectural preferences, he was never more British than when he chose Palladio for his master. Fifty years before this, the Earl of Burlington, who resented Wren's influence as deeply as Jefferson, summoned the architects at his beck and call to create a number of country houses in the manner of Palladio's "Villa Rotonda" at Vincenza. "Monticello" was unmistakably Burlingtonian.

* The Rockefeller-restored Capitol dates from an earlier period.

But Jefferson's domed country seat, finally completed in 1809, was far more than the reconstruction in the United States of a design found in Palladio's works; no archetype exists for the plan, and many of its features, such as the octagonal projections, were all but revolutionary in Federal times. To tell of the double doors of "Monticello" working simultaneously, of the dumb waiters, of the beds framed in alcoves, of the adroitly concealed staircases, and the hundred other revelations of Jefferson's ingenuity, is to recall that in this house he incorporated the findings of his ever inquisitive intellect, sharpened during the five years he served as our minister to the court of France.

Even in his youth, however, Jefferson was hankering after novelties. In 1771, some sixty years before fashion decreed the Gothic style for the villas of ambitious American businessmen, he thought of ornamenting a neighboring mountain with a battlemented tower, and planned, though he did not actually erect, "a small Gothic temple of antique appearance" to distinguish the site selected at "Monticello" for the graves of his family and servants.

"I am," Jefferson confessed to Madison, "an enthusiast on the subject of the arts. But it is an enthusiasm of which I am not ashamed, as its object is to improve the taste of my countrymen, to increase their reputation, to reconcile to them the respect of the world, and procure them its praise."

Gardens, he advised two young friends setting out on the Grand Tour of Europe, are "peculiarly worth the attention of an American, because it is the country of all others where the noblest gardens may be made without expense." When he himself was in England, he dashed from "Chiswick" to "Claremont," from "Stowe" to "Pains Hill," from "Moor Park" to "Kew," and from "Hagley" to the "Leasowes" in his eagerness to survey the lawns of the great estates. "The gardening in that country" he realized, "is the article in which it surpasses all the earth. I mean their pleasure gardening. This, indeed, went far beyond my ideas."

In France Jefferson duly admired "Marly," one of the châteaux destined to be leveled in the Revolution, and paused before "Bagatelle," the retreat of the King's devious brother the Comte d'Artois, but these were sights which a tourist might have visited, and other buildings inspected by the future president tell the secret of his personal taste. He seems to have been deeply moved by the work of Claude-Nicolas Ledoux, an architect who could be both simple and noble, for Jefferson remembered with unmistakable pleasure the day he spent at "Louveciennes," in the pavilion Ledoux fashioned for Madame du Barry, and he noted with reverence the gates Ledoux designed for the city of Paris. He was also charmed with the "Maison du Désert," the villa of a commissioner of water works who fancied passing his weekends in a house disguised as a ruined column. "How grand the idea excited by the remains of such a column!" exclaimed Jefferson, who could not forget that he had once toyed with a Gothic temple of antique appearance at "Monticello."

In Paris itself Jefferson was struck by the "Hôtel de Salm," a town house whose correct use of classic precedents flattered the Roman instinct in the American minister, but this was only one of many buildings whose influence on American architecture was to be no less profound than contemporary European politics on American history. "Here I am, Madam, gazing whole hours at the Maison Carrée, like a lover at his mistress," Jefferson wrote his good friend the Comtesse de Tessé from Nîmes in the spring of 1787.

> The stocking weavers and silk spinners around it consider me a hypochondriac Englishman, about to write with a pistol the last chapter of his history. This is the second time I have been in love since I left Paris. The first was with a Diana at the Château de Laye-Epinaye in Beaujolais, a delicious morsel of sculpture by M. A. Slodtz. This, you will say, was in rule, to fall in love with a female beauty; but with a house! it is out of all precedent. No, Madam, it is not without a precedent in my own history. While in Paris, I was violently smitten with the Hôtel de Salm, and used to go to the Tuileries almost daily, to look at it. The *loueuse de chaises,* inattentive to my passion, never had the complaisance to place a chair there, so that, sitting on the parapet, and twisting my neck round to see the object of my admiration, I generally left it with a torti-colli.

"From Lyons to Nîmes," Jefferson concluded, "I have been nourished with the remains of Roman grandeur. They have always brought you to my mind, because I know your affection for whatever is Roman and noble."

Trusting to his own affection for whatever was Roman and noble, Jefferson decided that the capitol of Virginia in Richmond might be patterned after the pride of Nîmes. He wrote Madison in the fall of 1785:

> We took as our model what is called the *Maison Carrée . . .* one of the most beautiful, if not the most beautiful and precious morsel of architecture left us by antiquity. It was built by Caius and Lucius Caesar,* and repaired by Louis xiv, and has the sufferage of all the judges of architecture who have seen it, as yielding to no one of the beautiful monuments of Greece, Rome, Palmyra, and Balbec, which late travellers have communicated to us. It is very simple, but it is noble beyond expression, and would have done honor to our country, as presenting to travellers a specimen of taste in our infancy, promising much for our maturer age.
>
> I have been much mortified with information, which I received two days ago from Virginia, that the first brick of the capitol would be laid

* Modern scholarship assigns 16 B.C. as the correct date.

within a few days. . . . Pray try if you can effect the stopping of this work.
. . . How is a taste for this beautiful art to be formed in our countrymen
unless we avail ourselves of every occasion when public buildings are
erected, of presenting to them models for their study and imitation?

The work was stopped, and Jefferson, who had asked Clérisseau, the
teacher of Robert Adam, to prepare a model of the "Maison Carrée" in
stucco, had the satisfaction of knowing that the new capitol of Virginia
based on this precedent would be the first example in the modern world
of a public building in the temple form. Not until 1807, twenty-two
years later, did Vignon begin work on the second such edifice, the Church
of the Madeleine in Paris.

Warm with this triumph, Jefferson was not offended to find that his
wishes were not exactly respected. "On account of the difficulty of the
Corinthian capitals, I yielded, with reluctance, to the taste of Clérissault
[sic] in his preference of the modern capital of Scamozzi to the more
noble capital of antiquity." Clérisseau, who appreciated the sacrifice of
the statesman's principles in the matter of capitals, could not refrain
from reminding him that "the love I have for my art is such that I
cannot tell you how satisfying it is for me to find a true lover of
antiquity."

It was in the role of a true lover of antiquity that Jefferson watched
over not only the planning of Washington, D.C., but also the beginnings
of the University of Virginia, whose campus was one of the supreme
achievements of American architecture. Unchallenged by the hundreds of
colleges founded in the next hundred years, it was not to be rivaled until
1938, when Frank Lloyd Wright began sketching the layout of Florida
Southern.

Though the concept of the university was even more truly the creation of Jefferson than the capitol of Virginia, he did not hesitate to
consult Benjamin Henry Latrobe, then the greatest of our architects, asking his advice on a series of pavilions and dormitories. "Now what we
wish," Jefferson made plain, "is that these pavilions as they will shew
themselves above the dormitories, should be models of taste and correct
architecture—and of a variety of appearance, no two alike, so as to serve
as specimens of orders for the architectural lectures." Latrobe, who could
not disagree with Jefferson's decision, devised two of the pavilions and
suggested the domed building or rotunda dominating the lawn, dormitories, and pavillions.

In 1819, seven years before the Palladian campus at Charlottesville
neared completion, one John Hartwell Cocke, a rugged planter who
fumed at the idiocy of cultivating no crop but tobacco in nineteenth-
century Virginia, risking his own idle capital in canals, watched the last
brick being laid at "Bremo," his Jeffersonian villa overlooking the James

Capitol, Richmond, Va., 1785-92 (Thomas Jefferson)

"Monticello," Charlottesville, Va., 1770-1809 (Thomas Jefferson)

Rotunda, University of Virginia, Charlottesville, Va., 1822-26 (Thomas Jefferson)

River. Though it is doubtful that Jefferson himself prepared plans for "Bremo," the mansion showed his influence. The owner not only asked the master of "Monticello" for hints, but hired two housewrights trained under his neighbor's supervision. The magnificent rough stone barn alone might be considered one of the masterpieces of American architecture; the house itself is one of the greatest of the Virginia mansions, its Tuscan portico at once subtle and majestic, its twin dependencies linked with the central block by serene balustraded walks.

Cocke, who raised the prestige of his family to new heights, was, as one might suspect, too aggressive a businessman to pose as a gentle philosopher. A ranting prohibitionist, he also dreaded the thought of aliens on the faculty at Charlottesville. And he was far too puritanical to rejoice in the splendid campus. It was all a "raree show," the rotunda and the pavilions, and he dared to alter "Bremo" itself in defiance of Jefferson's instructions. "Commenced taking off Roof of the House to be replaced by a new one to get rid of the evils of flat roofing and spouts and gutters, or in other words to supersede the Jeffersonian by the common sense plan," he noted in his diary.

L'ENFANT'S DEFEAT

Long, long before Cocke succeeded in remodeling the roof of "Bremo" to suit his own fancy, Benjamin Henry Latrobe, the architect Jefferson had consulted over the plans for the university, paused in his labors in Washington to consider the melancholy end of Pierre-Charles L'Enfant, the Frenchman who laid out the national capital. "Daily through the city," Latrobe remarked, "stalks the picture of famine, L'Enfant and his dog. . . . This singular man . . . had the courage to undertake any public work that might be offered to him. He has not succeeded in any, but was always honest, and is now miserably poor. He is too poor to receive any subsistence, and it is very doubtful in what manner he subsists."

The prospects of this city planner were not always so unflattering. In the summer of 1782, when the French minister at Philadelphia thought of giving a ball on the night of the Dauphin's birthday, the pavilion for the occasion was designed by L'Enfant. "One cannot imagine a building in better taste," conceded the Baron de Closen. "Simplicity is there united with an air of dignity."

Only twenty-three when he sailed as a volunteer for America in 1777, L'Enfant was wounded at Savannah, but not so severely as to despair of a career in the New World. The son of one of the tapestry designers at Gobelins, L'Enfant was trained both as an engineer and architect, and such was the joy of the guests at the French Legation that he was asked to decorate a room in Oeller's Hotel for the use of the Philadelphia

"Bremo," Fluvanna Co., Va., 1815-19

Assembly. An English traveler reported that this was "papered after the French taste . . . in the same style as lately introduced in the most elegant houses in London."

But L'Enfant had only begun to charm the ladies and gentlemen who presumed to set the fashions in the newest of the nations. When Caffieri's monument to General Montgomery was found to cast an eccentric shadow across the altar window of St. Paul's Chapel in New York, it was he who eased the minds of the vestrymen by inventing a superb altar screen, complete with thunderclouds, streaks of lightning, and the two tables of the Mosaic Law.

An even greater compliment was paid L'Enfant by the Society of the Cincinnati, who agreed that he was to design the eagle of the order and its diploma. Unfortunately, when sent to Paris on the happy errand of selecting the proper jeweler for the eagles, he revealed he was ignorant of the science of bookkeeping. "The reception which the Cincinnati met with soon induced me to appear . . . in a manner consistent with the dignity of the society of which I was regarded as the representative," he advised Hamilton. "My abode at the court produced expenses far beyond the sums I had at first thought of."

Though L'Enfant had already proved that he was unable to balance a budget, he was not overlooked by the solid men who anticipated New York State's adoption of the Federal Constitution, and he devoted his talent to the grand parade staged to hasten the decision of the legislators, fashioning the gigantic banquet pavilion which stretched 880 by 600 feet. A year later, when the Federal government was at last established, he made over the old New York City Hall into our first capitol. A novel feature was the pediment crowning the balcony and entrance; here crouched an eagle emerging from the clouds, and to render his patriotic significance unmistakable, thirteen stars filled the metopes of the frieze directly beneath. Within, L'Enfant tampered with the orders, devising capitals for the pilasters combining stars and rays.

Ten acres of Manhattan real estate were presented to L'Enfant in recognition of this achievement, but this gift he declined, having decided that he need stoop to no petty gains. Besides, he was consumed by the idea that he might lay out the national capital. "Although," he bravely wrote Washington in the fall of 1789, "the means now within the power of the country are not such as to pursue the design to any great extent, it will be obvious that the plan should be drawn on such a scale as to leave room for that aggrandisement and embellishment which the increase of the wealth of the nation will permit it to pursue at any period, however remote."

Whatever L'Enfant's failings, he was not mean, and the city of which he dreamed was not without grandeur. He did not forget five glorious fountains, an equestrian monument to Washington, a column in honor of our naval victories, another to recall the telling moments of our history, and he even remembered a temple for national thanksgivings. Perhaps Washington was correct in thinking that L'Enfant was "better qualified than anyone who had come within my knowledge, in this country."

Though scholars have discovered that the Washington plan is, after all, a recollection of that of Versailles, and have pointed out that the Capitol occupies the site of the palace, the White House that of the Grand Trianon, the Mall that of the Park, while East Capitol Street, Pennsylvania Avenue, and Maryland Avenue on the east, and Pennsylvania Avenue on the west, correspond to the Avenues of Paris, Sceaux, St. Cloud, and Trianon, all this must not obscure L'Enfant's subtlety in imposing a gridiron on the radial avenues beloved by the kings of France. Moreover, it is to L'Enfant that we owe the vista of the Capitol from the mall, and that of the White House from the Potomac, views which will surely carry his name down through the centuries.

In his own day, however, L'Enfant was in no danger of being overpraised, and even Jefferson, usually so understanding of the aims of an artist, was annoyed by the planner's insistence on houses being built at a certain distance from the street. "It makes a disgusting monotony," thought Jefferson. "All persons make this complaint against Philadelphia." The master of "Monticello" proceeded to discuss the wisdom of locating the Capitol at what is now the corner of Pennsylvania Avenue and Tenth Street, with the White House near by. In his opinion a public walk connecting the two buildings was all the planning required; the rest of the city might spread in unending rectangles

Businessmen and statesmen, too, got on L'Enfant's nerves. When one Daniel Carroll thoughtlessly erected a house across what was intended to be New Jersey Avenue, the planner was beside himself with anger. "It will always be found sound policy to conciliate the good will of any man, where it can be accomplished without much difficulty, inconvenience, or loss," Washington recommended. L'Enfant determined the house must be pulled down nonetheless. "Having the beauty and regularity of your plan in view, you pursue it as if every person or thing were obliged to yield to it," Washington commented.

In the end L'Enfant exhausted the patience of all of the influential men in the government. "I am thoroughly persuaded, that to render him useful, his temper must be subdued," Jefferson remarked. Washington was dismayed. "Losing his services . . . would be a serious misfortune," the President conceded. "At the same time he must know, there is a line beyond which he will not be suffered to go. Whether it is zeal, an impetuous temper, or other motives that lead him into such blameable conduct, I will not take upon me to decide—but be what it will, it must be checked."

Early in 1792 the unmanageable planner was dismissed from the service of the United States. Too proud to accept five hundred guineas and a lot in the center of the city for his labors, unwilling to descend to teaching military engineering at the Military Academy, he worked over the plans of Paterson, New Jersey, the manufacturing town which Alexander Hamilton and the other promoters of the Society for Useful Manufactures were founding. Then, his hopes once more raised, he began designing a truly magnificent town house in Philadelphia for the ambitious banker Robert Morris. Like so many of L'Enfant's projects, this was destined never to be completed. Late in 1795 Morris confessed that he was no less exasperated than Washington or Jefferson. "Although," he wrote the architect, "it was not my intention to have the marble you have introduced into this building, yet an inclination to indulge your genius induced me to permit so much of it. Had you executed my intentions instead of your own, my family would now have inhabited the house instead of being liable to be turned out of doors." A year afterward Morris discovered that L'Enfant was farther than ever from carrying out his instructions. "It is with astonishment I see the work of last fall pulled down in order to put up more marble on my house on which there is already vastly too much," he complained. The banker was then on the verge of bankruptcy.

Of brick faced with marble, the Morris town house recalled the Hôtel Biron in Paris; both were remarkable for pavilions with curved faces, and both were distinguished in a distinguished century, no matter if Benjamin Henry Latrobe, who was not the most considerate critic of his contemporaries, found it "impossible to decide which of the two is the madder, the architect or his employer." In all Philadelphia, the only house which might be compared to it, aside from the town and country establishments of the Binghams, was "The Woodlands," the newly remodeled estate of William Hamilton, grandson of the Andrew Hamilton who planned Independence Hall in his off hours from the law. Even today, when Hamilton's seat has been converted into the headquarters of a cemetery company, its lawn scarred by tombstones, and its fieldstone façade blackened by the fumes of the locomotives of the Pennsylvania Railroad, its two elliptical salons overlooking the Schuylkill suggest that the site was once the haunt of elegance.

Elegance—as even the most fervent admirers of L'Enfant must admit—was not apparent in the nation's capital at the dawn of the nineteenth century. Washington on the eve of the War of 1812 was a depressing sight to many gentlemen of taste. Gouverneur Morris sneered that this was the finest city in the world in which to live—in the future. As for the real-estate promoter Thomas Law, he was no less indignant. "When I walk over this city and see a bridge, with a wall only on one side—when I view the Patent Office with plank to its frameless windows—when I perceive the President's garden in gullies, and the rooms of his house unplastered—when the rain drips on my head through the roof of the Capitol . . . I ask—can these disgusting scenes to strangers, be pleasing to the citizens?"

THE DARING OF WILLIAM THORNTON

All of this must not blind us to the trials and triumphs of the architects laboring at the fearful task of pleasing both themselves and the politicians. The briefest summary of the history of the Capitol reads like nothing so much as a recital of grievances. William Thornton, who prepared the first designs, found it wise to retire in time to a job in the Patent Office.

A brilliant amateur who risked his income on the race track and his principal promoting steamboats, Thornton devoted what remained of his savings to cultivating Merino sheep. His wit he spent at Washington dinner parties, and everyone agreed that this West Indian Quaker, who had studied to be a physician in Edinburgh, had not forgotten what he had learned of the art of conversation in Paris. As an architect he may be seen at his very best at "Tudor Place" in Georgetown, the residence he completed in 1815 for Washington's step-granddaughter, Martha Parke Custis, the bride of one Thomas Peter. In this yellow-stuccoed adaptation of the Regency style of England, he displayed genuine discrimination in the design of the temple-like portico of the central block which so successfully dominates the wings. He was not half so daring in "The Octagon," the hexagonal Washington town house of John Tayloe, son of the John Tayloe of "Mount Airy," nor in his plans for "Woodlawn," the estate near "Mount Vernon" of Mrs. Peter's sister.

Thornton's success is all the more astonishing if you reflect that he might never have turned architect if he had not chanced to read one morning in a Philadelphia newspaper of a prize offered for the best design for a public library. "When I travelled," he admitted, "I never thought of architecture, but I got some books and worked a few days, then gave a plan in the Ionic order, which carried the day." He was then twenty-eight, and he was no more than thirty-one in 1792, the year he tried his luck in the contest for the national Capitol, the prize this time being either a gold medal worth five hundred dollars, or a lot of that value in Washington. "I lamented not having studied architecture," he afterward confessed, "and resolved to attempt the grand undertaking and study at the same time. I studied some months, and worked almost night and day, but found I was opposed by regular architects from France and various other countries." However, Thornton was battling against lesser odds than you might suppose.

Though you might assume that the competition for the national Capitol would attract only the most ambitious architects, such was far from the truth. A bridgebuilder whose bridges collapsed without warning, a carpenter who displayed a fascinating preference for windowless rooms—these were typical of the contestants. An exception was Etienne-Sulpice Hallet, a French professional who submitted a "fancy piece"—prior to the formal opening of the contest—inspired by the Panthéon in Paris. His final plans have been lost, as have Thornton's, but to him must be assigned the idea of a high central dome with balancing wings.

Since the unabridged chronicle of the Capitol would be incredibly detailed, the reader will be spared each and every recrimination of the various designers, but the plight of Hallet must not be ignored. He had all but won the competition when Thornton wrote in from the West Indies asking permission to send in his drawings after the closing date. This was granted, and in the spring of 1793 Thornton was notified that he was the winner. Critics have since judged that he must have based his design on a glimpse of Hallet's, but for all that, his vision of a great central rotunda satisfied Washington. "Grandeur, simplicity, and convenience appear so well combined in this plan of Dr. Thornton's, that I have no doubt," the President notified the commissioners of the Federal District, "of its meeting with that approbation from you, which I have given it under an attentive inspection."

Though the north wing was erected in accordance with Thornton's outline, as well as the exterior of the south wing, he was not allowed to build his own building. Of all people, Hallet was invited to superintend the construction, which he could not undertake without finding fault with Thornton's colonnades, stairways, windows, not to mention his floor plan. In the fall of 1794 Hallet was obliged to resign, but not before he had succeeded in laying a square instead of a round foundation for the central unit. This was later altered.

THE HOPES OF GEORGE HADFIELD

George Hadfield, who became superintendent when Hallet faded into the obscurity from which no scholar has rescued his last years, held on to the job until 1798, but not without twice offering his resignation before he was officially discharged. The son of a Leghorn hotelkeeper, he was the brother of the artist Maria Cosway, whose drawing room Thomas Jefferson haunted in Paris. Hadfield had studied at the British Royal Academy, had won his way to Rome on a fellowship, and what was even more rewarding, had earned the esteem of the American painter John Trumbull. It was Trumbull who recommended him to our government, though he lived to regret the day he persuaded him to settle in the United States. "I have always felt," said the American artist in his autobiography, "as if I had been instrumental in causing the ruin of this admirable artist and excellent friend; for if I had not been the means of inducing him to leave London, his connections there, who had some influence with the late king, George IV, might have procured him the execution of those extensive and splendid works which were committed to Mr. Nash. . . .

"Poor Hadfield," Trumbull recalled, "languished many years in obscurity in Washington." Yet his career was not quite so undistinguished as you might infer from his old friend's commiseration. "Arlington," the remodeled Doric mansion near Alexandria of Washington's step-grandson, G. W. P. Custis, was his design; so was the gracious Ionic City Hall of Washington, serving today as the district court house. Perhaps the loveliest of all his creations was the mausoleum in Oak Hill Cemetery that he fashioned for Washington's mayor, John Peter Van Ness. This was inspired by the Temple of Vesta in Rome.

THE TRIALS OF JAMES HOBAN

Though James Hoban, who succeeded Hadfield as superintendent of the Capitol in 1798, made no memorable alterations in that structure, he left his mark on Washington, for he designed the White House in 1792. Winning the competition for this building called for tact as well as talent. Thomas Jefferson, who submitted an anonymous design of his own patterned after Palladio's "Villa Rotonda," not only was positive which models should be followed, but felt obliged to force his taste upon the nation. For the President's house, he made plain, "I should prefer the celebrated fronts of modern buildings, which have already received the approbation of all good judges." He listed his favorites, including of course the front and rear elevations of the "Hôtel de Salm" in Paris.

Hoban's White House, which owed no debt to Jefferson's predilections, has sometimes been assumed to be a mere replica of "Leinster House" in Dublin, but a far closer parallel may be discovered with a plate for a gentleman's house in James Gibbs's *A Book of Architecture* Scholars have pointed out that the columns of the entrance façade of "Leinster House" are of the Corinthian order, while Hoban preferred the Ionic.

Only thirty-four the year he won the contest for the White House, Hoban was only twenty-two when he earned his first distinction, a medal from the Dublin Society for his drawings of brackets and roofs. Shortly thereafter, no one knows when, this talented youth from Kilkenny County landed in Charleston, and after designing the old State House

of South Carolina in Columbia, is said to have called on George Washington with a note of introduction from Charleston's merchant prince
Henry Laurens.

To catch the fancy of Henry Laurens was no doubt an easier task than
soothing the nerves of Abigail Adams, but Hoban eventually succeeded
in making the wife of our second President tolerably satisfied with her
surroundings. "Woods are all you see, from Baltimore until you reach
the city, which is only so in name," Mrs. Adams told her daughter not
long after settling in Washington.

> Here and there a small cot, without a glass window, interspersed
> amongst the forests, through which you travel miles without seeing any
> human being. In the city there are buildings enough, if they were com-
> pact and finished, to accommodate Congress and those attached to it; but
> as they are, and scattered as they are, I see no great comfort for them.
> The river, which runs up to Alexandria, is in full view of my window,
> and I see the vessels as they pass and repass.
>
> The house [Mrs. Adams continued] is upon a grand and superb scale,
> requiring about thirty servants to attend and keep the apartments in
> proper order, and perform the ordinary business of the house and stables;
> an establishment very well proportioned to the President's salary. The
> lighting, the apartments, from the kitchens to parlors and chambers, is
> a tax indeed; and the fires we are obliged to keep to secure us from daily
> agues is another very cheering comfort. To assist us in this great castle,
> and render less attendance necessary, bells are wholly wanting, not one
> single one being hung through the whole house, and promises are all you
> can obtain.

Logs were hard to come by for the grate fires, but Mrs. Adams faced
the future with her usual fortitude. "You must keep all this to yourself," she warned her daughter,

> and when asked how I like it, say that I write you the situation is beauti-
> ful, which is true. The house is made hospitable, but there is not a single
> apartment finished, and all withinside, except the plastering, has been
> done since Briesler came. We have not the least fence, yard, or other con-
> venience without, and the great unfinished audience-room I made a dry-
> ing-room of, to hang up the clothes in. The principal stairs are not up,
> and will not be until this winter. Six chambers are made comfortable;
> two are occupied by the President and Mr. Shaw; two lower rooms, one
> for a common parlor, and one for a levee-room. Upstairs there is the oval
> room, which is designed for the drawing-room, and has the crimson fur-
> niture in it. It is a very handsome room now; but, when completed, it
> will be beautiful.

"If," concluded Mrs. Adams, "the 12 years, in which this place has
been considered as the future seat of government, had been improved, as
they would have been in New England, many of the present incon-

veniences would have been removed. It is," she admitted, "a beautiful spot, capable of every improvement, and the more I view it, the more I am delighted with it."

THE GENIUS OF BENJAMIN HENRY LATROBE

Architects have seldom been lenient to their rivals, and Benjamin Henry Latrobe, who took Hoban's place as chief of the works at the Capitol, besides completing the White House, was not half so pleased with Hoban's achievement. Fretting one day at a colonnade suggested by Thomas Jefferson, he exploded. "The style of the colonnade he proposes is exactly consistent with Hoban's pile," said Latrobe, "a litter of pigs worthy of the great sow it surrounds, and of the Irish boar, the father."

Latrobe was ever sharp-tongued. "In spite of the unpopularity which politics will annex to the assertion," he observed, "the manners of Virginia are English. The English character, with some excellencies, has many faults. It is the most coldhearted and selfish of any nation I know." Latrobe himself was half-English. The son of a Moravian minister and a Pennsylvania girl who had been sent to school in England, he was packed off to a Moravian academy in Saxony, and did not settle down in Great Britain until after he had attended classes at the University of Leipzig and served in the Prussian Army.

No one could complain that he was untrained. Apprenticed first to John Smeaton, the engineer of the Eddystone Lighthouse, and later to Samuel Pepys Cockerell, one of the most successful architects of the day, in no time he became one of the best equipped practitioners in London. He was on the eve of establishing his reputation when suddenly, in 1795, perhaps because he was sick at heart over the death of his young wife, he quite England forever and set sail for the United States.

Had Latrobe remained in England, he would certainly have challenged the supremacy of Soane and Nash, the leaders of the coming generation; in America there was no one to match either his imagination or his experience, and it would be impossible to exaggerate the blessings of his example in our midst. Fortunately, he was not unappreciated. Though he secured few enough commissions at first—a prison in Richmond was perhaps the most important building he designed during the two years he tarried in Virginia—by 1799 he was watching over the progress of the Ionic colonnades of the Bank of Pennsylvania in Philadelphia. This was not only an admirable addition to the architecture of that city, but a truly revolutionary inspiration for architects unaware of the trend of taste in Great Britain. For the first time in American history a masonry vault dominated a monumental interior, and what was equally exciting, this was the first attempt in the United States to follow Greek instead of Roman precedent.

The Greek revival, which may be said to have begun in England in 1762, with the publication of the first volume of Stuart and Revett's *Antiquities of Athens,* did not catch the fancy of Americans until after Latrobe's death in 1820, an event which very properly closes the Federal period and introduces the romantic era. Even Thomas Jefferson, who was not one to believe that architecture must stand still, could not comprehend the fervor which seized Latrobe whenever he spoke of the remains of Greece. As long ago as 1771 Jefferson had meditated erecting a Grecian temple in the gardens of "Monticello," but that was before he contemplated the Roman relics in France and declared his loyalty to the Roman tradition.

Undaunted, Latrobe could not resist reminding Jefferson of what he conceived to be the Roman errors. "My *principles* of good taste are rigid in Grecian architecture," he told the President. "I am a bigoted Greek in the condemnation of the Roman architecture of Baalbec, Palmyra, Spalatro, and of all the buildings erected subsequent to Hadrian's regime. The immense size, the bold plan, and arrangements of the buildings of the Romans down almost to Constantine's arch, plundered from the triumphal arches of former emperors, I admire, however, with enthusiasm, but think their decorations and details absurd beyond tolerance from the reign of Severus downward."

Latrobe was a Greek, but a Greek troubled by the suspicion that modern requirements could not be satisfied by replicas. "Wherever," he told Jefferson, "the Grecian style can be copied without impropriety, I love to be a mere, I would say a *slavish* copyist, but the forms and the distribution of the Roman and Greek buildings which remain are in general inapplicable to the objects and uses of our public buildings. Our religion requires churches wholly different from the temples, our government, our legislative assemblies, and our courts of justice, buildings of entirely different principles from their basilicas; and our amusements could not possibly be performed in their theaters or amphitheaters. But that which principally demands a variation in our buildings from those of the ancients is the difference in our climate." And Latrobe ended by reaffirming his creed as an architect: "It is not the *ornament,* it is the *use* that I want."

Such was Latrobe's rational creed, but it would be inane to imagine that he was ever faithful to his own doctrine. Like all architects in all times, he could not always practice what he preached, and in 1799 he delighted the Philadelphia merchant William Crammond by designing him a Gothic mansion which was the first example in America of the Gothic revival, a style which, like the Greek revival, became exceedingly popular after Latrobe's death, and which, in its inception, had nothing whatever in common with the functionalism of the "genuine" Gothic of the Middle Ages.

Scholars may quarrel over the origins of the Gothic revival, but no one has yet denied that "Strawberry Hill," the tiny Gothic castle Horace Walpole commanded near London in 1749, was the first building to set the stamp of fashion on the rediscovery of the architecture of medieval times. The lord of this demesne, who knew nothing and cared less about the structural mathematics of Gothic vaulting, was anxious above all else to create a setting in which he might recall the romance of the past.

Like "Strawberry Hill," "Sedgeley," as William Crammond's retreat was named, was something of a stage-set, but there was a singular charm to the pointed arches of the colonnade encircling the otherwise conventional house, and to cultivated Americans weary of the formality of Georgian architecture, this design must have seemed quite as refreshing as that Grecian triumph, the Bank of Pennsylvania.

"Sedgeley" and the bank were being built when Latrobe was invited to superintend the engineering of the Philadelphia waterworks. Once the technical problems were solved, he amused himself creating a delicate Grecian pumphouse which stood on the site of the present City Hall. Having scored these three hits in only two years, Latrobe would not have been human if he had not been enchanted by his welcome in the Quaker metropolis, and in an oration delivered before the Society of Artists, he expressed the hope that here would rise the most glorious city in the world.

"If," he said, "a conviction can be wrought, and diffused throughout the nation, that the fine arts may indeed be pressed into the service of arbitrary power, and—like mercenary troops, do their duty while well paid—yet that their home is in the bosom of a republic; then, indeed, the days of Greece may be revived in the woods of America, and Philadelphia become the Athens of the western world." Calming the fears of Quakers who fancied that elegance and corruption were synonymous, he added that "the history of Greece refutes the vulgar opinion that the arts are incompatible with liberty. . . . Greece . . . lost her freedom" only after "she prostituted the fine arts to the gratification of vice."

Though Latrobe could not complain that the fine arts were prostituted to the gratification of vice in Washington, he was never so happy in the capital as in Philadelphia, and there were moments when he despaired of attaining the recognition for which he longed and to which he justly felt himself entitled. "Nothing," he told John Randolph of Roanoke, "has so much injured my utility to the public and to my family as the very prevailing notion that men who, unfortunately for themselves, are called men of genius, are incapable of the management of money. I, unfortunately, have, very undeservedly, acquired this nickname merely because I stand alone in a profession in which there is not room in our country for more than one, and which requires some portion of imagination. It is a mark upon me the effects of which I feel daily, and which keeps me from acquiring the independence which a dull usurer or a dealer in dry goods can easily and honorably attain."

No one, not even Jefferson who tactfully said he hoped the day would dawn when Latrobe would embellish "with Athenian taste the course of a nation looking far beyond the range of Athenian destinies," could quite console the architect for democratic America's distrust of intellectual prestige. "I shall at last make cloth, steam engines, or turn tailor for money," Latrobe cried, "for money is honor."

If Latrobe had not been an anxious artist, he might have been satisfied that America would remember his name for generations, for the Capitol as we know it is largely his. He it was who made over the western front of the central block, remodeled the portico on the east, added a domical roof with cupolas on each wing, and redesigned the interior of the south wing which once housed the Hall of Representatives and the Senate Chamber. All this, of course, was not accomplished without a struggle.

Not the least of Latrobe's worries were his arguments with Thornton. Shortly after he was appointed surveyor of buildings by Jefferson, he called on the original designer of the Capitol, but found that his courtesy was misunderstood. "I judged very ill in going to Dr. Thornton," Latrobe confessed to the President. "In a few peremptory words . . . he told me that no difficulties existed in his plan but such as were made by those who were too ignorant to remove them, and though these were not exactly his words, his expressions, his tones, his manners, and his absolute refusal to discuss the subject spoke his meaning more strongly and offensively than I have expressed."

Nor was Jefferson himself always appreciative of Latrobe's aims. To a friend the architect complained he was obliged to "introduce Corinthian columns into the House of Representatives, and put one hundred lights of glass into the ceiling, contrary to my declared judgment, urgent entreaties and representations. In other respects, however," Latrobe admitted, "the honor which the friendship of the great man has done me obliterates all feeling of dissatisfaction on account of these errors of a vitiated taste and an imperfect attention to the practical effect of his architectural projects."

Even the popular approval which greeted the "corn-cob" capitals in the Senate wing did not revive Latrobe's spirits. "These capitals," he said, ". . . obtained me more applause from members of Congress than all the works of magnitude or difficulty that surrounded them. They christened them the 'corn-cob' capitals, whether for the sake of alliteration I cannot tell, but certainly not very appropriately."

Having devoted ten years of his life to the Capitol, from 1803 to 1811,

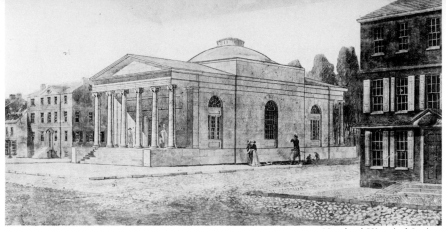

Bank of Pennsylvania, Philadelphia, Pa., 1799 (B. H. Latrobe)

Residence of William Crammond, Philadelphia, Pa., 1799
(B. H. Latrobe)

Residence of Robert Morris, Philadelphia, Pa., 1795
(P. C. L'Enfant)

and from 1815 to 1817 when his was the task of superintending the re-
building of both the Capitol and the White House after the devastation
of the War of 1812, Latrobe was bitterly disappointed on being forced to
resign from the government service in the Monroe administration. Planning the Chesapeake and Delaware Canal and designing steamboats for
the Ohio River traffic—these were trivial accomplishments by comparison. Closer to his heart was the commission for the Roman Catholic
Cathedral of Baltimore. For this he submitted two sets of drawings—one
Gothic, the other Roman in inspiration. The Roman plan was accepted,
but much altered following the dedication of the building in 1821. The
year before the consecration the architect fell a victim to the yellow fever
in New Orleans, just as the new waterworks he had conceived for the city
were nearing completion.

If no one in our republic prized Latrobe's gifts at their true worth,
this was not too surprising, for he was, as was only too evident, a generation ahead of his time, and Charles Bulfinch, who succeeded to his post
in charge of the Capitol, need not be ridiculed for failing to appreciate
the achievements of his predecessor. "At the first view of these drawings,"
he noted on gazing at Latrobe's plans, "my courage almost failed me—
they are beautifully executed, and the design is in the boldest style. After
long study," Bulfinch added, "I feel better satisfied and more confidence
in meeting public expectation. There are certainly faults enough in
Latrobe's design to justify the opposition to him. His style is calculated
for display in the greater parts, but I think his staircases in general are
crowded and not easy of access, and the passages are intricate and dark.
Indeed, the whole interior, except the two great rooms, has a somber
appearance." *

Fortunately for his own reputation, Bulfinch made few changes in Latrobe's scheme for the Capitol. Aside from introducing slight alterations
in the interiors of the wings, he was content to follow in Latrobe's footsteps. And when, in 1851, Thomas Ustick Walter was invited to create the
present dome and to plot the extension which includes the present north
and south wings, he, too, let well enough alone.

So much for Latrobe and the Capitol. In the rest of the nation, as in
Washington, talented architects from abroad were setting a higher and
higher standard for our native designers, and as in Washington, these
foreigners were often embittered. But the story of our architecture in the
Federal period is much more than a chapter of despair. Our native
architects, few of whom could compare to a Latrobe, were tempted by his
example and by that of other foreigners in our midst to all manner of
experimentation beyond the imagination of the colonial era. Moreover,
not all of the imported artists were necessarily disgruntled.

* These faults, says Latrobe's biographer, Talbot F. Hamlin, were really those of
Thornton.

THE FATE OF WILLIAM JAY

Of the Englishman William Jay, who whiled away seven years in the shadowy squares of Savannah before his premature death in Mauritius, we know little beyond the sorrowing comments of his father, a dissenting preacher who was not inclined to forgive the vagaries of his unconscientious son. He was cursed, lamented Father Jay, with "a large share of wit and humor, qualities always dangerous and commonly injurious to the possessor. . . . His comic powers drew him into company not the most friendly to youthful improvement." Young Jay may not have kept the most desirable company, but he had no trouble meeting the most desirable clients in Savannah. In 1817, the very year of his arrival, he is said to have designed what is now known as the "Owens House" for Richard Richardson, whose wife, a member of the pious and prosperous Bolton family, happened to be the architect's sister-in-law. Like the residence of Alexander Telfair, son of Governor Telfair, now the Telfair Academy, which he is supposed to have created in the following year, this was a casual adaptation of the Regency style so popular in the London of Beau Brummel. William Jay was not quite so inventive as John Nash in his recollection of classic splendors, but was equally adept at cutting costs by throwing up façades plastered with stucco, and undeniably elegant. He could even be noble, as he proved in the solemn Doric portico he is said to have conceived in 1818 for the town house of the merchant William Scarborough, later reconverted as a Negro school.

THE CHARLESTON OF GABRIEL MANIGAULT

Like Savannah, Charleston shared in the prosperity which blessed the former colonies once they were free of British restrictions on commerce, but unlike Savannah, Charleston had a native architect of real distinction. This was Gabriel Manigault, son-in-law of the difficult connoisseur Ralph Izard. An amateur who hesitated to follow the very latest styles, Manigault was nevertheless aware of the grandeurs of the Old World, having devoted the income from the family rice plantations to what must have been an excellent classical and legal education in Geneva and London. His finest work, the town house of his brother Joseph, dating from 1790, is still standing to tell of his appreciation of the delicacy on which the brothers Adam insisted when intent on charming clients as exacting as the Duke of Northumberland. The gardener's cottage might even have been inspired by one of the temples in the gardens of Stowe.

Unfortunately we have no means of ascertaining the name of the architect who designed the Charleston town house of the ambitious Rhode Island merchant Nathaniel Russell in 1811. Yet this three-story brick dwelling may be the city's supreme achievement in the Federal era. The oval drawing room on the first floor, the geometrical fancy of whose polygonal exterior is the delight of the garden, mirrors the anxiety of the unknown artist to realize in brick the most daring dreams of the day.

THE MONUMENTS OF ROBERT MILLS

Robert Mills, the first of our native architects to be trained for the profession, was seldom so ambitious. Two of his distinguished if prudent buildings remain to dignify the Charleston in which he was born. The Doric First Baptist Church was completed in 1822, the year in which Mills began the County Record (or "Fireproof") Building, finished five years later. Here neither the Doric portico itself, nor the high basement, nor the numerous blind arches reveal the genuine contribution of Mills to American architecture, but the bold, unmistakably American effort to simplify the composition.

All this, however, could not convince Latrobe that Mills, who had once labored as his draftsman, was a significant architect. He is, Latrobe told one of his fellows in the profession, "a wretched designer. He came to me too late to acquire principles of taste. He is a copyist, and is fit for nothing else. . . . But he has also his merit. He is a very snug contriver of domestic contrivances and will make a good deal of money. He wants that professional self-respect which is the ruin of you and me, and therefore we shall go to the wall, while he will strut in the middle of the street."

Which was not altogether fair to Mills. For although he never sighed for new horizons, he was much more than a clever copyist. And he was never so well off as Latrobe predicted. Once, when his wife's drawing and piano lessons failed to meet the requirements of the family budget, he was even reduced to begging the Baltimore merchant Robert Gilmor for a loan. "Unless you oblige me," said the frantic architect, "I shall scarcely be able to go to market."

The son of a successful tailor, Mills was evidently destined to follow his father's trade, but having fallen in with James Hoban, he set off for Washington in his company. There this young graduate of the College of Charleston met Jefferson, and for two years served as the President's draftsman at "Monticello." In 1803, when twenty-one, he went to work for Latrobe who was then planning the Chesapeake and Delaware Canal; in Latrobe's office, where he spent five years, he learned not only the fundamentals of architecture, but caught his master's fever for internal improvements. Aware of the inestimable advantages of canals and rail-

Residence of William Scarborough, Savannah, Ga., c. 1820 (William Jay)

"Hyde Hall," Cooperstown, N.Y., 1811-33 (Philip Hooker)

roads, too, he was one of the first to champion one of America's earliest railroads, that which ran from Charleston to Hamburg on the Savannah River.

But "The Internal Improvement of South Carolina," to quote the title of one of Mill's several essays devoted to canals, railroads, and lighthouses, was never so close to his heart as the art of architecture, nor were any engineering projects so noteworthy as the Bethesda Presbyterian Church in Camden, whose Doric portico he created in 1820, nor the Camden Court House he completed six years afterward. The Ionic portico of the latter was subsequently altered into four columns of the Doric order without genuine damage.

Mills, who was nothing if not a loyal South Carolinian, might well have preferred to labor only in his native state, but like all architects in all times, he was bound to answer the challenge of economics, and the prosperity of Richmond, which had more than doubled in size in the twenty years ending in 1810, tempted him nothward. In Richmond in 1812 he designed the best of all his town houses, that of John Wickham, the attorney who successfully defended Aaron Burr from the charge of treason. This stuccoed essay in the Regency manner, generously redecorated in the romantic era, is now open to the public as the Valentine Museum.

Architects may pause over Mills's town houses and churches, but most Americans will recall Mills as the designer of the Washington monuments in Washington, D.C., and Baltimore. Since the shaft on the Mall in the capital, begun in 1833 and completed only in 1884, twenty-nine years after his death, lacks the grand colonnade at the base which he considered essential, the Doric column at Mount Vernon Place in Baltimore, dedicated in 1829, fourteen years after the laying of the cornerstone, may be a more telling example of his skill. Though obviously influenced by the newly erected column in the Place Vendôme, it could scarcely be described as a replica, and its seemingly grotesque scale is peculiarly fitted to dominate the hillock on which it stands. Indeed, if you were asked to point out Mills's masterpiece, the Baltimore monument would be the best choice. Mills himself was positive that "the man of business, the statesman, the patriot, the warrior, while surveying the monument of Washington, will find a purer flame inspire his bosom, than does a pilgrim of Mecca, while worshipping at the tomb of Mahomet." And he proudly proclaimed that "the education I have received being altogether American and unmixed with European habits, I can safely present the design submitted as American."

Perhaps because he was half ashamed of remembering the splendors of Napoleonic France, Mills uttered an architectural declaration of independence. "I say to our artists," he solemnly announced, "study your country's tastes and requirements, and make classic ground *here* for your

Residence of Joseph Manigault, Charleston, S.C., c. 1790 (Gabriel Manigault)

Gate lodge, residence of Joseph Manigault

Dining room

art. Go not to the old world for your examples. We have entered a new era in the history of the world; it is our destiny to lead, not to be led. Our vast country is before us and our motto *excelsior.*"

THE TRIBULATIONS OF GODEFROY

Like most grandiloquent men in most times and places, Mills had to confess that his career was far less brilliant than his hopes. Too conservative to respond to the demands of the romantic era, he lived to see other men alter his plans for the Patent Office and Treasury in Washington. And in Baltimore itself, although the French refugee, Maximilien Godefroy, did not succeed in stealing the commission for the Washington Monument, he at least was a formidable competitor. It was Godefroy who designed the whimsical Gothic chapel in 1807 for the Sulpicians of St. Mary's Seminary. No matter if its barrel vault would have puzzled the master builders of the Middle Ages, the very rumor of its creation charmed Latrobe. "I am impatient to see it," wrote the genius of the Capitol. "I understand that it has at last crawled out of its chrysalis into a state of exquisite beauty. How did this miracle of conversion take place? I thought that your priests, God rest their souls! knew and were determined to suffer no beauty but that of holiness. Alas! what will become of my Cathedral? If ever it rises to a perceptible elevation above the ground, so as to overlook the buildings toward the college, it will sink again into the earth with envy of its child, the college chapel."

In 1815, when the citizens of Baltimore unveiled Godefroy's Egyptoid Battle Monument honoring the heroes of Fort McHenry in the War of 1812, the ceremony was not undignified. First in the parade was a detachment of horse, then the architect and the mayor, then two generals, then the clergy, then an antique car drawn by six white horses, and atop the car, festooned with drums and military standards, a model of the monument. This cavalcade moved to solemn music.

Three years afterward, when Godefroy's First Unitarian Church was opened in Baltimore, *The Port Folio,* then the most distinguished magazine in the nation, went into something like ecstasy over the arcaded loggia of the entrance. Its four Tuscan columns upheld a pediment featuring a terra cotta relief of the Angel of Truth. All this, reported the journal's correspondent, "will be acknowledged to approach nearer the perfection of architecture, than any other edifice in America."

But Godefroy, as his essays in the Gothic and Egyptian manner conclusively proved, was too far in advance of American taste to earn the national recognition he deserved, and there were days when he and his faithful American wife Eliza sank into the despair which blighted the hopes of nearly every alien architect in the Federal period. "I am weary more than I can express of this perpetual struggling with the stars for ignoble mutton chops and plebeian potatoes," Eliza cried. Her husband she likened to "a Corinthian capital, torn from its supporting column, and trodden under every careless foot."

Though we shall never know the answers to many of our questions concerning Godefroy's career—conscientious scholars have not yet been able to discover even the date of his death—he seems to have been dedicated to frustration long before he landed in the United States in 1805. He was then confident he had "found under the banner of American liberty consolation and resources against the storms that had destroyed my future." For he had "greeted the fall of the Bastille . . . as the dawn of hope," only to discover that the French Revolution in its ultimate stages was denying its principles. A mutinous veteran of the French Army, he was jailed for prophesying the end of the people's liberties; escaping with the blessing of a princess, he was recaptured, and released only on condition he set sail for America.

In Baltimore, even though he taught civil and military architecture at the Sulpican Academy, he found that what he earned as an architect could not begin to keep his family in comfort. Finally, after fourteen years of struggling, he departed for England, never to return to the United States. In his last years he was appointed the official architect of the Department of Mayenne in France; whether he made enough at that post to keep body and soul together we have no means of knowing, but most likely, he did not, for one of his wife's letters dating from that time is a melancholy document. "I for my part have no complaint to make of fate," Eliza declared. "Organized as my heart and affections are, to be the wife of such a man as Maxime, is more than my right of happiness— but oh, to see so much talent wrecked, so much genius thrown into utter darkness, such noble honor doomed to such a lot, that . . . is a mournful, a heart-rending contemplation."

THE GIFTS OF MANGIN AND RAMÉE

It is all very well to point out that the popular taste of America in the Federal period was far from mediocre, but the tragedy of Godefroy is no less poignant for all that. And if we possessed as many letters touching on the careers of Joseph-François Mangin and Joseph-Jacques Ramée, we might decide that those refugees in New York State were no less bitterly disappointed in America.

Since New York City in 1810 was already the first city in the country, with 96,000 inhabitants, you might suppose it would be far more splendid architecturally than either Philadelphia, Baltimore, or Boston, which ranked next in size. But possibly because New York could not come into

its own until the completion of the Erie Canal in 1825 insured the prosperity of which the trade of 1810 was only a foretaste, there were relatively few superb buildings in Manhattan in Federal times. An exception
was the City Hall, completed in 1812.

Usually attributed to the joint efforts of the native-born builder-
architect John McComb, Jr., and of the mysterious Frenchman Joseph-
François Mangin, the City Hall certainly owes not only the ease of its
staircase but the Louis XVI elegance of its exterior as well to Mangin,
who vanished from Manhattan in 1818 as casually as he had appeared in
1794. For in no other work of McComb do we find any hint of the
foreign influence so evident in this masterpiece in marble.

All of which must not be taken as a slight upon the ability of Mc-
Comb, who probably contributed his just share as supervisor of construction. An unusually competent craftsman in the late-Georgian vernacular, he was responsible for the handsome old Queens Building at
Rutgers University, and in 1807 could be peculiarly proud of the new St.
John's Chapel on Hudson Square, a church whose destruction in our
grandfathers' lifetime meant far more than the loss of a landmark.

Fortunately we are better acquainted with the European past of
Ramée than of Mangin. The eve of the Revolution found this apolitical
artist enrolled as one of the architects in the service of Louis XVI's
sinister brother, the Comte d'Artois, but so slight was his loyalty to any
political allegiance that he afterward designed not only an altar of civic
federation for the Jacobins, but also an Oriental tent for the discriminat-
ing British nabob, William Beckford. Tiring of the extremists, and of
their rhetoric, he fled first to Belgium, than to Hamburg where he created
the home of the stock exchange and a theater besides for French exiles
who fancied forgetting their trials in amateur performances. Still later he
scurried to the court of Denmark where he watched over the decoration
of Erichsen Palace and built the villas of Øregaard and Sophienholm.

Ramée might never have ventured to the United States if he had not
happened to come to the notice in Hamburg of David Parish, the
imaginative international banker who sank a significant fraction of his
capital in the undeveloped lands of upper New York State. In America
Ramée laid out the lawns of at least one villa along the Saint Lawrence,
but his triumph was the plan of Union College in Schenectady in 1813.
Though only two buildings were erected according to his designs, and
the plan itself rudely altered later in the nineteenth century, the very
suspicion of the architect's intentions is tantalizing, so charming is the
remembrance of Roman architecture in the stucco-covered brick walls of
North and South College. Had the plan been faithfully executed, the
rotunda built and the formal gardens set out, Union College might have
been almost as perfect an evocation of the ideals of the Federal period as
the campus of the University of Virginia.

Chapel, St. Mary's Seminary, Baltimore, Md., 1807 (Maximilian Godefroy)

Washington Monument, Baltimore, Md., 1814-29 (Robert Mills)

Fireproof building, Charleston, S.C., 1827 (Robert Mills)

THE AMBITION OF PHILIP HOOKER

The only ambitious native architect practicing in the environs of Schenectady was Philip Hooker, and he apparently was none too certain he could earn a living from tending uniquely to his profession; at least he held down one political job after another in Albany, and for thirteen years was city surveyor. A prudent craftsman, he was far from eager to follow the Grecian fashions of the romantic era, preferring to the end the Adamesque refinements of an earlier day. Both the capitol and the city hall he invented for Albany have been replaced, but the Ionic pilasters on the old Albany Academy of 1815 remain to persuade us of the sureness of his conservative taste. More daring than the Academy is Hooker's masterpiece, "Hyde Hall" at Cooperstown. The mansion of George Hyde Clarke, an Englishman who settled in America to supervise his landholdings, this was begun in 1811, but not completed until 1833. It is almost noble. In the center of its paneled stone façade is an astonishingly delicate portico of four unfluted columns with Grecian Doric capitals.

NEW ENGLAND IN THE AGE OF BULFINCH

Unlike Washington, D.C., Maryland, and New York, New England in the Federal period went ungraced by visits from foreign architects, which may account for the stubborn reluctance of the businessmen of Providence, Boston, Salem, and Portsmouth to build in any other style than an American version of the bygone glories of the Adams brothers. For all that, the architectural scene could scarcely be dismissed as dreary. Though the author knows of but one Gothic villa in Federal New England—that at Avon, Connecticut, of the shy art patron Daniel Wadsworth, son of the high-flying financier Jeremiah Wadsworth—there was, despite a disinclination to experiment with the latest styles, a genuine concern for magnificence in towns which had hitherto been remarkable merely for the discretion with which men of means hid their gains from the gaze of their fellow citizens.

In Rhode Island, as in no other state, merchant princes made the most of the opportunities they had been denied as British subjects. In Providence, no one was more adventurous than the Brown brothers, who turned from storekeeping to shipping and then to privateering to lay the foundations of a truly glorious fortune. There was Nicholas, who cornered the market for spermaceti; there was Moses, who launched the first American cotton mill; there was John, who in 1787 financed the voyage of the *General Washington* to Canton in hopes of snatching his due share and more of the newly opened trade with the Far East. Of no less consequence was their brother Joseph, whose zest in matters scientific led him to retire from the family's iron mills to conduct a significant series of electrical experiments, meditate on the mysteries of astronomy, and in the end teach philosophy at the College of Rhode Island, as the Brown-endowed Brown University was then known.

Though the money amassed by the Browns and their peers would in any event have tempted wise architects, the mansions on College Hill might have been far less pretentious if a member of the Brown family had not been himself an architect in his odd hours. This was Joseph, the creator in 1770 of the first building on the Providence campus of the College of Rhode Island, in 1774 of his own house on South Main Street, in 1775 of the First Baptist Meeting House, and in 1785, the year of his death, of his brother John's imposing residence on Power Street. A cool critic might point out that the college building was remarkable for no innovation, that the church was after all a skillful adaptation of a plate from James Gibbs's *Book of Architecture,* and that neither the Joseph Brown nor John Brown house was unduly subtle. Nevertheless, it would be absurd to overlook Joseph Brown's unique contribution. One of the first New England architects to realize the importance of a monumental façade, he may be said to have seduced the citizens of Providence with visions of splendor undreamed of in the colonial era.

To say that Joseph Brown's own house is no better than the typical Georgian pile is to forget that its brick front is enhanced with a curved baroque pediment of unusual dignity. And to observe that the John Brown mansion is also Georgian in inspiration is to convey no idea of its solid magnificence. Another brick house on the site might have been more refined, but it would not have dominated the city so successfully, and even today, some 200 years later, it is easily recognized as the home of a merchant prince of vast ambitions.

Equally presumptuous is the home of Nicholas Brown's son-in-law, Thomas Poynton Ives, dating from 1806. Its fourth story disappears, as does that of the John Brown house, behind the balustrade, but its solidity is even more marked, for it lacks the central projecting block with pediment, and the monumentality of its brick façade is emphasized by the semicircular portico added in later years.

The name of the builder of the Ives mansion has not been preserved, nor has that of the carpenter who in 1812 added the two-story Corinthian porch to the home of the merchant Edward Carrington, but it seems likely that the designer of Colonel Joseph Nightingale's mansion in 1792 was one Caleb Ormsbee. A square frame structure, with the hip roof and balustrade common to the John Brown and Thomas Poynton Ives houses, this is so superlative an example of late-eighteenth-century carpentry in the Georgian manner that it is no wonder it was shortly acquired by

Nicholas Brown himself. From its exquisite Palladian window above the entrance he could glance at the countinghouses of the city below.

It would be ungracious to criticize Providence for the conservatism of its taste. Its architects may have been prudent, but its moneyed men set a standard of ostentation which marked the emancipation of New England from the modesty enforced in the colonial period. In this expensive atmosphere, moreover, John Holden Greene found dozens of patrons for his delicate reminiscences of eighteenth-century English motifs. Each and every one of his houses on College Hill cannot be noted here, but something must be said of his St. John's Cathedral of 1810, in which he toyed, ever so casually, with lancet windows and other Gothic elements alien to the academic character of the design. This meant that he, like so many English architects of the late eighteenth century, was weary of repeating the façade of St. Martin-in-the-Fields.

Though no businessman of Salem was so farsighted as the Brown brothers, and though the mansions of this rival seaport were denied sites as glorious as those on College Hill, its architecture in the Federal period has plenty of dedicated admirers. And, if any one style may be called typical of the complex Federal era, it is not the Romanism of Jefferson and Ramée, not the Grecian note struck by Latrobe, but the cautious yet appealing manner evolved by the Salem carver Samuel McIntire.

Three-story cubical structures, whose hip roofs are hidden behind cornices and balustrades, the town houses created by McIntire and his followers resemble the Thomas Poynton Ives mansion, and like many of the best homes of Providence, follow the conservative plan of four rooms to a floor of the colonial period. But behind the five windows of their fronts, in the halls, in the parlors, in the dining rooms, and even in the bedrooms, the intricacy of the carving in the Adamesque vein is often arresting. This, rather than any structural innovation, may be said to be a peculiar contribution of McIntire.

There were many moneyed men to appreciate McIntire's gifts. *"Divitis Indiae Usque Ad Ultimum Sinum,"* was the motto on Salem's shield: "The Spoil of the Ind to the Uttermost Gulf." Troubled by the daring of New Yorkers in speeding the first American vessel to the Far East, local merchants financed the voyage of *The Grand Turk*. On her return from the Orient in the summer of 1787, the Crowninshields were inspired to sink their savings in the pepper of Sumatra, the Derbys and their peers were pleased with the profits from this and other Eastern staples, and Salem, even if its harbor was too shallow for ships drawing over twelve feet, was transformed from a relatively obscure seaport into a city which very nearly monopolized our commerce with the East Indies.

On Sunday when *The Grand Turk* set sail on one of its expeditions, the conscientious Salem minister William Bentley confessed he was embarrassed. "The previous invitations given to the principal gentlemen of the town, and the fame of a ship built in the town, and furnished with sails from our own manufactories urged a curiosity so strong that few people were left in our houses of worship." Yet Bentley could not complain, so natural was the gratitude of Salem to the great ship and its owner Elias Hasket Derby. Of an afternoon spent at Derby's farm at Danvers, Bentley wrote: "We envied nothing but his liberality to us, because we wished to do the same things. We felt no other emotions, than the innocence of rural life, the happy application of riches to facilitate agriculture, and the most ardent wishes to please a man, who had at once done us so much honor, and given us so much pleasure. Hypocrisy, meanness, envy and party, tho' evidently associated, agreed to hide themselves, and like owls fly the light."

It was for Elias Hasket Derby that Samuel McIntire conceived his most splendid town house. Pulled down in 1815 by Derby's timid children, only seventeen years after the last capital was carved, this was so far beyond the dreams of other businessmen that legend estimated the cost at eighty thousand dollars. In sober truth, the summerhouse, the outbuildings, and the frame mansion itself, vaguely reminiscent of Lord Burlington's design for General Wade's London residence, involved only $11,819. The Derby house might not have been half so magnificent, might not have featured an oval drawing room on the garden façade, and might not have boasted a fanciful Adamesque ceiling by the stuccoist Daniel Reynerd, had not the usually cautious McIntire been stirred to rival Charles Bulfinch, the Boston architect originally asked to design the setting for the Derbys' social life. If McIntire occasionally departed from the conventional colonial plan of four rooms to a floor, and ended by featuring lavish Adamesque ornament in many of his houses, the influence of Bulfinch must not be overlooked.

More typical of McIntire is the square three-story frame town house of Jerathmeel Pierce, dating from 1782, in which the only sign of elegance on the exterior, aside from the Doric pedimented porch and the fluted pilasters at the corners, is the balustrade atop the roof. More elaborate is the so-called Gardner-White-Pingree house of 1805. The brick façade is stark, but the interiors reveal the depth of McIntire's feeling for the Adamesque. These may strike us as curiously feminine for the needs of an undoubtedly masculine merchant in an aggressive seaport, but there is no question that Adamesque details were popular, for McIntire's precedent was followed on Chestnut Street, most of whose dignified mansions were erected after the carver's death at fifty-four in 1811.

Derby's grateful guest William Bentley was not exaggerating when he pronounced McIntire "one of the most ingenious men" of the town. "He was," Bentley tells us, "descended of a family of carpenters who had no claims on public favor and was educated at a branch of that business.

By attention he soon gained a superiority to all of his occupation & the present Court House, the North & South Meeting houses, and indeed all the improvements of Salem for nearly 30 years past have been done under his eye. In sculpture he had no rival in New England and I possess some specimens which I should not scruple to compare with any I ever saw."

McIntire was also a talented musician, Bentley reported, and as you might guess, was not without the social graces. "He had a fine person, a majestic appearance, calm countenance, great self-command & amiable temper. He was," Bentley concludes, "welcome but never intruded."

Unlike McIntire, Bulfinch was born to ease. The son of a distinguished physician who had the wit to marry an Apthorp, he was educated at the Latin School and at Harvard, and although obliged when a young man to enter the countinghouse of Joseph Barrell, he was not oppressed with the thought that he might one day have to earn his own living. "Except," he recalled, "about three months of hurried employment, when he [Mr. Barrell] was engaged in victualing a French fleet in our harbor, my time passed very idly, and I was at leisure to cultivate a taste for architecture, which was encouraged by attending to Mr. Barrell's improvement of his estate, and the [improvements] on our dwelling houses and the houses of some friends, all of which had become extremely dilapidated during the war."

In the summer of 1785, when twenty-two, Bulfinch set out on a Grand Tour of England, France, and Italy. Jefferson himself showed him over Paris. "I was," the future architect wrote, "delighted in observing the numerous objects & beauties of nature and art that I met with on all sides, particularly the wonders of Architecture & the kindred arts of painting and sculpture . . . but these pursuits did not confirm me in any business habits of buying and selling, on the contrary they had a powerful adverse influence on my whole after life."

In these early days, Bulfinch, like Gabriel Manigault of Charleston, fancied that a knowledge of architecture was but one of the accomplishments of a gentleman. "On my return to Boston," he remembered, "I was warmly received by friends, and passed a season of leisure, pursuing no business, but giving gratuitous advice in Achitecture, and looking forward to an establishment in life."

In the fall of 1787, when the Boston-owned *Columbia* set sail for Canton, opening the China trade, Bulfinch was one of the happy shareholders. A year later he married an Apthorp cousin, and the thought that he might eventually be reduced to designing churches and houses for money could never have crossed his mind. For all that, he was aware that there was a degree of luxury in architecture which his native Boston would never tolerate. Writing to his parents during a visit to Philadelphia in 1789, he noted that William Bingham's town house "is in a style which would be esteemed splendid even in the most luxurious parts of

Gardiner-White-Pingree house, Salem, Mass., 1810 (Samuel McIntire)

Parlor, Gardiner-White, Pingree house

Europe. Elegance of construction; white marble staircase, valuable paintings, the richest furniture and the utmost magnificence of decoration make it a palace, in my opinion, far *too rich* for *any* man in this country."

Meantime Bulfinch had set himself up as the first gentleman of New England in matters architectural; in 1792 he designed, apparently merely for the pleasure of sketching, the new mansion of his former employer Joseph Barrell in Charlestown. Though this house was afterward altered into the headquarters of the McLean Asylum for the Insane, and still later was taken down and rebuilt with many modifications in a neighboring town, we may, thanks to old photographs of the interior of the asylum, and to the reverent drawings of Ogden Codman, begin to appreciate the freedom with which Bulfinch departed from the conventional colonial plan of four rooms to a floor. Here he had the imagination to introduce a great oval drawing room between the sitting and dining rooms, an innovation which must have startled the merchant princes of Boston. The news in 1800 of the collapse of the Federalist political machine was scarcely more alarming.

Not so radical in design was Franklin Place, the crescent-shaped row of sixteen brick houses which he planned in 1793; here he aimed to recall the serpentine grandeurs of Georgian Bath. Demolished in the middle of the nineteenth century, Franklin Place might well have been preserved, not only because it set an amazing standard of elegance for Boston, but also because the architect was so gallant as to sink his entire fortune in the speculation. This proved to be a fatal error. Hard times set in, his partners backed out, the merchants who might have made their homes in the block hung back, and Bulfinch had to declare himself bankrupt.

Cool critics may claim that this failure had its happy side, forcing Bulfinch the amateur to turn into Bulfinch the professional. The architect could hardly have agreed. Stripped even of his wife's dowry, he had to move his family into his sister's house.

To describe all of the buildings credited or attributed to Bulfinch would be impossible in so slight a sketch as this of his career; this is unfortunate, for once he was driven to depend on his talents instead of his dividends to support his wife, he earned a wholly deserved reputation as the leading architect of New England, and it is doubtful that any New Englander since his time has surpassed him. Though occasionally provincial, as in designing the Connecticut State House of 1796, he was obviously fonder of Georgian splendor than Georgian thrift, and when creating the Massachusetts State House of 1798, drew on his memories of Sir William Chambers's "Somerset House" in London.

Attributed to Bulfinch are the three town houses of his creditor Otis, dating from 1796, 1801, and 1806. All three are standing today, but since the second and third have been subjected to minor alterations, not to mention the loss of a bow window, the first, which has been opened to the public by the Society for the Preservation of New England Antiquities, is worth the closest inspection. This three-story square brick mansion on Cambridge Street, crowned by a low hip roof, is a prudent effort if you will, but far from mean. Even if there are no elliptical saloons, and the plan is of the conventional central hall type, the restored Palladian window above the entrance porch is of unusually nice proportions, and there is more than a hint of elegance in the paneled embrasures of the windows. The most splendid private residence of the Bulfinch era is the country seat at Waltham of the Federalist governor, Christopher Gore. There is no evidence that Bulfinch was the author, but the ingenious plan of the brick villa which the Governor erected between 1797 and 1804 reiterates the challenge of the Joseph Barrell mansion of 1792. Flanked by one-story wings with recessed windows, the central block of three stories features a semicircular reception room on the ground floor, leading directly into an oval dining room, and these spheric experiments are repeated on the upper levels. Was a French architect involved here? This has been recently hinted. A comparison may be made with the château of Tauzia at Gradignan near Bordeaux, designed by Victor Louis in 1778. Gore Place is open to the public by the Gore Place Association.

No less of a miracle in brick is the Old Meeting House Bulfinch conceived in 1816 for Lancaster in western Massachusetts. To remember that the creator of this arched portico, of this cupola perched on these Ionic columns, was driven a second time into bankruptcy is to suspect that New England was not ready for the responsibilities of patronage.

In the midst of planning University Hall for Harvard and two buildings on the campus of Phillips Academy at Andover, Bulfinch was so imprudent as to speculate in the filling in of the Boston mud flats. Harrison Gray Otis and his associates, the architect bravely noted, "men of large capital, were able to wait for better times for the sale of their lands, from which they have since realized immense profit, but no sales could . . . be made by me, and demands were pressing with accumulating interest, so that I was obliged to surrender all property, and was even more reduced than before, and we were obliged to leave our neat and commodious home for a humbler and inferior one . . . my dear wife consenting to take charge of two young ladies as boarders, to add to our income."

You might suppose that the tragedy of Bulfinch was merely that of a gentleman who had not been sufficiently devoted to the care of his inheritance. Or you might more accurately guess that he failed twice in business because, reaching desperately for perfection in the art of architecture, he quite forgot that America at the dawn of the nineteenth century was a mechanic's rather than an artist's paradise.

One of the most successful architects in the New England of Bulfinch's day was Asher Benjamin, a clever carpenter from Greenfield,

Massachusetts, who hit in 1797 on the happy idea of publishing *The Country Builder's Assistant*. Though this was not the first book on architecture printed in America—a distinction which belongs to Abraham Swan's *British Architect,* issued in Philadelphia in 1775, thirty years after its original publication in London—Benjamin's was the first original American treatise, and so great was the need for builders' guides designed for American needs that this, and the six other handbooks bearing his name, ran into over forty editions. This may not have spelled wealth for the author, but it at least insured all the comforts of fame and the gratitude of innumerable carpenters across the nation.

As cautious as the canniest contriver of best-sellers, Benjamin was fearful of losing his audience if ever he surrendered to the latest styles, and a close study of his publications reveals that he clung fast to adaptations of the tried and true British models of colonial America. Once he felt that the village joiners were ready, however, he advanced from plates featuring Georgian and Adamesque examples to the Greek revival itself, and in one of his last books, dared to invent a new Grecian order for American use. There were economies to be realized in following this new fashion, he announced in 1833; what had once been a novelty was found to be "peculiarly adapted to the republican habits of this country."

Though none of the churches and houses Benjamin designed on the days when he was free from poring over the proof of a handbook could be compared with the triumphs of Bulfinch, not even the imposing Old South Meeting House of 1798 for Windsor, Vermont, nor West Church in Boston, he must not be belittled. He undoubtedly raised the standards of our builders, and if he was not a genius, he was at least an artist of considerable competence.

One of the most delightful examples of the influence of Benjamin is the First Congregational Church of Bennington, Vermont, dating from 1806. This exquisite white frame fabric, whose steeple harks back to the England of Gibbs and Wren, closely resembles Plate 33 in *The Country Builder's Assistant;* but the actual architect was not Benjamin but the carpenter Lavius Fillmore. He improved on the model, introducing a Palladian window instead of a stark fanlight in the belfry tower. A hundred other churches in New England might be less charming but for Benjamin's precedent.

We may save our deepest admiration for the geniuses whose ideas Benjamin retailed for rural consumption, but there is no good reason to scorn the common sense of the author of the first American builder's guide. His success was peculiarly American, and would not have surprised Benjamin Franklin himself, who once warned any and all European artists that our republic, for all the promise of great wealth in the future, was too utilitarian to pass for their promised land.

"Though there are," said Franklin, ". . . few people so miserable as

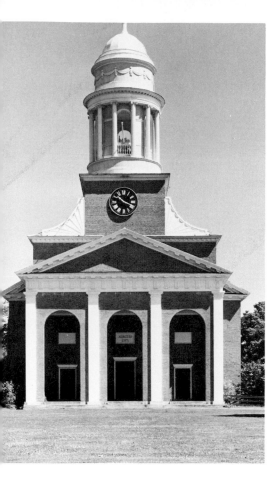

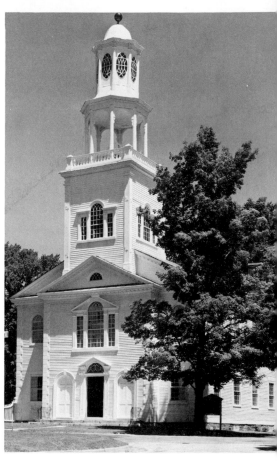

Left: Old Meeting House, Lancaster, Mass., 1816 (Charles Bulfinch) *Right:* First Congregtational Church, Bennington, Vt., 1806 (Lavius Filmore)

"Gore Place," Waltham, Mass., 1806

the poor of Europe, there are also very few that in Europe would be called rich; it is rather a happy mediocrity that prevails. There are few great proprietors of the soil, and few tenants; most people cultivate their own lands, or follow some handicraft or merchandise; very few rich enough to live idly upon their rents and incomes, or to pay the high prices given in Europe for painting, statues, architecture, and the other works of art, that are more curious than useful."

It was the great good fortune of America in the Federal period that so many foreign architects were so unwise as to disregard Franklin's advice.

CHAPTER FOUR

The Romantic Era, 1820—1860

THE ROMANTIC ATTITUDE

There was a time when critics felt they should apologize for the Grecian mansions, the Gothic castles, the Italian villas, and all the other manifestations of the romantic spirit in the American landscape. That time has passed. Though it is true that the owner of one estate on the Hudson River made a practice, whenever a bride spent the night in his home, of writing her name in white flowers across the fresh green moss in the tin pan that adorned his parlor table, we have learned that our great-grandfathers in the 1830's, '40's, and '50's worshiped something besides moonlight and ruins. Dynamite—intellectual, that is—was frequently concealed in the cellar of the most innocent castles.

The typical romantic plan bore no trace of the Federal preoccupation with elliptical exercises in geometry. Romantic homes were picturesque, but they were also comfortable. This meant that nothing so conservative as the colonial layout of four rooms to a floor represented the best work of the best architects. In fact, the injury to the traditional notion of formality was so serious that the modern concept of the free plan might be said to date from this period.

To speak of informality is to breathe one of the secrets of the romantics—their grudge against the Renaissance. Rebelling against the symmetrical façades of the great architects of France and Italy, and against the colonial perpetuation of that ideal, they were naturally drawn to the asymmetrical opportunities of the Gothic revival. And even if they—at first—failed to sense that the Gothic tradition was based on the structural integrity which the Renaissance had sacrificed in the quest for perfection of proportions—even if they gaily disguised the nature of

97

their materials by plastering brick to look like stone—they at least reminded America of the Gothic past, and so were the godfathers of the
organic architecture of the twentieth century which springs from Gothic
sources.

All of which must not make us forget that the romantic architects
were understandably anxious to lead their own lives in their own century.
Never for an instant did they suspect that they would one day be
relegated to the ranks of godfathers, however honorable the distinction.
They aimed—if we may hazard a guess as to the collective dream of a
generation—at introducing into architecture the fourth dimension, time
itself, and their Grecian, Gothic, Italian, Egyptian and other fantasies are
best remembered as so many invitations to explore the poetry of time.
No wonder, then, that the great figures of the romantic era refused to
deal in replicas, for an accurate reproduction would undo the spell on
which they set their hearts.

No one came closer to understanding the romantics than Congressman
Gulian Crommelin Verplanck of New York, who was at once an inde-
fatigable student of the tariff and the tried and true friend of the haunted
painter Washington Allston. Weary of all American attempts to work
over the themes of Robert Adam, Verplanck lectured the American
Academy of Fine Arts in 1824 on "that corruption of the Roman, or
rather Palladian architecture, which delights in great profusion of un-
meaning ornament, in piling order upon order, in multitudes of small
and useless windows, columns, and mean and unnecessary pilasters."

Having scolded Salem, in so many words Verplanck went on to insist
that men were meant to live in time as well as in space: the proper architecture for America would be rich in remembrance of other civilizations.
Paraphrasing Sir Joshua Reynolds, the Congressman wondered if even
the temples of Greece were as inspiring as the Gothic cathedrals with
"their peculiar and deeply interesting associations which, I know not
how, throw back the architectural remains of the Middle Ages to a much
remoter antiquity in the imagination than those of Rome and Athens."

Many Americans might not agree with Verplanck in his preference for
the Gothic, but so profound was the enchantment of the romantic styles
that citizens high and low displayed an astonishing concern for the art of
architecture. Torn between his passion for the Gothic and his reverence
for the Grecian, Henry Pickering, son of the Federalist politico, Timothy
Pickering, shed a tear when William Beckford in England unloaded (at a
fantastic profit) his fantastic Gothic castle. Pickering then sighed for the
day the American seacoast would rival the isles of Greece. "When," he
asked,

> . . . shall the homesick mariner from afar
> Descry upon thy promontories bold

And sea-beat coasts, the colonnade sublime
Glittering like Pharos in the moon's bright beams?

Equally impressed by the remains of antiquity was the painter Thomas Cole, who noted, after visiting the ruins of Paestum, that "railroads and canals are not the only works worthy of modern civilization." In Paestum "the citizen gazed with pride upon the marble triumphs of his native place; he loved it more than ever and felt his patriotism kindle as he gazed."

Somewhat more critical was Alexis de Tocqueville. He was surprised, on sailing into New York Harbor, "to perceive along the shore, at some distance from the city, a number of little palaces of white marble. . . . When I went the next day to inspect more closely the one which had particularly attracted my notice, I found that its walls were of whitewashed brick, and its columns of painted wood. It was the same story with all the buildings that I had admired the night before." Like de Tocqueville, James Fenimore Cooper felt that there might be too much of a good thing. He had "Otsego Hall" remodeled in the Gothic style, and smiled at the number of Grecian mansions along the Hudson River. "One such temple," he remarked, "well placed in a wood, might be a pleasant object enough, but to see a river lined with them, with children trundling hoops before their doors, beef carried into their kitchens, and smoke issuing, moreover, from those unclassical objects' chimnies, is too much even of a high taste."

A French traveler might be amazed, and an American novelist might be amused, but most Americans were proud of the Grecian colonnades of the better hotels. The thought of one such establishment, Congress Hall at Saratoga, was an inspiration to the journalist Nathaniel Parker Willis. "And now," wrote Willis, recalling the Saratoga season, "there was ringing of bells; and there were orders for the woodcocks to be dressed with pork chemises, and for the champagne to be iced, the sherry not—and through the arid corridors of Congress Hall floated a delicious toilet air of cold cream and lavender—and ladies' maids came down to press out white dresses, while the cook heated the curling irons—and up and down the stairs flitted, with the blest confusion of other days, boots and iced sangarees, hot water, towels, and mint juleps—all delightful, but all incomprehensible."

A Gothic setting might be more suitable for meditation, as Daniel Webster realized when he allowed his daughter to design the Gothic wing of his house in Marshfield, and as Washington Irving understood when he begged the artist George Harvey to fashion him at Tarrytown "a little nookery somewhat in the old Dutch style, quaint and unpretending." And nothing but the Gothic would do for the tragedian Edwin Forrest. When a rival from Britain dared to play Macbeth in New York, he provoked the Astor Place riots in which twenty New Yorkers lost their lives. Fortunately for Forrest, the incident does not seem to have shortened the lines at the box office; at least he was suspected of spending something like a hundred thousand dollars on "Fonthill Castle," his seat on the Hudson River. This granite fortress "combined the Norman and Gothic styles, softened in detail so as to embrace some of the luxuries of modern improvements," reported the actor's biographer. Here he celebrated the Fourth by reciting the Declaration of Independence "under waving flags and amidst booming guns." Here he dreamed of establishing after his death a home for decayed or superannuated actors or actresses of American birth, "all foreigners to be strictly excluded." All this might have come to pass, and the castle might not today be converted to the needs of Mount St. Vincent College, if Forrest had been content to divorce his wife in an undramatic manner. But he could not bear to enter a courtroom without staging a superb performance and after $200,000 had been lavished on attorney's fees, "Fonthill" had to be sold to satisfy his creditors.

No doubt the sensational Forrest divorce case frightened many a businessman from building a Gothic castle. No doubt, too, the occasional denunciations of the Egyptian style in the family magazines discouraged the promoters of the finer cemeteries from erecting gateways recalling the Nile. "Egyptian architecture," declared the *North American Review* in 1836, "reminds us of the religion which called it into being, the most degraded and revolting paganism which ever existed. It is the architecture of embalmed cats and deified crocodiles."

THE MESSAGE OF ANDREW JACKSON DOWNING

Fathers and mothers who worried over what surroundings in which to raise a family, puzzled whether to build in the Greek, the Gothic, the Italian, the Moorish, or the Egyptian manner, were grateful to Andrew Jackson Downing, the greatest of all the romantic critics. He interpreted the architecture of his generation with a grace denied to American commentators before or since.

Moreover, it was Downing who fired the ambition of New Yorkers for a vast public park. But for his insistence and that of Bryant, the Central Park which Frederick Law Olmsted laid out in 1857 might never have become a reality. Weary of the spectacle of city dwellers seeking the countryside in the vales of the city cemeteries, Downing denied that the beauties of nature were too fine for the average citizen. "Social doubters," he declared, "mistake our people and their destiny. If we would but listen to them, our magnificent river and lake steamers, those real palaces of the millions, would have had no velvet couches, no splendid mirrors, no luxurious carpets. . . . And yet, these our floating palaces and our monster hotels, with their purple and fine linen, are they not respected by the majority who use them, as truly as other palaces by their rightful sovereigns?"

Even though the architectural ideals of Downing's time are not those of our own, much of what he had to say is as pertinent in the day of the airplane as in that of the river steamer. "Attempts at great establishments are always and inevitably failures in America," he warned millionaires likely to forget that the gigantic mansions of one generation were often the white elephants of the next. And he, if not the architects whose achievements he hailed, was as conscientious as any twentieth-century theorist about expressing the nature of materials. "When we employ stone as a building material, let it be clearly expressed," he urged. "When we employ wood, there should be no less frankness in avowing the material."

Not too many years were granted Downing in which to weave his spell. He was only thirty-seven in 1852 when he died a hero's death in a steamboat disaster on the Hudson. The son of a nurseryman at Newburgh on the edge of the Hudson Highlands, he was scantily educated, threatened besides with the drudgery of clerking in a drygoods store before he joined his brother in the family business. But he was not to be a mere nurseryman for long. "The workman, the author, the artist, were entirely subjugated in him to the gentleman." A welcome guest in the summer retreat of the Austrian consul general, he had the wit to cultivate the family of Edward Armstrong, who dwelled in a Grecian villa at Devils Danskammer to the north of Newburgh. There he met an English gentleman, and what was almost as delightful, made the acquaintance of a British landscape painter with whom he sauntered again and again into the Highlands. The day was not far off when he was to publish the first of his books, a treatise on the theory and practice of landscape gardening. The very next year, in 1842, he issued a volume on cottage residences, and his fame was secure. In a Gothic cottage of his own design in Newburgh he settled down to dictate the taste of home owners from Maine to Missouri.

"He had," noticed one of his guests, "a natural fondness for the highest circles of society—a fondness as deeply founded as his love of the best possible fruits." He was pleased with the "magnificent ring" the Queen of Denmark forwarded in appreciation of his writings, but not overly pleased, since he was "marked by the easy elegance and perfect savoir-faire which would have adorned the Escorial." Save for the pile of letters on his writing desk, no sign of toil was tolerated in his home. At dawn he stole into the dining room to heap high with magnolias the breakfast plate of a favored guest; at dusk he darted out like a ghost from behind his Gothic bookshelves, alarming those of his friends who were unfamiliar with the machinery of Gothic novels.

Gentle in his home by the Hudson, he could still be a forbidding critic of what he considered erring taste. Perhaps because there were plenty of temples before he started his career, he was unmerciful with Americans who dreamed of sitting down to Sunday dinner midst memories of Athens. "The Greek temple disease has passed its crisis," he was happy to point out in 1846. "The people have survived it."

Downing was fonder by far of the Gothic. "There is," he remarked, "something wonderfully captivating in the idea of a battlemented castle, even to an apparently modest man, who thus shows to the world his unsuspected vein of personal ambition. But," he warned, *unless there be something of the castle in the man,* it is very likely, if it be like a real castle to dwarf him to the stature of a mouse." He could not approve of "a puny Gothic castle, built in a style which was warranted by feudal times and feudal robberies, for the habitation of a meek and quiet merchant, who has not the remotest idea of manifesting anything offensive or defensive to any of his peace-loving neighborhood."

He frowned, too, on houses that ignored their surroundings.

> To assist us in determining *what to build,* the character of the scenery itself should be considered. There is a fitness which natural construction and long association have bestowed on certain styles, as connected with particular kinds of landscape. Thus the Rural English cottage in fertile valleys, the Swiss cottage on the sides, or under the brow of steep mountains; the abbey and the villa in smiling plains; and the castle in bold rocky passes.
>
> We could [he went on] name a monstruous architectural absurdity in a neighboring state, in the shape of a large country residence, built in imitation of an old castle, with towers and battlements, *all of wood!* To render this specimen of folly and bad taste all the more glaring, the proprietor selected for its site the smooth green banks of one of the tamest rivers, in the flattest district in America, where the only warfare carried on is against oysters and woodcock! A man of imagination and wealth might be pardoned for building up, from the massive primitive rock, an imitation of a grand old Rhine castle on the top of one of the bold hills of the Hudson Highlands. One would, perhaps, from the keeping between the striking scenery and the edifice, find it difficult to believe that it did not actually belong to the past. But a wooden castle, in a flat meadow, is as much out of place as a knight in armor would be running a tilt in the Jersey pine barrens.

Since the castellated style, in Downing's opinion, never appeared "completely at home except in wild and romantic scenery," he recommended a milder, domesticated version of the Gothic—the "Tudor"—for those who could not gaze out of their bedroom windows onto crags and torrents, and for those in even more modest circumstances, he advised the "rural" Gothic. This last style, he explained, "harmonizes easily with the tall trees, the tapering masses of foliage, or the surrounding hills; and while it is seldom or never misplaced in spirited rural scenery, it gives character and picturesque expression to many landscapes entirely devoid of that quality."

Next to Gothic castles and cottages, Downing preferred Italian villas, whose towers crowned asymmetrical compositions which would have bewildered the masters of Renaissance symmetry. Though this style, like the Greek and the Gothic, originated in England, he did not attempt to describe its virtues as Britannic. "There are," he announced, "the men of imagination—men whose aspirations never leave them at rest—men whose ambition and energy will give them no peace within the mere bounds of rationality. . . . It is for such that the architect may safely introduce the tower and the campanile—any and every feature that indicates originality, boldness, energy, and variety of character." He concluded: "To find a really original man living in an original . . . house, is as satisfactory as to find an eagle's nest built on the top of a mountain crag, while to find a pretentious, shallow man in such an habitation, is no better than to find the jackdaw in the eagle's nest."

THE RISE OF ALEXANDER JACKSON DAVIS

All architects in all times have been fonder of eagles than jackdaws for clients; no exception were the ambitious designers of the romantic era, who yearned for Downing's approval, realizing that a chance word in one of his essays might persuade a patron to command a castellated villa. Few were called, fewer still were chosen.

Though Alexander Jackson Davis, on whom fell Downing's blessing, did not create all of the notable buildings of the romantic decades, he was not only the most prolific but the most influential architect of the time—so influential that he could afford to smile at the edicts of the master and design in the Grecian style if he liked. Like Downing, however, Davis was fonder of the Gothic and the Italian than the Attic mood; he also contributed most if not all of the Gothic and Italian illustrations for his friend's books.

Now and then, certain of forgiveness in Newburgh, Davis would forward a cut the master found too elaborate for the average home builder. "I find our people are foolishly frightened at a few crockets and finials," Downing once reminded his illustrator. Meanwhile the critic lived in dread that some other writer would "take up" his favorite designer. "I beg," he wrote Davis in regard to a particularly fine drawing, "you will not print it in the *Brother Jonathan,* or allow the editors of that or any other paper to write slang articles on taste in your name. I think it does you harm, and I do not hesitate to say this, as I am sure you are aware how entirely I have always endeavored, in my humble way, to advance your professional interests."

Had Davis been unkind, he might have replied that he was quite capable of advancing his own professional interests. To tell the truth, he was. Though he never outgrew a youthful fondness for Gothic novels, he succeeded so brilliantly in imposing his visions on the moneyed men of his time that he spent the last thirty-two of his eighty-nine years on earth in the most comfortable retirement conceivable—in a Gothic cottage of his own design set down on top of a modest but unmistakable mountain in the suburbs of New York City.

You might point to any number of reasons for Davis's astonishing success. No doubt he was astute in settling down in New York City, taking advantage of its ever increasing prosperity in the 1830's, '40's, and '50's. But perhaps it would be safer to say that he owed his rise in the world to the doggedness with which he labored to force into architectural form the darker dreams of the Gothic romancers. As tireless as Schedoni, the evil monk in *The Italian,* Davis would talk battlements one minute to a stove king from Albany and turrets the next to a James River planter.

Gothic was the language of Davis in his old age; Gothic was the vocabulary of his childhood. In his teens, enchanted with the unhappy heroines of Mrs. Ann Radcliffe's novels, he lived for the hours in which he could steal to the attic and sketch the mountainous retreats in which those ladies were imprisoned. For days he would puzzle over the plans of "some ancient castle of romance, arranging the trap-doors, subterraneous passages and drawbridges." Only at his older brother's urging would he pry open a book of history or biography, or ponder the riddle that was mathematics.

Though his father was a most conscientious theologian, being both editor and publisher of a Congregationalist review, young Davis—and this was delightful in someone who later became so industrious an architect—did not believe in laying too solid a foundation for the future. "I do not intend to trouble myself much about what business to follow as a livelihood, but jog along through the world without cares and at my ease," he wrote, when seventeen, to a favorite aunt. The year before, he had left his native New York City for Alexandria, Virginia, where his older brother was editing a newspaper. Helping set type did not keep him too busy to join a philodramatic society composed—so he told his aunt—"of the most respectable young men."

Davis's notebooks in these years reveal that while he and his friends were not unwilling to act out *Romeo and Juliet* or *The Merchant of Venice,* Shakespeare was not half so popular in Alexandria as the Gothic dramatists. Who, after all, could compare with Charles Robert Maturin, creator not only of that troubling novel *Melmoth the Wanderer,* but also of *Bertram,* a play complete with haunted towers? Charmed, Davis made sketches for what would have been the ideal sets for *Bertram.*

Perhaps because his romantic tastes alarmed his parents, Davis was obliged to return to New York in 1823. He was then twenty, and no doubt eager for a career on the stage. No one could deny that he was handsome, with his high forehead, his sensitive blue eyes, his sandy hair. When his money ran out on reaching Wilmington, his first thought was of the fine figure he would make addressing an audience. He got leave to use the lecture room of the local academy, then retired to the shadows of a decayed church on the banks of the Delaware and rehearsed the dramatic pieces he had memorized in Alexandria. That evening in the lecture room he was successful even beyond his hopes, for he raised more than enough cash to pay stagecoach drivers and landladies on the way home.

Davis no sooner was back in New York than he fled to the country to escape the yellow fever then raging in the metropolis. Idling away the long afternoons in a remote village, he chanced to look into a camera obscura, and, according to his diary, felt for the first time that his mission was to be an artist. He began "designing streets in Venice, conjecturing the fashions of gondolas, and planning interiors for churches, palaces, and prisons." When the epidemic subsided, and he could return to the city, he called on Rembrandt Peale, who told him that he was fated to be not a painter but an architect.

His means too modest for foreign travel, Davis got his architectural training in the studio of blustering John Trumbull who, rightly or wrongly, was positive that he had grasped the fundamentals of architecture in his afternoons off from painting the American Revolution. Whether Trumbull's teaching was inspired, or whether the courses at the old Antique School—the forerunner of our National Academy of Design—meant far more to the future architect, Davis easily made his way as a draftsman, sketching views of New York for the booksellers and preparing plans for that none-too-talented builder of churches, Josiah Brady.

But it was not in New York that Davis perfected his genius for rendering. In the winter of 1827, armed with a note of introduction from the affluent bridgebuilder and architect, Ithiel Town of New Haven, he moved to Boston where he was to spend nearly two years. When not hitting off the State House and the other new and noble monuments with his pen and pencil, he sought out the company of Dr. George Parkman, uncle of the historian, and of Dr. Jacob Bigelow, the public-spirited botanist who founded Mount Auburn Cemetery. Both Parkman and Bigelow were true lovers of architecture, and so anxious to encourage Davis that they opened to him their homes and their collections of architectural models, besides making it possible for him to study in the extensive library of the Athenaeum.*

* In later years, the two Bostonians were caught in tragedies. It was Parkman's lot to be murdered by Professor Webster, the crazed chemist of Harvard. As for Bigelow, he lost his mind—though only after translating *Mother Goose* into Latin—and then his

When, late in 1828, Davis returned to New York, he justified his patrons' highest hopes by becoming the partner of Ithiel Town, an opportunity for which many a young architect would have given his life's blood. Though Town was far from a great artist, he enjoyed a handsome income from his bridgebuilding patents, and putting his royalties to shrewd use, had acquired the largest architectural library in the New World. As his associate, Davis would have the privilege of consulting the publications of the greatest architects of France, England, and Italy.

What was even more exhilarating, Town set out on a Grand Tour of England and the Continent before the year 1829 was over, leaving Davis in complete charge of the Wall Street office. This, if ever, was a promising time to begin the practice of architecture. Latrobe, the greatest of our designers at the turn of the century, had already gone to his grave; of his peers, only Bulfinch lingered on, and his career was drawing to a close. Moreover, in literature and in painting as well, there were signs that America was on the eve of a civilization of her own. In the decade just past, Irving had brought out his *Sketch Book,* Cooper had published the first of his *Leatherstocking Tales,* and Poe had printed his early poems. Washington Allston, in Cambridgeport, was wasting his days flicking a morbid cigar before the never-to-be-finished canvas of Belshazzar's Feast, but Thomas Cole, the Chirico of the hour, would soon exhibit the first of his vast allegories.

Filled with wonder, like so many other Americans of his generation, at the remains of the ancient world, Davis turned to the Grecian style for the first of his commissions, a villa for the now forgotten poet, James Abraham Hillhouse of New Haven. This serene mansion, which stood at the head of Hillhouse Avenue until its demolition by Yale University, marked the liberation of American architecture from the last traces of Robert Adam's influence: the Salem style was now old-fashioned.

Having made a friend of a genuine poet, Davis did not rest until he got to know Willis and Cooper and Irving, and once, having just received a copy of Hillhouse's collected works, daringly thanked him with a poem obviously of his own invention:

> *Behold yon woodland seat! How deep, how grand*
> *The shadows of those groves! The graceful home*
> *Where he, the bard sublime, feeds his soul*
> *With visions high and solemn swelling thought.*
> *Methinks I hear, breathing from those dark shades*
> *The loud resounding echoes of his harp*

---

eyesight. The day was to come when he would totter through the gates of "Mount Auburn" on the arms of his friends; reaching the strange Sphinx Monument he set up in memory of the Civil War dead, he would finger it fondly.

Too long at rest, or only by the wind
Or chance alighting bird, touched into sound.

Meanwhile Davis could not resist completing other experiments with Grecian forms. In Middletown, Connecticut, he added the finishing touches to the Corinthian home of the Hong Kong trader Samuel Russell—a building today housing the honor students at Wesleyan. In New Haven, close by the Ionic retreat of Hillhouse, he and Town did yet another Ionic mansion for Aaron Skinner. This has been preserved, though slightly altered, as has Lafayette Terrace, the row of houses behind a Corinthian colonnade on Lafayette Street, New York, formerly credited to the firm. Farther down in Manhattan, the firm designed the old Customs House, whose Doric columns faced the offices of J. P. Morgan and Company, Inc.

Having shown such skill in the Grecian style, it was to be expected that Town and Davis would bid, and bid successfully, for state capitols. The old capitol of Indiana at Indianapolis has been razed, but that of North Carolina remains, its grandeur unchallenged in the century since the cornerstone was laid.

The canny New York auctioneer Philip Hone, who realized that grandeur was an asset in any summer hotel or clubhouse, hired Town and Davis to design him a marine pavilion at Rockaway. The venture failed, but Hone never regretted spending the money. Of his last day at the pavilion he wrote: "At eleven o'clock I retired to my room, lighted a cigar, and seated myself at the front windows. The view was unspeakably grand . . . and the lofty columns of the noble piazza, breaking the silver streams of light into dark and gloomy shadows, gave the edifice the appearance of classical antiquity."

Classical antiquity, however, no matter how much it might appeal to Mayor Hone, was never so attractive to Davis as the memory of the Middle Ages. On learning that Robert Gilmor of Baltimore, grandson of one of the founders of our East India trade, was about to build a mansion in the countryside at Towson, Maryland, he provided a Gothic castle which might have been the retreat of Amy Robsart, the forsaken heroine of *Kenilworth*. Never were plans more appropriate. Young Gilmor, whose idol was Sir Walter Scott, had only recently paid a call at "Abbotsford," and was uncommonly proud of the cane presented him by the laird himself.

"Glen Ellen"—Gilmor named the new house after his bride, Ellen Ward—is now no more. Long a ruin, it was completely demolished not so long ago to make way for Loch Raven Dam. Also missing from the American landscape today is another of Davis's dramatic achievements in the early 1830's, the old building of New York University on Washington Square. Samuel F. B. Morse, who happened to be living in one of its apartments while mulling over the invention of the telegraph, made it the subject of his fantastic painting, the "Allegorical Landscape Showing New York University." The now faintly remembered novelist, Theodore Winthrop, was equally affected by the sight of the Gothic towers of N. Y. U. They were the setting of his *Cecil Dreeme,* in which a young girl disguised as a gentleman painter to escape the clutches of a cynical millionaire, dies of a heart attack when he succeeds in spiriting her away to a lunatic asylum.

In the summer of 1835, barely three years after Town and Davis submitted their sketches of the building that troubled the imagination of Morse and Winthrop, the older partner withdrew from the firm, forcing Davis to face alone the panic of 1837 and the other inconveniences ahead of a romantic architect. But this was scarcely a calamity, since Davis had not only done most of the designing himself but also built up what might be called a mail-order business in architectural plans. Too busy to supervise most of his work, he trusted local carpenters and builders to carry out his ideas. To their credit it must be said that very few of the architect's dreams were insulted by slovenly craftsmanship.

Of course Davis genuinely enjoyed supervising his designs whenever the clients could afford inspection trips, just as he enjoyed using expensive materials instead of wood or the bricks he obligingly covered with plaster in imitation of stone. Such golden opportunities were rare, but in 1838 the highhearted merchant William Paulding, brother of Van Buren's Secretary of the Navy, was so kind as to ask Davis to design and supervise "Lyndhurst," a truly magnificent Gothic seat at Tarrytown. Free of his usual worries, the architect created a masterpiece: its graceful asymmetry, its complex massing have been rarely equaled in America, and never surpassed. Paulding himself was not uniquely responsible for all this, for a later owner wisely prevailed upon Davis to enlarge the mansion, and Jay Gould, in whose hands "Lyndhurst" ultimately passed, made no significant alterations. Today it belongs to the National Trust.

To be sure, "Lyndhurst" was not for every taste. Mayor Hone, whose heart leaped at a well-proportioned column, was unnerved by the extravagance of Paulding's estate. "It is," he noted in 1841, "an immense edifice of white or gray marble, resembling a baronial castle, or rather a Gothic monastery with towers, turrets, and trellises; minarets, mosaics, and mouseholes; archways, armories, and airholes; peaked windows and pinnacled roofs, and many other fantasies too tedious to enumerate, the whole constituting an edifice of gigantic size, with no room in it; great cost and little comfort, which, if I mistake not, will one of these days be designated as *Paulding's Folly.*"

More to Hone's liking was the Grecian town house of John Cox Stevens, who married a Livingston and founded the New York Yacht Club. When dining with the Stevenses in the winter of 1849, Hone could

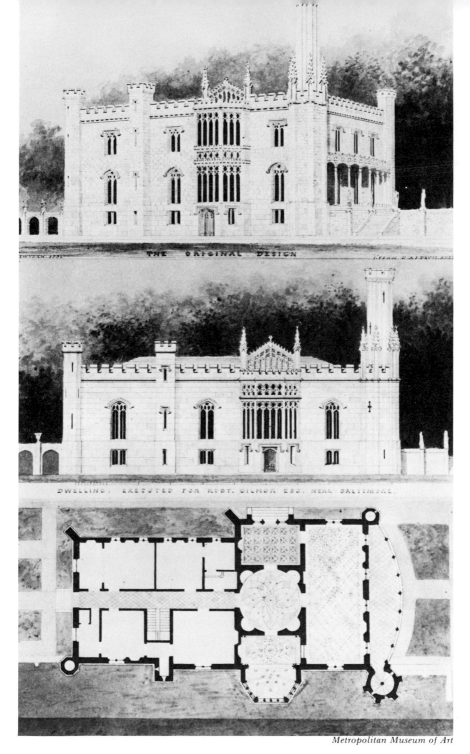

THE ORIGINAL DESIGN

DWELLING. EXECUTED FOR ROBT. GILMOR ESQ. NEAR BALTIMORE.

"Glen Ellen," Towson, Md., 1832 (Alexander Jackson Davis)

not say enough in praise of this Davis design. "The house is, indeed, a palace," he jotted down in his diary. "The Palais Bourbon in Paris, Buckingham Palace in London, and Sans-Souci at Berlin are little grander than this residence of a simple citizen of our republican city."

Today not a trace is left of the Stevens mansion, nor of "Murray Hill," the Gothic dwelling fashioned by Davis for W. H. Coventry Waddell on the northwest corner of Fifth Avenue and Thirty-seventh Street. Inspired by the view from her tower, which took in the harbor and the heights of Hoboken, Mrs. Waddell set her heart on the social splendors. She feted Irving, and Thackeray, too, and when a death in the family drove Maria Livingston Stevens out of society for a season, began giving *bals poudrés*. All these pleasures, however, came to an end in 1857, for her husband was so careless as to lose his fortune in the panic of that year. The house had to be sold, and the Waddells had to move to the St. Denis Hotel. For cold comfort in her hotel room, Mrs. Waddell may have thumbed through the pages of Ann Sophia Stephens' *Fashion and Famine*, a dime novel whose setting was "Murray Hill."

Unlike the Waddells, Davis seems to have had next to no financial worries; indeed, in 1842 and 1843, he had so much on hand that he asked Ithiel Town, who had retired to a Grecian villa on Hillhouse Avenue, New Haven, to return to the office to help with such commissions as the sternly Gothic Wadsworth Athenaeum in Hartford. And when Town resigned for the second time, there were plenty of clients, even though the Adams family never could make up its mind to ennoble Quincy with a mansion in the Italian style. Charles Francis Adams pleaded that the family had grown poor in public service.

The Adamses were hesitant, but the Livingstons were gracious. In 1843 Davis was invited by the widow of Edward Livingston, Jackson's Secretary of State, to begin what amounted to virtually a complete remodeling of "Montgomery Place" at Barrytown-on-the-Hudson. A pavilion was added on the north, a porch on the west, and a wing on the south, radically altering the exterior of the house in which Janet Livingston Montgomery, widow of the hero of Quebec, spent her last years. Not that Davis made changes which would have offended the original owner. Restraining for once his exuberant imagination, he toyed with festoons vaguely suggesting the Adam style so popular in the days before he had begun his career. In 1863, at the request of the Edward Livingstons' daughter, Cora Livingston Barton, he did still more work in the same vein, improving the east façade with the portico which makes "Montgomery Place" today the most fastidious home in Dutchess County.

Every other client of Davis in the forties and fifties begged for "modern" designs—fantasies either Grecian, Italian, Moorish or Gothic. In the Grecian style, Davis laid out the library of the University of North Carolina, now serving as the Playmakers' Theater, and the vast Ad-

"Lyndhurst," Tarrytown, N.Y., 1838-65 (Alexander Jackson Davis)

Dining room, "Lyndhurst"

ministration Building, now destroyed, of Davidson College not far away. He was also the adviser on the plans of three other architects for the present Grecian Capitol of Ohio.

In the Italian manner—which naturally became more and more fashionable as more and more businessmen's wives heard of "Osborne," Victoria and Albert's summer palace on the Isle of Wight—Davis designed the picturesque mansion in Brooklyn of the railroad builder E. C. Litchfield, treasurer of the first line to tie Chicago to the Eastern seaboard. Woefully neglected, the Litchfield towers are today Park Department headquarters in Prospect Park.

Very similar to the Litchfield house was the villa in Detroit of the real estate speculator Bela Hubbard. This was razed many years ago, like the equally Italian home of Lewis G. Morris at "Mount Fordham" in the Bronx. But "Locust Grove," Samuel F. B. Morse's seat just south of Poughkeepsie, is still standing to evoke Davis the conjurer of campaniles. And Davis' most imposing Italian design is still in use as the State Hospital for the Insane at Raleigh, North Carolina.

In the Moorish style Davis composed only one building, the long-ruined country home of Senator William S. Archer, one of Virginia's expansionists during the Mexican War. It was the Gothic tradition he turned to when asked by the carpet millionaire Alvan Higgins to draw the plans for "The House of Mansions," the row of houses that once startled the southeast corner of Fifth Avenue and Forty-second Street.

For Davis, of course, the Gothic was never a matter of archaeology, but merely the means of suggesting the poetry inherent in the passing of time. Such was the spirit in which, in 1846, he conceived the Bridgeport home of the leather dealer H. K. Harral. Preserved in all its original splendor by the last owner, "Walnut Wood" was given to the city in his will, only to be destroyed by a mayor who preferred a parking lot. It was difficult to know which to admire the more, the mirrored parlors featuring the statuary of Hiram Powers's rival, Chauncey Ives, or the intensely Gothic grand staircase, dining room, and bedrooms. The complete convenience of the plan was reflected in the asymmetry of the exterior.

There were other Gothic clients, not only in the neighborhood of New York but in points as far distant as Buzzard's Bay, the Blue Grass Country, and the banks of the James. In Rhinebeck there was the local banker Henry Delamater, whose cottage still fronts the Post Road. In Rye there was the broker William P. Chapman, whose seat is now the Glen Castle Country Club. In Tarrytown there was the merchant John J. Herrick, whose eyrie was only recently leveled after housing for many years the girls at Miss Mason's School. In Dobbs Ferry there was the silk importer E. B. Strange, whose estate has been turned into St. Christopher's, a school for boys. In New Bedford there was the mill owner, William J. Rotch, whose town house today belongs to the John M. Bul-

Residence of H.K. Harral, Bridgeport, Conn., 1846 (Alexander Jackson Davis)

Detail, bedroom, Harral residence

lards. In Lexington, Kentucky, there was the attorney Francis K. Hunt, whose "Loudon" is now known as Castlewood Community Center. In Newport there was the attorney Prescott Hall, whose "Malbone" became the summer home of the Lewis G. Morrises of our generation. And in Powhatan County, Virginia, there was the plantation owner Philip St. George Cocke, son of John Hartwell Cocke of "Bremo," whose "Belmead" became a Roman Catholic school.

One of the humane slaveholders, Cocke was a generous patron of Davis. He arranged for him to design the Gothic buildings of Virginia Military Institute—the officers' quarters, the mess hall, and the cadet barracks. This was a spectacular commission, and Davis did nothing so considerable in the Gothic at Yale, only Alumni Hall, now destroyed.

But Philip St. George Cocke thought he had not done half enough for the architect of "Belmead." "If," he once wrote Davis, "if I was autocrat or even emperor (like Louis-Napoleon in France), I should delight with your aid to build up the waste places, repair dilapidation . . . and beautify the goodly and glorious heritage of our Rip Van Winkle people. But recollecting that I am but a democratic unit, I must limit and control these flights of fancy."

Meantime Davis had found a new patron in the benevolent wholesale druggist Llewellyn Haskell, whose passion for wild scenery was responsible for Llewellyn Park, a real-estate development in West Orange, New Jersey. Here Davis laid out a castle for Haskell and the retreat for his own old age, both of which have vanished. However, the rustic gate lodge of the park remains, and the tiny cottage belonging to Mrs. Philip McKim Garrison. Glancing at those relics of the romantic era, surrounded by still innocent scenery, anyone might agree with the first chronicler of Haskell's venture, who wrote in 1859: "We thank Mr. Davis, the Michel Angelo of his time, for what he has done for us. No other man could have combined nature and art."

The Gothic hour was then almost over. At midnight on October 16, 1859, John Brown seized the arsenal at Harper's Ferry. "I expect to turn my peaceful lawn into a drill ground," Philip St. George Cocke warned Davis. "What hellish madness! . . ."

Except for a trifling commission here and there, Davis never again practiced architecture. Younger architects, guessing that many a rich wife was pining for the glories of the Second Empire, were designing palaces crowned with mansard roofs. This was heartbreaking to Davis, who complained again and again in his diary that the newer buildings of Manhattan were "wretched . . . despicable . . . depraved." He would like to have had a good talk about this with Philip St. George Cocke, but the master of "Belmead," a brigadier general at Manassas, had taken his own life in the first winter of the war.

Disconsolate, Davis retired to his hillside home at Llewellyn Park.

New York Yacht Club, now at Old Mystic, Conn., 1846 (Alexander Jackson Davis)

Capitol, Raleigh, N.C., 1833 (Town, Davis & Paton)

Residence of Henry Delamater, Rhinebeck, N.Y., 1844 (Alexander Jackson Davis)

Now and then he would have dinner with Peter Cooper, an old friend. Or he would go up to Pittsfield for a long walk with Herman Melville. Nature was always satisfying, if rarely as ominous as in the pages of Mrs. Ann Radcliffe. At the end of a winter's tramp, the architect would take down *The Italian* and relive the Gothic moments of his youth.

OF CARPENTERS AND A HOME FOR ALL

It is time to consider, first, the anonymous builders of the romantic decades, who owed much of their inspiration to the example Davis set the nation in picturesque composition, and second, his competitors in the architectural profession who, although they did not influence domestic design as directly as he did, created the country's churches, hotels, and prisons, three types of buildings in which he was not their equal. These rivals were especially prominent in Philadelphia and New Orleans, two citadels which he did not attempt to conquer.

We may never know who designed such minor miracles of the Greek revival as the William Hadwen and Nathaniel Banery houses of Nantucket, one with a Corinthian portico, the other in the Ionic style, facing the equally masterful three brick mansions of the Starbucks across Main Street; or guess who imagined such Gothic fantasies as the so-called Wedding Cake-house in Kennebunk, Maine, or the now vanished cottage of John B. Chollar in Watervliet, New York. Yet it is obvious that the unsung builders of the romantic era were quite as talented as their predecessors who fancied importing the essence of the Renaissance in colonial times. If the sureness of an architectural tradition is best tested, not by the work of the masters, but by that of the followers, the romantic movement will be remembered as long as Washington Square, New York, itself no mean achievement by obscure champions of the Greek ideal.

Local carpenters and masons were tempted by the poetic freedom of Davis and his peers. So, too, was that unforgettable figure, Orson Squire Fowler, who might never have launched the vogue for octagonal homes, if he had not been inspired by the Gothic and Italian villas about him. The son of a Congregational minister, Fowler was headed for the ministry himself at Amherst when suddenly blinded by the revelation of phrenology. Soon he and his brother and his sister were issuing tracts that told thousands the glad tidings of the new science. But phrenology was only one of their obsessions. The Fowlers taught their readers to revere mesmerists and clairvoyants, and to shudder at the damage done by tea, coffee, and tight-laced dresses.

It was in 1847 that Orson Squire Fowler made the discovery that an octagonal house "contains one fifth more room for its wall." Not one to be discouraged by the fact that octagons had existed for centuries, he

Residence of E. C. Litchfield, Brooklyn, N.Y., 1854 (Alexander Jackson Davis)

Gate lodge, Llewellyn Park, West Orange, N.J., c. 1855 (Alexander Jackson Davis)

proceeded to publish *A Home for All, or the Gravel Wall and Octagon Mode of Building, New, Cheap, Convenient, Superior, and Adapted to Rich and Poor.* "Why," he asked, "so little progress in architecture, when there is so much in all other matters? Why continue to build in the same SQUARE form of all past ages?" In all seriousness he defended the gravel wall as nature's own building material. "All that is wanted is stone and lime."

Fowler's own home on the Hudson is now destroyed. But hundreds of octagonal dwellings, from New York to Wisconsin, are still standing to tell the size of the audience reached by the Fowler publishing house. There is no way of knowing how many Americans smiled at *A Home for All.*

THE MESSAGE OF RICHARD UPJOHN

You might chuckle over Fowler's schemes to bedevil the public, but you could not question the sincerity of Richard Upjohn, the Englishman who ennobled our churches in the romantic period. "The object," he reminded Americans, "is not to surprise with novelties in church architecture, but to make what is to be made truly ecclesiastical—a temple of solemnities—such as will fix the attention of persons, and make them respond in heart and spirit to the opening service: The Lord is in His Holy Temple, let all the earth keep silence." No archaeologist, he refused to erect replicas in the New World of the cathedrals of the Old, and his finest achievements reveal that he was as conscious of the poetry of time past as Davis himself. This may have been the reason why Downing's favorite refused to compete with the Englishman in the ecclesiastical field.

The son of a surveyor, Upjohn was trained as a cabinetmaker, not as an architect, but this was no hindrance but a blessing. His churches were to tell of a rare sensibility to the possibilities of wood as a building material, a sensitivity that might not have been his, had he been apprenticed in the usual architect's office. In 1829, when at twenty-seven he set sail for America with his wife and child, he was not only a peculiarly talented but an extremely earnest young man. "Distress," he noted in his journal, "is not a proper subject for merriment or topic for invective."

He was not, he determined, to be a failure in the United States.

For the first few years Upjohn drifted from New York to Massachusetts to Maine, teaching drafting when he could and doing odd jobs in other architects' offices. His first real opportunity came in 1835 when Robert Hallowell Gardiner, the son of the last of the royal collectors of the customs at Boston, asked him to design a seat on the bank of the Kennebec at Gardiner, Maine. Gardiner, whose maternal grandfather had been one of the great landowners of Maine, might not have turned patron if his homestead at Gardiner had not been recently burned to the ground, but since a house was needed, he raised no objections when Upjohn created a Gothic mansion of stone—a picturesque dwelling that would have charmed Washington Allston himself, with whom Gardiner had attended Harvard.

Nathaniel Hawthorne admitted he was impressed by the Gardiner estate. "It well deserves the name of castle or palace," he decided in the summer of 1837, congratulating the owner on having spent sixty thousand dollars. The novelist was unaware that in this very year the architect was desperately in need of ready money.

"We have nothing to do here nor is there any means that I know of to meet rents and all the other expenses attending the keeping of a family . . . these *nothing to do* times," Upjohn wrote Gardiner from Boston that fall. Worrying over the depression, he begged his patron "to send me from 10 to 30 or even 50 bushels of the best eastern potatoes, three or four barrels of good keeping apples and anything else that can be obtained without cash. All my business is gone—all my means—nearly all my credit—seven of us in family—most of them growing fast and hungry—wood and coals—flour and all other stuff high—nothing to be got at without money."

Gardiner's answer has not been preserved. Perhaps he was so good as to abandon for a moment his favorite avocation, the keeping of accurate meteorological tables, and to save his architect from despair. In 1839 Upjohn was invited to create yet another Gothic home—a frame house this, but in Newport—for Gardiner's son-in-law, George Noble Jones. One of the many Southerners who haunted Newport in the summer months, Jones was the great-grandson of the fastidious Noble Wymberly Jones of "Wormslow Plantation," Savannah. To be the designer of his whimsical cottage on Bellevue Avenue was an enviable distinction.

Though neither the Gardiner nor the Jones house revealed that Upjohn was fond of gambling with the asymmetrical opportunities of the Gothic, only an erratic critic would think of stressing the conservatism of the architect's plans, so sure was his taste, so evident was his joy in the limitations of whatever material with which he worked. Moreover, if Upjohn had not been a discreet artist, he might not have enjoyed his peculiar success with the descendants of our finer families. Unlike Davis, who was as eager to persuade the creators of our new fortunes as the inheritors of our old, he seems to have been at his ease only when charming those who were not only rich but well born.

When Edward King, the grandson of one of the fashionable physicians of Newport in the eighteenth century, thought of building himself a villa in the resort, he turned to Upjohn in the summer of 1845. The architect's handsome Italian invention serves today as the People's Library. Later, when Henry Evelyn Pierrepont, a young gentleman whose father had left him sixty acres on Brooklyn Heights, not to mention a principality in northern New York, sensed that the time had come to endow his wife with the surroundings to which she was entitled—she was, after all, a granddaughter of John Jay—he, too, decided that only Upjohn could fashion a town house of the proper dignity.

Thanks to the ruthless determination of the planners of the present Brooklyn Heights Promenade, the Pierrepont house which Upjohn completed in 1857 has been demolished. This is a tragedy, for no other domestic design of the architect in the Italian manner, neither the restyling of Martin Van Buren's eighteenth-century residence at Kinderhook, nor the remodeling of the old Van Rensselaer mansion at Albany (since moved to Williamstown), may be compared to this serene brownstone overlooking the harbor.

But Upjohn, it must never be forgotten, was not an architect who happened to be an Episcopalian, but an Episcopalian who happened to be an architect. There could be no mistaking his reverence. A fervent High-churchman, he was so sensitive to the beauty of ritual that he often bewildered those who leaned toward the Low Church by his dogmatic insistence on deep chancels and every other architectural device that might enhance the mystery of the service. He was never quite certain that it was becoming for him to create houses of worship for dissenters, and when asked to provide plans for a Unitarian church in Boston, he refused. "Can we point out anywhere a class of men whose private life is more pure . . . than the Unitarians of Boston?" pleaded a tolerant Anglican, but to no avail. On another occasion he condescended to design a Presbyterian church—with grave misgivings. A rival glanced at the building and remarked that "he did it conscientiously, upon the ground that Presbyterians were not entitled to architecture."

But Upjohn could be generous. For country parishes that could not afford stone or even brick and plaster, he published a handbook of wooden churches that was a godsend to carpenters. This was a labor of love, for once he was established, he had more than enough work at hand. Few American architects have built more churches; no one has built better.

One of the finest of his ecclesiastical commissions is the Church of the Ascension, on the corner of Fifth Avenue and Tenth Street, New York, whose cornerstone was laid the year after the sketches for the Jones cottage at Newport. The entrance tower of this simple stone building is one of the architect's commanding designs. Searching for the precedent of this or any other feature may amuse a scholar, but prove nothing. Upjohn would always rather be imaginative than prudent, and he never hesitated to combine motifs from different eras of the Gothic past. Here the piers and trusses supporting the flat ceiling recall the Perpendicular style, while the tracery of the aisle windows follows that of the Decorated period. For once, incidentally, the architect was checkmated in the matter of a deep chancel. The rector, a conscientious Low-churchman, feared the worst and bought up the land in the rear of the plot. The vestry might surrender, but he never.

Perhaps Upjohn was happier designing the Church of the Holy Communion on Sixth Avenue and Twentieth Street. Though he had to be satisfied with a single aisle, instead of the three at Ascension, he introduced the cruciform plan, subtly accented by a corner tower, and secured the deep chancel on which he set his heart. He could be even prouder of St. Mary's Church at Burlington, New Jersey, which was consecrated in 1854, thirteen years after Ascension, nine years after Holy Communion. Ignoring Bishop Doane's plea for a mere reproduction of a favorite church in England, he submitted an invention of his own in Early English Gothic. His steeple so confidently dominates the crossing that the architect's skill in relieving the simplicity of the central tower with turrets is not at first apparent.

But Upjohn's masterpiece is Trinity, New York. This, the third church of the name on the corner of Wall and Broadway, may be said to be the very symbol in stone of the Anglican Communion in America. And it would have been a tragedy for Episcopalians if Upjohn had been merely consulted in the matter of repairing the sagging roof of the church then on the site. Haunted, as Phoebe Stanton has recently proved, by the achievements of A. W. N. Pugin in England, he may well have glanced with envy at an Ideal Church sketched by Pugin in his *True Principles*. There are obvious similarities.

Upjohn, who must have sensed that this was the golden moment, succeeded before the summer was over in persuading the vestrymen that it would be the height of idiocy to bother about the old building when the services of so devout an artist were available. Enchanted by the magnificence of the tower in his sketches—which bore a faint resemblance to that of St. Michael's, Coventry—they finally yielded to his demand for a deep chancel, and even tolerated a cross atop the spire. To many New Yorkers at the time, the cross was a Romish conceit, but Upjohn was so eager for this emblem of the High Church that according to family tradition he had it set in place before the vestrymen knew what was afoot.

Trinity, Downing decided, "will stand as far above all other Gothic structures of the kind in this country, as a Raphael's madonna before a tolerable sign painting." In the years that have gone by since the consecration on Ascension Day, 1846, critics have agreed that this is one of the greatest, if not the greatest church erected in America. Unhappily for Upjohn's peace of mind, however, there were those in the romantic

period who failed to appreciate the uncanny grace of Trinity's proportions. One such observer seems to have been Edgar Allan Poe. *The Broadway Journal,* of which he was one of the three editors, noted in 1845 that

> any structure of the so-called Gothic order must of necessity be an in-
> congruous work, unless it be an exact copy, and then it must be unfit.
> Trinity Church is a very showy building, and it seems to satisfy the senti-
> ment of the promenaders in Broadway very well; and it is also a very
> good object for the Wall Street brokers to contemplate, as they hurry
> to and from *the board,* reminding them, by its tall spire, to look up,
> occasionally. But considered as a work of architectural expression, as a
> house of worship, and consuming money which should be devoted to
> religious purposes, it reflects but little credit upon those who have had
> the responsibility of its erection.

Upjohn, who apparently made no reply to the squib in Poe's review,
was so seldom satisfied by his own attainments, and so far from certain
that the romantic was the only valid approach to architecture that he
dared remind his colleagues of the then wholly forgotten beauties of the
colonial period. "May we not gain a valuable lesson while contemplating
these works of our forefathers?" he asked an architects' convention. "Old
and quaint as they are, will we not see by comparing them with the
works of our own hands that their authors regarded the law of harmony
between a building and its surroundings better than we do at the present
day?"

RENWICK: ARCHITECT AND YACHTSMAN

There were other architects in those days who designed admirable
churches. One of the most talented and most erratic was James Renwick,
Jr. His father was a comfortable professor at Columbia, his mother was a
Brevoort, and his wife was an Aspinwall. So he kept two steam yachts, one
for fishing off the Florida coast, and the other for cruising farther from
home.

These were luxuries which Renwick fairly earned, if the Gothic castle
he created in 1851 for C. T. Longstreet of Syracuse be given its due. For
this clothier, who reaped a fortune shipping ready-made suits to California at the height of the Gold Rush, he invented a fantastic fortress of
stone, very likely inspired by "Hafod," the villa in the wilds of Wales that
haunted the author of "Kubla Khan." Anyone who has even seen himself caught in the quiverings of the conspicuous mirrors of the grand
staircase will be dismayed to learn that the Longstreet mansion has recently been leveled by Syracuse University.

Renwick's masterpiece, Grace Church, New York, may be considered
safe for all time from the wreckers. Next to Trinity, no building on Man-

Left: Residence of C.T. Longstreet, Syracuse, N.Y., 1851 (James Renwick, Jr.)
Right: Trinity Church, New York City, 1846 (Richard Upjohn)

Rectory, Grace Church, New York City, 1847 (James Renwick, Jr.)

hattan Island is dearer to Episcopalians than this fanciful Gothic monument on Broadway at Tenth Street. In the social history of New York Grace has a niche of its own; the sexton, over a hundred years ago, was the sleek and happy Isaac Brown who admitted that the Lenten Season was "horridly dull," but then "we manage to make our funerals as entertaining as possible." Even prior to its consecration, the social standing of Grace was undeniable, as Philip Hone, a vestryman of Trinity, recognized when he noted in his diary that

> the pews were sold last week, and brought extravagant prices, some $1200 to $1400, with a pew rent on the estimated value of eight per cent; so that the word of God, as it came down to us from fishermen and mechanics, will cost the quality who worship in this splendid temple about three dollars every Sunday. This may have a good effect; for many of them, though rich, know how to calculate, and if they do not go regularly to Church, will not get the worth of their money.
>
> This is to be the fashionable Church, and already its aisles are filled (especially on Sundays after morning services in other Churches) with gay parties of ladies in feathers and mousseline-de-laine dresses, and dandies with moustaches and high-heeled boots; the lofty arches resound with astute criticisms upon gothic architecture from fair ladies who have had the advantage of foreign travel, and scientific remarks upon acoustics from elderly millionaires who do not hear quite as well as formerly.

Renwick, who was twenty-eight in 1846 when Grace opened its doors, was not quite twenty-five when he secured the commission to ennoble what had been until then a prize parcel of real estate in his mother's family; the only training the young Columbia graduate had received was in engineering, first on the construction of the Erie Railroad, later on the Croton Aqueduct. Perhaps success came too easily, for he was to wobble disastrously in his later practice. St. Patrick's Cathedral, begun in 1858 and dedicated in 1879, was a commendable essay in the Gothic, but lacked the whimsical charm of Grace and its crudities foretold the errors to come.

For all that, nothing could be sillier than to scold the genius who created the Smithsonian Institution in 1846. This picturesque composition in the Romanesque manner, no matter what its failings as an exhibition hall, is one of the ideal stage sets of the romantic era. This was understood even by the sculptor Horatio Greenough, who was not one to approve of fantasy in any form.

"Suddenly," Greenough declared, ". . . the dark form of the Smithsonian palace rose between me and the white Capitol, and I stopped. Tower and battlement, and all that medieval confusion, stamped itself on the halls of Congress, as ink on paper! Dark on that whiteness—complication on that simplicity! It scared me. Was it a specter, or was I not another Rip Van Winkle who had slept too long. . . . I am not about to

Residence of J.B. Chollar, Watervliet, N.Y., c. 1848

Whaler's Church, Sag Harbor, N.Y., 1844 (Minard Lafever)

criticize the edifice. I have not quite recovered from my alarm. There is still a certain mystery about those towers and steep belfries that makes me uneasy. This is a practical land. They must be for something. Is no *coup d'état* lurking there?"

THE MERITS OF MINARD LAFEVER

Minard Lafever, who like Renwick was famous for churches, could not possibly have conceived of a building which so perfectly captured the mood of Byronic defiance. Ill-educated, starved for knowledge in his youth, he was as earnest as the other was suave. At nineteen he walked fifty miles from his home in upstate New York to purchase his first architectural treatise, and so highly did he prize the fundamentals that in later life he published five handbooks for carpenters and builders. In these he popularized choice Grecian and Gothic details besides advertising his major achievement, the rich Gothic Church of Holy Trinity, Brooklyn. This, the heart's desire of Edgar John Bartow, a devoted Episcopalian who made a fortune in the paper business, was not opened until 1847 when the architect was forty-nine. It was at Bartow's urging that Lafever created the lovely little stone bridge over Montague Street, Brooklyn, now demolished.

To Lafever have also been attributed the Whaler's Church and the Benjamin Hunting house at Sag Harbor. The first is Egyptian in inspiration, the second, Grecian. Neither of these frame buildings suggests that their creator was once a mere carpenter, so subtle are the details and so perfect the proportions.

JOHN HAVILAND, CONTRIVER OF PRISONS

Like Lafever, John Haviland reached our artisans by means of an excellent handbook, but his forte was not churches but prisons. A native of Somersetshire, first cousin to the dark-minded painter Benjamin Haydon, he got his start in the office of James Elmes, an architect best remembered today for the handsome book he published on the sights of Regency London. Wandering to St. Petersburg—his aunt was the wife of Alexander I's minister of marine—he came across our minister, John Quincy Adams, who invited him to the United States. In 1823, at thirty-one, he watched the cornerstone being laid of the Eastern Penitentiary, Philadelphia, the monument on which he built his fame in the New World.

"The Penitentiary," remarked a Philadelphia admirer, "is the only edifice in this country which is calculated to convey to our citizens the external appearance of those magnificent and picturesque castles of the Middle Ages which contribute so eminently to embellish the scenery of

Doorway by Minard Lafever   *Courtesy of the New-York Historical Society*

Europe." Its gateway originally filled by a massive wrought-iron portcullis and double oaken doors studded with projecting iron rivets, embellished besides with buttresses and pinnacles, the Eastern was an awesome Gothic pile, fit to confine Sir Brian de Bois-Guilbert himself. Yet it was not only an ominous but even a revolutionary design. Its corridors radiated from a central observation point, and its inmates were subject to solitary confinement. Penologists from Prussia, Russia, France and England traveled to Philadelphia to behold and admire. Only Charles Dickens was stirred to horror.

"In its intention," said Dickens, "I am well convinced that it is kind, humane, and meant for reformation: but I am persuaded that those who devised this system of prison discipline, and those benevolent gentlemen who carry it into execution, do not know what it is they are doing. I believe that very few men are capable of estimating the immense amount of torture and agony which this dreadful punishment, prolonged for years, inflicts upon the sufferers. . . . There is a depth of terrible endurance in it which none but the sufferers themselves can fathom, and which no man has a right to inflict upon his fellow-creature."

Dickens shuddered at the ritual prepared for new inmates. "Over the head of every prisoner who comes into this melancholy house, a black hood is drawn; and in this dark shroud, an emblem of the curtain dropped between him and the living world, he is led to the cell from which he never again comes forth, until his whole term of imprisonment has expired." Prisoners just released were visited with fits of trembling, Dickens was told. "Well, it's not so much a trembling," confessed a guard, "though they do quiver—as a complete derangement of the nervous system."

No wonder Dickens, who could not bring himself to excuse the inhumanity of the penologists of his century, was impatient with Haviland the architect. In New York he pronounced the Tombs—one of Haviland's rare experiments in a mood other than Gothic—a "dismal-fronted pile of bastard Egyptian, like an enchanter's palace in a melodrama." A more thoughtful critic might join Dickens in condemning the practice of solitary confinement, yet realize that the challenge of penal reform was too vast to be met by one generation, much less by one architect. Moreover, the chain of romantic prisons erected by the creator of Eastern in the county seats of New Jersey and Pennsylvania added, as did Eastern, to the evidence that America was dissatisfied with previous solutions, and—this is something which high-minded humanitarians often forget— only in dissatisfaction are satisfactory answers to social problems conceived. Finally, reformers of the Dickens persuasion could not begin to appreciate the American yearning for the picturesque; this was a need which Haviland filled with such subtlety that he was one of the most popular architects of Philadelphia, rivaled only by William Strickland, Thomas Ustick Walter, and John Notman.

THE PHILADELPHIA STORY

Though the steeple of Independence Hall and St. Stephen's Church on Tenth Street prove that Strickland could design in either Georgian or Gothic, the Grecian was his favorite style. This was not surprising. His taste was formed by Latrobe. The son of one of Latrobe's carpenters, he himself was apprenticed to the master at fifteen, at the very moment that the Chesapeake and Delaware Canal was being planned in the office. If he had not gone fishing on the day he was supposed to be rubbing the mold off the walls of the Latrobe residence, he might have lasted longer than two years, but even in this interval he learned enough to realize that a canny architect might be expected to double as an engineer. There came a time, in 1824, when the Pennsylvania Society for the Promotion of Internal Improvements, newly founded by the aggressive local Whigs, dispatched an engineer to England to report on the new canals and railroads, and to Strickland fell this splendid mission.

All this was long after the days when the architect was driven to

Eastern State Penitentiary, Philadelphia, Pa., 1829 (John Haviland)

Tremont House, Boston, Mass., 1829 (Isaiah Rogers)

sketching "victorious commodores and other notorieties" for the shop windows, or painting street views in oil which, if he was lucky, he managed to trade for "two hams, ten dollars, and a box of segars." Strickland's struggle for recognition did not end even in 1818 when his design was accepted for the home of the Second Bank of the United States. What might have been a triumph was marred by Latrobe's ill-substantiated claim that the plan was really his own. But the building, bounded by Chestnut and Library, Fourth and Fifth streets, was at last completed in 1824, and it was then universally agreed that the creator of this magnificent Doric pile for the omnipotent bank was one of the first artists of America.

James Fenimore Cooper, who claimed that the Bourse in Paris was the most distinguished monument of the nineteenth century, was undeniably awed. "Next to this exquisite work of art, I rank the Bank of the United States," he declared. "There are certainly a hundred buildings in Europe of a very similar style, and of far more labored ornaments; but I cannot remember one in which simplicity, exquisite proportion, and material, unite to produce so fine a whole." As for Vignon's Church of the Madeleine, "I do not believe it will ever produce so pleasing an effect as this chaste and severe little temple of Plutus."

Even if the bank cost something less than the $500,000 rumored to have been invested in its marble tellers' counters, marble floors, marble-faced walls, and marble porticoes, it told superbly of Philadelphia's ambition to supplant New York as the financial capital of the nation, and Strickland, who was only thirty-seven the day the Library Street portico was completed and the bank open for business, might have been excused for boasting of his commission. But such was his modesty, that he half-apologized for his masterpiece. He had been haunted by the Parthenon, he confessed to readers of *The Port Folio,* and like his old master Latrobe, was occasionally troubled by the challenge of reconciling Grecian forms with nineteenth-century functions. "In selecting this example as a model for a building such as a bank," he said, "it becomes a difficult task for an architect to preserve *all* the characteristics of a Grecian temple. . . . The flanking columns of a Grecian building produce a decidedly beautiful feature. . . . But they cannot be applied with the proper effect to places of business, without a sacrifice of those principles which have a constant application to internal uses and economy."

Strickland may have been dissatisfied, but not his fellow Philadelphians. In 1833 the Naval Asylum was dedicated. This was a surprisingly successful compromise of Grecian ideals and American needs. In 1834 the Merchants' Exchange was opened. Its noble façade on Third Street, a rounded Corinthian portico two stories high, was crowned by a tower recalling the Choragic Monument of Lysicrates. As if these and other local commissions did not mean he was overworked, he designed

Second Bank of the United States, Philadelphia, Pa., 1824 (William Strickland)

"Oak Alley," Vacherie, La., c. 1836

Washington's tomb at Mount Vernon. He was busy besides with engineering projects, such as improving the Chesapeake and Delaware Canal and surveying the Wilmington and Susquehanna Railroad.

The greatest of all his opportunities, the Capitol of Tennessee, came in 1845. Settling in Nashville, he died there in 1854, five years before the last stone was set and the fine marble interior was completed in what must be accounted one of the most beautiful of all our state houses, second only to that of North Carolina. The Corinthian columns of the twin porticoes were the work of a man who had carefully considered the Erectheum, and the cupola, like that of the Merchants' Exchange, showed that he had studied the Choragic Monument of Lysicrates. But it would be wrong to suppose that he was merely a scholar. He was also a poet who sympathized with the American longing for the Grecian past.

The New South was moved by these memories as was no other section of the United States. The Capitol of Kentucky, completed in 1830 by Strickland's pupil, Gideon Shryock, evoked the temple of Athena Polias at Priene in Iona, and the mansions of the great planters were often equally reverent. One of the subtlest of these plantation houses was "Gaineswood" at Demopolis, Alabama, erected in 1842 for Nathan Bryan Whitfield. One of the most magnificent was "Rattle and Snap," built near Nashville in 1845 by George Polk, brother of the fighting bishop Leonidas Polk.

Moving in this world, Strickland could scarcely avoid making plans for Grecian homes at Nashville. According to tradition, he created "Belmont," the somewhat Italianate residence of the lawyer Joseph Acklen—later the main building of Ward-Belmont College for Women— as well as "Belle Meade," the spare but commanding plantation house of William Giles Harding. Harding, who kept a deer park of four hundred acres on his four thousand-acre estate, might have passed for the ideal client of the New South. A breeder of blooded stock who bragged of being born in a log cabin, he was all the cannier a farmer for not being overly educated. He was said to have been the first to ship a load of hay to New Orleans, and he was one of the original promoters of the Nashville and Chattanooga Railroad.

Meanwhile in the Philadelphia which Strickland had left behind him, the genius of Thomas Ustick Walter did not go unrecognized. Walter was prized for his highly imaginative designs for Moyamensing Prison—the central block was Gothic, the Debtors' Jail, Egyptian—for his delightful sketches for the hamlet of West Chester—for his labor in creating the cast-iron dome of the Capitol in Washington, and above all, for his success in collaborating with Nicholas Biddle, the banker who was determined to dictate the architectural as well as the financial trend of the times.

Biddle's quarrel with Jackson over the Bank of the United States has been given its due in all the textbooks, but the banker's concern for the fine arts has been overlooked. One of the great connoisseurs of the romantic era, he was fonder of the geometry of Attic temples than the simple arithmetic of his ledgers. "The two great truths in the world," he stated in his diary, "are the Bible and Grecian architecture." This was something he may have discovered at Princeton, from which he was graduated in 1801, when only eighteen, or perhaps in Paris, where he served our minister John Armstrong as secretary, or maybe in London, where he rendered the same service to Minister James Monroe, but most likely in Greece itself, which he explored at twenty-three. Though he turned editor on his return to America, directing the policies of the discreet but influential *Port Folio,* neither journalism nor the presidency of the Bank of the United States, a prize awarded him the year before Strickland's plans for the Philadelphia offices were completed, could quite satisfy his ambition. "Man is really very little superior to a brute," he decided in his European travels. If mankind in the New World were to be saved from oblivion, architecture might perform the miracle— provided Biddle were allowed to supervise the work in progress.

The banker could not wait for long. When the will of merchant Stephen Girard was read, authorizing the spending of two million dollars to house a school for orphans, Biddle had himself elected president of the college's board of trustees. There were Philadelphians who murmured at this, but President Biddle was pleased. "For the first time since the days of Pericles," he reflected, "architecture was introduced into city politics."

With Biddle heading the board, the orphans were not likely to be cheated out of their architectural rights. "This building," he said,

> might be after the most approved fashion of barns and almhouses—large and shapeless and cheap, and when it was finished, many men, worthy and discreet citizens, would rejoice that so large a mass of stone had been piled at so small a cost, and then go their ways and be as they were yesterday. But they have sounded little of the depths of our nature who do not know that in every mind, however rude, there is a keener sympathy with the forms of the external world, a stronger sensibility to the harmonies, both of art and nature, than shallow thinkers imagine, and the cultivation of that sentiment, the diffusion of a love for the beautiful and the graceful, contributes to make men wiser and gentler and happier than much that is taught in the schools and is called knowledge. I thought then that instead of one of these commonplace structures, I would endeavor to obtain a perfect model of the simple, chaste, and pure architecture of the ancients. . . . My life has been one of great labor, but I have rarely labored so much for any other object.

He was not pleased with the plan that Walter first submitted. This was for "a large, showy building, wanting simplicity and purity," and

Biddle had made up his mind that what was needed was a Grecian temple with elegant Ionic colonnades on all four sides. Scholars have since discovered that the architect's original conception was daring and original, but these scholars have not enjoyed, as Walter did, a heart-to-heart talk with the determined banker.

While Biddle was willing to consider the merits of Walter's scheme, "to which the natural self-love of a young artist attached him . . . I endeavored," he recorded in his diary, "to excite his ambition to achieve something beyond his plan or the plan of anyone else, in order to take advantage of this rare opportunity of immortalizing himself by a perfect, chaste specimen of Grecian architecture. He was inclined to listen with confidence in me, and he had worked at the Bank of the United States, where I was chairman of the building committee. He behaved perfectly well about it, no one could have done better. He removed his own plans and came at once into my views and prepared all the necessary drawings and seconded me with great cordiality."

Nor was this all that Walter did to smooth the way. "The architect has since told me that several of them [the board] said to him: We do not like to oppose Mr. Biddle, but cannot you help us to get those ideas of Greek architecture out of his head, and accordingly he made plans and estimates for them to persuade me out of this plan."

When the struggle was over, and the marble temple completed, Biddle was satisfied that "Philadelphia now possesses the most beautiful building now standing, for of all the ancient structures resembling it, there is not a single one standing in sufficient preservation to compare with it, and modern buildings of the same class are mostly disfigured by some departure from the true and ancient simplicity."

Biddle may not have been an impartial critic, but this classroom building, flanked by the four dormitories, was one of the triumphs of the Greek revival in America, no matter if a perverse echo harassed the orphans' instructors. It is just possible that Walter, surveying the capitals on the colonnades, modeled after those of the monument of Lysicrates, may have wondered whether his original plan would have been half so splendid.

No one could deny that Walter had traveled far. Only twenty-nine when the cornerstone of Girard was laid in 1833, he had once thought of abandoning architecture for bricklaying—which was his father's and his grandfather's calling—and this, even after he had begun studying in Strickland's office. But now, with the achievement of Girard College behind him, he was asked to watch over "Andalusia," the country seat on the banks of the Delaware on whose lawn Biddle laid aside the cares of the Bank of the United States. This was one of the magnificent country homes of the North, so complete a remodeling of the residence of the banker's wife that Walter may have raised no objections when Biddle insisted that the portico recall that of the Theseum at Athens.

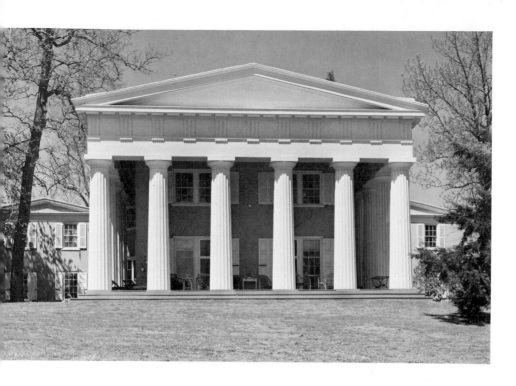

Residence of Nicholas Biddle, Andalusia, Pa., 1833 (T.U. Walter & N. Biddle)

Girard College, Philadelphia, Pa., 1833 (T.U. Walter)

Nothing so magnificent was ever attempted by John Notman, yet this Scottish-born contemporary of Walter can scarcely be omitted from any consideration of Philadelphia in the romantic era. In 1837, when twenty-seven, Notman succeeded in designing what may have been the first Italian villa in the United States. This American answer to the achievements of Schinkel and Persius in Germany, and of Barry in England, was built at Burlington, New Jersey, on the bank of the Delaware, to please Bishop George Washington Doane, the prelate who commissioned St. Mary's Church. Remembered in our day as the author of the hymn, "Fling Out the Banner, Let It Float," Doane was pitilessly publicized in his own time for his supposed mismanagement of the finances of a church school. The charges could not be proved, but they embittered the Bishop's stay on earth. For all this trouble John Notman may have been in some way responsible. The envious we have always with us; there were those who envied Doane his chocolate-colored villa behind whose façade was secreted a library in the gentlest Gothic taste. It has been destroyed.

Notman has gone down in history as "a one-bottle man," meaning that he could down a bottle of brandy at a sitting; nevertheless he managed to draw the plans for Philadelphia's Athenaeum, the president's house at Princeton, and an imposing number of Gothic churches and Italian villas in and around the city before his death in 1865. One of his admirers was Henry Austin of New Haven, who found the Italian villa ready-made for adaptation. Following the Philadelphian's example and that of A. J. Davis, he acquired a comfortable reputation in New Haven and its environs for his mansions in the Italian manner. Many of these have survived, as has the Egyptian entrance he conceived in 1845 for the Grove Street Cemetery.

ROMANTIC NEW ENGLAND

Neither Boston nor Providence in the romantic decades could compare with New York or Philadelphia. The first bloom of prosperity had been rubbed off in the Federal era, and the dividends from the new cotton mills went in many cases to the very families who had already established their eminence and built their town houses on Beacon and Power streets.

Not that either Providence or Boston was insignificant. In the former city, Russell Warren and James C. Bucklin designed in 1828 the Arcade whose Ionic colonnades of granite concealed a two-story skylighted interior with unusually graceful cast-iron balconies, while in near-by Bristol Warren honored the descendants of slave traders by planning monumental mansions for the De Wolfe dynasty.

Boston could be proud of the Bunker Hill Monument conceived by the one-time mason and quarrier, Solomon Willard, of St. Paul's Church and the Quincy Market, Grecian essays in Quincy granite by Alexander Parris, and above all, of the formidable Doric Custom House, imagined in marble by Ammi Burnham Young. Nor was this all, since Isaiah Rogers built in Boston the first great American hotel, the Tremont House, beneath whose Doric portico Charles Dickens, often so skeptical of American ways, paused long enough to remember that the hotel had "more galleries, colonnades, piazzas, and passages than I can remember, or the reader would believe."

But Young, who could not hope to find in Boston the rewarding commissions to which he was entitled, moved finally to Washington where he filled Mills's position as architect to the government, dictating the design of countless customs houses and post offices across the nation, now repeating his classic triumphs, now daring to impose Italianate façades. As for Rogers, he left for New York shortly after the Tremont House was completed, and once the Astor House was erected on lower Broadway, found himself swamped with orders for Grecian hotels up and down the land. He ended his days in Cincinnati, but not before he had endowed New York with his Ionic Merchants' Exchange on Wall Street. Its façade was ultimately incorporated in the National City Bank Building by McKim, Mead and White.

THE ROMANTIC SOUTH

Though Boston could not command the services of even those architects who grew up in New England, the Deep South drew dozens of ambitious draftsmen in the decades preceding the Civil War. From Natchez to New Orleans mansions bordering the Mississippi revealed the magnificent incomes of the luckier masters of cotton and sugar plantations.

In Natchez itself, where nearly all of the newly rich of Mississippi made their homes, the parade of town houses was a splendid thing—so splendid you might forget that the majority of Southerners had no economic interest in the slavery on which all this luxury was based. Four of the finer Grecian houses in Natchez were "D'Evereux," "Melrose," "Dunleith," and "Stanton Hall." the first belonged to the planter William St. John Elliott, the second to the attorney John McMurran, the third to the banker Charles Dahlgren, and the last to the cotton broker Frederick Stanton.

But by all means the most extraordinary sight in the village was "Longwood," the octagonal villa in the Moorish manner that the Philadelphia architect Samuel Sloan invented for the planter Haller Nutt. Nutt's father, a Virginian who had studied medicine with Rush in Philadelphia and toured the Near East before settling in Mississippi, founded the family fortunes when he perfected a new variety of cotton. His son, who increased the family income by making his own improvements on Whitney's cotton gin, looked forward to long years of rereading his favorite Greek, Latin, and Hebrew authors under the domed rotunda one hundred feet high. This was not to be, as the war broke out before Longwood was half-finished.

Not every planter was so cultivated as Haller Nutt. Though an occasional descendant of a great family in the Old South moved to the lower Mississippi Valley in hopes of reviving the waning prestige of his name, and though certain accomplished Creoles made the most of Jean-Etienne Boré's discovery of the proper method to refine sugar, many of those who suddenly became rich in the Deep South as suddenly emerged from obscurity. So the story of architecture in this area on the eve of the Civil War is largely if not wholly the chronicle of the newly rich.

To trace the Barrow family of Louisiana back to the North Carolina of the eighteenth century is not half so rewarding as to stress the achievements of the Barrows in and about Saint Francisville in the nineteenth century. Whoever came upon "Greenwood," the mansion of William Ruffin Barrow, whose encircling columns, two stories high, were reflected in the stagnant lake on the lawn, would agree that this was one of the great country houses of America. Not every Barrow built so well, but no traveler with a taste for the picturesque would regret visiting "Afton Villa," the Gothic seat which David Barrow, first cousin of the master of "Greenwood," completed nineteen years later in 1849. Both houses have been destroyed by fire.

Many another plantation house along the river would tell the same story of the wonders accomplished by architects, known and unknown, for the creators of the fat new fortunes of the romantic decades. Probably the most beautiful of all was "Belle Grove," built in 1857 by one Henry Howard for John Andrews, Jr., a planter about whose origins little or nothing has been learned, except that he was a Virginian by birth. In its day "Belle Grove" may have been the most magnificent mansion in America. Until recently, when tramps or urchins set fire to its strawberry-stucco façade, and its Corinthian capitals toppled, it was our most enchanting ruin, even more tantalizing than the remains of "Windsor Plantation" to the north of Natchez.

Nearer New Orleans, at the end of an avenue of twenty-eight ancient live oaks, stands "Oak Alley," the only house on the river that could have rivaled "Belle Grove." But it has been saved from the havoc that may be wrought by time, and the twenty-eight Doric columns that encircle the former home of the planter J. T. Roman are almost as immaculate as in 1836, the year in which this grove was settled. Since Roman came from a Creole family already distinguished before the dawn of the romantic era—the venerable Whig governor, André Roman, was his brother—his

"Greenwood," St. Francisville, La., c. 1830

"Longwood," Natchez, Miss., 1860 (Samuel Sloan)

"Belle Grove," White Castle, La., 1857 (Henry Howard)

home can scarcely be considered an architectural expression of the yearnings of the newly rich. But this may be only an exception to the rule that the great buildings of the Deep South were monuments to the ambition of speculators here today and gone tomorrow.

As for New Orleans itself, it exhibited no symptoms of anemia in the romantic decades. Its population, which numbered only 8,000 in the year of the Louisiana Purchase, swelled by 1820 to 41,000, and by 1860 to 160,000. By 1840 it was second only to New York as a port.

One of the most talented of the designers who descended on New Orleans was one James Harrison Dakin of Hudson, New York, who had been a pupil of Alexander Jackson Davis, and drawn plates for Minard Lafever's handbooks. He created the exotic Gothic capitol of the state at Baton Rouge in 1847. His brother Charles B. Dakin collaborated with James Gallier, Sr., the Irish-born genius who reached the city in 1834 at thirty-six after a stint in the office of Town and Davis and year of partnership with Lafever. Together C. B. Dakin and the elder Gallier executed the St. Charles Hotel, the Merchants' Exchange, and Christ Church, all of which have been demolished. But the City Hall, an Ionic design in marble for which the elder Gallier was alone responsible, has survived, and so have the twin Pontalba Apartments on Jackson Square, brick buildings with cast-iron balconies which his son and namesake is said to have conceived in 1849 for the Baroness Pontalba.* The French Opera House, by the younger Gallier, was destroyed by fire early in this century.

In so brief an account as this of American architecture there is no space for the vernacular of the Vieux Carré. Nor can anything be said of the persistence in the lower Mississippi Valley, from Saint Genevieve, Missouri, to New Orleans, of the building tradition of the earliest French settlers, even though their insistence on raised ground floors and on porches encircling their homes created a precedent which artisans and architects alike were bound to observe. Only thus could man defend himself from humidity and heat.

None of the romantic architects took notice of the presence in Louisiana of the few but commendable examples of the Franco-Spanish academic style, such as the Cabildo and the Presbytère on Jackson Square, New Orleans, both of which dated from the 1790's. Nor did our architects acknowledge the existence in the Southwest and the Far West of the Spanish missions of Texas, New Mexico, Arizona, and California. Perhaps this was because the romantic insistence on the poetry of time past was so deeply influenced by British thought that it could not conceive of the magic of French or Spanish times. Or perhaps this was because of the traditional romantic dislike of the survival of the Renaissance in all its

* Samuel Wilson, Jr. suggests that the Pontalba was begun by Gallier and the exterior redesigned and executed by Henry Howard.

forms. Whatever the reasons, the dismissal in those days of the reincarnation of Spanish forms by Indian craftsmen was unfortunate.

PROPHETS OF MODERN TIMES

In romantic times our architects were criticized, not for neglecting the achievements of French and Spanish civilization in the New World, but for daring to experiment with the poetry of time in any of its aspects. The most unfriendly critic of the romantic movement was the sculptor Horatio Greenough, the very man who disparaged Renwick's Smithsonian Institution. "I contend," wrote Greenough, "for Greek principles, not Greek things." Defining beauty as "the promise of function," he warned the nation that "the men who have reduced locomotion to its simplest elements, in the trotting wagon and the yacht *America,* are nearer to Athens at this moment that they who would bend the Greek temple to every use."

These and other pronouncements of Greenough have been reread in our era with such passionate interest that he has been portrayed as one of the great American critics, a precursor of Louis Sullivan himself. But if the mark of a good critic is his understanding of the art of his own time, Greenough is disappointing. He could refer to Mills's Washington Monument as "a symbol of huge aspiration and classic impotence," and he could speak of Upjohn's Trinity Church as "the puny Cathedral of Broadway, like an elephant dwindled to the size of a dog."

Greenough died five years before the first practical passenger elevator was installed in the cast-iron Haughwout Building, New York City, but it is hardly likely that he would have noticed the device. He was oblivious of all the technical advances of the romantic period toward the architecture of the twentieth century. He said nothing of the balloon frame type of construction, introduced in Chicago in 1833, even though this method of nailing upright timbers marked a revolution in carpentry. And he never mentioned the erection in 1848 in New York City of James Bogardus's factory, the first complete cast-iron building. This was all the more unfortunate because this invention, whatever its defects, foretold the steel frames of our skyscrapers. Perhaps Greenough was offended by what Bogardus termed the "happy adaptability" of cast iron to ornament and decoration. Or perhaps he was displeased to learn that the inventor had received his inspiration in Italy, while "contemplating the rich architectural designs of antiquity." Yet he might have listened to the claims of an American who hit upon so ingenious an idea while traveling abroad.

"Such a building," Bogardus pointed out, "may be erected with extraordinary facility, and at all seasons of the year. No plumb is needed, no square, no level. As fast as the pieces can be handled, they may be adjusted and secured by the most ignorant workman; the building cannot fail to be perpendicular and firm. And if, for some strange reason, a client was not satisfied, the cast-iron pile could always be carted away. "It follows that, a building once erected, it may be taken to pieces with the same facility and despatch."

There are hundreds of cast-iron office buildings still standing in Lower Manhattan. But even more significant is the record of the violent arguments over cast iron in the early meetings of the American Institute of Architects. The Institute, founded in 1857 by Upjohn, Walter, and the other leaders of the profession to take the place of the earlier American Institution of Architects, survived one of the angriest sessions in its history when young Henry Van Brunt delivered his paper on cast iron in December, 1858.

"This," Van Brunt told his colleagues, "is called an iron age—for no other material is so omnipresent in all the arts of utility. . . . But architecture, sitting haughtily on her acropolis, has indignantly refused to receive it, or receiving it, has done so stealthily and unworthily, enslaving it to basest uses, and denying honor and grace to its toil." Calling for an "architecture of strict mechanical obedience," he saw no reason why "that much reviled material," cast iron, might not be "ennobled." After all, the "purest eras" were "those in which building material had been used with the most honest regard for its nature, attributes, and capacities."

In another generation the age of steel would be upon us, and with the problem of the elevator already solved, architect William LeBaron Jenney planned what is commonly called the world's first skyscraper, the Home Insurance Building of 1883–85 in Chicago. In its odd way this was a *Gothic* building: the idea could have come from the *Discourses on Architecture* of the French Gothic revivalist Eugène-Emmanuel Viollet-le-Duc. In this book, put into English by Van Brunt in 1875, Americans were called upon to take another look at the cathedrals of the Middle Ages. Said Viollet of those cathedrals: "Walls disappeared and became only screens, not supports."

Van Brunt read his paper in the twilight of the romantic era. The spell was undone before the young men marched away in the spring of 1861, and when the survivors came straggling home in the summer of Appomattox, there were new problems, new answers.

Gone was the world in which Alexander Jackson Davis had been so startlingly successful. But this world could never be forgotten, no matter if very few of the new architects remembered Davis's name, and fewer still comprehended his longing for the fourth dimension. The Grecian villas, the Gothic cottages, and the Italian mansions were too numerous to leave no trace, even if many of the most beautiful examples were demolished before the century was over. Moreover, Hawthorne would always be read, and he understood, as did no one else, the mood of Davis and his followers. "No author, without a trial," said Hawthorne in the preface to *The Marble Faun*, "can conceive of the difficulty of writing a romance about a country where there is no shadow, no antiquity, no mystery, no picturesque and gloomy wrong, nor anything but a commonplace prosperity, in broad and simple daylight, as is happily the case with my dear native land."

We may not sigh in the twentieth century for a "picturesque and gloomy wrong," but we cannot hope to understand the architects of the romantic decades if we forget how anxious they were to create the setting that Hawthorne desired.

CHAPTER FIVE

The Age of Elegance, 1872–1913

THE LOST WORLD

Two fountains played, one of cologne and the other of champagne, at a ball given by a fashionable Manhattan broker, and Mrs. Ellet, the author of *The Queens of American Society,* a wiser and a sadder woman since Appomattox, admitted that "changes, and changes not for the better" were unsettling the social fabric. There had been those Brazilian guests at a *bal masqué* who donned headdresses of small gauze balls, each ball imprisoning a firefly; worse yet, there had been that American lady who made her entrance into a ballroom wearing on her forehead a lyre of tiny gas lights, the gas supplied from a reservoir concealed in her gown. "These leaders of gayety flutter in the admiring gaze of the stupid and ignorant masses, but they are not worthy to be named in the same category with those who can boast better claims to distinction than merely the possession of money."

All this may have been true, and indignation only too natural, but jeremiads, however justified, have seldom succeeded in altering the trend of the times. For better or for worse, the millionaire was the American hero in the decades between Lincoln's assassination and Wilson's inauguration. His pomp and circumstance were admired by millions who could never hope to dwell in a palace on Fifth Avenue. Commodore Vanderbilt might brag that "the law, as I see it, goes too slow for me when I have the remedy in my own hands"; but who could complain when he hitched his superb parlor car, *The Duchess,* in the rear of the *Flying Devil* and roared down the tracks with engineer Jim Wood at the throttle?

Since plutocrats no longer meet with the reverence which Commodore Vanderbilt demanded as his due, it is not exactly easy to sympathize with the Astor who is said to have remarked that "a man who has a million is almost as well off as if he were rich." And it is hard to explain the phenomenal influence of Andrew Carnegie's favorite philosopher, Herbert Spencer. "There is a notion," said Spencer, ". . . that all social suffering is removable, and that it is the duty of somebody or other to remove it. Both these beliefs are false." One of those who shared the philosopher's distrust of government intervention was the attorney Joseph H. Choate, who persuaded the Supreme Court in 1894 that any income tax was unconstitutional. "In striking," he declared, "at the corporations, in attempting to confiscate their property, you injure, not the wealthy—they can now stand it—but the widows and the orphans."

The tentative income taxes imposed by the Civil War were repealed as early as 1872, and it was not until 1913 that the Sixteenth Amendment was ratified. In these taxless years—our age of elegance—a Henry Adams might murmur, and a Theodore Roosevelt might growl, but millionaires could not possibly imagine that the day would come when the electorate would approve of checks on private enterprise. Wilson's "New Freedom" and Roosevelt's "New Nationalism" were equally unthinkable.

In this taxless world our architects, like all architects in all times, were dreamers not of dreams but of realities, and the problem of designing magnificent mansions could not be long ignored. To point out that the problem might have been solved without soul-searching is to forget that it was not so much the North as New England which forged the moral convictions of the Civil War years. In the sermons, speeches, poems, essays, and novels of the New England intellectuals, you would come across a hundred passages stirring your conscience to one that told you that it was a fine thing to spend your income on the delights of this world. So it was that many an architect became self-conscious when he turned to the task before him.

While the New England influence on our civilization waned before the century ended, and even William Dean Howells, in many ways more of a Brahmin than the Brahmins, felt obliged to desert Boston for New York in 1891, the Boston-bred distrust of magnificence was evident in the work of as sophisticated a novelist as Henry James. He was dismayed by the spectacle of Newport in 1904 when he revisited his native land after over twenty years of exile. Depressed by "the distressful, inevitable waste" represented by what he was pleased to call "white elephants . . . all cry and no wool, all house and no garden," he vastly preferred the "high refinements" of Farmington, Connecticut, to all that was bold and new on Bellevue Avenue.

Had James been a less passionate pilgrim to the Old World, had he been aware of the struggles of the American architects who were his contemporaries, he might have pronounced a direct verdict on the Newport of the early twentieth century. Something, after all, had been achieved in the 1880's and '90's. The millionaire in search of a palace had been taught to trust the arbiters of taste, and the designers had learned something themselves about scale and proportion.

Back in the days of the Grant administration, no one could tell which way architecture was traveling, or why. There were those who suggested that the mansardic was the ideal style for the New America. Was it? It was true that the mansard roof, first introduced on a Fifth Avenue mansion in 1850, could be seen everywhere as more and more Americans were fascinated by the Paris of the Second Empire. There were also those who swore that John Ruskin's favorite Venetian Gothic would be our salvation. Would it? It was true that the great English critic had taught many an American architect to venerate the Grand Canal.

The United States Hotel at Saratoga, perhaps the supreme example of the mansardic style—it was certainly so considered in the 1870's, for its piazza was littered with the ashes of Commodore Vanderbilt's cigars—has been demolished, and so has its mansardic rival, the Grand Union, in whose pier glasses you could have caught the reflection of crinolines only slightly less extravagant.

Sad to say, the mansardic town house on Rush Street, Chicago, of Cyrus Hall McCormick, whose Lake Superior sandstone façade, was blackened and chipped by the smoke and cold of three-quarters of a century, has also recently been leveled. Yet this, the boldest and best of all the designs of architects Cudell and Blumenthal, was once the most sumptuous home in the Middle West, and here, in the spring of 1880, the biggest businessmen of the city gathered with their wives to salute the twenty-first birthday of McCormick's oldest son. On this occasion the gifted caterer Kinsley prepared three enormous floral ornaments, a horseshoe, a lyre, and a fountain, all three executed with exquisite care.

However, all mansardic fans may rejoice in the fact that the B. F. Allen mansion of 1865–69 in Des Moines, Iowa, has been saved. This banker's paradise was perhaps the grandest design of the Chicago hotel architect W. W. Boyington.

As far as we know, no floral tributes were paid the Venetian Gothic, perhaps because it was deemed more appropriate for public buildings than for private palaces. In New York City the finest of all Venetian designs was the now vanished National Academy of Design, completed in 1865 by Peter Bonnett Wight, one of Ruskin's most faithful disciples in the New World. However, it was in Philadelphia that the Venetian flowered with the happiest indifference to the American landscape; there the firm of Furness and Hewitt, who swore by both Ruskin and his fellow Goth in France, Viollet-le-Duc, declared their independence from

Residence of B. F. Allen, Des Moines, Ia., 1865-69 (W. W. Boyington)

Pennsylvania Academy of Fine Arts, Philadelphia, Pa., 1872-76 (Furness & Hewitt)

Residence of William Carson, Eureka, Calif., 1884 (S. & J.C. Newsom)

the Quaker tradition of decorum by conceiving the Pennsylvania Academy of Fine Arts in 1872, and the Provident Life and Trust Company in 1879. The very best work of Furness and Hewitt may be too petulant for the taste of the late twentieth century, but this may be a reflection on us; if we are unnerved by the impudence which marks so many of their creations, if we are particularly outraged by their parodies of Gothic construction, it may be because we have no other way of acknowledging the threat of their imagination.

Certainly no one could describe as imaginative the writings of Charles L. Eastlake, the Englishman who dictated in these years the fashions of American interiors. An uncompromising utilitarian with a strange predilection for encaustic tiles, he preached the homely doctrine that "to fulfil the first and most essential principle of good design, every article of furniture should, at the first glance, proclaim its real purpose." But sincere tables and chairs are likely to be as ill at ease as guests who have never learned to turn a compliment, and Eastlake's furniture has sadly dated. So, too, has the Victorian kitchenware of which he was an enthusiastic promoter. "There has been," he was willing to believe, "a great improvement of late years in the design of ordinary water jugs."

You may forgive a self-made man for failing to share Eastlake's passion for ordinary water jugs. You may also forgive the founders of our dynasties for thinking that neither the mansardic nor the Venetian Gothic style was the ideal solution to the problem of the palace. There were many millionaires who felt inclined to design their own homes, paying little or no attention to the architects they happened to hire. One of these ambitious capitalists was Potter Palmer, a Quaker from Albany County, New York, who made good in Chicago, amassing one of the handsome fortunes of the Middle West from merchandising, hotelkeeping, and speculating in real estate.

Though Palmer is known to have consulted an architect, the angry Gothic castle that stood until recently on Lake Shore Drive was a revelation in Wisconsin granite of his very own dreams. "The age of Pericles seems to be dawning," commented the Chicago *Inter-Ocean*. The French dandy, Boni de Castellane, was not quite so kind. Chilled by the gloom of the porte cochere, he decided that the castle was "sumptuous and abominable." Almost as brave as Palmer was the California lumberman William Carson, who in 1884 commissioned the brothers S. & J. C. Newsom to build him the belligerant frame castle still standing in Eureka.

Like Palmer and Carson, William Henry Vanderbilt was a millionaire with a mind of his own where architecture was concerned. Furthermore, he was entitled to respect. Though he inherited no more than $90,000,000 of the $105,000,000 which his father the Commodore accumulated, first in shipping and then in the New York Central and other railroads, the

Grand Union Hotel, Saratoga Springs, N.Y., 1872

Trinity Church, Boston, Mass., 1872-77 (H. H. Richardson)

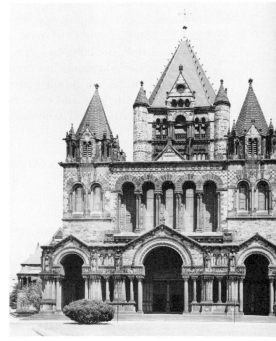

City Hall, Albany, N.Y., 1880-82 (H. H. Richardson)

younger Vanderbilt ran the family fortune up to $200,000,000 before he died in 1885, and this in only eight years. He was suspected of spending $3,000,000 on the block-long triple brownstone mansion stretching from Fifty-first to Fifty-second Street on the West side of Fifth Avenue which he began building in 1879 for himself, his wife, and two of his daughters and their husbands.

"The country, at this moment, is just beginning to be astonishing," declared the critic who signed the commentary which accompanied the glorious picture album of *Mr. Vanderbilt's House and Collection.* This private home "may stand as a representative of the new impulse now felt in American life. Like a more perfect Pompeii, the work will be the vision and image of a typical American residence, seized at the moment when the nation begins to have a taste of its own. . . ." Conceding that the "exterior can hardly be said to make any architectural pretension" and that "the style—for those who are particular about a style—may be called Italian Renaissance," the critic made the most of the interior, where "the garish light of noontide is tempered by massive embroideries and picture frames." Lingering in Mr. Vanderbilt's drawing room, he noted two statuettes of solid ivory. "Both are completely adapted for parlor meditation. They are completely elegant, refined, and artistic, without deep mythological meanings to disturb the equipose of the evening caller." But it was in Mrs. Vanderbilt's bedroom that he sensed "the culmination of everything elegant, delicate, and fresh. . . . The furniture is the most choice, the most elegant, that the mansion contains. . . . In this exquisite room, where silver toilet services, embroidered silks, and delicate hangings vie with masterly paintings to refresh the attention, it would seem that dreams must be propitious, and the waking pleasant. Among the fragile glitter of the upholsterer, where everything seems to start bright and crisp from the hands of the artificer, there is one worn-looking object, and only one: it is the little Bible."

THE RISE OF RICHARDSON

Though we have no way of knowing what Henry Hobson Richardson, the genius then working a revolution in American architecture, thought of the William H. Vanderbilt residence, it is hardly likely that he would have joined in the snickering to be heard in the parlors of our intellectuals. He was not one to scold a millionaire for bragging. If he had not rejoiced in the economic expansion of the United States, had not felt his heart beat faster at the thought of our railroads, our mills, and our mines, he could never have adapted himself so easily to American conditions. He was trained at the Ecole des Beaux-Arts, but the first building he planned on his return from Paris was scarcely Parisian. A house for himself on Staten Island, it was indistinguishable from the mansardic efforts of his ill-educated rivals in New York—proof that he did not choose to flaunt his superb education; proof, too, that he realized he could not hope to become one of the leaders of his profession if he did not first suffer the headaches of the average practitioner.

Since Richardson eventually dominated, as did no other designer, the trend of the 1880's, and since his success was based on the massive and dignified translations he rendered of the fierce ambitions of our millionaires, it may not be a mistake to point out that here was an architect with a dignity of his own. The great-grandson of Joseph Priestley, the discoverer of oxygen who fled to America when a British mob, outraged by his sympathy for the ideals of the French Revolution, fired his house and laboratory, Richardson may have inherited the coolness with which he stared at the financial worries that plagued the beginning of his career. He was for a time in real need, but no one who met him on Fifth Avenue could guess that he was distressed. "He wore his clothes," we are informed, "with an indescribable air of ease." And he was gay when he told his troubles to his landlady. "Look at me," he said. "I wear a suit made by Poole of London, which a nobleman might be pleased to wear, and—and—and I haven't a dollar to my name."

The architect's self-confidence could, of course, be traced to the calm of his childhood on the family plantation at Saint James Parish, Louisiana. Sent to Harvard when West Point ruled that a speech defect unfitted him for a military career, he was so urbane a representative of the planter aristocracy that he was inevitably elected to the Porcellian Club.

To glide over this Southerner's conquest of Cambridge would be foolish, for it was at Harvard that he formed the intimate relationships which drew him in later years to Boston, when he might have settled in New York. A year ahead of him was Henry Adams, for whom he was to design a house in Washington; in his own class of 1859 he met the brother of his future wife besides making a friend of James A. Rumrill, whose rise in the Boston and Albany was to spell a number of commissions for railway stations.

In the summer of his graduation Richardson traveled in England, Scotland, and Wales. Then, positive that engineering was not, as he had at first supposed, to be his chosen profession, he entered the atelier of Jules-Louis André at the Ecole des Beaux-Arts. For the next five years he was to force his romantic talents into an academic pattern.

Since certain dogmatic critics have shuddered at the influence of the Ecole, it is worth recalling that Richardson himself thoroughly approved of the formal education he received in Paris; he was bitterly disappointed when the Civil War, blocking remittances from Louisiana, forced him to leave off studying. "I have," he wrote his fiancée in New England, "taken a decided step. I have given up all hope of aid from home. I begin next week, or as soon as possible, to work for my living. . . . How I have suffered from it you will never know, for you know not how I love my art."

He earned his living in the office of Théodore Labrouste, the brother of the architect of the Bibliothèque Sainte-Geneviève, but after hours was so loyal to the Ecole that he joined his friends in the atelier even if he could no longer afford to enroll in their classes. Incidentally, he was never an unqualified admirer of Viollet-le-Duc; when the students rioted over the great medievalist's appointment to the staff of the Ecole, the American was so far from welcoming his emphasis on the functionalism of the Gothic cathedrals that he threw himself in the thick of the demonstration. For this he was jailed, though in a private cell, thanks to his almost perfect clothes from Poole's.

"I can't say how long I will remain in Europe," Richardson told his fiancée. "It depends on various things . . . and you would prefer to have me remain a few months longer in Europe than to return to America a second-rate architect. Our poor country is overrun with them just now. I will never practice till I feel I can at least do my art justice."

Back in the United States in the fall of 1865, the twenty-seven-year-old architect labored in near obscurity for seven years before winning the competition for Trinity Church, Boston. This design fixed not only his own reputation but the course of American architecture for nearly two decades. Others may have dreamed in odd moments of the drama inherent in boldly simplified masonry construction, but it was Richardson who showed that this was one way to bring order out of chaos.

In the architect's own words, Trinity was "a free rendering of the French Romanesque," in plan a Latin cross with a semicircular apse added to the western arm, but such terms convey no idea of the grandeur of the mass of Dedham and Westerly granite, trimmed with Longmeadow freestone, which dominated Copley Square; nor do they begin to suggest the richness of the interior lit by John La Farge's windows. Besides, the very word "Romanesque" is misleading, implying that Richardson was an archaeologist, borrowing a vocabulary for one of his own. In fact, in his frequent use of broad arches and other medieval accents to secure the dramatic emphasis on which he set his heart, he was less of a revivalist than a romantic.

In the meantime he got on splendidly with Robert Treat Paine, chairman of Trinity's building committee. Paine, who was one of the original stockholders in the Calumet and Hecla copper mines, called on Richardson in 1884–1886 to remodel the interior of his country house at Waltham. But no building loomed as large in Paine's life as the granite mass on Copley Square. An ex-Unitarian, he worshiped this monument to the Episcopal Church with the fervor of a true convert. "I wonder," Paine afterward wrote, "if any Building Committee ever took more pleasure in their task than did I. Five years: Brooks always on fire with

Ames Monument, Laramie, Wyo., 1879 (H. H. Richardson)

interest and delight in all the great questions; Richardson, a noble genius in architecture, with infinite patience in making plan after plan . . . declaring that art was infinite, and that he could go on improving time after time."

The "noble genius" could not be said to have labored in vain. Trinity was no sooner consecrated in the winter of 1877 than Richardson found he was swamped with commissions, even in this depression year. He was especially favored by the family of the late Oakes Ames of North Easton, Massachusetts. Though it was true that Congressman Ames was censured by the House of Representatives for offering Union Pacific stock to other members, the guilty man may have been less reprehensible than the standard account of the Crédit Mobilier scandal would suggest. The vigilant liberal Wendell Phillips believed that he was "one of the most honest, patriotic, devoted, and far-sighted men" that Massachusetts had sent to Washington.

Whether Phillips was biased or not, the bedeviled Congressman was an aggressive representative of an aggressive family. His father had been the first of the Ameses to rise high in the world, founding the shovel works which was the source of their wealth, and watching over the business so carefully that it was worth $200,000 by the time he surrendered control to Oakes and his brother Oliver, Jr. They in turn ran their inheritance up to $4,000,000 before the Civil War broke out, and this was only the beginning of their moneymaking, when their investment in Union Pacific was still in the future.

What Richardson thought of the career of the Ames brothers may never be known, but we may guess, from the monument he designed in their memory, erected near Laramie, Wyoming, in 1879, that he was one of their admirers. A pyramid of random ashlar (the technical term for stone blocks of random size), this was a blunt answer to the railroad promoters' critics. The only decorative relief was supplied by Augustus Saint-Gaudens, who sculpted the medallions of the brothers' heads.

However, it was in the little town of North Easton that Richardson paid his deepest reverence to the family. Here, within earshot of the shovel factory, he designed not only the railroad station (for the Old Colony, later the New Haven System), but a town hall in honor of Oliver Ames, Jr., a library in remembrance of his brother Oakes, and a gate lodge and gardener's cottage for the home of Oliver, Jr.'s son, Frederick Lothrop Ames. It was no accident that he did so much for a dynasty whose wealth was a reflection of the new industrial age.

"The things I want most to design," Richardson once exclaimed, "are a grain elevator and the interior of a great river steamboat." He was never asked to shape either of these phenomena of the nineteenth century, but his eagerness suggests how happy he must have been to reach an acceptable formula for our railroads. Though the North Easton sta-

Gate lodge, residence of F. L. Ames, North Easton, Mass., 1881 (H. H. Richardson)

Crane Memorial Library, Quincy, Mass., 1883 (H. H. Richardson)

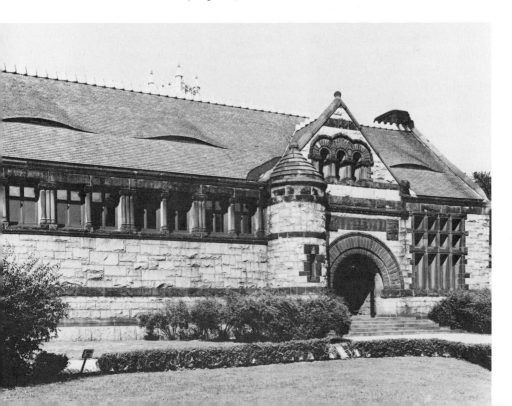

tion, completed in 1882, is not a masterpiece on the order of the Boston and Albany station at Chestnut Hill which he finished two years later, it is a challenging statement in granite, and its porte cochere, even if not so dramatic as that of Chestnut Hill, reveals his peculiar skill in simplifying. Chestnut Hill is gone.

There is no space to comment on all of Richardson's railroad stations; most of them served to mark the beginning of the business day for Boston's commuters on the Boston and Albany, and only one, that at New London, is located in what could be called a city. They tell, however, what might have happened everywhere if big business had been willing to hire great architects instead of timid draftsmen to carry out its building program.

Unfortunately, the wholesale store of Marshall Field and Company, Chicago, the greatest of all Richardson's designs for the business world, is no longer standing, having been wrecked in 1930, just forty-five years after the last block of granite was set in place. This gigantic seven-story business block was created for the coolest of Chicago businessmen, and a less imaginative architect would never have dared to sketch anything so imposing as the unrelieved arches of the fourth story. But Richardson, perhaps because he sensed that the merchant prince was about to create the greatest of Chicago fortunes—$120,000,000, no less—did not hesitate to dramatize his client's success.

Especially impressed was Louis Sullivan, the Chicago architect who was to come closer than anyone to finding the ideal solution for the setting of the businessman at work. Agreeing with everyone else that the structure was "massive, dignified, and simple," he likened it to an oasis. "Four-square and brown it stands," said Sullivan, "a monument to trade, to the organized commercial spirit, to the power and progress of the age, to the strength and resource of individuality of character; spiritually, it stands as the index of a mind, large enough, courageous enough, to cope with these things, master them, absorb them, and give them forth again, impressed with the stamp of a large and forceful personality."

But it is time to notice what Richardson did for Harvard in the era of President Charles Eliot. His Sever Hall of 1880 is easily *the* monument of Harvard Yard. Nearby the architect paid his respects in 1882 to the Law School that Eliot was reorganizing with Austin Hall.

Richardson's greatest civic achievements—the Albany City Hall of 1882 and the Pittsburgh Court House and prison which he did not live to see finished—were among the most unaffected compositions of the nineteenth century. Indeed the City Hall's tower is so unabashed an expression of the power of granite that the people of New York must forever regret that Richardson was not asked to plan the entire State Capitol across the park instead of confining himself to the Senate Chamber and various internal and external details. Even more dramatic—and equally

Chicago Architectural Photographing Company

Marshall Field Wholesale Store, Chicago, Ill., 1885-87 (H. H. Richardson)

Allegheny Co. Court House and Jail, Pittsburgh, Pa., 1884-87 (H. H. Richardson)

simple—is the conception of the Pittsburgh unit which he began in 1884. Thinking of this granite mass, he felt he was near fulfilling his mission. "If they honor me for the pigmy things I have already done, what will they say when they see Pittsburgh. . . ?"

Meantime Richardson had proved that a public library could be as monumental as a city hall, and once again he had set a high standard in his work for the Ameses of North Easton. Though the Oakes Ames Memorial Library completed in 1879 was not quite so successful an essay in simplification as the Quincy Library of 1883, the architect's command of granite was evident.

Richardson was equally important as a domestic architect. Rewarding his old patrons, he reached one of the threatening moments in his career the day in 1881 he sketched the gate lodge of the F. L. Ames estate at North Easton. Low-slung and boulder-faced, centered on an ominous arch, this was a building strangely prophetic of the earth-bound dwellings of Frank Lloyd Wright.

Richardson was not half so inspired in 1884, when he began planning the adjoining town houses in Washington of John Hay and Henry Adams—possibly because he was well aware that millionaires made much more sympathetic clients than ambitious intellectuals. "As for the house," Adams complained to a friend, "Richardson has turned down the worst carvings, and although I cannot pretend to think them all appropriate, I say as little as possible on the subject." Today a hotel occupies the site.

Richardson's greatest town house was conceived for a self-made millionaire, the Chicagoan John J. Glessner, whose farm machinery business (now merged with International Harvester) was then expanding at an alarming rate. This granite residence, completed in 1887, the year after the architect's death, may seem a somber design with too few windows, but only to those unfamiliar both with the site and plan. An unornamented façade was the ideal answer to the smoke and cinders of the location, on Prairie Avenue on the brink of the right-of-way of the Michigan Central Railroad. Moreover, the mansion was not so dark as you might think; inside, an ample courtyard, relatively safe from the grime of the steam locomotives, provided adequate lighting.

Meantime Richardson was experimenting—though without quite the high confidence of his disciples, McKim, Mead and White—with shingled cottages whose informality was perhaps better suited to modern times than to the age of elegance. One of these was the gardener's cottage on the Ames estate. This, like the shingled dwelling he finished in Cambridge in 1883 for Mrs. M. F. Stoughton, mother of the historian John Fiske, proved that he might have solved the architectural problems of the middle class as readily as those of the very rich. The example was not lost on the leaders of the younger generation of architects.

But it was at Newport, the summer capital of our millionaires, that

Boston & Albany R.R. Station, Chestnut Hill, Mass., 1881-84 (H. H. Richardson)

Residence of W. Watts Sherman, Newport, R.I., 1874-76 (H. H. Richardson)

Doorway, residence of John J. Glessner, Chicago, Ill., 1885-87 (H. H. Richardson)

Richardson conceived the greatest of all his domestic designs. This was the half-timbered mansion dating from 1874, of William Watts Sherman, a young man of immense means whose father had been a partner in the respectable New York banking house of Duncan, Sherman and Company. As for young Sherman himself, his first wife had been one of the Wetmores of Rhode Island, whose fortune had been amassed in the Far Eastern trade; his second was one of the Browns of Providence.

Scholars have pointed out that the Sherman villa owes much to the example set in England by Norman Shaw, who grew so indignant at the spectacle of Victorian confusion that he returned to the half-timbered tradition of Elizabethan times. This is not the same thing as saying that Shaw was a mere mimic—indeed he was a supremely inventive artist— nor may Richardson be accused of copying from English sources. If influence there was, it was recoined. The architect was never more sure of himself than the day he decided on pink stucco between the timbers, or puzzled out the meeting of the impressive brick chimney with the massive granite walls of the first story.

As we all know, the workers of miracles are seldom the most sensible of men, and Richardson was no exception. The victim of a disease which left him with the waistline of an elephant, he was so gallant that he wore bright yellow waistcoats. And he ate and drank with the bravery of a man who has read many times over his own death sentence.

"I have been told," wrote his good friend Augustus Saint-Gaudens,

> that although afflicted with a trouble for which he was absolutely prohibited stimulants, he once drank a quart of black coffee on his way to Pittsburgh, in order to be in good condition when he met the committee to arrange for the building of that masterpiece, the jail and courthouse.
>
> At any rate, whenever I visited [him] . . . he would say before dinner: "S-S-Saint-Gaudens, ordinarily I lead a life of abstinence, but tonight I am going to break my rule to celebrate your visit, you come so rarely." He would thereupon order a magnum of champagne which, as none of the family drank it, had to be finished by him and me. Unfortunately I am very moderate in such matters, and the result was the consumption of virtually the whole magnum by my good friend. This had to be accompanied by cheese, which was also proscribed by the doctor, and of this he ate enormous quantities. The proceeding doubtless occurred every night, as he always arranged to bring home a guest.

Another of Richardson's acquaintances, thinking of the zest he displayed when he raced through France, Italy, and Spain on a vacation trip with Phillips Brooks, and marveling at the schooners of iced beer he downed in Venice, declared that he would "never take the time to die." But the architect could not always be as gay as he appeared to Saint-

Gaudens. "There is a lot of work to do, isn't there?" he once asked. "And *such* work! And then to think that I may die here in this office at any moment." The moment came in the spring of 1886, when he was not yet forty-eight.

THE RICHARDSONIANS

There were architects in the coming generation who forgot that Richardson had brought order out of chaos, and preferred to believe that the designer of Trinity Church was the gloomy eulogist of a dusty decade. And there were critics who professed to admire Richardson while deploring his influence—as if any genius were responsible for the performance of those who parodied his gifts. The truth was that he had transformed American architecture.

Though Shepley, Rutan and Coolidge, who inherited his practice, could not always maintain his standards, they were so deeply moved by his example that they created one country house of which the master might have been proud. This was the tremendous, boulder-hewn residence at Dedham, Massachusetts, of the mill owner G. A. Nickerson. As for their contemporary, Bruce Price, as long as he was under Richardson's spell, he could design moving tributes to the Ames gate lodge like the entrance lodge to Tuxedo Park, New York.

Another of Richardson's disciples was William Appleton Potter, son of Bishop Alonzo Potter of the Episcopal Church, and brother of yet another bishop, Henry Codman Potter. Trained as a chemist in New York and Paris, young Potter did not dream of turning architect until the day he entered the office of his brother Edward Tuckerman Potter, a genuinely talented Gothic designer who had learned much from Richard Upjohn's son and gone on to plan Mark Twain's curiously Ruskinian residence at Hartford.

William Appleton Potter earned a certain reputation before falling under Richardson's influence, but did not begin to come into his own until 1885, the year before the master's death, when he sketched the amazingly free rendering of St. Mary's Church at Tuxedo Park, New York. This ingenuous chapel for the luxurious, yet wild setting of Pierre Lorillard's colony in the Ramapo Mountains, a fantastic blending of boulders and shingles, was perhaps his greatest achievement, but the granite masses of St. Agnes' Chapel, New York City, and of Princeton's Alexander Hall are not likely to be soon forgotten, no matter if the former was recently demolished.

There were other commanding talents who learned much from Richardson. One of these was Clarence Luce, whose shingled town house in Springfield, Massachusetts, for the rifle manufacturer W. H. Wesson might not have been so serene a composition without the precedent of the Watts Sherman villa. Another was the devoted Anglo-Catholic W. Halsey Wood, whose granite masterpiece, the Peddie Memorial Baptist Church of Newark, New Jersey, could scarcely have been conceived with any other model in view than Trinity. Then there were John Calvin Stevens and William R. Emerson, neither of whom might have come upon their solutions for suburban and summer homes if the older man had not dramatized the virtues of simplification.

THE EARLY WORK OF McKIM, MEAD AND WHITE

But of all the followers of Richardson the least imitative and by all means the most inspired were Charles Follen McKim, William Rutherford Mead, and Stanford White. No other architects in American history have been more deeply admired—or more often damned—than these three. No other architects have been more successful in baffling critics who insist that the only genuine artists are those who ignore the trend of their times.

The truth is, that McKim, Mead and White cannot be classified as easily as glib commentators would prefer. Ending their career as the champions of the formal tradition of the Renaissance, they began by designing an astonishing number of summer homes and casinos for summer resorts which belong, for want of a better word, to what is known as "modern" architecture. Usually of shingles, often left unstained, these have weathered out the decades so gracefully that it would be foolish to deny that their creators were as sensitive to the nature of materials as the most gifted architects of the West Coast in the twentieth century.

Henry James might have been thinking of one of these informal designs of McKim, Mead and White, so admirably suited to the needs of the prosperous middle class, when, in *An International Episode,* he spoke of the Newport villa visited by Percy Beaumont and Lord Lambeth. "The house," we are told, "had a veranda of extraordinary width all around it, and a great many doors and windows standing open to the veranda. These various apertures had, in common, such an accessible, hospitable air, such a breezy flutter within of light curtains, such expansive thresholds and reassuring interiors, that our friends hardly knew which was the regular entrance, and, after hesitating a moment, presented themselves at one of the windows."

The three young architects who were so successful in their beginnings were not only supremely perceptive but superbly trained. No doubt the best prepared of the three, and certainly the most purposeful, was McKim, who may have inherited his dogged streak from his father, an abolitionist notorious in his day for his skill in smuggling runaway slaves across state lines. No lackadaisical student either at Harvard or at the Ecole des Beaux-Arts, young McKim made up his mind on his return to talk H. H. Richardson into a job, and in this he had no particular trouble, for once his mind was made up, he was irresistible. The opportunity was priceless, for the older man at that very moment was completing the drawings of Trinity.

Stanford White, who also served as one of Richardson's draftsmen at the time of the building of Trinity Church, was as imaginative and enthusiastic as McKim was cautious and reflective. The son of Richard Grant White, a literary critic who teased the Tweed Ring, doted on the violin, and published what was once thought to be the definitive edition of Shakespeare's plays, young White was no less versatile than his father. On a minute's notice he could design a necklace sure to create a sensation in the most crowded ballroom, a picture frame fit for the portrait of an exquisite beauty, or a magazine cover for thousands to spot in the newsracks; he was responsible for the covers of *Scribner's, The Century,* and the old *Cosmopolitan.* He might have been a painter, and his eye was quick to detect the picturesque accents in almost any landscape, whether in France, which he enjoyed visiting with his good friend Augustus Saint-Gaudens, or on the New England seacoast, which he and McKim and Mead explored in 1877, sketching on their way the then utterly neglected remains of our colonial architecture.

One of White's assets as an architect was his uncanny talent for attracting attention. He had, as his good friend the critic John Jay Chapman observed, "the same divine frenzy for making himself known that great politicians are born with. Disraeli, for instance, had this instinct. . . . Popularity is a gift; but it is also a profession and has a technique of its own. Stanford White," thought Chapman, "was one of these dynamic trumpeters. He was pervasive. Not a day passed without one's hearing something new about him. His flaming red head could be seen a mile; and every night at the Opera he would come in late, and sit for an hour in the center of the house, not purposely advertising himself, but intuitively knowing that every millionaire in town would see him, and that the galleries would whisper, and the very supers on the stage would mutter, 'There's Stanford White.' "

Thinking of White and his clients, Chapman decided that "his relation to the merchant class and to the swell mob was of a personal, galvanic kind. He excited them, he buffaloed them, he met them on all sides at once, in sport, pleasure, antiquities, furniture, decoration, bibelots, office buildings, country houses, and exhibitions."

William Rutherford Mead, who lived on until 1928, nineteen years after McKim's death and twenty-two years after White's, was another sort of person altogether. He once said that it took all his time to keep his partners from "making damn fools of themselves," and it was true that he was the level-headed member of the firm, the man who could argue McKim out of an obstinate mood, or pop up with a sensible suggestion when White was overly optimistic. The brother of the sculptor Larkin Goldsmith Mead and the brother-in law of William Dean Howells, he earned his own reputation for what White's son has called "that instinctive sense of scale and proportion which makes the development of the elevations follow naturally and logically from the plan."

Long before the firm was founded, Mead traveled to Italy to see for himself the monuments of the Renaissance, having decided, shortly after he was graduated from Amherst, that it would be wise to spend a year and a half with his brother in Florence. No doubt Russell Sturgis, the architect in whose office he was then a draftsman, shook his head over the young man's decision. Sturgis, who eventually abandoned the practice of architecture for the pleasure of writing architectural history, was so extravagant in his admiration of the Gothic tradition of structural integrity that he never could conceal his contempt for what he believed to be the false gods of Florence, Rome, and Venice. Nor could he, in later years, keep from cursing McKim, Mead and White for spreading the Italian gospel.

In 1879, when McKim, then thirty-two, Mead, thirty-three, and White, twenty-six, set up their office, New York was urban but not urbane. There were New Yorkers who felt that their city, despite the labors of Upjohn, Davis, and their peers, was not the metropolis it might have been. One of these dissatisfied natives was Edith Wharton. Recalling the Manhattan of the 1870's in her autobiography, she confessed she despaired of that "cramped horizontal gridiron of a town without towers, porticoes, fountains or perspectives, hidebound in its deadly uniformity of mean ugliness." She added: "How could I understand that people who had seen Rome and Seville, Paris and London, could come back to live contentedly between Washington Square and the Central Park?"

Come back of course they did, and McKim, Mead and White eventually met the challenge presented by the most fastidious of New Yorkers in search of town houses. But the very earliest work of the firm was mostly created for the countryside—the countryside at that strange and wonderful moment when, as James has reminded us, an English nobleman might set foot on a Newport veranda without being instantly confronted by a butler.

Perhaps because the founders of the dynasties did not fully realize what they had accomplished, perhaps because too many Americans were unwilling to acknowledge the gulf which threatened to separate rich and poor, the very wealthiest of the clients of McKim, Mead and White built houses which were big, if you will, but informal in character. This unexpected informality has charmed the most solemn critics in the twentieth century.

Even in the grandest of their early designs, the vast residence at Mamaroneck, New York, which the partners completed in 1885 for Charles J. Osborn, the confidential broker of Jay Gould, they were so willing to relieve the tedium of housekeeping that they provided a plan whereby one wing might be used in winter, the other in summer. Not that they ever fell under the delusion that labor-saving devices were the end-all of architecture. They were artists first and engineers afterward; proof of this was the enchantingly romantic composition of the Osborn estate. Set on the edge of Long Island Sound, its evocative towers and beckoning archway might have pleased Alexander Jackson Davis himself, while the blending of stone and shingles showed that they had learned all that Richardson had to teach. All this, it should be said, was largely the work of White; he left his signature on the waterfront façade—a mosaic of stone set in stucco which told that the decorative genius of the firm had watched over the scheme from beginning to end.

Also attributed to White is the shingled villa at Cornwall, Pennsylvania, which was completed in 1881 for Robert Percy Alden, a young gentleman with a delightful income springing from his family's interest in the local iron mines, and from his wife's descent from the Warrens of Troy, New York. The Warrens were not unfamiliar with the best in architecture. Long ago they asked A. J. Davis to design them a Gothic castle atop Troy's Mount Ida. White may or may not have been warmed by this recollection, but he made one of his most daring advances toward the twentieth century when the time came to ponder the fenestration of the Alden house in Cornwall. The east end of the living room he turned into a glass wall; at least that is the best description of the glass area, broken, it is true, into a pattern of myriad panes.

But if you are to be absolutely certain of White's handiwork in these early days, you must look for the mosaics he introduced in so many of his designs. One of the best of these decorative highlights, a fantasy of bits of broken glass set in stucco, was created for the stables of the summer home of Cyrus Hall McCormick, the inventor of the reaper, at Richfield Springs, New York. Dating from 1882, the McCormick mansion was one of the happier achievements of the firm in the shingled style, and it is an alarming reflection on the taste of the reaper king's descendants that they have allowed both house and stables to disintegrate until the former, when last seen by the author, was no more than a somber ruin.

Two other shingled houses bearing White's telltale mosaics have been treated with genuine reverence. One huge, the other modest, these were planned in 1883 for Newport, a community which was always aware of the reaches of the partners' talents. It is hard to say which is the more brilliant solution, the mansion of Robert Goelet, nephew of the Peter Goelet who collected stocks, pheasants, peacocks, and Manhattan real estate with apparent indifference, or the cottage of Samuel Colman, a gentle painter famous in his day for rendering the Hudson River's beauties at dusk.

The most ambitious of White's Newport commissions in these years, however, was the casino that he completed in 1881. This vast shingled clubhouse fronting Bellevue Avenue, whose lawn was until recently the scene of the national tennis tournaments, and in whose theater so many stars faced the most polite audience of their careers, might never have become a reality if James Gordon Bennett, Jr., the irreverent publisher of the New York *Herald,* had not been having a row with the board of governors of the Newport Reading Room. One of Bennett's friends, a British army officer who had been dared to ride a polo pony into the Reading Room's front hall, won the bet but found the next morning that his guest card was no longer valid. Brooding over this affront, the publisher decided there was but one way to avenge his honor, and that was to ask White to design a glorious casino.

No architect could have refused this invitation; no architect could have given a gayer answer than White. Though the Bellevue Avenue façade was unprovocative, there was nothing sedate about the enormous archway which led into the courtyard, and there was something slightly flippant about the wicker-like wooden screens framing the generous piazzas that encircled this open space. As for the tower to the south of the entrance, its charm was nothing less than humiliating if you happened still to belong to the Reading Room.

Bennett gazed on all this and was pleased, so pleased that he called on the firm to plan the interiors of his new steam yacht, the 226-foot *Namouna.* And when his brother-in-law, the cotton broker Isaac Bell, Jr., built a house on Bellevue Avenue not far from the casino, White was the architect. Once again, he insisted on a shingled frame; this time there was a piazza upheld by incredibly delicate bamboo columns.

So far White's contribution to the firm has been emphasized, but it would be a mistake to suppose that McKim was his inferior, no matter if he was never quite so fanciful. Certainly no one was more anxious than McKim to simplify the designs of our houses. Over this challenge he worried for years, as may be seen by comparing an early sketch* for an unidentified country home (now in the McKim, Mead and White Collection of the New-York Historical Society) with his final achievement in the shingled style, the summer residence at Bristol, Rhode Island, of William Gilman Low.

Though no floor plan has survived for the drawing at the Historical Society, the capricious outline of the elevation, from wing to wing, and from story to story, proves that McKim at the outset of his career was already thinking in twentieth-century terms of the unconfined flow of

---

* This may be an elevation of the unexecuted Thomas Dunn house, 1877.

Casino, Newport, R.I., 1881 (McKim, Mead & White)

Residence of Isaac Bell, Jr., Newport, R.I., 1883 (McKim, Mead & White)

Interior, residence of Isaac Bell, Jr.

Courtesy of the New-York Historical Society

space. But this, he seemed to realize, was not enough. In the Low house
he daringly reduced the façade to a sheer triangle. Since this is the kind
of gambling that appeals to the best of our architects today on the West
Coast, it is hard to believe that the design dates from as long ago as 1887,
or that the owner was the nephew of a trader who sent clipper ships
from New York to Canton. It has been destroyed.

The Low house was apparently the last design of McKim, Mead and
White in the shingled style, and if the only excuse for studying the past
was to find the answers to the problems of the immediate present, the
later work of the firm might be dismissed as of no interest to anyone
except antiquarians. Such a decision would be a blunder. For the past
cannot be clipped as casually as you would a newspaper. Nor can the
present be captured by the fastest presses. Tomorrow is often upon us
before we expect it, and the architects of tomorrow may find much to
admire—for reasons we may not even imagine—in the later work of
McKim, Mead and White.

We can, however, try to understand why the firm altered its approach.
The partners knew what they were doing.

THE IMPORTANCE OF RICHARD MORRIS HUNT

While McKim, Mead and White were building their informal houses
in the countryside, our millionaires—and their wives—were coming to
appreciate that something could be said for formal manners. Ward
McAllister said it in Newport, and said it with authority. When he gave
picnics on his farm, he was as careful of the champagne he chose, and of
the *filet de boeuf piqué,* as if he were on Fifth Avenue. He was not to be
trifled with, this great and good friend of Mrs. Astor. He has told us that
"a dinner obligation once accepted, is a sacred obligation. If you die before the dinner takes place, your executors must attend the dinner."

McAllister may be amazing, but he is accurate when he recalls in his
autobiography the little world that he knew so well in the late nineteenth
century. "Up to this time," he said,

> for one to be worth a million of dollars was to be rated as a man of
> fortune, but now, bygones must be bygones. New York's ideas as to values,
> when fortune was concerned, leaped boldly up to ten millions, fifty mil-
> lions, one hundred millions, and the necessities and luxuries followed
> suit. One was no longer content with a dinner of a dozen or more, to be
> served by a couple of servants. Fashion demanded that you be received
> in the hall of the home in which you were to dine, by from five to six
> servants, who, with the butler, were to serve the repast. . . . Soft strains
> of music were introduced between the courses, and in some houses gold

Courtesy of the New-York Historical Society

Unidentified sketch by Charles Follen McKim, undated

Residence of W. G. Low, Bristol, R.I., 1887 (McKim, Mead & White)

Residence of C. J. Osborn, Mamaroneck, N.Y., 1885 (McKim, Mead & White)

replaced silver in the way of plate, and everything that skill and art could suggest was added to make the dinners not a vulgar display, but a great gastronomic effort, evidencing the possession by the host of both money and taste. . . . Orchids, being the most costly of all flowers, were introduced in profusion.

Perhaps the most typical, and certainly the most splendid family in McAllister's ken was that of William Kissam Vanderbilt, grandson of the Commodore. His wife, the former Alva Smith of Mobile, Alabama, nursed an ambition the like of which can scarcely be imagined in the twentieth century. Though she could not pretend to be disappointed in her husband's dividends from the New York Central System, she was grieved as a bride to discover that Mrs. William Astor, then the un-crowned queen of American society, had no intention of including the Vanderbilts in her set. There was a remedy to this, Mrs. Vanderbilt decided. She made up her mind to humble the House of Astor by staging the most brilliant ball in the annals of Manhattan.

As the appointed evening—the twenty-sixth of March, 1883—drew near, Mrs. Astor's daughter Carrie was so innocent as to join a few of her friends in practicing the steps of the Star Quadrille. Daily the girls rehearsed, and with each day, the anticipation grew keener. There were to be four sets of twin stars, in yellow, blue, mauve, and white; on their foreheads electric stars would twinkle; down their backs their hair would stream, glowing elfinlike. Not until the partners in the quadrille had drilled themselves to perfection did Mrs. Vanderbilt let it be known that inasmuch as Mrs. Astor's calling card had never been deposited in her salver, she could not properly invite either Miss Carrie or her mother to the *affaire de luxe*. Faced with this ultimatum, Mrs. Astor thought not of the loftiness of her name, but only of the happiness of her daughter. A footman in the blue livery of the House of Astor delivered a visiting card to a butler in the maroon livery of the House of Vanderbilt. Now no one could ignore the Commodore's descendants.

As for the ball itself, the broker Henry Clews conceded that "it may not have been quite so expensive as the feast of Alexander the Great at Babylon, some of the entertainments of Cleopatra to Augustus and Mark Antony, or a few of the magnificent banquets of Louis XIV, but when viewed from every essential standpoint, and taking into account our advanced civilization, I have no hesitation in saying that the Vanderbilt Ball was superior to any of those grand historic displays of festivity and amusement."

Revolutionary may be the best adjective to describe the house in which the ball was held. Here, on the northwest corner of Fifth Avenue and Fifty-second Street, stood an exception to the brownstone fronts in which our millionaires were accustomed to conceal their rise in the world—a glistening château of Caen stone which satisfied so superbly the needs of a railway king of the age of elegance that neither Fifth Avenue nor American architecture could ever be quite the same again.

Earnest critics have scoffed at the Vanderbilt château, have reminded us that Mrs. Vanderbilt's architect, Richard Morris Hunt, was inspired by the monuments of the early Renaissance in France, and have even pointed out that here and there the design was reminiscent of the Château de Blois and of the town house at Bourges of the fifteenth century capitalist Jacques Coeur. They have said all this and more, these serious-minded students, but they have not succeeded in proving that the Vanderbilt château was a replica. A replica it decidedly was not. While it was true that the architect had returned to the past for guidance, what he had accomplished in this, the first "eclectic" design in American architecture, was to plan a house in the manner of sixteenth-century France to suit the wants of a nineteenth-century millionaire.

Charles Follen McKim, who was not the least intelligent of the partners of McKim, Mead and White, did not need to be told that Hunt had found the answer which architects had been seeking ever since Appomattox. McKim made a habit of strolling up Fifth Avenue late at night to gaze again and again at the Vanderbilt château. He said he always slept better for the sight of it; having taken a look at it, he was ready to return home for another cigar before going to bed.

It would be pleasant to imagine that the architect whom McKim so deeply admired lived a life free from cares, but this would not be the truth. Even though Hunt was spared the usual financial worries of a rising practitioner—his wife was one of the Howlands of the New York shipping firm of Howland and Aspinwall—and even though he died of nothing less elegant than the gout, aggravated by a cold he caught while attending one of the Vanderbilt weddings, he was too conscientious a designer not to worry over the standards of his office. "You have not got long to live, you won't live half long enough to be a really accomplished architect," he warned his pupil George Browne Post. "You have got to work at day, and you have got to work at night. When you wake up at night you have got to think about it." When he spotted Post on the dance floor of an evening, he was more than indignant. "What are you doing here?" he asked. "You ought to be at home sketching."

There were bitter moments, too, when Hunt calculated the depth of the eternal chasm between architect and client. "The first thing you've got to remember," he admitted, "is that it's your clients' money you're spending. Your business is to get the best result you can, following their wishes. If they want you to build a house upside down, standing on its chimney, it's up to you to do it and still get the best possible result."

Perhaps it was just as well that his childhood was serene. The son of a congressman from Vermont who moved in the very best Washington society, mixing with Webster and Bancroft, the architect spent his earliest schooldays in the comfortable worlds of New Haven and Boston. Those were the days when he and his brother William Morris Hunt—later to turn painter and to despair of the prospect for painting in the United States—chose for one of their playmates the future novelist Theodore Winthrop, and for another, the future attorney Joseph Hodges Choate. In the meantime, Congressman Hunt had died and William had come down with a troublesome cough; vexed by this illness, and reassured by the return on the family investments in Middle Western real estate, Mrs. Hunt thought it might be the wisest thing to take the family to Europe. She did. Settling in Geneva in the fall of 1843, when Richard had just turned fifteen, the Hunts moved to Paris three years later when the architect began studying, in the office of Hector-Martin Lefuel, for the entrance examination of the Ecole des Beaux-Arts.

Like Richardson, Hunt could never complain that the Ecole was a narrowing influence; while in Paris he learned something about painting in Couture's studio and something about sculpture in Barye's, and when he went traveling, whether in Egypt, in Palestine, in Turkey, or down the valley of the Loire with Lefuel's notes in hand, he learned more. Finally, at twenty-six, he went to work as a government inspector of architecture with Lefuel's blessing, his old master having been appointed imperial architect. He even had the honor of helping him design the new Pavillon de la Bibliothèque at the Louvre.

Like Richardson, Hunt might have enjoyed the happiest of careers in France if he had not been attracted by the challenge of the United States. "It has been represented to me," he wrote his mother while correcting the drawings for the Pavillon,

> that America was not ready for the fine arts, but I think they are mistaken. There is no place in the world where they are more needed, or where they should be more encouraged. Why, there are more luxurious houses put up in New York than in Paris! At any rate the desire is evinced and the money spent and if the object is not attained it is the fault of the architects. Why should not our public hotels, I should like to know, rival or even surpass the palaces of Europe? It is the same in painting or any branch of the arts, merit must eventually command its position with us. There are no greater fools in America than in any other part of the world: the only thing is that the professional man with us has got to make his own standing.

So it was not in the least extraordinary that Hunt joined the newly formed American Institute of Architects shortly after his return to America in 1856, nor was it surprising that when one of his first clients, the dentist Eleazar Parmly, balked at paying a 5 per cent commission, he went to court to demand what he considered the proper compensation. He lost the case, for the jury rendered a verdict of $2\frac{1}{2}$ per cent, but he made it plain that an architect could stand up for his rights. He was always a man with a manner, and cautious patrons now and then wondered if he were "safe."

Perhaps this was the reason that his progress was far from meteoric. Or perhaps the reason was that, after his many years in France, he found himself baffled by the American environment. For over three decades he offered one solution, and then another to the problems of our society, rejecting them one by one as he discovered they failed to suit the requirements of his clients. One of his very first designs was the now vanished little Studio Building at 51 West Tenth Street, but this retreat for artists in the French vernacular set no style in Manhattan, and neither for that matter did the now missing Stuyvesant Apartment House of 1869 on Eighteenth Street, even though this last (which owed much to the example of Viollet-le-Duc in France) is said to have been the very first French flat building in New York. Nor was Hunt any happier when he came to plan private houses. As early as 1861 he was experimenting with clapboarding as in the Newport home of John Noble Alsop Griswold— now the Newport Art Association—but he could not be playful if he tried, and this no more represents the true Hunt than does the half-timbered house he conceived in 1872 for another Newporter, the railway financier and art collector Henry G. Marquand.

It was only in 1879, in his fifty-first year, that he came to imagine what would please Mrs. Vanderbilt. His career, for our purposes, may be said to begin on the day in 1881 when the Vanderbilts moved the last of their belongings into their new and noble château at 660 Fifth Avenue. "She's a wonder," Hunt remarked of his great and good friend Alva. "It is as much as one man's brain can do to keep up with the Vanderbilt work."

He was summoned shortly after this by Alva's father-in-law, William Henry Vanderbilt, and for the first, and luckily, the last time, made a mistake in dealing with America's most magnificent family. Hearing that a mausoleum was needed for the remains of the Commodore and his descendants, he drew the plans for a funeral chapel so extravagant that Alva herself would have been charmed. William Henry Vanderbilt was horrified. "You entirely misunderstood me, Mr. Hunt," he said. "This will not answer at all. We are plain, quiet, unostentatious people, and we don't want to be buried in anything as showy as that would be. The cost of it is a secondary matter, and does not concern me. I want it roomy and solid and rich. I don't object to appropriate carvings, or even statuary, but it mustn't have any unnecessary fancy work in it."

No objections were raised to the second set of plans. This was fortunate, for thanks to Hunt, no American family has ever been buried with quite the pomp of the House of Vanderbilt. Even if the mausoleum was not quite so showy as the architect intended, it was unmistakably splendid, a stone chapel "roomy and solid and rich" in the manner of St. Gilles at Arles. Set down on top of one of the highest hills of Staten Island, above the old Moravian cemetery at New Dorp—the very village from which the Commodore had sprung—it enjoyed a surprising view of New York Harbor. What was more, the site was picturesque. Olmsted himself planted the firs along the drive leading to the summit.

No one who had heard of the Vanderbilt Mausoleum, no one who had passed by the Vanderbilt château on Fifth Avenue, could imagine that Hunt would be long unemployed. He was invited to Newport in 1888, two years after the mausoleum was completed, to create the first palace the resort had seen. This was "Ochre Court," the glorious early Renaissance château of Ogden Goelet, brother of the Robert Goelet for whom McKim, Mead and White planned the shingled "Southside," Confined to a small but choice lot on the cliffs, "Ochre Court" was an admirable advertisement in limestone of the Goelets' investments in New York City real estate. As for the great iron gates, they suggested that the curtain had just risen—so contagious was the designer's enthusiasm for this stage set.

There were those who murmured that a country house as luxurious as this would insult the dearest traditions of New England, but Paul Bourget, the French novelist who visited Newport shortly after the Goelets began entertaining at "Ochre Court," was enchanted by the sight of this and the other palaces by Hunt. "These," Bourget declared, "are not weak imitations, pretentious and futile attempts, such as in every country bring ridicule upon braggarts and upstarts. No. In detail and finish they reveal conscientious style, technical care. Evidently the best artist has been chosen, and he has had both freedom and money. Especially money!"

Bourget might have been thinking of "Ochre Court" as he wrote these lines. Or he might have been referring to "Belcourt," the great lodge, including the inevitable grand ballroom, which Hunt conceived in the style of Henri IV for Oliver Hazard Perry Belmont, son of the August Belmont who had long been the American representative of the Rothschilds. But there were other palaces by Hunt at Newport. In 1892, the year in which he planned "Belcourt," he was studying and restudying the drawings for two other monumental summer homes, "Marble House" for the W. K. Vanderbilts, and "The Breakers" for W. K.'s brother, Cornelius II. Perhaps because he felt that Cornelius was too dutiful a millionaire to approve of the highest flights of an architect's imagination, or perhaps because he resented the fact that the Cornelius Vanderbilts had chosen his pupil George B. Post to design their Henri IV château in Manhattan on the southwest corner of Fifth Avenue and Fifty-eight

Street, "The Breakers" was a gigantic but chilly palace in the manner of sixteenth-century Genoa. "Marble House," echoing the late eighteenth century in France, was really more imposing even if not half so vast. Behind its Corinthian colonnade Alva Vanderbilt plotted the marriage of her daughter Consuelo to the ninth Duke of Marlborough.

In the meantime Hunt had not been altogether forgotten on Fifth Avenue. In 1891 he was asked to design two more town houses. The southeast corner of Sixty-first Street was brightened by yet another château in the early Renaissance style of the valley of the Loire, this time in brick and limestone, for Elbridge T. Gerry, whose mother was a Goelet. The northeast corner of Sixty-fifth Street was dignified by a double house for Mrs. Astor and her son John Jacob Astor, and here again, as Hunt's biographer Alan Burnham has pointed out, the architect was recalling the Loire. Though the formality of the Fifth Avenue façade was vaguely reminiscent of the seventeenth-century Château de Maisons, more than one detail might have been inspired by Chambord or Blois.

Since Hunt was always at his best when he toyed with the early French Renaissance vocabulary—since his most sensational commission, the W. K. Vanderbilt town house, was in that style, as well as the most successful, "Ochre Court"—it was to be expected that the most stupendous of all his creations should be an American version of one of the châteaux of the Loire. This was "Biltmore," the castle near Asheville, North Carolina, of George Washington Vanderbilt, the younger brother of Cornelius and W. K.

There was nothing suburban about either "Biltmore" or its owner. You could find plenty of millionaires who were willing to spend most of their incomes on country homes, but this Vanderbilt sacrificed not only his income but his principal as well—something like $4,100,000 of it—on this 130,000-acre domain in the Great Smoky Range. Though he could not claim to be too familiar with the eleven million specimens in his arboretum, he grew valiant when he thought of what he might accomplish as the patron of scientific forestry and farming. He hired Gifford Pinchot to watch over his timberland, and when he remembered that his employees deserved a village of their own, he built one, with school buildings, a shopping center, and a hospital as well. "He employs more men than I have in my charge," admitted Benjamin Harrison's Secretary of Agriculture.

George Vanderbilt's brothers lived in large houses, but even they may have been amazed when they reached "Biltmore" for the housewarming on Christmas Eve, 1895—five years after the project was begun, five months after the architect had died—and discovered that the foundations of this vision in Indiana limestone covered five acres. It was indeed a tribute to Hunt and to Olmsted, who laid out the pleasure gardens, that the castle looked as though it had always belonged to the site. Henry James, who was often puzzled by the dreams of our moneyed men, confessed that this was "a thing of the high Rothschild manner."

THE LATER WORK OF McKIM, MEAD AND WHITE

As for McKim, Mead and White, they could not have been surprised by "Biltmore." They had long ago come to appreciate Hunt's contribution, and they had already made up their minds that their own approach to the problem of the palace would differ from his, no matter if they had learned from him that the past might be re-examined. Hunt owed his success, there could be no doubt of that, to his talent for imagining something approaching the ultimate in magnificence. But McKim, Mead and White reasoned that elegance was just as desirable, and as they watched him move from castle to castle, from Fifth Avenue to Newport and on to Asheville, they began to suspect that Alva's favorite seldom worried whether the interiors he created were livable. Where, for instance, in all "Biltmore" was there a comfortable, intimate room in which Vanderbilt could relax? Indeed, with the exception of "Ochre Court," Hunt's gorgeous settings could not be measured by a human scale.

Finally, McKim, Mead and White were none too certain that the *early* French Renaissance of which their rival was so fond offered the perfect inspiration. It was showy enough, but was it splendid? Edith Wharton expressed the firm's point of view when she argued in her very first book, a treatise on *The Decoration of Houses,* that architecture and decoration could be set right "only by a close study of the best models"— and these, she made plain, were "chiefly to be found in buildings erected in Italy after the beginning of the sixteenth century, and in other European countries after the full assimilation of the Italian influence." Of the firm's loyalty to the Renaissance there could be no question. Not that they were narrowly Italian in their preference; occasionally they turned for suggestions to the Renaissance forms of France, of England, or of the American colonies, reveling in the richness of this pageant.

One of the noblest creations of the firm in their new manner was their very first, the complex of five town houses (originally six) which they completed for the railroad promoter Henry Villard and four of his friends in 1885. However, these five houses on Madison Avenue between Fiftieth and Fifty-first Streets are slated to be dismembered, the firm of Emery Roth and Sons having decided that a new hotel on the site was essential. Public-spirited New Yorkers protested in vain that the group should be saved as a place to entertain distinguished foreign guests. The only concession made by Emery Roth and Sons was to promise that a

Residence of W. K. Vanderbilt, New York City, 1881 (R. M. Hunt)

Brown Brothers

Dining room, "The Breakers," Newport, R.I., 1892 (R. M. Hunt)

"Biltmore," Asheville, N.C., 1895 (R. M. Hunt)

few fragments might be kept from the wreckers and exhibited to the public on perhaps six days a year.

Legend has it that Joseph M. Wells was the draftsman in the office who advised this abrupt reorientation of the firm's approach, but too much must not be made of this, since White himself is credited with the final appearance of the Villard grouping. Moreover, it was White who invited Augustus Saint-Gaudens to sculpt the superb setting of the clock on the Villard stairs, and White who saw to it that Maitland Armstrong fashioned the mosaicwork in the ceiling of Villard's marble entrance hall. Wells, who was a direct descendant of Sam Adams, seems to have shared his Revolutionary ancestor's distrust of luxury. "The Renaissance ideal," he complained, "suggests a fine and cultivated society, with its crowds of gay ladies and gentlemen devoted to the pleasures and elegances of life— which excites my admiration, but not my sympathies." He had the chance to become a partner, but declined, respectfully but humorously, because, he said, he could not afford to "sign his name to so much damned bad work."

Wells, of course, would have been the first to blast the ridiculous assumption that the masterpieces of McKim, Mead and White and of their fellow eclectics were so many replicas, but as the taunt is still heard, the charge might as well be examined. It is even argued that the Villard complex is a duplicate of the Cancelleria palace in Rome, though how such a statement could be made by anyone who had compared the two buildings is difficult to imagine. To begin with, the plans of the two are totally unlike, the American building U-shaped, the courtyard opening on Madison Avenue, while the supposed archetype is a trapezoid enclosing a cortile. Perhaps the only real resemblance lies in the detailing about the windows. This leads to the only possible conclusion, that the firm was guilty of nothing more reprehensible than the desire of creating a palace in the manner of Bramante for the needs of an American railroad financier.

These needs were satisfied, even more fully than Henry Villard would have liked. Forced out of the management of Northern Pacific before his house was quite finished, he was embarrassed by the declining earnings of the railroad and exasperated by the threatening crowds that gathered outside the courtyard on Madison Avenue. The crowds never could understand that the man they suspected—wrongly—of abusing his stockholders occupied only the southernmost wing of the block-long brownstone edifice. Nor could they realize that he had moved into this palace, so his son Oswald Garrison Villard has told us, to save money on hotel bills.

Henry Villard may have been inconvenienced by the splendor of his town house, but McKim, Mead and White had every reason to be delighted in their creation. They had arrived; they knew it; enlightened New Yorkers knew it; in fact everyone knew it who was worth cultivating,

North end, Villard Group, New York City, 1885 (McKim, Mead & White)

Clock on stairs, residence of Henry Villard, New York City, 1885 (McKim, Mead & White)

and when the contract was let early in 1887 for the new Boston Public Library, they were inevitably awarded the prize.

This was McKim's opportunity, as the Villard group had been White's, and the austere but superb façade of the library on Copley Square—facing Richardson's Trinity Church on which both partners had collaborated in their youth—proved that it was next to impossible to decide which of the two was the greater architect. Though it was obvious that McKim had glanced at Henri Labrouste's Bibliothèque Sainte-Geneviève in Paris, the Boston Library bore only a superficial resemblance to the supposed "original"; like the Parisian example of forty-odd years before, this was a symmetrical composition based on Renaissance precedents, but here the fenestration was far more emphatic, thirteen great bays whose dignity could not be denied. What was most important of all, McKim understood that he could not begin to realize his highest hopes without the co-operation of his fellow artists, no matter how skillfully he himself dealt with the great granite block. So Saint-Gaudens was invited to sculpt the seals of the library, the city, and the commonwealth above the entrance, and Sargent, Abbey, and Puvis de Chavannes were persuaded to decorate the walls of the upper floor, the delivery room, and the main corridor.

This was a splendid commission, but it was only one of many. The time had come for McKim, Mead and White to work their will on Manhattan, and the city surrendered without a sigh, so perfect was the partners' understanding of the mood of the 1890's. Despite the depression of 1893, these were the years when more and more of our businessmen, marveling in spite of themselves at the money they had amassed, were willing to consider what luxury had to offer, and as they passed by Henry Villard's home on Madison Avenue, they could not help thinking that the firm could stage, as could no one else, the pageant which the city could at last afford.

Perhaps the most ruthless, and certainly the most intelligent of the new millionaires was William C. Whitney of the traction ring. As Henry Adams observed, he "had thrown away the usual objects of political ambition like the ashes of smoked cigarettes: had turned to other amusements, satiated every taste, gorged every appetite . . . until New York no longer knew what most to envy, his horses or his houses." New Yorkers had every reason to admire his town house on the northeast corner of Fifth Avenue and Sixty-ninth Street. Though a gloomy brownstone, it was gaily and sumptuously redecorated within by Stanford White.

Perhaps the most sensational newspaper publisher of Whitney's generation was James Gordon Bennett, Jr., of the New York *Herald,* and he too turned to Stanford White when the day came for the newspaper to move its offices uptown to Herald Square. The plans were not unworthy of the Newport Casino, and those who knew their way around

University Club, New York City, 1899 (McKim, Mead & White)

Boston Public Library, Boston, Mass., 1887 (McKim, Mead & White)

Verona could understand how much trouble White had taken to design something in the manner, but not imitative of the Palazzo del Consiglio.

Perhaps the most gifted caterer of the hour was Louis Sherry, and he too thought of McKim, Mead and White when he built a restaurant and hotel on the southwest corner of Fifth Avenue and Forty-fourth Street. In his dining room the ladies' jewels were bound to have come from Tiffany's, and Tiffany's as well had insisted on our architects' providing the setting for their merchandise. A palace from the hand of White which suggested the elegance of Venice, the Tiffany Building was even less like the Palazzo Cornaro than the Herald Building was like the Palazzo del Consiglio; both testified to the wealth of the tradition in which White was so adept.

It was a contagious thing, this craving for the riches of the Renaissance, and by the turn of the century you could scarcely venture down any of the principal streets of the city without noting that McKim, Mead and White had passed this way. There was the old Madison Square Garden and the Madison Square Presbyterian Church to tell of White's delight in ornament; there was that new town house by McKim, so rich, so scrupulous, for John Innes Kane, who was one of John Jacob Astor's descendants; last but not least, there were the clubs. It was White who planned the Century, through whose doorway passed nearly all the distinguished artists and writers of the day, and White again who conceived of the Metropolitan, said to have been founded by J. P. Morgan in a huff at the old Union, while it was McKim who fashioned the Harvard Club, a Georgian version this time of the Renaissance theme, and McKim who imagined the University Club. This, which will always be remembered as one of the truly magnificent buildings of New York, could never be mistaken for the Palazzo Strozzi in Florence, no matter if Da Majano and Cronaca would have been happy to sign so marvelous an evocation of the Florentine spirit. Here it was that J. P. Morgan decided at the end of a dinner for Charles M. Schwab that United States Steel must be launched, and of course McKim was asked to design Morgan's library—of which the banker complained more than once that the building was not his, but the architect's.

So it was no wonder that McKim was obliged to create the Pennsylvania Station and to lay out the new Columbia University on Morningside Heights, and not in the least puzzling that the firm came to enjoy the greatest prestige of any architects in our history. You may argue— and the partners would probably have agreed—that not every building for which the firm was responsible was a masterpiece, but you must remember that the standards of McKim, Mead and White were remarkably high considering the volume of work which passed through the office.

The critic John Jay Chapman could not forget this when he wrote of White's swimming "on a wave of prestige that lifted him into view like a

Triton that typified the epoch. If you were walking down Fifth Avenue and caught sight of a Turkey red curtain at the upper window of a new Renaissance apartment, you knew who it was who hung his flag there. If you went to a Charity Ball, and saw on the stage a set of gilt twisted wooden columns eighteen feet high and festooned with laurel, you looked about till you found Stanford on top of a ladder draping a tapestry."

You were sure, too, to come upon White in the cultivated countryside. He was the one who conceived of the charming casino at Rhinebeck in which John Jacob Astor IV played tennis and went swimming. The casino, like "Rosecliff," the gorgeous palace on the cliffs of Newport which White planned for Mrs. Herman Oelrichs, the daughter of James Graham Fair of the Comstock Lode, might have been suggested by the Grand Trianon at Versailles, but far too many freedoms were taken for either to be judged a facsimile. The latter has been presented to the New-port Preservation Society.

White was no more bound by precedent than an earthquake or a hurricane, and when, in 1906, he came to design a "colonial" home at Southampton for James L. Breese, a gentleman of leisure who had once, long ago, dallied with the idea of turning architect himself, he sketched a frame house of an easy elegance far beyond the imagination of the best of our craftsmen prior to the Revolution. The plan, as anyone can tell at a glance, is formal; indeed, nothing could be farther removed from the modern concept of flowing space than this setting aside of special rooms for special uses. However, it is wise to remember that nothing could be more convenient in an age in which servants were plentiful. Edith Wharton was well aware of this. "Privacy," she pointed out in *The Decoration of Houses,* "would seem to be one of the first requisites of civilized life, yet it is only necessary to observe the planning and arrange-ment of the average house to see how little this need is recognized. Each room in a house has its individual uses: some are made to sleep in, others are for dressing, eating, study, or conversation; but whatever the uses of a room, they are seriously interfered with if it be not preserved as a small world by itself."

The colonial revival, incidentally, may be said to have originated in the office of McKim, Mead and White. One of the partners' finest designs in this style was their very first, the Newport residence created in 1886 for Henry Augustus Coit Taylor, son of the omnipotent Moses Taylor of the City Bank of New York. But "colonial" is not the correct label. There were frame houses erected in the colonial period, and there were, occa-sionally, noble chimneys, but no one, before the days of our indepen-dence, had conceived of a frame house of this dignity. Perhaps the only specifically "colonial" attributes of the Taylor mansion were the entrance porch, which might have been suggested by a stroll in Portsmouth, New Hampshire, and the dainty, Adam-like festoons above the window

Courtesy of the New-York Historical Society

Salon, residence of Mrs. Herman Oelrichs, Newport, R.I., 1902 (Designer: McKim, Mead & White)

frames, which might have been called to mind by a visit to "Kenmore" at Fredericksburg, Virginia. This Newport monument has vanished.

More than likely, McKim was responsible for the Taylor residence; at least its restraint showed his influence. To McKim also may be attributed two of the greatest country houses in the firm's history. Dating from 1891, these were planned, both of them, for Edwin D. Morgan, grandson and namesake of the banker who served as New York's Republican governor in the Civil War. One was erected at Wheatley Hills, Long Island, the other at Newport.

Huge, rambling, U-shaped, the Morgan house at Wheatley Hills covered one of the gentle knolls in the neighborhood of Roslyn. You entered under an archway made doubly inviting by a graceful cupola, and found yourself in a secluded courtyard, with the family wing on your right and the servants' quarters on your left. You glanced at the window frames, you took in the stucco walls, and you sensed that the architect had learned to cherish the Georgian remains in the Philadelphia countryside.

Residence of James L. Breese, Southampton, L.I., 1906 (McKim, Mead & White)

Library of J. P. Morgan, New York City

Residence of E. D. Morgan, Newport, R.I., 1891 (McKim, Mead & White)

But you could not claim that he was in the least imitative. And if you recalled the early work of the firm, you could realize that he was tempted now and then by the informality of the shingled style.

The plan of the Morgan house at Newport was far more formal: two projecting wings joined by an Ionic colonnade met you as you came down the drive across the rustic stone bridge. But McKim's sympathy for a site was never more evident; you might have thought the villa had grown out of the cliff to which it clung, so perfectly did the rough stone columns surrounding the semicircular living room at the rear blend with the rocks below.

These were real achievements, the two Morgan houses, and if you had asked the partners, you might have learned that this sort of thing was far more satisfying than the praise which greeted each and every sketch on their drafting boards. You could hardly pick up a newspaper in those days without coming across a reference to McKim, Mead and White. When the White House was remodeled during Theodore Roosevelt's administration, they were in charge; when Jefferson's Rotunda at the University of Virginia was rebuilt after a fire, White supervised the restoration; when L'Enfant's plan for Washington was resurrected by Daniel H. Burnham of Chicago, McKim shared in the enterprise; and when, in 1893, Chicago opened its World's Fair, the firm did not need to remind anyone of its responsibility for the success of the exposition.

The partners might have imagined that the future of American architecture was fixed forever along Renaissance lines, had they not been well aware that the firm's reputation, high as it was, had to be defended by an unending struggle. J. P. Morgan was fortunately willing to underwrite McKim's dream of an American Academy in Rome, yet there were millionaires who thought twice before signing checks; worse than that, there were clients who liked to believe they knew exactly what they wanted.

When Mrs. Clarence Mackay, daughter-in-law of one of the principal shareholders in the Comstock Lode, begged White one morning to join her at luncheon in the sitting room of her suite in the Waldorf-Astoria, he may have been pleased to learn that the firm had been selected to design the Mackays' country house at Roslyn. Later, as the work progressed, and he dashed to and from Newport to consult on first one change and then another in the plans, he may have been delighted at the thought that this was to be a sizable château, with wine racks in the cellar for 21,900 bottles. Flattered, White ransacked Munich, Dresden, Berlin, and Vienna; Florence, Palermo, and Malta; Barcelona, Burgos, Seville, Cordova, and Madrid; Oporto and Lisbon; Brussels, Amsterdam, and London; Bordeaux, Marseilles, and Paris in the hope of finding the ideal chairs, the irreproachable tapestries for this $840,000 commission.

Mrs. Mackay made it more than plain that she had ideas of her own. "I do mean a very severe house," she instructed the architect. "The style of the full front view of Maisons-Lafitte comes nearest to what I mean."

He would do well, she added, to prepare two sets of drawings for the library, one in the Italian manner, the other Louis XV. As for Mr. Mackay, he was often frightened. "In regard to the remaining moose-heads which you strongly advise me to buy, and of which I understand you made a hurried inspection, you seem to forget the main point, viz: the price," he told White.

Finally the Mackays were reassured. "Although it may be a calamity to you," they were informed in 1900, two years before the house was finished, "you must acknowledge that, in the end, you will get a pretty fine château on the hill, and with the exception of Biltmore, I do not think there will be an estate equal to it in the country."

Not everyone could be convinced. Colonel Oliver H. Payne of Standard Oil was actually upset by the bill White submitted for decorating the Fifth Avenue mansion of young Payne Whitney, the Colonel's nephew. "I know," the architect apologized,

> that all kinds of small extras have crept in and that the changes I made in the treatment of the smaller rooms have added over a hundred thousand dollars to the price of the house, and I have dreaded to speak to you about it until the house was far enough finished for you to see the result, as although I feared that you would be angry at first, I thought if you saw the money had been wisely spent and that I had given Payne and Helen a house to live in which was really of the first water and could stand in beauty with any house in the world, that you would forgive me and I believed in my heart that you would in the end approve of what I had done, but your saying to me yesterday that you could not see where the money has gone has taken all the sand out of me and made me very unhappy, for I know from the character of the work and in comparison with other houses that it is not extravagant. However, I must not say more until you receive and go over the accounts tomorrow, but I am sure you will not find it as bad as you think.

Colonel Payne was furious, but not for long. How could he stay angry when the Payne Whitneys were pleased? "I am dreadfully sorry about the fits the Colonel gave you and can't quite see what it was all about," Helen Whitney wrote White. We may imagine her horror the morning after June 25, 1906, when she learned that White had been murdered by the Pittsburgh playboy Harry Thaw. White had invited his son to join him that evening atop the Madison Square Garden.

THE RIVALS OF McKIM, MEAD AND WHITE

Though there were few architects who dared, as White did, to challenge a client by running $100,000 over an estimate, there were even fewer who could hope to rival the partners in their inspired moments.

The art of architecture can never be reduced to a formula, and many of those who, following the precedent of McKim, Mead and White, rediscovered the Renaissance were either too prudent or too heedless to achieve anything resembling a masterpiece. Yet it would be stupid to neglect Ernest Flagg, who came back from the Beaux-Arts to plan the Singer Tower in New York, and other festive experiments with steel and glass. And it would be silly to ignore Horace Trumbauer, or his brilliant draftsman, the black Julien Abele, whose finest work, such as "Miramar," the Newport residence of Mrs. Alexander Hamilton Rice—an Elkins by birth, she was previously married to a Widener who went down with the *Titanic*—revealed that Abele had studied, carefully and profitably, the legacy of Gabriel and the other masters of the French eighteenth century. Finally, it would be absurd to pass over the accomplishments of Carrère and Hastings, Charles A. Platt, and Warren and Wetmore.

Trained at the Ecole des Beaux-Arts and in the drafting room of McKim, Mead and White, John Merven Carrère and Thomas Hastings had little enough in common as far as their inheritance was concerned. The former, whose father was a Baltimore coffee merchant of French descent, spent his childhood in Rio and his school days in Switzerland before coming across his future partner in Paris. The latter stemmed from a long line of New Englanders, earnest men all of them. His grandfather was a composer of sacred music, and since he wrote the tune for "Rock of Ages," his name may still be found in almost any hymnbook. His father was the pastor of the West Presbyterian Church in New York, the very church in which Henry M. Flagler of Standard Oil worshiped.

The firm might not have been founded as early as 1885, when Carrère was only twenty-seven, and Hastings twenty-five, if Flagler had not decided that his pastor's son was the only architect who could translate into laths and plaster something of his own passion for the future of Florida. The state was then undeveloped, a haven for difficult and distinguished men of means like the Evert Winthrop of Constance Woolson's *East Angels*. Flagler determined that the time had come to transform the peninsula from a retreat for the happy few into a tourist resort for the millions. Hotels would have to be erected, not only extravagant but glorious, to tempt the first travelers on the Flagler railroad.

The very first of the Flagler hotels, opened early in 1888, was the Ponce de León at Saint Augustine. This has usually been described as an example of the Spanish Renaissance, but the label is no more revealing than the sticker on a suitcase. Though two towers with belfries loomed above the courtyard, as towers should in a Spanish town, there was no precedent in any time or country for the gaiety with which Carrère and Hastings attacked this commission. Like the Spaniards who built the near-by fort of San Marcos, they were well aware of the advantages of coquina, the local shell rock, and with it they faced the hotel walls; but ly a Spaniard realizing for the first time in his life that he was Spanish could have struck the wild note of the decoration of the Ponce. In 1977 the hotel become Flagler College.

We now know, thanks to Jean Murray Bangs's research on Bernard Maybeck's work, that he was the draftsman in the office who conceived of all the incandescent ornament of the hotel, forcing Carrère and Hastings to take liberties over which they may have had more than one anxious moment. For the firm was never again to design anything as rash as this hotel; to be coolly competent, that was to be their highest aim, and if they did better than they intended, it was because they were artists in spite of themselves.

While McKim, Mead and White were drawn to one and then another aspect of the Renaissance, in Italy, France, Spain, England, and the British colonies, Carrère and Hastings usually, though not invariably, found their inspiration in the Renaissance as developed in France alone. It was the early seventeenth century they remembered in 1898 when they came to create "Blairsden," the villa at Peapack, New Jersey, of C. Ledyard Blair, one of the princes of the Lackawanna Railroad. This was a grandiose scheme which might have been grand if only the interiors had been elegant and the terraces of the gardens had been given greater architectural emphasis. It was the seventeenth century, especially Perrault's façade of the Louvre, that they recalled in 1897 when they won the competition for the New York Public Library. Later it was the eighteenth century that the firm evoked in 1914 when it designed the palace of the steel magnate Henry Clay Frick at Fifth Avenue at Seventieth Street. This, too, was an elegant advertisement for the city, though more prudent, less eloquent than the greater mansions of McKim, Mead and White.

Three years before the Frick commission came into the office, Carrère was struck down and killed by a taxicab, but Hastings lived on until 1929, meditating, often with surprising insight, on the role of the architect in America. "Copying," he observed, "destroys progress in art, and all spontaneity. The problem solved makes style." And he added that "our Renaissance must not be merely archaeological, the literal following of certain periods of the style. To build a French Louis XII or Francis I or Louis XIV house, or to make an Italian *cinquecento* design, is indisputably not modern architecture."

There may have been days when Hastings was worried by the challenge from Chicago, whose architects were coping, as had no New Yorker, with the problem of business buildings expressing in their structure the revolution wrought by the elevator and the steel frame. He was anxious for the Public Library to be as truthful as any Chicago skyscraper; he used no steel in the great marble edifice except where wood might have been inserted, and he was proud of the forthright rear elevation of the Library, with verticals boasting of the stacks behind.

There may even have been more than one moment when Hastings

doubted he had done right to swear allegiance to the Renaissance, for he defended his point of view so vigorously that you might have thought he knew he was in the wrong. "What an inspiration there is," he cried, "in working for and with one's own time! . . . Whoever demands of an architect a style not in keeping with the spirit of the time is responsible for retarding the normal progress of the art." The spirit of the twentieth century, he always pointed out, was forged by the Renaissance. "Whatever we now build, whether church or dwelling, the law of historic development requires that it be Renaissance. All branches of art have contributed to the embellishment of this style; no other is so expressive of the age in which we live."

If Charles Adams Platt were stricken with doubts such as those which tormented Hastings, he left no evidence of it in writing, and it is extremely unlikely that he was ever so distressed. He came from a more comfortable family than Flagler's protégé; his father was an affluent New York attorney; his mother was a Cheney, of the silk manufacturing dynasty at Manchester, Connecticut. Since there had been two notable engravers in the Cheney family, his parents could not very well complain when he began studying the art of etching in New York and Paris, and since there was no need for him to earn his own way, no one hurried him into a career. He was nearly thirty before he thought of turning toward architecture; overcome by the beauty of the gardens of Italy, he came home in 1893, when thirty-two, to write a book on the subject. That, marvelous as it may seem, was as close as he came to undergoing anything like formal training for the profession.

Idling away his afternoons by the fountains of the "Villa Lante" or on the stairs of the "Villa Farnese" at Caprarola, Platt learned far more of the art of architecture than if he had been slaving over a drafting board in the best of schools. His eyes were sharp; his taste was almost matchless; and when he returned to America, haunted by the spell of Vignola, he was too wise an artist to condescend to design a replica. Guided by his own irreproachable instinct for perfection of proportion, he succeeded quickly, and with apparent ease, in creating a number of noble country homes in the Italian manner.

To dare to simplify a façade in the hope of emphasizing the charm of an already symmetrical composition is to accept a dangerous invitation, but Platt in his superb moments was not an architect who hesitated. Neither, apparently, did his clients, who included many of our most fastidious men of means. In Cleveland in 1907 he was asked to design a mansion for William G. Mather of the steel dynasty; in Lake Forest in 1908 for Harold and Edith Rockefeller McCormick, whose income flowed from both International Harvester and Standard Oil; and in Grosse Pointe in 1910 for Russell A. Alger, Jr., son of the Michigan lumberman who headed the War Department in McKinley's cabinet. Fortunately

Hotel Ponce de León, St. Augustine, Fla., 1888 (Carrère & Hastings)

Residence of John Jay Chapman, Barrytown, N.Y., 1914 (Charles A. Platt)

situated on the shores of Lakes Erie, Michigan and Saint Clair, these were three of the truly magnificent houses of the age of elegance, and it would be a stale and stupid amusement to quarrel over their respective merits. Michelangelo, the author of the Palazzo dei Conservatori, might not have been too critical of the bold horizontal accent of the cornice over the entrance to the Mather residence, and certainly no American could find fault with the serene window frames of the Alger house. As for "Villa Turicum," the retreat of the McCormicks, house and gardens were in their way as remarkable an expression of a formal standard of living as the rejected plans of Frank Lloyd Wright of an informal existence. It is now no more.

"Sylvania," the estate at Barrytown-on-Hudson of the critic John Jay Chapman, was on a more modest scale than "Villa Turicum." Here there was no Palladian pavilion in the gardens, and no cascade, but the great portico facing the river was fine and emphatic, and the terrain sloped so beguilingly down to the Hudson that there could be no doubt that the architect was an accomplished landscapist. He meant what he said when he pointed out that "the essential truth in country house architecture is that house and garden together form a single design. They cannot be separated."

Platt's success, of course, was proof that McKim, Mead and White had been wise to teach America the lesson of the Renaissance. Possibly McKim was thinking of all that the firm stood for in the minds of younger men when he composed, one spring morning in 1909, a note of welcome to Lawrence Grant White, Stanford's son, who was then completing his studies at the Ecole des Beaux-Arts.

"Uncle Sam," McKim encouraged young White, "is now proud of what is being done, and is going to demand the very best that millions can purchase; and there is no fear of falling back into the degenerate order of things which has heretofore always existed. Mr. Hunt was the pioneer and ice-breaker who paved the way for recognition of the profession by the public; and now his successors are paving the way for 'vous autres,' who are to come home and design the *really great works*. . . .

"When you get through with your work on the other side and come home ready to build, you will find opportunities awaiting you that no other country has offered in modern times. The scale is Roman, and it will have to be sustained."

Perhaps it was fortunate that McKim died in the year in which this note was written, for he was spared the grief of witnessing the end of the age of elegance. You might say that the age came to an end in 1913 with the ratification of the Income Tax Amendment to the Constitution, but you should not make too much of this as an answer to the question. The first income tax under the Sixteenth Amendment, a timid thing compared with the legislation of our time, was only one of many signs that the rampant individualism responsible for big spending was threatened with extinction. In the business world itself, the titans were dying off, and the admittedly gifted men who took their places were no more than the efficient servants, with limited powers, of the great corporations. Perhaps because these new masters of industry would rather drive a shrewd bargain with their workers than alienate trained hands by swamping the market with cheap labor from abroad, Congress was not kept from passing the Immigration Acts of 1921 and 1924, which drastically reduced and then all but eliminated the quotas on which we had counted in the past. What this meant in terms of the supply of household help must be evident to all of us; what this meant in terms of architecture may be told by the number of families who have found it more convenient to live in apartments than in homes of their own, and in three or four rooms, instead of ten or twelve.

But the age of elegance was probably over by the beginning of the Big Change—to borrow Frederick Lewis Allen's phrase for the tack we have taken since the redistribution of incomes was foreshadowed by the Sixteenth Amendment. Very few palaces have been built since 1913; though the eclectic tradition lingered on, it was only the palest shadow of its former self, as anyone can tell by comparing the meek homes— French, English, or what you will—that cluster around our country clubs with the mansions of the 1890's.

What is sadder by far, you cannot possibly count all the extraordinary buildings planned for formal living which have been scrapped in our informal era. Of the survivors, many have been mauled by real estate speculators anxious to modernize a masterpiece; others, more fortunate, have been made over to suit the needs of every conceivable organization, from a labor union in search of a rest home for its members to a religious order in quest of another nunnery or monastery.

If Richardson were to come back to earth, he would find that the Watts Sherman villa was turned into an Old People's Home for Baptists, and the Glessner residence into a research center. As for Hunt, he would discover that the W. K. Vanderbilt château—like the residences of W. K. Vanderbilt, Jr., by Stanford White, of Cornelius Vanderbilt by George B. Post, the W. H. Vanderbilt block and his own designs for John Jacob Astor and Elbridge T. Gerry—had been pulled down to make way for changes along Fifth Avenue. At Asheville, Hunt would learn that "Biltmore" was now a museum to teach a younger generation what life was once like in the United States; at Newport he would hear that "Ochre Court" had been converted into a Roman Catholic college for girls, and "The Breakers," like "Marble House," was opened only to satisfy the curiosity of tourists who could dream of, but never experience a ball staged by, Ward McAllister.

Carrère and Hastings might not be surprised if you informed them that the Frick mansion was a museum, for such had been the intention of the millionaire in the first place, but they might be amazed if you told them that the Blair estate at Peapack was serving, like "Ochre Court," the educational program of the Roman Catholic Church.

The founders of the firm of McKim, Mead and White might be the most bewildered of all. How could they have told that the E. D. Morgan home at Wheatley Hills would one day be altered beyond recognition for householders of modest means? Or how could they have known that the Mackay estate would be leveled and the R. Percy Alden house at Cornwall would be saved from destruction only because it could be converted into a vacation retreat for members of the International Ladies Garment Workers Union? Or how could they have guessed that James L. Breese's residence at Southampton would be turned into an economics study center for Amherst students?

In Manhattan the partners of McKim, Mead and White would look in vain for Sherry's, the Herald Building, the Madison Square Presbyterian Church, old Madison Square Garden, and the Kane and William C. Whitney houses, all of which have been pulled down. And if they strolled on, they would come upon the remains of the Tiffany Building, its capitals shaved away to suit a collector of parcels of Manhattan real estate. Further north, if they knocked at the door of the Payne Whitney mansion, they would be reminded that it had been stripped of its furnishings before being turned over to the French Delegation to the United Nations. Their only consolation would have been the requiem for Pennsylvania Station, pulled down in 1963. On hand to protest the demolition were two champions of modern architecture, Philip Johnson and the widow of Eero Saarinen, who admitted that the later work of McKim, Mead and White was incomparable.

As for Warren and Wetmore, who spent ten years on the elegance of Grand Central Station, as lovingly detailed as their New York Yacht Club nearby, they would have felt they had labored in vain on this great contribution to the city planning of New York. For in 1963 Emery Roth and Sons, abetted by Walter Gropius and Pietro Belluschi, paid their homage to this Park Avenue landmark by erecting between it and the New York Central Building to the north the tactless tower of the Pan-Am Building.

From all that has been said, it is quite apparent that we have been exploring a civilization only casually resembling our own. We have been glancing at the very world in which Edith Wharton's Lily Bart suffered her degradation. Lily Bart, as you may remember if you have recently reread *The House of Mirth,* fell from grace the day she was seen leaving a gentleman's lodgings, to which she had gone on the innocent mission, safely performed, of taking a cup of tea. On the eve of this misstep, she

Grand Central Station, New York City, 1903-13 (Warren & Wetmore)

New York Public Library, New York City, 1902-1909 (Carrère & Hastings)

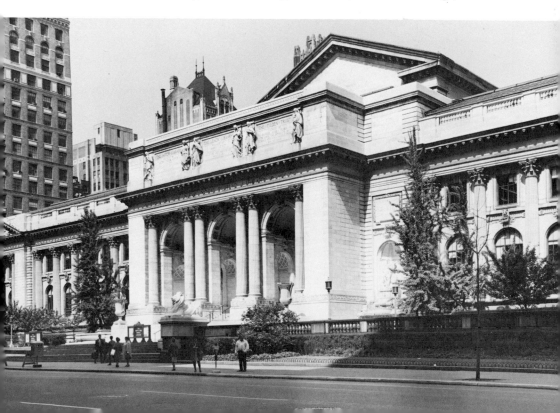

had sent on her personal maid from Tuxedo Park to the estate at Rhine-beck at which she was to be a guest.

No one today in Lily Bart's circumstances would think of traveling with a personal maid, and no one, to tell the truth, would care to build buildings on the grand scale of the age of elegance. But this does not mean that either architects or clients were foolish.

Perhaps we should stop scolding our grandfathers for spending money which after all was theirs to spend. Pageants have their place, and America without a palace would be as poor a thing as a parade without a banner.

Interior, Pennsylvania Station, New York City, 1906-10 (McKim, Mead & White)

CHAPTER SIX

The Chicago Story

1

THE CHICAGO SETTING

While McKim, Mead and White and their followers were enchanting the leisure class of the East with palace after palace, other architects were solving other problems in Chicago. Though the businessmen of Chicago played as important a part in our architecture as their Eastern competitors, their ideal of the good life was not so broad as to admit that luxury was desirable, and you might not be wrong in assuming that there was no leisure class in the Middle West in the Eastern sense of the term.

According to the Chicago novelist Henry B. Fuller, the typical successful businessman was an earnest figure. Take, for example, old Erastus Brainerd, the banker in Fuller's *Cliff-Dwellers* who "had never lived for anything but business. . . . He never dreamed of anything but business— he had never worn a dress coat in his life. He wrote about nothing but business—his nearest relative was never more than 'dear sir' and he himself was never more than 'yours truly'; and he wrote on business letterheads even to his own family."

Fuller might have patterned Erastus Brainerd after P. D. Armour, for that great meat packer admitted that he had no other interest in life but his business. "What other interest can you suggest to me?" he asked a reporter who wondered why, having got so rich, he did not retire. "I do not read. I do not take any part in politics. What can I do? Besides," he added, "I think it is well for me to remain in business in order to set an example to the younger men who are coming up around me." He liked to get down to work "before the boys with the polished nails show up," and he usually stuck to his desk from six in the morning until six at night.

Armour was a model Chicagoan, no doubt of that. "The bare figure of leisure, when exposed to the public gaze, was expected to be decorously draped in the garment of strenuous endeavor," Fuller complained of his native city. "People were required to appear busy even if they were not."

That there was room for improvement did not occur to P. D. Armour's great rival, Gustavus F. Swift. "Chicago," said Swift, "is the finest city in the world for the moderate, natural, average man of affairs. The New Yorker who says Chicago is a city of no luxuries is probably one of that constantly growing number who are insatiable in their greed for the softer things of life. To those men who have families and who find in their homes the greatest of their pleasures, Chicago offers all that New York offers, and in my opinion, more. A man can get wholesome food in Chicago more cheaply than he can in the East, and he can live as well on a smaller amount of money. I do not go in for luxuries myself," he made plain. "Chicago is good enough for me. I can spend my money fast enough here."

There were not many Chicagoans who shared Fuller's longing for broader horizons. "This town of ours," he sighed, "labors under one peculiar disadvantage: it is the only great city in the world to which all its citizens have come for the one common, avowed object of making money. There you have its genesis, its growth, its end and object; and there are very few of us who are not attending to that object very strictly. In this Garden City of ours every man cultivates his own little bed and his neighbor his; but who looks after the paths between?"

Chicago, then, is not the sort of city in which artists are encouraged. But artists who need to be encouraged are not those whose names are remembered in generations to come. And Chicago, it must never be forgotten, has made the greatest contribution of any city to the art of designing business buildings. Here the metal skeleton was developed on which all skyscrapers ever since have been based; here, as nowhere else, the metal skeleton proved a real incentive.

Perhaps the great Chicago millionaires should be forgiven for tending to nothing but their business. The very grimness of their devotion freed them from the restraint of tradition, and when the time came for them to invest their capital in improving real estate, they felt next to no reluctance in following where their daring architects chose to lead. They were fortunately willing to brag, these millionaires, even if they had misgivings about putting on Eastern airs.

TALLER AND TALLER

Ever since that day in 1857 when the first practical passenger elevator was installed in the cast-iron Haughwout Building in New York City, restless architects had been dreaming of tall buildings whose walls might be no more than curtains enveloping metal frames. Meantime more than one designer regretted the divorce of architecture from engineering on which the leaders of the age of elegance insisted. There was always the threat that the engineer and not the architect would shape the cities of tomorrow, and it was exasperating to think of what had been accomplished in London, where the Crystal Palace of the Exhibition of 1851 promised a new world of cages of glass and iron. In Paris, too, there had been gigantic halls of glass and iron for the world's fairs of the Second Empire and the Third Republic. At home, the opening of the all-steel Brooklyn Bridge in the spring of 1883 taught even the dullest draftsman that a revolution in building methods could not be long delayed. Steel, as the engineers were well aware, could carry loads far beyond the capacity of iron.

With out natural resources we could not long escape leading the world in steel production. Even though our mill owners were unaccountably reluctant to introduce the Bessemer or Kelly process, by 1900 our mills were producing as much steel as those of Germany and Great Britain combined. It was only meet and right that this new building material should be treated with simple respect in Chicago, a city dedicated as no other to business enterprise.

In New York, where the making of money was not so much an end in itself as the means toward an end, business buildings were likely to look like apologies for the industrial revolution rather than advertisements of our technological progress. The confusion of Richard Morris Hunt and of his pupil George Browne Post was typical. The nine-story Tribune Building designed by the former in 1873 was partly iron-framed behind its brick façade, but this was a secret from the public. The iron age was denied by this Old World town hall, stretched as in a nightmare beyond its intended dimensions. As for Post's St. Paul Building of 1899, then the highest in the city, it could be described as a curiously elongated classical column. Its architect was not an inventor, but the prisoner of proportions governing bases, shafts, and entablatures.

There were, of course, the business buildings of McKim, Mead and White. But these were tributes to the elegance made possible by American enterprise rather than to the enterprise itself. Aside from these, the only business block of extraordinary merit in late-nineteenth-century Manhattan was the De Vinne Press Building on Lafayette Street conceived by Babb, Cook and Willard in 1885. Since this was a brick structure of only six stories, it offered no challenge in the interpretation of height. Its grave simplicity could, however, have served as a model for the tallest of skyscrapers.

New York architects might pay little or no attention to the problem of expressing our business civilization *at work*. Not so, their colleagues in

Haughwout Building, New York City, 1857 (J. P. Gaynor)

Home Insurance Building, Chicago, Ill., 1885 (William Le Baron Jenney)

Monadnock Building, Chicago, Ill., 1891 (Burnham & Root)

Chicago. Out there, it was understood that a skyscraper was a commission worth battling for. Refinements might be eliminated on an instant's notice. An unidentified Chicago designer smiled when asked what would happen if an architect presumed to sacrifice one of the stories of a business building to "the exigencies of architecture." "Why," said the designer, "the word would be passed, and he would never get another to do. No, we never play these tricks on our businessmen. They are too wide-awake."

This might have been a bleak world, in which the architects were no better than the businessmen's flunkies, if for every client who played the part of a bully, there had not been a designer who stood up for his rights. One of these was William Le Baron Jenney, a native of Fairhaven, Massachusetts, who had been trained as an engineer in Paris and promoted to major on Grant's and Sherman's staffs. Moving to Chicago, he earned a reputation for eliminating dark rooms from the business blocks he erected, and—so one of his contemporaries thought—"disposed of matters easily in the manner of a war veteran who believed he knew what was what." To Jenney must go the credit for planning one of the revolutionary buildings in the history of metal frame construction.

In 1883 he was asked by the Home Insurance Company to contrive a ten-story building for the southwest corner of LaSalle and Adams streets. This was the decade in which such property soared from $130,000 the quarter-acre to $900,000. Impressed by this, Jenney invented a skeleton framework, using wrought iron up to and including the sixth story, and Bessemer steel beams above that level. What this proved was that elevator-equipped business buildings could reach inconceivable heights. Walls were no longer needed to perform the old function of support: they could be as thin as silk.

Whether the skeleton did *all* the work of the walls in the Home Insurance Building is a technical matter. There are those who insist that Jenney did not achieve this result until 1889, in the Second Leiter Building, later the main Chicago outlet of Sears, Roebuck and Company. However the argument may be settled, it would be silly to pretend that Jenney's feats of engineering were works of art. Louis Sullivan, who worked for a time in his office, did not hesitate to declare that his old master was "not an architect except by courtesy of terms."

There are those who argue that the honor of conceiving the first *completely* self-supporting office building should be awarded William Holabird. Though Holabird failed to graduate from West Point, he picked up more than a smattering of engineering there and in Jenney's office, where he met his partner Martin Roche. In 1886 the two young men laid out the never-to-be-forgotten Tacoma Building on the northwest corner of LaSalle and Madison streets. This was not the first steel frame office building, since cast and wrought iron as well as Bessemer steel were used, but it was the first example of the riveted skeleton. Its L-shaped plan made possible an outer exposure for every office, and its thin terra cotta walls suggested the delicacy that could be won by telling structural facts. Its demolition in 1929 was a far greater tragedy than that two years later of the Home Insurance Building.

Holabird and Roche went on to crowd the Loop with many more buildings that set standards in both architecture and engineering. One of the best of all was the University Club of 1909, still standing on the northwest corner of Monroe and Michigan. This was no omen of structural progress to compare with the Tacoma, but a singularly inventive Gothic setting for a club, owing no more to actual examples of the Middle Ages than the clubs of McKim, Mead and White to the models of the Renaissance.

Unlike Holabird and Roche, whose claims to the invention of the skeleton frame were as real as the cash payments to the contractors on the job, Leroy Sunderland Buffington of Minneapolis staked his hopes of immortality on a patent for a "cloudscraper" he was granted in 1888. It was Buffington's boast that he had thought of a twenty-two-story building in 1881, inspired, so he said, by a passage in Viollet-le-Duc, where the great French critic hinted that "a practical architect might not unnaturally conceive the idea of erecting a vast edifice whose frame should be entirely of iron, and clothing that frame, preserving it, by means of a casing of stone."

The truth, according to Dr. Dimitris Tselos, was that Buffington knew next to nothing about skeleton construction until he happened on an article which Jenney had written in *The Sanitary Engineer* of December 10, 1885. This, then, was the "inspiration" for the patent of 1888. Deep in debt to Jenney, Buffington labored under even greater obligations to one of his own draftsmen, the talented Harvey Ellis, whose renderings of the Richardsonian projects of the firm were so sensitive. Ellis was a genius but a drunkard. "You must remember that I've been preserved in alcohol for twenty years," he told a friend who complimented him on looking so young.

THE WORK OF BURNHAM AND ROOT

You might say that Buffington and his draftsman Ellis were dreamers whose hopes remained unfulfilled, but you could not describe in those terms the Chicago firm of Burnham and Root. Here were two architects whose will was done. Aside from Louis Sullivan, there was no designer who approached them in understanding and solving the problem of business buildings.

Of the two partners Daniel Hudson Burnham was the more ambitious. "My idea," he once told Louis Sullivan, "is to work up a big business, to handle big things, deal with big businessmen, and to build up a big organization, for you can't handle big things unless you have an organization." The grandson of a Congregational minister, and the son of a wholesale druggist who moved to Chicago from western New York, he had dreamed of making a million as a merchant, tried his luck at mining out West, and finally turned into a plate glass salesman before, in 1872 at twenty-six, he joined the Chicago architectural firm of Carter, Drake and Wight.

It was in this office that Burnham met John Wellborn Root, four years younger but far wiser in the ways of architecture. The son of a Georgia drygoods dealer who made and lost a fortune in New York City, Root had been trained by James Renwick, Jr., the designer of Grace Church, and given his chance as a draftsman by J. B. Snook, the architect of Commodore Vanderbilt's Grand Central Station. But perhaps he learned the most of all in the office of Carter, Drake and Wight. Peter Bonnett Wight, the most stimulating of the partners, was one of the most intelligent and one of the most faithful of Ruskin's disciples in the United States. Before settling in Chicago he had designed the National Academy of Design in New York in the Venetian Gothic manner that the master had made popular.

Root, Louis Sullivan decided, "was not of Burnham's type." Here was "a facile draftsman, quick to grasp ideas, and quicker to appropriate them; an excellent musician; well-read on almost any subject; speaking English with easy exactitude of habit . . . and vain to the limit of the skies. This vanity, however, he tactfully took care should not be too obtrusive. . . . His temperament was that of the well-groomed free-lance, never taking anything too seriously, wherein he differed from his ponderous partner, much as a dragon fly and mastiff. Nor had he one tenth of his partner's settled will, nor of said partner's capacity to go through hell to reach an end."

Perhaps it was just as well that Burnham was in earnest. Founded in 1873, the very year in which the collapse of Jay Cooke and Company warned investors that an ominous depression was upon us, the firm of Burnham and Root might not have survived but for his perseverance. In 1874 Burnham succeeded in persuading John B. Sherman, one of the magnates of the stock yards, that this was a wise time to begin building a sixty-thousand-dollar house. Two years later he married Sherman's daughter Margaret.

Meantime Root was reaching conclusions of his own as to what American architecture might become. "American students," he believed, "have at least this advantage, that while they have no great national art history, they certainly have no ignoble history; for all that has been done up to the present counts for nothing."

We were not, he held, bound by the traditions of Europe. *"Periods and styles* are well enough, but you may be sure that whenever in the world there was a period or style of architecture worth preserving, its inner spirit was so closely fitted to the age wherein it flourished that the style could not be fully preserved, either by people who immediately succeeded it, or by us after many years."

As for business buildings, they presented problems very different from those of houses, whether large or small. "It would seem," he said, "that ordinary discretion should teach us that the relation between dwellings and trade-palaces is the relation between an orchestra and a brass band. Whatever is to be spoken in a commercial building must be strongly and directly said. The very style of ornament should be simple enough, and the scale large enough, to be easily comprehended."

Even if Root were simply another brash young man in his contempt for all that passed for tradition in American architecture, he was a typical representative of the Chicago school in his distrust of periods and styles. And in his demand for simple and direct business building he was expressing the innermost convictions of Burnham and Root at the start of their career.

The start was not brilliant, but then you must not judge architects by their beginnings but by their major achievements. Fortunately for the reputation of the firm, the Montauk Building, a ten-story brick structure designed in 1882 for the northwest corner of Monroe and Dearborn streets, has been long since demolished. It looks crude enough in the old prints for no one to regret its destruction; its only merit was a matter of engineering—the so-called "floating raft" foundation, a concrete slab reinforced with iron rails which Root devised as a means of spreading the load and allowing for easy settlement in the uncertain Chicago soil.

Three years later, Burnham and Root confronted the Loop with a masterpiece. This was the Rookery, whose emphatic composition and delicate ornamentation proved that the partners had stared long and lovingly at the creations of H. H. Richardson. One of the greatest of these, of course, was the Marshall Field Wholesale Store, begun the very moment the Chicagoans were completing the plans for this skyscraper. But Richardson, who neglected the challenge of engineering, would never have thought of inventing a great cage of glass and iron to serve as a lobby. To this feat Frank Lloyd Wright paid his respects in 1906, when he decorated the entrance with a staircase and landing of marble inlaid with gold.

Burnham and Root were more directly influenced by Richardson in 1891, when they came to design the Women's Temple and the Masonic Temple, two skyscrapers long since vanished. They were unmistakably more original in 1889 when Root, dared by Burnham to suppress for once his love of ornament, sketched the unrelieved sixteen stories of the

Monadnock Building on the southwest corner of Jackson and Dearborn. Of masonry construction, the Monadnock, despite its floating raft foundation, ignored the technological advances of which so much was made by Jenney and Holabird and Roche. The threatening thing was the building's bareness: to be bold without being brutal is not given to every architect as it was to Root in this instance.

Like the Monadnock, the Reliance Building on North State Street is still standing. Its deliberately exploited skeleton framework, conceived in 1890, but not completed until 1895, five years after Root's death, indicates that the partners were well aware that none of the calculations of the engineers could be overlooked if a skyscraper was to fulfill all expectations. Here the decorative note in the horizontal bands of terra cotta was so welcome, and the modulation of the projecting bays so clever, that the building may be remembered as one of the greatest in the history of the firm. Certainly "Chicago windows"—so architects describe horizontal windows in which a single pane fills the entire area with the exception of narrow movable sashes at either end—have been rarely used with a greater understanding of their dramatic effect. And to Burnham and Root themselves must go the credit for all of this, even if much of the responsibility was entrusted to their draftsman Charles B. Atwood.

SULLIVAN AND THE SKYSCRAPER

But the unchallenged master of the skyscraper, equally imaginative whether solving the riddles of engineering or expressing the answers in architectural form, was Louis Henri Sullivan. Unhappily, he was seldom willing to accept Chicago as it was: to the end of his days, despite the Pullman strike and the other signs that all was not for the best in the best of all possible worlds, he insisted on believing in the perfectability of human nature. "The beauty, the passion, the glory of the past shall merge into a new beauty, a new passion, a new glory as man approaches man, and recognizing him, rejoices in him, and with him, as born in power," he prophesied in his autobiography, declaring that "never . . . has there been such sound warrant for an attitude of optimism."

Perhaps Ralph Waldo Emerson was not a little to blame for the architect's confusion. Sullivan was born and grew up in the neighborhood of Boston, at a time when the spokesman for transcendentalism was taken very seriously, and more than one passage in the architect's autobiography may be said to bear the trace of the essayist's influence. Here, probably, was the source of Sullivan's unbounded faith in human nature, for the philosopher from Concord was not one to emphasize the evil that is in all of us. Nor was he afraid of simplifying the most complex issues. "The intellectual life," he declared, "may be kept clean and healthful if man will live the life of nature and not import into his mind difficulties which are none of his."

To the twentieth century this dictum of Emerson's may sound dangerously like philosophy made easy. But Sullivan, for that matter, came close to laying down the rule for architecture made easy when he announced that "form follows function." Very fortunately, his designs were all of them too personal to be reduced to a formula of this sort; no one was less rigid than he at the drafting board.

All his life, however, this superb individualist was hoping to discover a set of regulations to which he could give his wholehearted allegiance, never suspecting that if he silenced his unrest he would be assassinating the better part of himself. No passage in his autobiography is more pathetic than that in which he tells of his joy in coming across his tutor in mathematics in Paris, Monsieur Clopet, who advanced the notion of demonstrations so broad as to admit of no exception. "Instantly the words had flashed," he recalled, "there arose a vision and a fixed resolve. . . . If this can be done in mathematics, why not in architecture? The instant answer: It can, and it shall be! *No one has—I will!*"

No one was more vague than Sullivan when he dreamed of what architecture might be; no one was more accurate when he put pencil to paper or criticized his own work or that of others. As a boy in Boston, he could not be confined by the horizon of either his father, an Irish dancing master who seems to have been overly reverent to book learning, or of his mother, a gentle pianist who must have sighed now and then for the decorum of her native Geneva, Switzerland. At twelve the architect gazed with a wonderful irreverence at the buildings of Boston. "Some said vile things, some said prudent things, some said pompous things, but none said noble things." His own buildings were noble, perhaps for the very good reason that he never succeeded in becoming the conformist he idealized.

The architect's autobiography is the record of his quest for an absolute alien to his temperament. At Boston's English High School he fell under the influence of the disciplinarian Moses Woolson, who had, he recollected, "the authority and pugnacity of a first mate taking on a fresh crew." At the Massachusetts Institute of Technology, then under the conservative leadership of William R. Ware, he missed the dogmatic teaching of his high school idol.

Quitting M.I.T. at the end of a year, he went looking for a job in Philadelphia. "Once settled down in the large quiet village, he began to roam the streets, looking quizzically at buildings as he wandered. On the west side of Broad Street a residence, almost completed, caught his eye like a flower in the roadside. He approached, examined it with curious care, without and within. Here was something fresh and fair, a human note, as though some one were talking. He inquired as to the architect and was

told: Furness & Hewitt." Fortunately, since the uncompromising individualism of this firm answered his inner need, he found work in their
office. Frank Furness he admired as one who "made buildings out of his
head." He also rejoiced in John Hewitt, who "made of Louis a draughts-
man of the upper crust, and Louis's heart went out to lovable John in
sheer gratitude."

Dismissed from Furness and Hewitt during the depression which followed the collapse of Jay Cooke and Company in 1873, Sullivan ventured
to Chicago where "in spite of the panic, there was stir: an energy that
made him tingle to be in the game." For a few months he labored in the
office of William Le Baron Jenney. Then, in the summer of 1874, he set
sail for the Ecole des Beaux-Arts, bound once more in search of fixed
principles.

Although Hunt, Richardson, and McKim all learned much at the
Ecole, Sullivan may have got even more out of his stay in Paris. Confronted with the highest standards in the world in architectural training,
he had to confess that he was too romantic an artist to follow the accepted classical tradition. "There came," he wrote of himself, "the hover-
ing conviction that this great school, in its perfect flower of technique,
lacked the profound animus of a primal inspiration. He felt that beneath
the law of the school lay a law which it ignored unsuspectingly or with
fixed intention—the law he had seen set forth in the stillness of the
Sistine, which he saw everywhere in the open of life."

He was to find an ideal partner on his return to Chicago. Early in
1879, when not yet twenty-four, he entered the office of Dankmar Adler, a
German-born Jew twelve years his senior who fully appreciated his
genius, and what was even more important, fought for his rights in the
aggressive city which Sullivan worshiped without understanding. The
founding of the partnership of Adler and Sullivan on the first of May,
1880, meant that a great artist would be relatively free of the usual worries of his profession.

Adler was less of an artist than Sullivan, but it would be unwise to
under-rate his accomplishments. The son of a rabbi who eventually
headed Congregation Anshe Ma'ariv in Chicago, Adler grew up in Detroit, where he had the benefit of free-hand drawing lessons from Gari
Melchers' father. Later he practiced drafting in more than one Detroit
and Chicago architectural office before seeing service in the Civil War in
Kentucky, Georgia, and Tennessee; as a draftsman in the Topographical
Engineer's Office of the Military Division of Tennessee, he laid the
foundation for his unusual understanding of engineering. Back in
Chicago when the war was over, he went into partnership with one
Edward Burling. Together they did a big business in the building boom
following the Chicago Fire. Adler was practicing alone, however, in 1879
when Sullivan joined his office; this was the year in which he was com-

pleting the plans for the Central Music Hall that stood on the present site of the retail store of Marshall Field and Company. A six-story theater and business block, the Central Music Hall was famous for the upward curve of its orchestra floor, one of the devices adopted by Adler for insuring the diffusion of sound.

Adler was so widely respected for his insight into acoustics that in the winter of 1885 the firm was commissioned to remodel the old Exposition Building in Grant Park for use as a temporary grand opera house. This was a greater opportunity than either he or Sullivan could have recognized. So successful was this design with its fan-shaped plan and sloping ceiling that its promoter, a businessman by the name of Ferdinand E. Peck, conceived the idea of the Auditorium—a structure combining a four-hundred-room hotel with business offices and a hall seating four thousand. This, the greatest civic project in America since the founding of Washington, was entrusted, as was only reasonable, to Adler and Sullivan.

In the very beginning, in the summer of 1886, Sullivan fancied gable roofs, dormers, and corner pinnacles. But gradually, as he came to consider the Marshall Field Wholesale Store by Richardson then nearing completion in the Loop, he simplified these sketches until he reached the magnificent solution still dominating Michigan Boulevard, Congress Street, and Wabash Avenue. Of solid masonry construction, the Auditorium made no use of the steel frame which Adler and Sullivan were to exploit with such confidence in their skyscrapers; to this, only purists could object, so expertly were the stories of the façades grouped under high arches.

There were, of course, engineering problems. One of the most vexing was that of the seventeen-story tower on the Congress Street side, which weighed fifteen thousand tons. To allow for even settling, Adler was obliged to load this tower artificially with pig iron and brick. And then there were the acoustical questions, solved all of them by Adler with his usual success.

At last, on the evening of December 9, 1889, the Auditorium was opened. The house was packed, the boxes filled with the George M. Pullmans, the Marshall Fields, and the other seigneurs of the city, all of whom were struck, at least for the moment, by the sumptuousness of Louis Sullivan's imagination. So were the guests of honor, the President and Vice-President of the United States. Glancing now at the distant galleries, now at the gorgeously decorated elliptical arches above him, Benjamin Harrison only half-listened to Adelina Patti's trilling of "Home, Sweet Home." He leaned over and nudged Vice-President Morton by the elbow. "New York surrenders, eh?" said the President.

You could certainly forgive Louis Sullivan for feeling that all of his troubles were over. He had spent himself inventing the ornamentation of those golden arches, and his originality was apparently appreciated by the biggest businessmen in the audience. He could scarcely foresee that this opera house, then the most brilliant advertisement of the city, would be abandoned in only thirty years, not because its usefulness was over, but simply to satisfy the caprice of Samuel Insull, who insisted on the opera company's moving away from Michigan Avenue. Happily, not too long after, the Auditorium Building, thanks to Marshall Field III and the Rosenwald Fund, was given to Roosevelt College; the opera house itself was restored by Harry M. Weese.

But it was just as well that Sullivan the idealist was not immediately disillusioned. In the ten years following the completion of the Auditorium, he was to fix his attention on the skyscraper. "How," he asked, "shall we impart to this sterile pile, this crude, harsh, brutal agglomeration, this stark, staring exclamation of eternal strife, the graciousness of those higher forms of sensibility and culture that rest on the lower and fiercer passions?" He decided that the tall office building "must be every inch a proud and soaring thing, rising in sheer exultation that from bottom to top it is a unit without a single dissenting line." This might be a description of any one of his skyscrapers; having gracefully solved all of the structural problems, he enriched his designs with more than one trace of the ornament which was so personal and so poetic an expression of his genius.

One of the greatest of his skyscrapers was his first, the Wainwright Building in St. Louis, completed in 1891 for Ellis Wainwright, one of the city's wealthier brewers. Here, to quote the architect's own words, "the steel frame . . . was first given authentic recognition and expression." There was no mere utilitarian solution of a utilitarian problem. The lower stories of this vertically accented block were made massive, and the corners emphasized, not for structural reasons, but to delight the eye. The architect's aim was not to let "form follow function," but to dramatize the function, which was new, in a new way. He wisely relieved the bareness of the red brick piers which rose above the Missouri granite base by inserting lovingly decorated terra cotta panels beneath the windows and by capping the building with the gayest of friezes beneath the simple cornice.

The Guaranty Building in Buffalo, which Sullivan finished four years later, was the most eloquent expression of the ideal of the architect. Here the ornament was even richer, the vertical accent even more arresting, the composition even more successful. The walls were of a rich red terra cotta, studded with one of the master's most ingenious decorative conceits, and the top story, with its round windows sunk in lush, flower-like patterns, was an enchanting climax.

Meantime the firm had not been idle in Chicago itself. There was the Schiller Theater of 1892, which in our time was handed over to the

Auditorium, Chicago, Ill.

Interior, Auditorium, Chicago, Ill, 1889
(Adler & Sullivan)

Detail of Congress Street façade

wreckers, like the Stock Exchange Building of 1894, whose bold arches forced pedestrians to forget what might have been the monotony of tiers of Chicago windows; last, but not least, there were the two tombs Sullivan designed for Graceland Cemetery. One of these, dating from 1889, was an Egyptoid block of Quincy granite, an austere but splendid monument to Martin Ryerson, father of the Martin A Ryerson who watched over the growth of the Art Institute. Close by was the sepulcher he fashioned in 1890 for Carrie Eliza Getty, whose family had benefited by shrewd investments in local real estate. But there was no thought of gain or loss in the architect's mind when he came to decorate this cube of Bedford limestone with its four round arches; never in all his career was he more subtle than when he sketched the lacelike patterns circling the arches, nor was his feeling for proportions keener than when he thought of filling the octagonal panels above these arches with eight-pointed stars.

Sullivan executed yet another memorial in 1892, this time in St. Louis, a delicate tribute in limestone to Charlotte Dickson Wainwright, wife of the promoter of the Wainwright Building. In the very next year he was made aware that neither his tombs nor his skyscrapers entitled him to any special consideration in his adopted city. The Chicago World's Fair opened its gates.

THE WORLD'S FAIR AND THE CHICAGO PLAN

Perhaps the best clue to the World's Fair was given by Mrs. Astor's friend Ward McAllister. He believed that Chicago might learn a lesson in her hour of triumph. "The contact of New York and Chicago society during the World's Fair cannot help but open the eyes of our Western natives to our superiority," he told reporters. "I do not wish to belittle Chicago in using the word 'superiority.' The society of Chicago is behind that of New York, but there is no reason why it should not eventually catch up. Chicago is moving in the right direction, and should be encouraged in every way."

No one was more eager to encourage Chicago in this new direction than Daniel Hudson Burnham. When his partner Root died in the midst of the preparations for the Fair, Burnham came to the conclusion that the "originality" of the Chicago School was very much of a mistake. Enchanted by the "pure ideal of the ancients"—so he translated the aims of Richard Morris Hunt and McKim, Mead and White—he begged forgiveness for the romantic skyscrapers of his youth. "We have been in an inventive period, and have had rather a contempt for the classics," he dogmatized. "Men evolved new ideas and imagined they could start a new

Left: Guaranty Building, Buffalo, N.Y., 1895 (Adler & Sullivan) *Right:* Schlesinger & Mayer Building, now Carson, Pirie, Scott & Co., Chicago, Ill., 1904 (L. H. Sullivan)

Transportation Building, World's Fair, Chicago, Ill., 1890 (Adler & Sullivan)

• Chicago Architectural Photographing Company

school without much reference to the past." That he now knew to be an error.

Burnham, who surrendered the planning of the Fair to Hunt, McKim, Mead and White, and the other Easterners working in the eclectic manner, was not one to criticize his new-found friends. Once the Easterners were on the scene, he went out of his way to apologize for what he conceived to be the cultural inferiority of the Middle West. This sort of thing did not sit too well with Richard Morris Hunt. "Hell," he interrupted Burnham, "we haven't come out here on a missionary expedition. Let's get down to work."

In this uncritical atmosphere, the Easterners were guilty of designing buildings which added nothing to their reputation. Hunt's domed Administration Building was unworthy of the creator of the W. K. Vanderbilt house on Fifth Avenue; McKim, Mead and White's Agricultural Building was no more than a parody of the skill they had displayed in the Villard group. The same thing could be said of the achievements of the lesser men.

True, the lagoons conceived by Frederick Law Olmsted were splendid; true, the classic motive carried out with a uniform cornice line induced a remarkable harmony; true, this was a grand show, the most successful of all American fairs. And for artists who liked to bask in mutual admiration, this was a glorious moment. "Look here, old fellow," the sculptor Saint-Gaudens called out at the end of a conference in which Hunt, McKim, and the rest had had their say, "do you realize that this is the greatest meeting of artists since the fifteenth century?"

The public was stunned and pleased, too. But there were those who raised a word of warning; one of these was the architectural critic Montgomery Schuyler. "Arcadian architecture is one thing and American architecture another," he cautioned. "Men bring not back the mastodons nor we those times."

Save for the Fisheries Building in the Richardsonian manner by the Chicagoan Henry Ives Cobb, the only exception to the prevailing white and classic pattern of "The White City" was Louis Sullivan's Transportation Building. Though its round arches complemented the adjacent Roman façades, this was a highly personal phenomenon in this impersonal setting. Of richly colored plaster, it was a revelation of the architect's command of an intensely individual decorative sense. Nowhere was this more evident than in the grand entrance. An oblong, framing five receding half-circles, it was covered with gold leaf, set off by arabesques in orange, red, and yellow stucco.

These two disobedient buildings did not fail to catch the eyes of French visitors to the Fair. "The only things they had a good word for were the Transportation Building and parts of the Fisheries Building," noted the critic Russell Sturgis. "As for the Roman colonnades, they sneered at them as being the school work of their authors, revived for the purpose, and they intimated very plainly that this returning to their schoolboy work signified merely the adoption of what was easiest and quickest done."

No doubt it was the facility of the eclectics which most deeply distressed Sullivan. He had always believed, as a romantic artist should, that a work of art was a sacrifice, and anyone could tell that the White City was the monument of untormented minds.

Sullivan was willing to concede that "Burnham performed in a masterful way, displaying remarkable executive capacity. He became open-minded, just, magnanimous. He did his great share." But the architect of the Transportation Building could not forget for an instant that the White City was the antithesis of his ideal.

He shuddered when he thought of the vast numbers who had passed through the turnstiles.

> These crowds were astonished. They beheld what was for them an amazing revelation of the architectural art, of which previously they in comparison had known nothing. . . . They departed joyously, carriers of contagion, unaware that what they had beheld and believed to be truth was to prove, in historic fact, an appalling calamity. For what they saw was not at all what they believed they saw, but an imposition of the spurious upon their eyesight, a naked exhibitionism of charlatanry in the higher feudal and domineering culture, conjoined with expert salesmanship of the materials of decay. . . .
>
> The damage wrought by the World's Fair will last half a century from its date, if not longer. It has penetrated deep into the constitution of the American mind, effecting there lesions significant of dementia.

This was the final judgment of a great architect. Yet there is no reason why it should be accepted without reservations. Sullivan was an idealist who failed to reckon with reality—a wiser man would, for instance, have expected that a World's Fair be shot with politics, and been pleasantly surprised if a single building were distinguished. Moreover, a keen observer of the social scene would have understood that the eclecticism fostered by McKim, Mead and White was a reflection of the life led by the leisure class in the East; in the Middle West, where the popping of champagne corks was not heard every day in the year, the pageantry of the Renaissance might attract, but could scarcely hold a vast audience.

As for the mediocrity of much of the eclectic work of the twentieth century, this might be blamed, not on the Fair, but on our refusal to understand the implications of the social legislation of the Wilson administration. The income-tax amendment to the Constitution and the other checks on private enterprise were working a revolution in the

economy we had inherited from the age of McKinley. Many an architect—and many a client—could not comprehend what had happened,
and, like baffled men in all times, preferred what they took to be the
tried and true to the threat of the new and unknown.

Finally, the quarter-century in Chicago following the World's Fair
was much more brilliant than you would suppose from Sullivan's testi-
mony. Even though he had little to do in those years, and the level of
industrial architecture suffered in consequence, this was the period in
which Barry Byrne, Dwight H. Perkins, Guenzel and Drummond, George
W. Maher, Purcell and Elmslie, Walter Burley Griffin, and Frank Lloyd
Wright himself planned a surprising number of buildings.

Sullivan, then, may have overemphasized the damage done by the
Fair, so far as architecture was concerned. The White City and city
planning is another story altogether. As Christopher Tunnard has reminded us, D. H. Burnham would never have dreamed of his famous
"Chicago Plan" if he had not first gazed upon Olmsted's lagoons. Though
only partially carried out, this scheme of Burnham's, elaborated by his associate Edward H. Bennett, was responsible for the dramatic development
today of Chicago's lake front. Yet another offshoot of the Fair was the
revival, by Burnham and McKim, of the L'Enfant plan for Washington.

The man behind these radical alterations of the topography of
Chicago and Washington was, of course, a well-nigh irresistible promoter.
Quite rightly, Burnham has been identified with one of the pleas he made
on behalf of the Chicago Plan. "Make no little plans," he warned one
audience. "They have no magic to stir men's blood. . . . Make big plans;
aim high in hope and work, remembering that a noble, logical diagram
once recorded will never die, but long after we are gone will be a living
thing, asserting itself with ever-growing insistency. Remember that our
sons and grandsons are going to do things that would stagger us. Let your
watchword be order and your beacon beauty."

This was Burnham at his best. At his worst he could appeal to another
side of his fellow Chicagoans. "Beauty has always paid better than any
other commodity, and always will," he argued when asked to explain the
Chicago Plan to the businessmen of the Merchants' Club. "You all
know," he went on, "that there is a tendency among our well-to-do
people to spend much time and money elsewhere, and that this tendency
has been rapidly growing in recent years. We have been running away to
Cairo, Athens, the Riviera, Paris, and Vienna because life at home is not
so pleasant as in these fashionable centers. . . .

"Does anyone," he asked, "grown rich in the mines, the forests, or the
plains of our country come here to live, or even linger for the sake of
pleasure? Does he not pass through the city, remaining only so long as
he is compelled to, so that we get the benefit neither of his money nor of
his presence among us?" He succeeded, incidentally, in making Chicago
the best-planned city in the Western Hemisphere.

If Sullivan had been as willing as Burnham to talk to businessmen on their own terms, he would never have watched, as he did, his practice dwindle. Though all great architects have been poets, the very greatest have had to double as salesmen in order to survive.

SULLIVAN'S LAST YEARS

Like all architectural firms, Adler and Sullivan were dismayed by the depression which followed the failure of the National Cordage Trust in the spring of 1893. First the office force was cut and then the partners themselves were embarrassed. At the height of this anxiety, Adler was beguiled into retiring from the profession. Offered a handsome salary by the millionaire valve and plumbing manufacturer, R. T. Crane, he agreed to head the Crane sales staff.

Perhaps because he realized how deeply he was indebted to Adler for shielding him from the business world outside the drafting room, Sullivan could never forgive his partner for deserting him, and when Adler, early in 1896, barely six months after the partnership was dissolved, begged him to let bygones be bygones and resume their relationship, he refused. This was a tragic decision. In practice by himself until he died of apoplexy in the spring of 1900, Adler never again executed a major commission. As for Sullivan, he went his own way, bewildered.

Although his imagination was undulled, he was baffled by what he discovered to be the spirit of Chicago. As he afterward admitted, "he was too young to grasp the truth that the fair-appearing civilization within which he lived was but a huge invisible man-trap, man-made. Of politics he knew nothing and suspected nothing, all seemed fair on the surface. . . . He had also heard vaguely something about finance and what a mystery it was. In other words, Louis was absurdly, grotesquely credulous. How could it be otherwise with him? He believed that most people were honest and intelligent. How could he suspect the eminent? So Louis saw the real world upside down."

Perhaps, then, it was nothing short of a miracle that he succeeded in designing, in the twenty-nine years that were left to him after he and Adler separated, the loveliest skyscraper so far in New York, the greatest of all department store buildings, and a series of astonishing banks for small towns in Indiana, Ohio, Iowa, Wisconsin, and Minnesota. These last were conceived in a time when he was sick at heart, worried over making both ends meet, and a heavy drinker. "He lived alone most of his life," commented one of his closest friends, "and when he drank, he drank alone."

Sunk in the shadows of Manhattan's Bleecker Street is the Bayard or Condict Building, completed in 1898. This was a twelve-story tower of unhesitating verticality, but Sullivan was not satisfied with dramatizing a feat of engineering. In between the steel shafts bearing the weight, he inserted terra cotta mullions incrusted with his charming decoration. "Ornament, when creative, spontaneous, is a perfume," he said.

In 1899, when the Chicago drygoods firm of Schlesinger and Mayer asked him to create the building on the northeast corner of State and Madison streets occupied today by Carson, Pirie, Scott and Company, he began by sketching twelve stories emphasizing the horizontality of the "Chicago windows." But so simple a solution bored him, and he sheathed the first two stories in a marvelous envelope of decorative cast iron. As a business building this has never been equaled.

This was his last major commission. Defeated, so he reasoned, in our cities, he turned to the country towns of the Middle West. Nine miniature business blocks and banks in Indiana, Iowa, Ohio, Wisconsin, and Minnesota told of his struggle for survival. Since he did not know how to be inadequate, all but one of these buildings were exceptional. Three of the most provocative were the National Farmers' Bank at Owatonna, Minnesota, 1908; the Merchants' National Bank at Grinnell, Iowa, 1914; and the People's Savings and Loan Association at Sidney, Ohio, 1918. All three were of brick; terra cotta was, as usual, the medium in which he freed his decorative instinct.

Perhaps the best of all was the bank at Owatonna. Centered on two conquering round arches, this was composed in one of those moments when the architect regained faith in himself. In this Minnesota village were clients who understood exactly what he was about. The officers of this bank, to quote the president, "believed that an adequate expression of the character of their business in the form of a simple, dignified, and beautiful building was due to themselves . . . and their patrons. . . . Further than this, they believed that a beautiful business house would be its own reward." Mistrustful of architects who followed precedents or took their inspiration "from the books," they decided on Sullivan after discovering the tedious mistakes of his rivals in the architectural magazines. In our time Harwell Harris made no mistakes when he restored it.

The bankers of Owatonna were braver men than they realized. The business community, stunned by the brilliant social program of the Wilson administration, was already frowning on buildings that expressed the convictions of individuals. Precedents were being followed everywhere, not because they were stimulating to designers, but because they offered some sort of guarantee.

There was a time when Sullivan insisted that "the lifting of the eyelids of the world is what Democracy means." In his last years he confessed that this was a creed to which few members of his profession conformed. "American architecture," he had to admit, "is composed, in the hundred, of 90 parts aberration, eight parts indifference, one part poverty, and one part Little Lord Fauntleroy. You can have the prescription

Tomb of Carrie Eliza Getty, Chicago, Ill., 1890 (L.H. Sullivan)

National Farmers' Bank, Owatonna, Minn., 1908 (L. H. Sullivan)

filled at any architectural department store, or select architectural millinery establishment."

Sinclair Lewis has told us how deep Sullivan was buried at the time. The Gopher Prairie in which Carol Kennicott fought the good fight for what looked like broad horizons was certainly not far distant from Owatonna, but the type of architecture on which she set her heart had nothing in common with the art of the master of the Auditorium. "In all the town," said Lewis of Gopher Prairie, there was "not one building save the Ionic bank which gave pleasure to Carol's eyes." As for the new house of which she dreamed, it was nothing if not conventional. "She babbled of a low stone house with lattice windows and tulip beds, of colonial brick, of a white frame cottage with green shutters and dormer windows."

When Louis Sullivan died in the spring of 1924 in an undistinguished hotel on Chicago's South Side, he had no reason to think he would be remembered. He is scarcely forgotten today, but that is not the same thing as saying that this generation has spelled out the principles for which he stood. Though eclectic skyscrapers are now hopelessly out of fashion—the last distinguished example, Cass Gilbert's Woolworth Building in New York City, dates from as long ago as 1909—it is hardly likely that Sullivan would approve of the tall buildings that pass for the last word in 1978. Stripped of all ornament, they are monuments to the insistence of certain of our big business executives on solutions as impersonal as chemical formulas. It is only in our domestic architecture, and then only on the West Coast, that anything resembling the individualism he championed is endemic.

THE SKYSCRAPER SINCE SULLIVAN

The architects of the notable skyscrapers since Sullivan may be praised for meeting the demands of businessmen intent on besting every available inch of floor space; they may even be admired for providing, as they sometimes have, a dramatic setting for the masters of our corporations. But they cannot be said to have triumphed, as did Sullivan, over the laws of economics.

The completion in 1930 of the New York Daily News Building by Howells and Hood marked the beginning of the present trend. In this rhythmically vertical mass there was no trace of the influence of the great styles; what was even more striking, ornament was discarded as unnecessary. The very same thing might be said of the horizontally accented McGraw-Hill Building at the other end of Forty-second Street, designed by the same firm in 1931. As statements of the facts by an architect working under intense economic pressure and complying with the setbacks enforced by the new building code, these were emphatic, even powerful monuments. But the poetry of Sullivan was missing; no one could tell that an individual had planned these buildings.

A similar criticism could be made of the Philadelphia Saving Fund Society Building, completed by Howe and Lescaze in 1932, and of the Rockefeller Center development on which Reinhard and Hofmeister, Corbett, Benjamin Wistar Morris, Harmon and MacMurray, and Hood and Fouilhoux collaborated. Rockefeller Center, with its open spaces welcoming the crowds of Fifth Avenue, represented at least an advance in city planning. No such praise could be given the Empire State Building, conceived by Shreve, Lamb, and Harmon in the dawn of the Great Depression.

In recent years the planners of our skyscrapers have been more skillful in dramatizing the feats of engineering on which their art depends, but the creators of these glass and steel cages have also come close to reaching total anonymity. "Untouched by human hands" would not be a harsh description of the marble and glass tower of the United Nations, completed by Wallace K. Harrison and his associates in 1950.

Who knows, the sight of this bleak tower and of the dozens of sterile skyscrapers erected in Manhattan in the postwar years may have provoked the recent interest in Art Deco—the lavish type of decoration applied to a number of business buildings in the 1920s. The architects of Art Deco took their cue from either the Exposition des Arts Décoratifs in Paris in 1926, or from the venturesome experiments of certain German expressionists. Perhaps the best example of Art Deco in New York was the Barclay-Vesey Building of 1923–26 by McKenzie, Voorhees and Walker. Not that the Barclay-Vesey could be compared with something as remarkable as Peter Behrens's design for the German dye trust I. G. Farben in Hoechst.

The battle pro and con anonymous architecture will be reviewed in the next chapter, but this may be the place to point out that there have been a few exceptions to this impersonal approach to the tall building. One of these was the Hallidie Building of San Francisco, planned by the eclectic Willis Jefferson Polk in 1918. Forgetting in this instance the Roman grammar he had learned in the office of D. H. Burnham, Polk fashioned a façade of glass whose bareness was relieved by fanciful cast-iron moldings. Another remarkable exception was the Singer Building at 561 Broadway in New York, completed by Ernest Flagg in 1904. Like Polk, this Beaux-Arts graduate understood that a glass wall may be a boring thing if the art of decoration is forgotten.

Anonymity, it must be admitted, never held any charms for Frank Lloyd Wright. Trained in Sullivan's office, and even more of an individualist than his master, he was to reveal again and again that his contempt for utilitarian answers was as deep as his understanding of utilitarian questions. "The machine should build the building," he declared. "But it is not necessary for that reason to build as though the building, too, were a machine." In the eyes of architects who were fonder of formulas than of their own ambition, he was a perfect nuisance. It is true that his ambition was alarming.

YOUNG FRANK LLOYD WRIGHT

Wright is credited, even by his enemies, with being the greatest architect of the twentieth century. He is the greatest artist to emerge from the Middle West, the only one who may be said to have conquered Chicago. One reason for his success is that he always knew exactly what he wanted. "You've got to have guts to be an architect!" he has said. "People will come to you and tell you what they want, and you will have to give them what they need."

"Early in life," Wright has confessed, "I had to choose between honest arrogance and hypocritical humility. I chose honest arrogance, and have seen no reason to change." This passionate preacher came from a family whose members had again and again urged their convictions from dissenting pulpits. His grandfather, a Welsh hatter turned farmer in the New World, led a Unitarian congregation in Wisconsin until told the Church proposed to "try" him for his unorthodox opinions. "You need not," he declared. "If I am intrusive, I will get out. I cannot quell my spirit." The architect's father, a New Englander who went west to teach music after finding no substance in either medicine or law, was also a circuit rider, at first under Baptist and later under Unitarian auspices.

That a good sermon must hold everyone's attention was the great lesson of Wright's childhood. His father was none too successful at any of his callings, and the parents separated when the architect was a boy. His mother was the one who watched over him and his two sisters. He has described himself as "the sentimental son of a sentimental mother grown up in the midst of a sentimental family planted on free soil by a grandly sentimental grandfather . . . the Welsh pioneer."

Born at Richland Center, Wisconsin, in 1867, Wright could never see any reason to apologize for his native state. "The real American spirit, capable of judging an issue for itself upon its merits, lies in the West and Middle West," he believed, "where breadth of view, independent thought and a tendency to take common sense into the realm of arts, as in life, are more characteristic. It is alone in an atmosphere of this nature that the Gothic spirit of building can be revived." Whether or not the Middle West is all that the architect says it is, it is true that he was quite as aggressive as any of the Chicago millionaires who were the folk heroes of the region in his childhood.

There is more than one echo of P. D. Armour in Wright's autobiography. At twenty-one he was, so he claims, "the best-paid draftsman in the city of Chicago." Being simply the best draftsman would have been enough to cheer the heart of any other beginner in the profession, but Wright was aware, as Sullivan never was, of the struggle for survival in our big cities. He realized that an artist who sang small might never be heard at all.

He was only twenty when he quit the School of Engineering at the University of Wisconsin to look for work with an architect in Chicago. Before the year was out, after convincing two other firms of his ability, he was settled in Sullivan's office. "You've got the right kind of touch, you'll do," admitted the master.

"About 10.30 the door opened," Wright wrote of those days in the Adler and Sullivan office. "Mr. Sullivan walked slowly in with a haughty air, handkerchief in his nose. Paying no attention to anyone. No 'good mornings.' No words of greeting as he passed from desk to desk. Saw me waiting for him. Came forward at once with a pleasant 'Ah! Wright, there you are,' and the office had my name. And evidently, in Sullivan's unusually pleasant address, also my 'number.' "

For six years Wright served Adler and Sullivan as draftsman, and in 1891, when only twenty-four, designed for the firm the town house on Astor Street of the real estate speculator James Charnley. Here, the architect has told us, he "first sensed the decorative value of the plain surface." This symmetrical brick structure, still standing, though extended on the south side, proved that Wright was capable of achieving a dignity seldom seen in our residential streets. Despite the restrictions of his contract, he began planning houses on his own. This was something that Sullivan could not tolerate. "Your sole interest is here, while your contract lasts," he claimed. In 1893 Wright opened his own office.

Shortly after this, D. H. Burnham offered the young architect the opportunity of studying four years at the Ecole in Paris, then two years in Rome, all expenses paid and his family supported in the meantime. On his return, he would step into a job with D. H. Burnham and Company. "Another year, and it will be too late, Frank," the older architect warned.

"Yes, too late, Uncle Dan," Wright admitted. "It's too late now, I'm afraid. I am spoiled already. I've been too close to Mr. Sullivan. He has helped spoil the Beaux-Arts for me, or spoiled me for the Beaux-Arts, I guess I mean."

"You are loyal to Sullivan, I see, Frank, and that is right," Burnham put in. "I admire Sullivan when it comes to decoration. Essentially he is a great decorator. His ornament charms me. But his architecture? I can't see that. The Fair, Frank, is going to have a great influence in our country. . . . I can see all America constructed along the lines of the Fair, in noble, 'dignified' classic style. The great men of the day all feel that way about it."

"No," Wright interrupted, "there is Louis Sullivan, he doesn't. And if John Root were alive, I don't believe he would feel that way about it. Richardson I am sure never would."

"Frank," Burnham declared, "the Fair should have shown you that Sullivan and Richardson are well enough in their way, but their way won't prevail—architecture is going the other way."

"But, it is essentially the uncreative way . . . isn't it?" Wright asked. "No, Mr. Burnham . . . I can't run away . . . from what I see as mine."

So ran the conversation as Wright remembered it many years afterward in his autobiography.

Then, as ever, Wright was the champion of what he labeled "organic architecture." An organic building, he has told us, is designed from within outward. The cathedrals of the Middle Ages are excellent examples; so, too, are the wooden structures of Japan. "The Japanese," the architect has insisted, "have never outraged wood in their art or in their craft."

What Wright scorned as inorganic is best represented by the triumphs of the Renaissance. In this arch-individualist's eyes, the Italian masters and their followers were the slaves of precedent, and their finest façades one-dimensional. This may sound prejudiced, but being biased could never embarrass this architect, who knew a thing or two, it must be admitted, about the perfection of proportions that the Renaissance idealized.

"Democracy needed something basically better than the box," Wright claimed. "So I started out to destroy the box as building." In his very earliest houses in the Chicago suburbs, he conceived of walls as screens instead of barriers. He also emphasized, as did no one else, the texture of whatever materials he was using. And he never forgot that a building should appear to grow easily from its site.

These early earth-bound houses have often been criticized as too dark, and it is true that the broad eaves he favored often made for gloomy interiors. The furniture he designed for these houses has also been disparaged, and by no one more sharply that Wright himself. "I have been black and blue in some spot, somewhere, almost all my life from too intimate contact with my own furniture," he admits.

Perhaps it does not matter very much if these and a hundred other charges again Wright be substantiated. If anyone has earned the right to blunder now and then, it is this inventor who could never see anything to be proud of in repeating an experiment successfully performed. Besides, even if the freedom of planning which has been saluted as one of the great discoveries of domestic architecture of the mid-twentieth century dates from the era of Alexander Jackson Davis, it is undeniable that Wright promoted something like a revolution by breaking down, as he did in his earliest work, the compartments that passed for rooms in the

American house. Planning of this sort was novel when servants were plentiful; today, when servants have vanished, it is imperative.

Throughout his career, Wright discovered that the clients who best understood his aims were, more often than not, self-made businessmen. One of these was Frederick C. Robie, a Chicagoan who made his fortune dealing in bicycles and sewing machines. For him in 1909 Wright designed one of the greatest of his Prairie style houses. A long low brick mass that clung to the earth with stubborn allegiance, its plan was one of the best exhibits of the architect's talent for forcing space to flow as easily as water.

Seven years before the sketches were made for the Robie house on Chicago's South Side, another rising businessman, Ward M. Willitts of the railway supply firm of Adams and Westlake, called on Wright to build his house in the North Shore suburb of Highland Park. This was an airier, lighter structure than the Robie residence, even though the plan was not quite so novel. And the symmetrical façade of stucco accented by wood strips was uncannily serene.

The soap manufacturer Darwin D. Martin of Buffalo was another independent businessman completely satisfied by a Wright design. Recently restored to serve as the president's house of the branch of the state university, it now allows us to imagine the first fine moment in 1904 when the Martins occupied the premises. That was the very year in which the architect completed the austere but compelling Administration Building in Buffalo for the Larkin Company of which Martin was the secretary. The Larkin Building has been pulled down, which is indeed unfortunate, for in this brick pile Wright showed how carefully he had read William Morris. "I believe machines can do everything—except make works of art," Morris had argued.

While Robie, Willitts, and Martin were businessmen challenging the established families of Chicago and Buffalo, B. Harley Bradley of Kankakee, and Avery Coonley of Riverside were the masters of fortunes already created. But Wright was not embarrassed by the thought of having to please gentlemen with unearned incomes at their disposal. For Bradley, the scion of a plow manufacturing dynasty, he sketched in 1900 a villa whose interior was delightfully simplified and whose provocatively pitched eaves answered the angles of the adjacent river bank. For Coonley, whose wealth, like that of Bradley, was derived from farm machinery, he invented one of the most elaborate designs of his career, a low, ever-spreading structure with sunken gardens and pools mirroring the fanciful ornamentation he conceived for the plaster covered walls. The symmetry of the Coonley house was classic—in the sense that the greatest artists of the Renaissance would have understood. In 1912, three years after the Coonley estate was completed, he designed a playhouse for the Coonley children; here the trellis stretching over the central block let fall on the gaily colored windows a light that was as picturesque as the

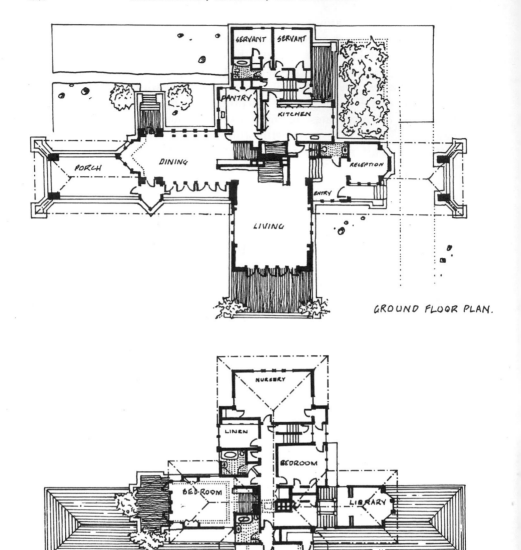

Plan of residence of Ward M. Willitts, Highland Park, Ill., 1902 (Designer: Frank Lloyd Wright)

landscaping which Frederick Law Olmsted had dreamed of, over half a century before, for this fortunate Chicago suburb. The house itself has suffered by recent alterations.

Meantime it was in Oak Park, the suburb in which Wright himself

Residence of Ward M. Willitts, Highland Park, Ill., 1902

Residence of Frederick C. Robie, Chicago, Ill., 1909 (Frank Lloyd Wright)

made his home, that most of his work was carried to completion. Of the Oak Park commissions the most famous was Unity (Universalist) Church, an uncompromising bid for prominence in poured concrete which still dominates the center of the town. As whimsical as Unity Temple was forbidding were the Midway Gardens which the architect laid out in 1914 on the South Side of Chicago. These pleasure grounds were, however, destroyed shortly after the Eighteenth Amendment put an end to drinking in public.

WRIGHT'S CONTEMPORARIES, MODERN AND UNMODERN

Though Wright was the greatest architect of the Chicago School, he did not stand alone. Nor can his rivals be slighted as so many imitators of his mannerisms. In recent years scholar after scholar has investigated the early twentieth century in the Middle West, and we now know something about the characteristics of Dwight H. Perkins, Guenzel and Drummond, Barry Byrne, and the others including Walter Burley Griffin and Purcell and Elmslie who were aware of Louis Sullivan's legacy. Sullivan to the contrary, architecture in Chicago did not die with the Fair.

Certainly Walter Burley Griffin deserved the reputation he was winning in America on the eve of the First World War. He is usually, and perhaps rightly, identified as the winner of the competition in 1912 for the plan of Canberra, the capital of Australia, a stroke of luck which unfortunately removed him from America for the rest of his life. He died in 1937 at sixty-one while working on the plans for the library of Lucknow University, and most, though not all, of his designs were executed in Australia and India.

Griffin was a graduate of Wright's office. But this does not mean that he borrowed his vocabulary as casually as he might his rubbers or raincoat. He shared certain of Wright's objectives, as did his wife, the former Marion Mahony, who spent eleven years as the master's draftsman. In the four years he himself collaborated with the inventor of the Prairie style, he came to acquire an almost magical sympathy for the nature of materials, and a poetic reverence for the possibilities of a site.

Griffin may have done his greatest work on continents other than our own, but before leaving the United States he succeeded in creating one of the irreplaceable houses of the twentieth century. This was the residence of the real estate speculator J. C. Melson in Mason City, Iowa, planned in 1912. A fantasy in rough stone on the brink of what had once been the town ash heap—altered at his suggestion into a romantic ravine—this showed a command of stone which Wright was not to equal for many years, not, indeed, until the building of "Taliesin West." Mason City may one day regret that no public protest was made over the re-

Unity Temple, Oak Park, Ill, 1906 (Frank Lloyd Wright)

Interior, Unity Temple

modeling of this masterpiece by the present owner. Since the negative for our illustration was taken, nearly every trace of the architect's intentions has been obliterated.

Like Griffin, the firm of Purcell and Elmslie made far too great a contribution to American architecture to be omitted from this brief survey. While Griffin was encouraged by Wright, William Gray Purcell and the late George Grant Elmslie drew their inspiration directly from Sullivan. Purcell, who stepped into the office of the creator of the Auditorium for three months following his graduation from Cornell, knew all there was to be learned about modern architecture on the West Coast as well as in his native Chicago, for he spent almost two years with John Galen Howard in San Francisco. In 1910, ready to build his own reputation, he asked Elmslie, who had been Sullivan's trusted assistant for twenty-one years, to join him in partnership. The firm, which went under the title of Purcell, Feick and Elmslie until 1913, when George Feick abandoned the profession, was then renamed Purcell and Elmslie. It was not dissolved until 1922, on Purcell's retirement. In the dozen years of its existence, it set standards in its best work that Wright alone could equal and that no one surpassed.

Elmslie came closer than anyone to understanding Sullivan, and the firm was loyal, as was none other, to his principles. This was especially evident in the terra cotta encrusted interior of the Woodbury County Court House at Sioux City, Iowa, completed in 1917 in collaboration with William L. Steele, Connoisseurs could tell that Sullivan owed much to Elmslie. It was the younger man who designed not only much of the decoration of the Guaranty and Bayard buildings, but also all of the ornamental work of the Schlesinger and Mayer Store.

Since it was Elmslie who suggested the great arches of Sullivan's Owatonna bank, the new firm could hardly avoid specializing in banking houses for country towns. The finest of these, the Merchants National Bank of Winona, Minnesota, carried to completion in 1911, was an achievement with which Sullivan himself could have found no fault. The brick façade, in spite of the stretch of glass lighting the banking room, was one of the most coherent compositions of the Chicago School. And there was true elegance in the blazes of terra cotta over the entrance and at the sides.

For all their success with public and commercial buildings, Purcell and Elmslie were at their best with private houses—the very branch of his practice which was of such slight interest to Sullivan that he did not hesitate to let Wright work up any domestic commissions that came into the office. One of the most charming houses conceived by Purcell and Elmslie was the **T**-shaped frame cottage at Moylan-Rose Valley, Pennsylvania, of Purcell himself. Though this was erected as long ago as 1918, its warmth and ease were prophetic of the aims of the most advanced architects of the West Coast in our time.

There was next to no ornament applied to this bungalow; neither was there any trace of Elmslie's decorative instinct in the greatest of all the houses created by the firm, the residence at Woods Hole, Massachusetts, of Harold C. Bradley, son-in-law of the benevolent Chicago millionaire Charles R. Crane. Dating from 1912, twenty-five years after McKim planned the simplified summerhouse at Bristol, Rhode Island, of W. G. Low, this could be compared with the very best of the early work of McKim, Mead and White. Like the Low house, this shingled invention of Purcell and Elmslie was meant to weather any storm of the coast and its **T**-plan, allowing the utmost enjoyment of the view, was so well suited to the promontory overlooking the ocean that you might think the Bradleys settled on the site long before the first blueberry bush clung to the windswept hillside.

Though the partnership was disbanded ten years after the Bradley house was finished, the firm's influence could not be so easily dated. Bertram Goodhue, who posed as a repentant sinner at the close of his prosperous career as Ralph Adams Cram's associate, may have been thinking about what Purcell and Elmslie accomplished when he confessed he could no longer derive any pleasure from eclectic work. Said Goodhue: "The discovery of reinforced concrete and the invention of the steel frame put, or so I think, all historic forms on the blink, so that Gothic-detailed office buildings, like the Woolworth Building, or that Classic-detailed public buildings . . . are equally absurd."

Whatever the future may think of Ralph Adams Cram, there can be no doubt that he was highly regarded in the 1920s. He got his share of honorary degrees from college presidents who were impressed by his scholarly if uninspired Gothic churches, and he would remind the young of his achievements by displaying his honorary degrees on the title pages of his books. Were the young impressed? This is doubtful. In any event he did his best to keep the young in their place. "I took the position," he recalled, in speaking of the years when he was head of the school of architecture at MIT, "that my function was not to get men into the architectural profession but to keep them out." There was always the danger that the young might try something "modern." "The modernist idea in the field of art," he argued at the close of his autobiography, "has its own place and it may and should go to it. Its boundaries are definite and fixed, and beyond them it cannot go, for the Angel of Decency, Propriety and Reason stands there with a flaming sword."

Cram's contemporary, Addison Mizner, who struck it rich in the Florida Land Boom of the 1920s, did not take himself half so seriously, which may be one reason why the Spanish stage set he created for the millionaires wintering in Palm Beach has its appeal for those who can scarcely imagine what it meant to enter Mizner's Everglades Club on the arm of Paris Singer of the sewing machine dynasty. If Wright was the Wagner of twentieth-century American architecture, Mizner was its Offenbach. Two of his most expensive houses, "Playa Riente," where Mrs. Hugh Dillman—once the wife of Horace Dodge—found her refuge from the climate of Grosse Pointe, and "El Mirasol," where Mrs. E. T. Stotesbury of Philadelphia held her court, have vanished, but Worth Avenue, where the Duke of Windsor felt completely at home, is still there to tell something of his ambition.

One splendid client beyond Mizner's reach was the Chicago millionaire James Deering of International Harvester who decided in 1914 to build the serene "Villa Vizcaya," a palace on Biscayne Bay at Miami. His architect was F. Burrall Hoffman, a graduate of the Carrère and Hastings office, who knew how to evoke a Venetian villa on the Brenta for this fastidious Chicagoan; the great formal garden was the work of Diego Suarez. Now a museum, "Villa Vizcaya" was originally intended to house Deering's vast collection of antiques.*

WRIGHT YESTERDAY AND TODAY

Unfortunately for the 1920's, Frank Lloyd Wright was the only prominent architect who dared to design in what Goodhue referred to as "the freer styles, those less hampered by rules." For this he paid a penalty; hounded by creditors, he was saved from bankruptcy only by the intervention of a few of his good friends, headed by the Darwin D. Martins. Nor was this his only embarrassment. "Taliesin," his home in the Wisconsin hills went up in flames for a second time, and his second wife had him thrown into the county jail at Minneapolis before permitting the divorce which made possible his marriage to his third and last wife, the former Olga Lazovich of Montenegro.

Wright braved the 1920's by insisting that now or never was the time

---

* Perhaps the most alarming sight in the Florida of the 1970s is Miami's Fontainebleau Hotel, a vast pile of concrete boasting a Getting-To-Know-You Room, where boys may meet girls and girls, boys. This was conceived in 1954 by Morris Lapidus, who might well have planned the sets for a James Bond movie. Of late, Lapidus has had to face the competition in the hotel field offered by John Calvin Portman, Jr., who got his start with the Hyatt Regency Hotel of 1967 in Atlanta, a futuristic fantasy sponsored by the Pritzker family of Chicago. "It's hard to sell just a pillow," remarked one of the Pritzker executives. "You have to sell some sizzle, too." The sizzle was also evident in Portman's Detroit Renaissance Center, which opened in 1977, featuring the Detroit Plaza Hotel surrounded by the glass towers of office buildings for Ford and other employees.

Residence of J. G. Melson, Mason City, Ia., 1912 (Walter Burley Griffin)

Merchants' National Bank, Winona, Minn., 1911 (Purcell, Feick & Elmslie)

Residence of H. C. Bradley, Woods Hole, Mass., 1912 (Purcell & Elmslie)

to experiment with untried methods of construction. This was, if you will, the innocence of Woodrow Wilson suggesting in the last days in the White House that his ideal successor would be a labor leader, but it was also the conviction of an artist who had done more than dabble with engineering. The Imperial Hotel at Tokyo, over which he labored from 1916 to 1922, seconded by Paul Mueller, a veteran of the Adler and Sullivan office, withstood, exactly as he intended, the earthquake of 1923, and he could say—who could contradict him?—that this was because the hotel was balanced like a tray on a waiter's fingers.

Wright's houses in the early 1920's were designed according to what has usually been described as the "textile block" system. In simplified language this means that they were built of precast cement blocks, reinforced by metal, over which he allowed his decorative impulse to stray with a gay indifference for the canons of his rivals. The most brilliant of all these textile block houses was "La Miniatura," conceived in 1923 for Mrs. George Madison Millard, whose husband, an executive of McClurg's Bookstore, Chicago, had seventeen years earlier asked him to build one of the Prairie style designs at Highland Park. Sunk in a ravine at Pasadena, California, "La Miniatura" provided an almost Persian surprise, with a pool reflecting the picturesque impress on the blocks; what was more important, its decidedly vertical elevation proved that Wright would never again return to the manner of his early Chicago successes.

There were few other commissions in this decade, and in his idle moments the architect brooded over the dislike for big cities which he had never outgrown since his first sight of Chicago. "Broadacre City"—so he labeled the model of the decentralized metropolis of his dreams when it was exhibited in 1935—told of his longing for an America minus her skyscrapers, a strange new land in which there would be no cities at all in our sense of the word, but thousands of villages combining, as he believed, the advantages of both urban and rural environment.

Wright may have been mortified by the neglect of the 1920's; if so, he must have been amazed by the revival of interest in his work which took place at the very time when the American people re-elected Roosevelt in 1936. The New Deal's emphasis on redistribution of incomes was answered immediately by this artist, who planned house after house for Americans of middling though not surprising wealth in the late thirties.

The architect had traveled far since the days of the Prairie style, as you could tell by glancing at one of the many excellent examples of the medium-sized house in this period, the country home at Libertyville, Illinois, of the newspaperman Lloyd Lewis, completed in 1940. The Lewis house was of course intimately related to the landscape, in this instance to the bank of the creeklike Des Plaines River. But this long, low-slung narrow design on the river bank was as asymmetrical as the early houses

"La Miniatura," residence of Mrs. George M. Millard, Pasadena, Calif., 1923 (Frank Lloyd Wright)

"Taliesin East," Spring Green, Wis., 1925 (Frank Lloyd Wright)

were symmetrical. And though the flow of space from one living quarter to another was as easy as ever, the broad eaves of Wright's early work were missing; instead there were trellises over the porches. Much, then, had been gained and nothing lost, for the architect's instinct for materials—here he built of brick and light wood sheathing—was as faultless as in the beginning of his career.

The Lewis house was a thing of beauty constructed on a modest budget. "Falling Water," the retreat at Bear Run, Pennsylvania, of the Pittsburgh department store executive Edgar J. Kaufmann, was a magnificent monument erected with no thought of expense, and Wright was never for a second unaware that this was one of the great opportunities of a lifetime. Since all photographs of "Falling Water"—including those in this book—give a false impression of the grandeur of this design, it may not be a mistake to point out that the house was built mostly of rough stone; the white concrete slabs cantilevered over the tumbling mountain stream which gives the estate its name were simply the bold projections of the porches, projections unhappily overemphasized by the best of lenses.

This is the most famous modern house in the world, and not undeservedly, for no other architect in recent times has wooed and won a site so spectacular. But "Falling Water" is something more than the perfect answer to a romantic question; its irregular, asymmetrical plan is contrived with amazing cunning to reflect the informal existence of a Pittsburgh executive on his weekends in the country, and is as admirable an expression of the casual manners of our day as the Breese house by McKim, Mead and White of the formality of 1906.

The most famous of all modern office buildings is also the work of Wright—which is just what you should expect, since the inventor of "Falling Water" has never cared to believe that he was merely a domestic architect. In his opinion there is no good reason for forcing the employees of a great corporation to labor in surroundings which are hygienic and nothing more, and in the Administration Building for the Johnson Wax Company of Racine, Wisconsin, begun in 1936, the year the Kaufmann house was completed, he proved he had no intention of saving his greatest surprises for men of great wealth. Without, the Johnson headquarters is an apparently windowless brick pile, curiously curved; within, the typists, once they lift their eyes from the keys, gaze not on the usual bare ceiling, but on lily-pad columns vanishing into pyrex glass tubing, from which the daylight gently descends.

This was not the only occasion on which Wright bent over his drafting board for the greater glory of S. C. Johnson and Son. In 1949, ten years after the Administration Building was finished, he conceived the Research Tower next to the firm's offices. Often described in technical terms as a web of glass spun around a hollow reinforced concrete stem,

Residence of E. J. Kaufmann, Bear Run, Pa., 1936 (Frank Lloyd Wright)

Living room, residence of E. J. Kaufmann

this was as eloquent an advertisement of the corporation's quest for new products as its companion building of the working conditions at Racine.

Meantime in downtown San Francisco, just off Union Square, Wright had shown that not even a gift shop need be trivial. Perhaps the most beautiful design of his career was the windowless façade of brick he composed in 1949 for V. C. Morris, the owner of a store specializing in glassware. Behind the startlingly simple round-arched entrance lay a snail-like ramp tempting customers to a ceiling of glass bubbles.

You might say that Wright paid a moment's homage to the arches of the Sullivan bank at Owatonna before sketching the Morris shop front, but you could not trace any particular precedent in the campus of Florida Southern College at Lakeland, unless it were an occasional backward glance at his own experiments in textile blocks and poured concrete. Linked by arcades that recalled the arabesques of "La Miniatura," the Chapel, the Library, and the Administration Building of Florida Southern were so many improvisations on the theme suggested by the climate. Never before were reinforced concrete blocks thrust, as here, into forms that might have been created, not by man, but by the tropical heat.

Because he believed that education was too serious a matter to be entrusted to educators, Wright saw to it that the Administration Building at Florida Southern was fixed on the brink of a pool whose dazzling reflections made anything as conventional as the usual gestures of authority unthinkable. You could imagine an amiable teacher sitting beside this pool, but you could not conceive of a merely respectable academic figure tolerating this, the gayest campus in America, for an instant.

Florida Southern was a glorious invitation, even for this ambitious architect. The layout called for sixteen units, not all of which have been completed. This was most unfortunate, for the publicity that greeted the Pfeiffer Chapel of 1940, the Roux Library of 1942, the Administration Building of 1948, and the Industrial Arts Building of 1952 was such that no board of trustees in its right mind could think of abandoning the program.

No church has been so generous to Wright, but he has not been forgotten by the Unitarians, in whose pulpits both his father and his grandfather were preachers. In 1951 he created the First Unitarian Meeting House at Madison, Wisconsin, and to make sure that the houses of worship of tomorrow would in no way resemble those of yesterday, insisted on a roofline that might have been patterned after a dropped handkerchief. This was not an eccentric note; the interior of the auditorium was as warm as it was original, and his feeling for materials—this long, low, broad-eaved design was built of the rough stone of the Wisconsin hillsides—was everywhere evident.

Research Center, Johnson Wax Co., Racine, Wis., 1951 (Frank Lloyd Wright)

Interior, Administration Building, Johnson Wax Co., 1939 (Frank Lloyd Wright)

But to speak of Wright's architecture without describing the two country houses he planned for his own use would be as vain as to tell the tale of Merlin without a word as to his cavern. The greatest achievements of this enchanter have naturally enough been monuments to himself. "Democracy," he has not hesitated to tell us, "can live by genius only. Its very soul is individuality."

Twice damaged by fire, "Taliesin East," his retreat in the hills of Spring Green, Wisconsin, has been rebuilt with the devotion Wagner might have spent rewriting the score of a demolished opera. This was not simply because the architect was fond of his home. Here was the evidence in rough stone, evidence he would have last through the ages, that he meant what he said when he announced that "no house should ever be *on* any hill or *on* anything. It should be *of* the hill, belonging to it, so hill and house should live together each the happier for the other."

You may, if you are able to resist the spell of this shrine, wonder if the day has not passed for mottoes in any American home, even here. You may even suspect that Wright fell under the influence at one time or another of Elbert Hubbard. In this you may not be mistaken. The architect once designed a house in Buffalo for the sister of the author of "The Message to Garcia." Very likely, he decided he had much to learn about publicity from the supersalesman who retired from the Larkin soap company to found the incredibly successful Roycroft Press.

It is just possible that it was Hubbard who taught Wright there was no easier way of attracting attention than wearing one's hair long and sporting flowing ties. After all, the nation listened when the editor of *The Philistine* preached: "Wear thy hair long: it is a sign that thou art free." Wright may have listened more attentively than anyone else, for he and Hubbard were one in their admiration for the teachings of William Morris.

Possibly, too, the architect might never have dreamed of ending his days as a patriarch surrounded by young admirers if he had not been aware of what the founder of the Roycroft Press accomplished at East Aurora. The Taliesin Fellowship of future architects come to learn the secrets of the profession from the master had more than a little in common with the Roycrofters—in Spring Green as at East Aurora, young people were obliged to recognize that, as Hubbard put it, "all work is respectable, including the dirty work."

No doubt, if Hubbard had lived long enough to visit "Taliesin East," he would have been pleased to find the sayings of great men printed broad on the walls for the edification of all guests. There were no numbers on the doors of the rooms in the inn at East Aurora that he built to house the worshipers who flocked to observe the press in action. Instead, the rooms were *named*—"named after the famous men and

V.C. Morris Store, San Francisco, Calif., 1949
(Frank Lloyd Wright)

Detail, façade, V.C. Morris Store

women of all time—Socrates, Edison, George Eliot, Beethoven, William Morris, and Susan B. Anthony."

Whether Hubbard, who will be remembered less as a philosopher than as a pioneer in the advertising business, would have appreciated the beauties of "Taliesin East" is another matter. He might have been baffled by the sight of a house designed to suit the needs of an individual who differed so radically from the average American reached by the publications of the Roycroft Press.

Wright's ambition, as you may have guessed long before this, was far too fierce to resemble that of the average American. You can sense this at "Taliesin East." For once you grow used to the uninterrupted flow of space, to the touch which blends one building material with another, and to the wizard-like identification of site with stone, you will have to admit that this house was peculiarly his own because it never could be finished as long as he lived. Though begun in 1925, the present "Taliesin East" is a dateless structure, constantly rebuilt and altered to meet the master's whims and the demands of the students who joined the Fellowship.

"Taliesin West," Wright's refuge in the winter in the Arizona desert near Phoenix, is sure to perplex historians who insist on such things as dates. First laid out in 1938, its seemingly disobedient plan, spreading carelessly through the sands, tells that the architect has never recognized either any limit to his building operations or to the size of his staff.

Built of red desert stone, its lines dotted against the horizon, and its planes broken with diabolical accuracy, "Taliesin West" might be the last glad sight on the road to hell, so strangely is it identified with this, the most unfriendly site in the United States. Wright was ninety-one when he died in 1959, and could not complain, with eight hundred-odd projects brought to completion, that he had been neglected in the United States. If, occasionally, a design looked hurried, who could object? In his eighties he was as keen as in his twenties, as you could tell from glancing at the Douglas Grant house in Cedar Rapids, Iowa, dating from 1951, or the H. T. Mossberg house in South Bend, Indiana, dating from 1952. By 1955, when he was eighty-eight, he at last conquered that conservative citadel Lake Forest, Illinois, with the home of the broker Charles F. Glore. And in the year of his death he was watching the completion of the Guggenheim Museum in New York, whose snail-like ramps told the twentieth century that a museum could be entertaining.

"Who gains promotions, boons, appointments," William James once asked, "but the man in whose life they are seen to play the part of live hypotheses?" He could have been describing the master of "Taliesin West." Such was Wright's daring that we could never tell which way he would leap tomorrow. We have only known that he landed with both

Administration Building, Florida Southern College, Lakeland, Fla., 1948 (Frank Lloyd Wright)

First Unitarian Meeting House, Madison, Wis., 1951 (Frank Lloyd Wright)

Interior, First Unitarian Meeting House

feet on the ground, fixing with the stare of a basilisk anyone who doubted his missision here on earth.

Frank Lloyd Wright was indestructible. No tragedy could stay his step, not even the horror of July 4, 1914, when a crazed handyman from Barbados set "Taliesin East" on fire and murdered not only Wright's mistress Mamah Borthwick Cheney, the wife of one of his Oak Park clients, but also two of her children and four others on Wright's staff.

Study and office, "Taliesin West," Phoenix, Ariz., 1938 (Frank Lloyd Wright)

Entrance from west, "Taliesin West"

Interior, living room

CHAPTER SEVEN

Modern Times

THE MODERN MUDDLE

If the aims of modern architecture are frequently misunderstood, the architects may be to blame, and so may the critics. Though the author may be guilty of adding to this confusion, he cannot resist discussing what are, in his opinion, the three major fallacies of modern architectural criticism.

The first fallacy may be described as the *temporal* fallacy. According to this notion, the architect is bound by some sort of higher law to express the spirit of his time. The Swiss architect Le Corbusier, who had his brilliant moments, may be more responsible than anyone else for this dictum's widespread acceptance. As you may remember, if you have read *Vers une architecture,* Le Corbusier sang something like a hymn to airplanes, steamships, office furniture, typewriters, fountain pens, and Gillette razors. These, he said, were so many incarnations of our time. Architecture should be equally obedient.

To this theory many objections may be raised. First of all, no one can help expressing in one way or another the spirit of his time. More than likely, the temporal fallacy is based on a misunderstanding of the preface to Taine's history of English literature. You may recall that the great French historian found the key to cultural history in race, environment, and the spirit of the age—"*la race, le milieu, et le moment.*" It is no exaggeration to say that cultural history has never been the same since Taine made this discovery. But that is not the same thing as saying that all artists are dutybound to fit into such a framework. André Gide, who protested that he, for one, was interested only in artists who fought against the spirit of their times, could not help singling out for special praise those who were misunderstood because they provided answers to questions not yet asked.

The influence of the temporal fallacy is not confined, of course, to the work of those who have read Taine. You may observe this influence merely by taking a walk in your home town. All too many piles of glass and steel across the land symbolize the conviction of well-meaning architects that such materials must be used, not because they are appropriate—they often are—but because they are the materials of our time. Inside these buildings human beings have been roasted many times over in the noonday sun: air conditioning, while expensive, is not infallible. And then there are the smudges of fingerprints on the omnipresent glass doors.

The second fallacy may be described as the *intellectualistic* fallacy. According to this notion, the architect is not like other men. He is a hyperintellectual who dearly loves to argue the premises of post-Newtonian physics. Buildings created by such designers cannot, of course, be properly appreciated by the average man who merely likes or dislikes the look of things. According to Sigfried Giedion, the Bauhaus planned by Walter Gropius is just such a building. It is an expression of the "conception of space-time." We must never forget, says Dr. Giedion, that "space in modern physics is conceived of as relative to a moving point of reference, not as the absolute and static entity of the baroque system of Newton." All this would delight any scientist with a sense of humor. For scientists have been taught that post-Newtonian physics may be of more help in measuring time on planets beyond our ken than in walking up and down a flight of stairs on earth.

Following in the footsteps of the earnest Dr. Giedion, Robert Venturi has been spellbound by the possibilities of *Complexity and Contradiction in Architecture,* to quote the title of his recent treatise. Venturi has made the discovery that the "double-functioning element" may be a thrilling ingredient in modern architecture. In common every-day English, this is a little like saying that a door has two functions: it can let you in and it can let you out. Venturi's ideas are obvious, and his buildings are banal, a fact of which he boasts in public. It is his prose that is complicated, requiring, as one of his best friends admits, "professional commitment and close visual attention." In his *Learning from Las Vegas,* he went into rapture over the Strip, but his rapture was purely intellectual. It is hard to believe that he ever trusted his luck at the gambling tables.

The third fallacy may be described as the *moral* fallacy. Even though there is no evidence that the most beautiful building in the world—you may make your own selection—has improved anyone's morals, this has not stopped certain modern critics from suggesting that more than one problem that has been perplexing mankind could be solved on the drafting board. Lewis Mumford, for instance, has referred to the modern American kitchen as "the moral flower of that long discipline of the spirit which Western man has undertaken during the last millennium under the forms of monasticism, militarism and mechanism."

Like that of the temporal fallacy, the influence of the moral fallacy is felt every day in the week. Open almost any ambitious architectural magazine, and you will be told that the best sermons of the twentieth century are preached in glass and poured concrete.

If you doubt that these three fallacies are popular, if you think the public understands what modern architecture is all about, strike up a conversation with almost any architect. Before you know it, he will fall back on the temporal fallacy, and start telling you that unless we express the spirit of our times we are in danger of going back to Williamsburg for inspiration, or worse yet, to the Ecole des Beaux-Arts.

The truth, of course, is that traditionalism today is worse than a lost cause—it is unfashionable. In fact it is so unfashionable that only a young man with a martyr complex would dare to remind his classmates in architectural school that it was time to turn back the clock.

The battle of the twentieth century, which is fierce enough to amuse anyone who recollects that this is not the first time that artists have disagreed about art, is not over whether we should build in the modern or in the traditional manner, but over what kind of modern is worth building. In spite of the fact that a poll of a hundred architects might give an innocent observer the impression that there are no fewer than a hundred varieties of American architecture, it is safe to say that there are only two brands marketed in our generation by designers positive they are accomplishing a mission. One of these brands might be labeled Veblenite, after the economist Thorstein Veblen. The other might be labeled Jacobite, after the philosopher William James.

VEBLEN VERSUS JAMES

In case you have not dipped into Veblen's *Theory of the Leisure Class* since your college days, you may wonder what he has to do with specifications and other worries of the architectural profession. But if you take the trouble to read over his remarks on the evils of conspicuous consumption, you will discover that his dread of luxury is shared by more than one modern architect. It was Veblen, after all, who remarked at the height of the age of elegance that "considered as objects of beauty, the dead walls of the sides and backs of [New York apartment houses] left untouched by the hand of the artist, are commonly the best feature of the building."

The mortal enemy of exuberance, Veblen made a point of preferring machine-made spoons to hand-wrought silver spoons. "The case of the spoons is typical," he said. "The superior gratification derived from the use and contemplation of costly and supposedly beautiful objects is, commonly, in great measure a gratification of our sense of costliness masquerading under the name of beauty."

Veblen was too emphatic a critic to be rejected as of no account even by the bitterest of his enemies. Yet it must be said that his horror of conspicuous consumption was something quite different from the irritation of a common-sense American appalled by the wastefulness of our economy in the days before the income tax checked the extravagance of the very rich. What he deplored was not the spending of foolish sums of money but the expression of untrammeled individualism in any form. A ruthless individualist himself, he dreamed of a world in which we should all conform to a pattern laid down by an omniscient legislator who knew what was best for the average man.

As an anti-individualist, Veblen looked forward to the day when the small town businessman would be extinct. One of his pet projects in the First World War would have set up a mail order system under the Post Office with that very end in view. And if he had had his way, the old ladies would have been taxed out of footmen and coachmen.

William James delivered a different message to the American people. He was positive that a conscious striving for splendor was foolish. But then so was the worship of austerity for austerity's sake. As flexible as Veblen was inflexible, he liked to think that "truth *happens* to an idea. It *becomes* true, or is *made* true, by events."

Unlike Veblen, who as the social scientist David Riesman has reminded us, "did want men to live by bread alone, provided Consumers' Research had studied the ingredients and no middle man had made a profit on the loaf," James thought nothing was gained by throttling individuals for the mere pleasure of throttling. "The personal and romantic view of life," he said, "has other roots besides wanton exuberance of imagination and perversity of heart. It is perennially fed by the *facts of experience*." He liked to repeat the saying of a carpenter who found that there was very little difference between one man and another, but what little there was, was very important. "This distinction," James remarked, "seems to me to go to the heart of the matter."

Though there is no way of knowing what he would have thought of the final answers implied in Veblen's punitive program, he could scarcely have approved of the economist's drastic remedies. "There is," James declared, "no complete generalization, no total point of view, no all-pervasive unity, but everywhere some residual resistance to verbalization, formulation, and discursification, some genius of reality that escapes from the pressure of the logical finger, that says *hands off* and claims its privacy, and means to be left to its own life."

James insisted that theories were only instruments, *"not answers to enigmas, in which we can rest.* We don't lie back on them," he made plain, "we move forward, and on occasion, make nature over again by their aid."

Since neither James nor Veblen ventured into architectural criticism, no one can tell exactly what would have been their likes and dislikes. But that should not stop us from stealing their names as symbols. After all, they were far apart in their conception of the role of the artist in the modern world, and probably would not object if we set them arguing after their death. They might even be amused to see their names scrawled across this sort of blackboard:

Veblenite Architects	*Jacobite Architects*
Cool	Warm
Impersonal	Personal
Anti-individualistic	Individualistic
Dogmatic	Casual
Absolutist	Pragmatic
Worshipers of the machine	Tolerant of the machine
Spellbound by modern materials, such as steel and glass	Fonder of the texture of materials than of their modernity
Experts at factories, sanitariums, and other impersonal buildings.	At their best in domestic work
Willing to disregard the site	Haunted by the site

To simplify matters still further, you might say that a Veblenite would rather listen to the answers of the machine, a Jacobite to the questions of man. There is, of course, something to be said for both points of view. Whether that something will be said in this book is something else. The author is not without his own bias.

ENTER THE VEBLENITES

The most prominent of all our Veblenites was Walter Gropius. Though he may not have read a word of Verblen in all his life, no modern architect has come closer to sharing the economist's suspicion that, epidemic for epidemic, the Black Plague would be more pleasant than rampant individualism. As long ago as 1923, when he was forty-one, Gropius reached the conclusion that "architecture is a collective art." He added that "the dominant spirit of our epoch is already recognizable although its form is not yet defined. The old dualistic world-concept which envisaged the ego in opposition to the universe is rapidly losing ground. In its place is rising the idea of a universal unity in which all opposing forces are in a state of absolute balance."

A state of absolute balance, he might have added, is not easily discovered in this world. In any event the individual was in need of reorientation. "Collective architectural work," he declared, "becomes possible only when every individual, prepared by proper schooling, is capable of understanding the idea of the whole, and thus has the means harmoniously to co-ordinate his independent, even if limited activity with the collective work."

A native of Berlin, he was so fortunate, when only twenty-six, as to become one of the assistants of Peter Behrens, the designer not only of the austere German Embassy in Saint Petersburg, but of the headquarters of the I. G. Farben Trust and the majestic turbine plants of the A. E. G., the electricity trust of Imperial Germany. These were achievements that should have inspired any assistant.

There is every reason to believe that Gropius would have been a happier man and a greater architect if he had been able to follow the example of his master and build an unlimited number of factories. But such was not the case. Aside from the Hall of Machines at the Deutscher Werkbund Exposition of 1914—which was, after all, an ideal factory, rather than a factory in operation—he is remembered for no more than two such buildings in his native Germany. Of these two, the more famous was the first, completed in 1914 for the Fagus shoe-last works at Alfeld near Hanover. This was far more than an honest expression of a steel box with glass walls. One of Gropius's admirers, who worships nothing so much as honesty, has pointed out that the glass and steel walls were cleanly joined at the corners, without the intervention of piers. Perhaps it would be more accurate as well as more flattering—we choose our friends for other reasons than their fresh-laundered shirts and their credit ratings—to suggest that the designer had done his best to think in novel terms of novel needs.

In 1919 the creator of the Fagus works was to make the most of an opportunity such as seldom comes to artists who are honest and nothing more. Appointed director of the Grand Ducal Art School and Arts and Crafts School of Weimar, he reorganized both institutions, united them under the title of Staatliches Bauhaus (or State School of Architecture), and in 1925 saw to it that the Bauhaus moved to Dessau. There he had the satisfaction of building the school's headquarters, a glasswalled shed that struck some observers as one of the masterpieces of twentieth-century architecture. Very like a factory, it was a genuine *tour de force*, ever so much more dramatic than the Fagus plant.

The day of the Belgian Henry van de Velde, who had championed the rights of the individual craftsman at Weimar before the war, was gone foreover. Gropius had decided that if the artist was to survive in the modern world, he must be the servant of industry. Coordination and integration became the watchwords of the school, and efficiency-plus the goal of the program. All this Veblen would have been bound to approve, for he was arguing at this time that the engineers (or efficiency experts) would have to rescue American business from the wastefulness of the captains of industry.

If you believed in the message of the Bauhaus, and there were many who did, the wise architect was the man who looked forward to designing radiators or doorknobs for the prefabricated buildings of tomorrow— in which there would be no trace of the hopes and fears of man in search of his personality. Whether this reasoning was valid could not be proved: the worldwide depression crippled Germany and German architecture, and Gropius was forced to flee from Hitler's Reich, first to England and then to the United States in 1937.

Were all the artists whom Gropius invited to the Bauhaus happy in this environment? This is doubtful. Lyonel Feininger, the American-born painter who returned to the United States when Hitler came to power, was baffled by the dogma that ruled that art and engineering should be chained as one. "A genuine engineer would never care to interfere in artistic matters," he claimed. "And even the greatest engineering skill can never take the place of the divine inspiration of art." Count Harry Kessler, the great connoisseur who counted Gerhart Hauptmann, Hugo von Hofmannsthal, André Gide, and Jean Cocteau among his closest friends, was even more depressed when he contemplated an exhibit in Paris of the Bauhaus products. *"Arme-Leute-Kunst"* (freely translated, *art for the deserving poor*) was his comment. Kessler recognized that Gropius could never rise to the level of Peter Behrens, or for that matter that of Henry van de Velde, whom he had championed in prewar Weimar.

The master of the Bauhaus was not unknown in the New World. In 1932 the Museum of Modern Art of New York staged an exhibition of the so-called International Style in which particular attention was paid to Gropius and his fellow Veblenites Oud of Holland, Le Corbusier of Switzerland, and Miës van der Rohe of Germany. This salute from the museum staff could not be ignored. After a stay in England, Gropius was invited to head the School of Architecture at Harvard University.

As Gropius could not help noticing, there were designers in America who excelled at impersonal buildings and yet were unwilling to be dogmatic. Easily the most successful of these was Albert Kahn. The favorite architect of Packard, Chrysler, Ford, and General Motors, he was obliged to maintain a staff of as many as four hundred to handle his factory business, which ran as high as a million dollars a week in 1929. Best remembered as the inventor of "the daylight factory," he proved he was an innovator as early as 1905, when at thirty-six he completed Building Number Ten at the Packard plant in Detroit. In this, his first reinforced

Apartment houses at 860-880 Lake Shore Drive, Chicago, Ill., 1951 (Ludwig Miës van der Rohe)

Crown Hall, Illinois Institute of Technology, Chicago, Ill., 1954 (Ludwig Miës van der Rohe)

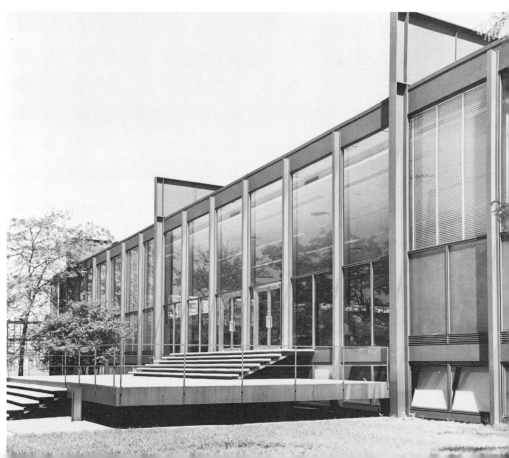

concrete factory, he made a feature of the extensive window openings which were to be his trademark.

Although Kahn rejoiced in the success which came to him, he refused to lay down the law for his rivals, even when, as in 1938, he was responsible for 18 percent of all architect-designed building in the United States. "Architecture," he announced more than once, "is 90 percent business and 10 percent art." And he was never afraid to confess that he was a lucky individual. "When I began," he used to say, "the real architects would design only museums, cathedrals, capitols, monuments. The office boy was considered good enough for factories. I'm still that office boy designing factories. I have no dignity to be impaired."

There was no universal formula, of that Kahn was convinced. "Evolution is preferable to revolution," he told critics who questioned the "reuse of well-tried forms" in his nonindustrial work. Of all his buildings, his favorite was the Clements Library at the University of Michigan, in which he paid homage to the later work of McKim, Mead and White. In the General Motors Building of 1920 in Detroit he saluted the later, Renaissance accomplishments of Daniel H. Burnham.

Kahn's reluctance to play a solemn role might not have distressed the earnest Veblenites if his industrial architecture had been no more than the clever calculation of costs per square foot. But the truth—and this was exasperating—was that his factories were often works of art. Perhaps the best of all was the Dodge Half-Ton Truck Plant at Warren, Michigan, completed in 1938, four years before his death. A shed of glass and steel, this was as graceful as it was spare.

Faced with Kahn's phenomenal success as a businessman and as an artist, Gropius refused to abandon his lifelong crusade against the evils of individualism; in Cambridge as in Dessau he called on his pupils to be true to the collective gospel. "A building designed by one man and carried out for him by a number of purely executant assistants cannot hope to achieve more than a superficial unity," he insisted. He also hesitated to expose his students to architectural history. "When the innocent beginner is introduced to the great achievements of the past, he may be too easily discouraged from trying to create for himself."

There were times when Gropius felt his voice was unheeded. "Today," he announced in 1952 on his retirement from fifteen years of teaching at Harvard, "the architect is not the 'master of the building industry.' Deserted by the last craftsmen (who have gone into industry, toolmaking, testing, and researching), he has remained sitting all alone on his anachronistic brick pile, pathetically unaware of the colossal impact of industrialization. The architect is in a very real danger of losing his grip in competition with the engineer, the scientist, and the builder unless he adjusts his attitude and aims to meet the new situation."

To prove what might be accomplished if a number of designers joined

Residence of Philip Johnson, New Canaan, Conn., 1949 (Philip Johnson)

Residence of Walter Gropius, Lincoln, Mass., 1938 (Walter Gropius)

hands and freely abandoned all hope of expressing their respective personalities, Gropius persuaded certain of the most promising of his admirers to enter into TAC, or The Architects' Collaborative, a kind of architectural corporation of which he was chairman of the board. Though this group put up several private houses at Lexington near Cambridge, its most important commission was the Graduate Center at Harvard, built in 1950. Consisting of eight concrete units whose walls were of limestone and buff-colored brick, this did not make quite the impression on the public that Gropius could have wished. No one as yet has doubted that this was an anonymous performance, but there have been misgivings as to the appropriateness of the design for Cambridge. The buff-colored brick and limestone were sure to weather wearily in the smoky air, and more than one observer came away positive that the members of TAC were utterly indifferent to the nature of materials.

But as his friend Dr. Giedion rightly observed, the idea of teamwork was "part of Gropius's very nature as well as of his actions." If he could not always be the captain of the team, at least he could play the game. One team he joined was that of Emery Roth and Sons, who asked Gropius and Pietro Belluschi, once head of the School of Architecture at MIT, to collaborate on the Pan-Am Building in New York City. This undistinguished and unnecessary skyscraper signed the death sentence for Grand Central Station in 1963. Although the engineers Reed and Stem, along with Colonel William J. Wilgus, had done their best to complement the work of the architects Warren and Wetmore, devising delightfully gradual ramps down to the tracks, and skirting traffic around the station by ramps that led up to Forty-sixth Street, the Pan-Am Building insured the congestion that until then had been shrewdly avoided. It also banished from men's eyes the focal points provided by the station and Warren and Wetmore's New York Central Building to the north. Park Avenue was now deprived of its dignity.

Less damage to the American landscape was done by the three houses which Gropius and his partner from the Bauhaus, Marcel Breuer, conceived in 1938–39 for Lincoln, Massachusetts. One of these was meant for Gropius, another for Breuer, and the third for Professor James Ford of Harvard. It was immediately obvious that Gropius and Breuer were bewildered by the traditional American friendliness for frame construction. The timber of the vertical sidings on all three houses was painted a glistening white, so that on bright days it could scarcely be distinguished from cardboard or poured concrete.

Marcel Breuer, who began practicing on his own in 1940, was equally indifferent to texture in the two houses he built for himself in New Canaan, Connecticut. He was not the most sensitive of architects, as you could tell by his cry in the 1920s that "even if I try, I can see no chaos in our time." And although he was impressed, like so many other architects, by Le Corbusier's campaign in the 1950s to turn architecture into a form of sculpture, he could never capture the lyrical enthusiasm of his Swiss contemporary. His Saint John's Abbey of 1962 in Collegeville, Minnesota, was more theatrical than dramatic, and his Church of Saint Francis de Sales of 1967 in Muskegon, Michigan, was a ponderous essay in concrete. As for the Whitney Museum in New York of 1966, its concrete forms were gigantic rather than appealing. It is curious that he never realized that one of the needs of the Whitney would be elevators vast enough to transport the huge canvases of the American expressionists. In fact, the elevators were so cramped that one giant painting of Gottlieb had to be removed from its frame and rolled up before it could be placed on exhibition.

Ludwig Miës van der Rohe, who had the honor of taking Gropius's place at the Bauhaus shortly after the founder withdrew to go into private practice, was a far more interesting architect than either Gropius or Breuer. Ever meticulous, ever exacting, he had the intelligence in 1920–21 to invent a peerless formula for a skyscraper. The floors were cantilevered out from the central core of this unexecuted project, and the curtain walls were only a frame holding giant panes of glass. The formula was magical in Miës's hands, but it was a formula to which he was faithful, perhaps too faithful, until the day he died in 1969.

The limitations of Miës were evident in the statement he issued in 1924, when he was only thirty-eight. "The whole trend of our time," he said, "is toward the secular. The endeavors of the great mystics will be remembered as mere episodes. Despite our greater understanding of life, we shall build no cathedrals. Nor do the brave gestures of the romantics mean anything to us, for behind them we detect their empty form. Ours is not an age of pathos; we do not respect flights of the spirit so much as we value reason and realism. . . . We are concerned today with questions of a general nature. The individual is losing significance, his destiny is no longer what interests us. The decisive achievements in all fields are impersonal, and their authors are for the most part obscure. They are part of the trend of our times toward anonymity."

Here was a man for whom the other world had no appeal. And here was a man, no matter how accurate he might be in designing business buildings, who could never design a *private* house: privacy was one of the antique virtues.

Though Miës will always be identified with the trend toward anonymity that he so bravely championed in this statement to the press, he has made—perhaps in spite of himself—an individual contribution to modern architecture. The son of a stonemason at Aachen, at nineteen he talked the fashionable Berlin furniture designer Bruno Paul into giving him a job, and from that day forward was not neglected. Welcomed by Peter Behrens, the industrial pioneer in whose office he worked side by side with Le Corbusier, he proceeded in 1929 to plan the German pavilion at the Barcelona Exposition.

An undeniably elegant structure of Roman travertine, this was one design by Miës of which Veblen could not have approved. The architect was guilty in this instance not only of using expensive materials, but also, so it seemed, of enjoying the confusion of critics who caught him in the act. There was even a pool lined with green Tinian marble in the courtyard of this deceptively simple masterpiece.

The Barcelona pavilion was not forgotten, nor were his superb if demanding Barcelona chairs, when he arrived in the United States to begin a new career in 1938. Named head of the department of architecture of Chicago's Armour Institute, later reorganized as the Illinois Institute of Technology, he began laying out its campus from 1942 to 1954. Here, in what had been a slum neighborhood bordering the right-of-way of the New York Central tracks, he provided an astonishing exhibit of meticulous craftsmanship in brick, steel, and glass. The campus might *almost* pass for a series of factory buildings built by and for a crew of automatons. Almost, but not quite. While Saint Savior's Chapel might better be used as a dental laboratory than as a church, there is a compelling fascination in Crown Hall of the architectural school. His accuracy in this instance was delightful and the flexibility of the plan enviable.

Miës was not half so successful when it came to designing for Dr. Edith Farnsworth, a well-to-do Chicago physician, a weekend cottage on the bank of her favorite creek at Plano, not far from O'Hare Airport. This was a bleak thing: it led to a lawsuit between him and his disappointed client.

Perhaps because he could imagine the requirements of landlords easier than he could those of an individual, he was entirely at ease in 1951 when planning the twin apartment towers at 860–880 Lake Shore Drive. These two bare but splendid buildings—curtains of glass hung on steel—were a more welcome and dramatic addition to D. H. Burnham's lake front.

Equally exciting is the Seagram Building on Park Avenue, New York, completed in 1955 with the assistance of Philip Johnson, who, with Henry Russell Hitchcock, had arranged the International Style show of 1932. No corner was cut on 860–880 Lake Shore Drive or the Seagram Building, and Miës was always at his best when no expense was spared. It is in his minor housing developments, such as Lafayette Park in Detroit and the Colonnade Apartments in Newark, that one feels that the formula has been tried once too often. It is said that he never once gazed out of a taxi window in Chicago. He was forever oblivious of the environment: this led to certain mistakes, like the Home Federal Building in Des Moines, a bank so formal as to take no account of the fact

Styling Building, General Motors Technical Center, Warren, Mich., 1948-56
(Eero Saarinen Associates)

Dodge Half-Ton Truck Plant, Warren, Mich., 1938 (Albert Kahn Associates)

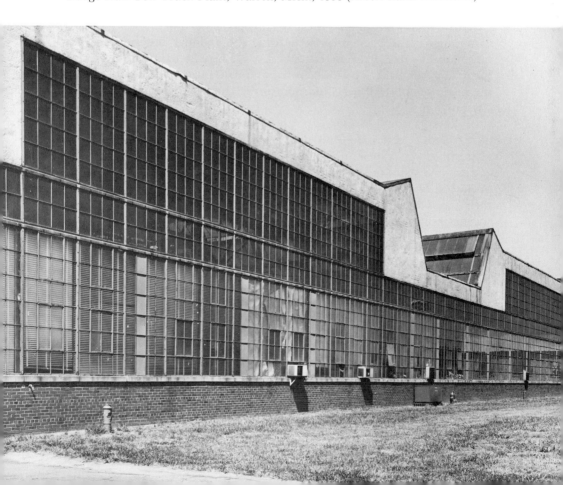

that the customers may wear neither jackets nor neckties on summer days.

His old friend Philip Johnson did not follow his career with blind admiration. "Miës is such a genius," he told a group of students not so long ago at Yale. "But I grow old! And bored! My direction is clear: eclectic traditionalism. This is not academic revivalism. There are no classic orders or Gothic finials. I try to pick up what I like throughout history. We cannot *not* know history."

While anyone would be glad to hear that Johnson did not sympathize with Gropius's dictum that architectural history was an unnecessary encumbrance, the preceding paragraph is not the best summation of Johnson's career. *If at first you do not succeed* may be his motto; for he has turned here, turned there, and there seems to be little consistency to his ambition.

Although the Miësian pleasure pavilion he built for himself at New Canaan, Connecticut, in 1949, a wall-less glass and steel box, is the perfect showpiece for a fastidious bachelor's entertainment of his friends, the typical Johnson-designed residence is likely to be no more warm and welcoming than an induction center. Johnson may be merely pompous, as in the Kline laboratory and science center at Yale, or banal, as in the New York State Theater at Lincoln Center. Or he may do an indifferent curtain wall skyscraper like the Investors Diversified Service Building in Minneapolis, and then surprise us with the ominous but inviting glass towers of Pennzoil Place in Houston. At his best he has been more than surprising, as in the Roofless Church at New Harmony, Indiana, and in the intricate and charming addition to the Dumbarton Oaks Museum in Washington, D.C.

Johnson's friend Miës may not have *invented* the curtain wall—as we have noted, eclectics like Polk and Flagg had already experimented with glass-walled skyscrapers in which the decorative element was far from forgotten—but Miës did come close to patenting the idea with his 1920–21 project in Berlin. This is not to say that he must be held responsible for the ravages of the curtain wall epidemic in recent years, when unimaginative designers have decided that it was the answer for every question, much as the builders of brownstone fronts in the New York of a hundred years ago refused to consider any other alternative for private dwellings. Perhaps the most notorious propagandist for the curtain wall is Ieoh Ming Pei, once an associate professor under Gropius at Harvard, who earned his share of publicity when the 10,344 panes of glass in his John Hancock Tower in Boston began popping out and it was also discovered that the inner core of the skyscraper was in need of strengthening against "rare wind conditions." Incidentally, Pei had no mercy on the adjacent Trinity Church by Richardson. Lawyers for Trinity, who found the foundations of the church were endangered, have added to the legal difficulties that Pei has encountered.

But the most *financially* successful proponents of the curtain wall are the firm of Skidmore, Owings and Merrill, whose skyscrapers may be seen in nearly every city from New York to San Francisco. There is no doubt that this firm admires Miës, but they have never succeeded in erecting a single building that does more than prove that imitation is the sincerest form of flattery. In Chicago, when SOM moved in on the campus of the Illinois Institute of Technology, they indicated that they had no intention of studying local requirements: Crerar Library, whose entrance slopes down to receive all of the slush and ice that is sure to accumulate in a Chicago winter, is only one of their mistakes. Competent, but never inspired, they could use the Miësian vocabulary without comprehending his grammar. At the campus of the University of Illinois–Chicago Circle, they tried their heavy hands on concrete. In New York, thanks to their example in Lever House on Park Avenue, SOM made sure that this once gracious avenue would become bleak. *Somitis*—so one might label the peculiar inflammation that is eating away at the core of so many American cities—makes one look back with longing at the Park Avenue of McKim, Mead and White and Warren and Wetmore, when Manhattan was a livable island. Now and then SOM will decide to be *original,* as in their eccentric plans for the U.S. Air Force Chapel at Colorado Springs. Perhaps their only handsome building is the translucent Beinecke Library at Yale, a treasure house for rare books, and here, so the library staff tells us, they quite forgot, until the last minute, to include the ducts for air conditioning.

The late Louis I. Kahn, who died at seventy-three in 1974, deserves to be taken more seriously. Although one of his apologists· has claimed that "we are indebted to Kahn for a re-evaluation of the problem of man," he was not so naïve as this would lead you to believe. A native of the island of Oesel in Estonia, he brought a Baltic austerity to American architecture that was sorely needed in the years when Minoru Yamasaki was celebrated for designs on the order of the McGregor Center at Wayne State University. Trained at the University of Pennsylvania, where he came under the influence of Paul Cret, the designer of the Detroit Institute of Arts, he was intended to be a monumental architect. Although his Unitarian Church in Rochester, New York, is no more ethereal than a machine-tool shop, and although he had no instinct for decoration— his Kimbell Museum in Fort Worth boasts a parking lot with lights that are no more arresting than trash cans—he could be graceful and noble, as in the library for Exeter Academy at Exeter, New Hampshire, of 1972. This may be even more important that his famous Salk Center of 1962 at La Jolla, California. His eyes, unfortunately, were not always alert. When he conceived the slate-covered façade of the Stern dormitory at Bryn Mawr in 1966, he seems to have overlooked the fact that the slate he fancied looked all too much like tarpaper on a sunny day. However, he could not be pretentious if he tried. He was never guilty of anything so silly as Max Abramowitz's Philharmonic Hall or W. K. Harrison's Metropolitan Opera at Lincoln Center, New York.

But the most significant of all our Veblenites is Eero Saarinen, who was only fifty-one when he died in 1961. He was the son of Eliel Saarinen, the Finn who played so prominent a role in the arts and crafts movement of Helsinki before the First World War. "Hvrittäsk," his estate at Luoma, was one of the commanding country houses of Europe, and his Helsinki railroad station will not be easily forgotten. Then, placing second in the competition for Chicago's Tribune Tower, won by John Mead Howells and Raymond Hood, he moved to the United States, where George Booth, the Detroit philanthropist and newspaper owner, called on him to plan the buildings of the Cranbrook schools at Bloomfield Hills, Michigan. At Cranbrook he was at his best in Kingswood School for Girls, completed in 1930. This was an extraordinarily graceful achievement, as feminine as his last Finnish work had been masculine. While at Cranbrook he also founded the art academy where Harry Bertoia and Charles Eames started on their careers as furniture designers. But the most talented graduate was young Eero. With his famous womb chair and the contributions of Bertoia and Eames, Michigan became preeminent for modern furniture.

"Our architecture," Eero was to declare not long after his graduation from Yale, "is too humble. It should be prouder, much richer and larger than we see it today. I should like to do my part in expanding that richness." This was the confession of faith of a perpetually dissatisfied man, and although Eero Saarinen could commit blunders like the American Embassy in London and the War Memorial in Milwaukee, he became one of the major architects of the twentieth century. For a time he was under his father's spell. Then, when in 1948 he came to design the General Motors Technical Center at Warren, Michigan, he revealed that he was the equal of Miës as a meticulous artist. No matter how many objections may be raised to impersonality in fields other than industrial architecture, it is hard to imagine a factory as anything else than an impersonal complex, and a research center, the very place where the ideas are perfected for the factories of tomorrow, can hardly escape being Veblenite. To Eero Saarinen—in association with the Detroit firm of Smith, Hinchman and Grylls—must go the credit for having designed one of the Veblenite landmarks. For the steel-framed units of the project, whose walls are filled with brick or glass, are not the bleak objects with which a less sensitive architect might have been satisfied. The glazed ceramic and sand-molded bricks of the Research Center have been tinted in wild and happy colors, from burnt orange to ultramarine, and visitors

Residence of Miss Ellen Scripps, La Jolla, Calif., 1917 (Irving Gill)

Residence of Warren D. Tremaine, Santa Barbara, Calif., 1948 (R. J. Neutra)

are not likely to forget the electric gaiety enveloping machines as forbidding as dynamometers. What Miës thought of all this we do not know: we know only that he abhorred color all his life.

Another great adventure of Eero Saarinen as an industrial architect was the oxidized steel headquarters of the John Deere Company at Moline, Illinois, completed three years after his death. Here a parallel could be made with the work of Kenzo Tange, his Japanese contemporary. But business buildings were not the only buildings that Eero could create. When invited to make a contribution to the campus at Yale, he revealed that he could be at once fancy-free and tactful. The Ingalls Hockey Rink, which might have been inspired by the hull of a Viking ship, was a tribute to his imagination. Tributes to his discretion were two new colleges at Yale, Morse and Stiles, where he invented dormitories that did not insult, but in fact complemented the conservative neo-Gothic buildings nearby.

But there was another avenue to be explored by Eero Saarinen. He was to recognize the daring of Le Corbusier. This Swiss, whom we too quickly characterized as a Veblenite when talking of the International Style exhibit at the Modern Museum, could never quite fit into the discipline of Gropius and Miës. He wrote easily, perhaps too easily, and since he had once spoken of a house as a *"machine à habiter,"* was for a time believed to be a mechanistic designer. This was not the case. He had also described architecture as *"le jeu savant, correct et magnifique des volumes assemblés sous la lumière."* What was this but an invitation to conceive of architecture as a form of sculpture, to turn back to what Gaudí had accomplished in the Church of the Holy Family at Barcelona, or Eric Mendelsohn in the Einstein Tower of the Weimar Republic? Le Corbusier was not without a sense of humor. He had praised our silos before he visited America but, once here, he preferred the palaces of McKim, Mead and White, deciding that the Renaissance in New York was more than worthwhile. "It is so well done," he exclaimed, "that you might almost believe it was the real thing." This message may have dismayed the prigs among our architectural historians, but it must have pleased Saarinen, who knew what architecture as sculpture might mean.

Although Saarinen said nothing in print about Le Corbusier's Unité d'Habitation at Marseilles, where the rooftop was nothing if not a sculptural essay, nor about Notre Dame du Haut at Ronchamp, where Le Corbusier again broke all the conventions of the International Style, he was to pay his own respects to this new trend in the John Foster Dulles Airport at Chantilly, Virginia, not ready for traffic until two years after his death. The year before this, the TWA Terminal at Kennedy airport, which may be the greatest of all Saarinen's works, was open to the public. This was a lyrical prelude to air travel, as elegant in its way as the best of Stanford White.

So it was not surprising that Saarinen stubbornly refused to design

Library, Phillips Exeter Academy, Exeter, N.H., 1972 (Louis I. Kahn)

Interior, Library

another curtain wall when CBS selected him as the architect of their skyscraper on Sixth Avenue. The granite piers that finally rose in 1965 might have suggested to Kevin Roche and John Dinkeloo, who took over the office on his death, that conventionality was not the equivalent of immortality, but their work has been as disappointing as Saarinen's was amazing. We have seen the Ford Foundation Building of 1967, lacking the cornice on which Louis Sullivan would have insisted ("Watch the terminals," he told Wright), and worse yet, the Knights of Columbus Building of 1969 in New Haven, a square with four triumphant towers devoted to toilets.

Le Corbusier has not had on every American architect the inspiring influence he had on Saarinen. While Paul M. Rudolph paid loving attention to Le Corbusian principles in his Endo Pharmaceutical Building of 1966 at Garden City, Long Island, and proved how graceful he could be in the New Haven Parking Lot of 1962, he was content in the Art Center for Colgate at Hamilton, New York, merely to recall the outline of Le Corbusier's monastery of Sainte Marie de la Tourette. Of late he has grown more ponderous, as in the concrete campus at North Dartmouth, Massachusetts, for the South Eastern Massachusetts Technical Institute and in the Brydges Public Library of Niagara Falls, New York. He has always been more inventive, however, than the firm of Kallman, McKinnell and Knowles, whose Boston City Hall of 1962–67 owed almost too much to the example of the monastery. To Bostonians with a sense of humor the City Hall will always be known as "Fortress Boston."

So much for the Veblenites of the East and the Middle West. The Veblenites of California have labored under conditions so different from those facing their confederates in other parts of the United States that it would be unwise to proceed without saying what it means to be an architect in Los Angeles or San Francisco.

To begin with, it would be foolish to forget that California is the state in which most Americans would prefer to live—if they could. From 1940 to 1970, the population of California rose from nearly 7 million to over 19 million. Already from 1900 to 1930, the population had climbed from nearly 1.5 million to nearly 6 million, proving that the climate, the scenery, and the economic opportunities were irresistible long before the aircraft plants laid out their assembly lines.

This onrush has had an influence second only to that of the newly rich in the days before the income tax. For the climate alone cannot explain the fascination which the fine art of architecture has for so many citizens of California. The genial sun—genial despite the recent smog menace in Los Angeles—may make it much easier for designers to experiment with window openings, but it has nothing to do with the social standing of the brighter members of the profession, who enjoyed—at least

Salk Center, La Jolla, Calif., 1959-62 (Louis I. Kahn)

in the 1950s—a notoriety granted on the East Coast to successful stage producers. What is more, Western architects are less self-conscious, less troubled by the unwritten laws that threaten their conscientious brethren elsewhere. "No one has ever asked me to design a *modern* house," one of the bright young men of San Francisco—an émigré, incidentally, from Philadelphia—told the author.

Since it is hard to live by rules in a land where the sun itself is so agreeable that grim commands are not likely to be remembered twenty-four hours later, California is a paradise for Jacobites and a singularly stimulating place for Veblenites too, who cannot always be as strict as they would prefer.

One of the most deserving Veblenites of California was the late Irving Gill, a native of Syracuse, New York, who before his death at sixty-six in 1936, proved that he was one of the interesting architects of the early twentieth century. An intransigent individualist, he might have ended as a Jacobite had it not been for his didactic impulse. Gill was never so austere as he would have liked to appear. Perhaps this was because he learned in Louis Sullivan's office that there was nothing so delightful as breaking one's own commandments.

He might never have moved from Chicago to the West Coast if he had not had an unfortunate collision with Frank Lloyd Wright. Gill was so indiscreet, so Wright tells us, as to show up for work sporting the hairdo and the flowing black tie which the future lord of "Taliesin" had made very much his own. "This had been the case with others often enough," Wright tells us, "but in this instance the affair suddenly seemed to me more like caricature. I regarded him for a moment and said, 'Gill, for Christ's sake, get your hair cut.' This common enough exhortation, to which I have been subjected in nearly every province of the United States, was not pleasantly said. Gill was as rank an individualist as I and he quit then and there. But his individual character came out to good purpose in the good work he did later in San Diego and Los Angeles. His work was a kind of elimination which if coupled with a finer sense of proportion would have been—I think it was, anyway—a real contribution to our so-called modern movement."

In his passion for elimination Gill resembled his contemporary in Austria, Adolf Loos, who published a most interesting essay in 1898 entitled *Ornament and Crime*. "A modern man who tattoos himself is a criminal or a degenerate," Loos pointed out. "There are prisons in which 80 per cent of the prisoners show tattoo marks. Tattooed men who are not in prison are latent criminals or degenerate aristocrats." Arguing from this premise, the Austrian architect demonstrated to his own satisfaction that the slightest trace of ornamentation in a building was proof of a criminal tendency on the part of the designer. "The progress of civilization," he thought, "is synonymous with the stripping of all orna-

Palace of Fine Arts, San Francisco, Calif., 1915 (Bernard Maybeck)

First Church of Christ Scientist, Berkeley, Calif., 1912 (Bernard Maybeck)

Interior, First Church of Christ Scientist

ment from objects of every-day use. I intended to bring new joy into the world with this discovery, but the world has not thanked me for it."

Gill could be almost as dogmatic as Loos himself. "We must," he said, "boldly throw aside every accepted structural belief and standard of beauty, and get back to the source of all architectural strength—the straight line, the arch, the cube, and the circle—and draw from these fountains of art that gave life to the great men of old.

"Every artist," he felt, "must sooner or later reckon directly, personally, with these four principles. . . . The straight line borrowed from the horizon is a symbol of greatness, grandeur, and nobility; the arch patterned from the dome of the sky represents exultation, reverence, aspiration: the circle is the sign of completeness, motion, and progression, as may be seen when a stone touches water; the square is the symbol of power, justice, honesty, and firmness." With all this at our command, "we must not weaken the message of beauty and strength by the stutter and mumble of useless ornaments."

There were to be no moldings for pictures or plates in the ideal modern house, which was to be a dustless place, minus baseboards, paneling, or wainscoting. "We should," he said, "build our house simple, plain, substantial as a boulder, and leave the ornamentation of it to nature, who will trim it with lichens, chisel it with storms, and make it gracious and friendly with vines and flower shadows as she does the stone in the meadow."

Gill was a much better architect than you would guess from reading this prescription for a modern house. The many buildings he designed in Los Angeles, San Diego, and La Jolla have mellowed gracefully, and the artistry with which he simplified the interiors and exteriors of his stucco and concrete houses is as obvious today as it may have been puzzling yesterday.

Until not so long ago, the best of Gill could be seen at La Jolla, the resort on the edge of the Pacific near San Diego. There he laid out the Bishop School for Girls and there, in 1917, he built the finest of all his houses for Miss Ellen Scripps, sister of the founder of the Scripps-Howard newspaper chain. Though this was hardly so light and so airy a thing as Le Corbusier would erect in France in the next decade, the skill with which the American practiced the doctrine of elimination was such that anyone could tell that the two architects were dreaming much the same dreams. Miss Scripps's memory and the cause of modern architecture would have been better served if her house had not fallen into the hands of the local art museum, whose board of directors saw fit to "modernize" this masterpiece by altering the fenestration so that next to nothing may be guessed of the designer's intentions.

Had it not been for the example which Gill set here and elsewhere in Southern California, Richard J. Neutra might not have enjoyed so soon

Residence of D. B. Gamble, Pasadena, Calif., 1909 (Greene & Greene)

Residence of C. H. Wolfe, Catalina Island, Calif., 1928 (R. M. Schindler)

the success which was his. Not that Neutra was ill trained. A graduate of the office of Adolph Loos in his native city of Vienna, he reached Los Angeles in 1925 at thirty-three, after an apprenticeship with Eric Mendelsohn in Berlin and Holabird and Roche in Chicago. From Mendelsohn, whose temperament was too romantic for his taste, he seems to have learned little, but from Holabird and Roche he acquired an awesome respect for the business methods of the giant architectural organizations of the skyscraper age. Though he arrived in Chicago too late to meet D. H. Burnham, he decided then and there that the great organizer was one of his heroes.

Even in the benign climate of California, he aimed at, but did not always succeed in, organizing the lives of his clients. The ideal Neutra house was one in which no magazine was ever carelessly dropped on a table, and in which ashes were removed from ashtrays on a second's notice. He was disappointed one day to discover that a woman he trusted had insisted on asking the Jacobite William Wilson Wurster to design her new home in West Los Angeles. When he was invited to take a look, he was mortified to find a double-hung window in the teakwood living room. "If you had had me, I should never have allowed that," he pointed out. "That, my friend, is just why I didn't have you," he was told.

"Earnest reform," he noted with regret in one of his books, "may ever so often be interrupted by caprice." Not one to indulge his own caprices, or to approve of those who enjoy themselves with no thought of the ultimate consequences, he was stirred by the "minutely standardized" dwellings of Japan, but offended by the "Renaissance myth of genius. . . . In our own age, which is so much committed to both industrialism and collectivism, and also is advancing in a knowledge of physiologically based psychology, we shall have to rectify this picture of heroic, independent creation."

Although he might have been happier building railroad terminals, airports, and factories, he did plan a great number of houses. These testified not only to his taste but to his determination. His golden opportunity came in 1929 when Dr. Philip M. Lovell, then at the start of his sensational career as a body-builder and dietician, asked him to lay out a house atop one of the Los Angeles hills. Here was a cage of glass and steel and concrete, contrived with exasperating accuracy.

An even more surprising example of the mechanistic artistry of Neutra was the mansion he planned in 1949 at Santa Barbara for Warren Tremaine, the son of a General Electric executive from Cleveland. Its site as cultivated as that of the Lovell house was stark, this mansion was set off from a polite grove on the property by flower beds as precise as any to be found in the Japanese rock gardens of sophisticated children. Just above the flower beds the reinforced concrete beams jut out beyond the masonry walls—as electric a sight as the curtain falling at the end of

Residence of Warren Gregory, Santa Cruz, Calif., 1927 (W. W. Wurster)

Institute for the Behavioral Sciences, Palo Alto, Calif., 1954 (Wurster, Bernardi & Emmons)

a desperate second act. The interior of this, the most elegant achievement of the Veblenites, is so cool, so patient, that its perfections may not be immediately recognized.

But there is another side to the architect—a side to which neither he nor his admirers paid much attention before his death in 1970. When dealing with wood and plaster instead of the steel and concrete he usually preferred, Neutra could be surprisingly casual and warm. These were the materials he used in 1943 when he and his consultant Eugene Wilson laid out the Channel Heights Housing Development at San Pedro near Los Angeles. Channel Heights in its time may well have been the most ingenious example of low-cost housing in the United States. The site was bleak—six hundred acres overlooking Los Angeles Harbor, surrounded by countless spectral oil derricks. But the six hundred units were spaced with a rare regard for the charm of variety, and, best of all, timber served a playful purpose, whether on the balconies of the units, or in the public telephone stands.

ENTER THE JACOBITES

California was the promised land of the Jacobites, and nowhere else in the United States have so many architects built so many buildings telling in their warmth and ease the individuality of their creators. Frank Lloyd Wright, who always believed that "there should be as many types of houses as there are types of people," was always at home on the West Coast: he turned to California in the 1920s when there was little or no chance for his type of architecture in the rest of the country.

Wright was the greatest of all the Jacobites, but it would be a mistake to pass over other men who sensed, as he did, the need for the exception "as necessary to prove any rule both useful and useless." No architect was more disobedient—and hence more of a Jacobite—in our century than Bernard Maybeck.

More than any other modern architect, he was conscious of the yearning for the fantastic that will not be suppressed in any age. In sticks and stones he kept writing until his death in 1957 a new *Mother Goose*. Without asking anyone's permission he would write a set of variations on a Tudor or Corinthian theme, and since whatever he remembered was his own, what he recalled was neither Gothic nor classic but Maybeck. He could be compared in this respect with Alexander Jackson Davis, the greatest of our romantics, though Davis never stressed, as he did, the texture of the materials involved.

Five years older than Wright, Maybeck was intimately associated, as the lord of "Taliesin" was not, with the masters of the age of elegance. A graduate of the Ecole des Beaux-Arts, he was always proud of his education. On his return to New York, where he was born, he worked for a time in the office of Carrère and Hastings, supervising the Ponce de León Hotel at Saint Augustine. Not long afterward he moved to the West Coast, and in 1899 laid the foundation of the School of Architecture at the University of California. Four years later he was practicing for himself.

In 1910 he was asked to design the First Church of Christ Scientist in Berkeley. One of the half-dozen great churches in America—Christ Church, Lancaster County, Virginia; the Synagogue at Newport, Rhode Island; Trinity, New York; Trinity, Boston; and Unity Temple in Oak Park, Illinois, come instantly to mind—this was too brilliant an invention to fit into the usual categories. It could not be classified as Chinese, even though its gables vaguely resembled the rooflines of a pagoda. Nor could it be described as Gothic, even though more than one tracery might have been drawn by an inspired Tudor craftsman.

Five years later, when Maybeck created the Palace of Fine Arts for San Francisco's Panama-Pacific Exposition, he proved he was closer to the romantic painter Thomas Cole than to any architect past or present. Like Cole, who portrayed the glory and the damage done by time to a picturesque site in the five canvases of "The Course of Empire," Maybeck could not ignore poetic associations. "I find," he announced, "the keynote of a Fine Arts Palace should be that of sadness, modified by the feeling that beauty has a soothing influence. . . . Great examples of melancholy in architecture and gardens may be seen in the engravings of Piranesi . . . whose remarkable work conveys the sad minor notes of old Roman ruins covered with bushes and trees."

In the sixty-odd years since the palace was erected, much of its plaster flaked off and much of its stucco crumbled, but the peach-hued Corinthian columns surrounding the peach-hued dome of the octagon—which had its own peach-hued Corinthian columns—gleamed so compellingly in the sunlight that the Golden Gate Bridge nearby was easily overlooked. It became as ruinous as Maybeck intended. But it also became the symbol of San Francisco, and recently it has been refaced. Would Maybeck complain about this? Perhaps.

While the creator of the Palace of Fine Arts will always be considered as the most provocative of the early Jacobites of California, it would be unwise to pass over the brothers Charles Sumner Greene and Henry Mather Greene. Dismissed once upon a time as mere propagandists for the bungalow style so popular in the early twentieth century, Greene and Greene deserve to be remembered, not for spreading the bungalow cult, but for forcing their generation to recognize that this often humble dwelling could be made a work of art.

The brothers Greene were natives of Saint Louis, where they attended the Manual Training School of Washington University before completing their architectural education at the Massachusetts Institute of Technology. But their real education may be said to have begun when they moved to California, where they made plain in their many houses in Pasadena that no one was warmer or more inventive than they in conjuring with the texture of timber. With exquisite patience they fashioned built-in furniture or toyed with the play of light in gable trellises. In a sense they re-created the early work of McKim, Mead and White.

Perhaps the greatest of all their designs was the mansion in Pasadena completed in 1909, of David Berry Gamble, son of one of the founders of Procter and Gamble. Here there was more than one hint of the Orient in their use of trellises. And here they spent themselves not only on built-in cabinets but on serenely paneled walls. Another fine example of their artistry was the winter home at Ojai of Charles M. Pratt of the Standard Oil dynasty.

The brothers Greene might have fancied that theirs was a lost cause in the 1920s if R. M. Schindler, a brilliant Austrian, had not settled in California at that time. Once a student of Otto Wagner in Vienna, Schindler went to work for Wright in 1918, when twenty-eight, and superintended the Barnsdall house in Los Angeles. In practice for himself, he showed that, though an admirer, he was never an imitator of Wright. Tempted in 1926 by the experiments of *De Stijl* in Holland, he built for Dr. Philip M. Lovell, later the client of Neutra, an ingenious beach house of plaster suspended by iron rods on concrete frames. Two years later on Catalina Island he was at work on his greatest achievement, a plaster and wood house of dateless charm for the schoolmaster C. H. Wolfe.

Schindler died in 1953 at sixty-three, but only after advertising his hostility to the slogans of the Veblenites. "Functionalism," he complained, with its white stucco, stainless steel, glass, and poster color schemes is here more out of place than anywhere else on this continent." He felt that the so-called International Style promoted by the Museum of Modern Art threatened the existence of all he believed in. "Problems of form as such are completely dismissed," he argued. "The classical mode of set forms for columns, architraves, and cornices is replaced by a stereotyped vocabulary of steel columns, horizontal parapets, and corner windows, to be used . . . both in the jungles and on the glaciers."

Yet another protest against dogma in any form was made by William Wilson Wurster, the founder in 1945 of the firm of Wurster, Bernardi and Emmons in San Francisco. "There is," he said, "always more than one answer." In fact his approach was so pragmatic that he once advocated cutting down the cost of all present-day building so as to make it easier for the architects of tomorrow to replace the work of those of our time.

Ever a critic of the collective ideal of Walter Gropius, Wurster believed that "architecture is individual effort even when expressed in

Schuckl & Co. offices, Sunnyvale, Calif., 1942 (W. W. Wurster)

Residence of R. M. Shainwald, Atherton, Calif., 1948 (Wurster, Bernardi & Emmons)

Living room, residence of R. M. Schainwald

group action. For the emerging result of the group comes from the sum of the individuals." Certainly no one could easily mistake a Wurster design for that of anyone else. His work, and that of the firm he directed in San Francisco, was marked not only by an appreciation of the carpenter tradition of the area, but also by a willingness to go to almost any extreme to reveal the richness of texture of local woods.

His education in architecture may be said to have begun when he was a boy in Stockton. His father, one of the local bankers, spent his holidays with his son watching the construction gangs at work during the building booms. By 1913, when Wurster entered the University of California on the eve of his eighteenth birthday, he was already committed to his lifework. On his graduation—he shipped in the engine room of more than one freighter during the First World War—he labored in San Francisco and Sacramento in the offices of various architects and engineers, then took a year off exploring Europe, and in 1923 went to work in New York for the eclectic firm of Delano and Aldrich. By 1924 he was back in San Francisco and by 1926 he was in practice for himself.

Wurster made his appearance in 1927 with the farmhouse he designed

Plan of residence of R. M. Shainwald, Atherton, Calif., 1948 (Designer: Wurster, Bernardi & Emmons)

Residence of Weston Havens,
Berkeley, Calif., 1941 (H. H.
Harris)

Living room, residence of Weston Havens

for the Warren Gregorys at Santa Cruz. As gentle an introduction into modern architecture as one could desire, this was so unaffected a house that it was immediately evident that here was an architect too subtle to fit into anyone's dogma. He could glance at the older buildings of Monterey—and, indeed, into any part of the California past—and decide how easily they could fit into the California present. He could not help sharing the experience he acquired; in 1944 he became the dean of the School of Architecture at the Massachusetts Institute of Technology; by 1950 he was head of the school at Berkeley, reminding the students again and again that the designer of anyone's house is a privileged person. "Families heading for the divorce courts," he said, "don't build houses. Houses are built by husbands and wives in the happiest period of their lives, and architects, unlike lawyers or doctors, have to be thankful that they are dealing with optimists." There was, he discovered, one sure way of telling whether one of his own houses was successful: the owner would decide that he had thought of everything himself. "At such a time," he confessed, "I smile and feel wonderful all over." There is certainly no need to emphasize the tact, the diplomatic talent, that he brought every day to the office.

His practice was constantly growing in San Francisco, even when he was spending the winters in Cambridge, and the formation of Wurster, Bernardi and Emmons could no longer be postponed. Of the two younger partners, Theodore C. Bernardi, trained at the University of California, was especially gifted at contriving apparently unsophisticated but in reality consciously rustic private houses, while Donn Emmons, who prepared at Cornell, excelled in simple but strangely elegant interiors.

Wurster and his partners were so prolific—or perhaps we should say so popular—that it is not the easiest thing to summarize the activities of the firm. The most famous example of Wurster as an industrial architect is the Administration Building he planned in 1942 for the Shuckl Canning Company at Sunnyvale, south of San Francisco. Its redwood frame might be a sheet drawn taut, it is so slight, and the trellises over the horizontal windowstrips add accents so subtle that this is likely to be remembered as one of the incomparable business buildings of the twentieth century.

But Wurster, Bernardi and Emmons have been most prominent as domestic architects, and the houses they designed in and about the bay of San Francisco ran into the hundreds. Many of these were without parallel in the art of bringing the outdoors in and the indoors out—a feat often attempted in our time and often bungled. The cottage of the real estate promoter I. Schuman at Woodside, conceived in 1949, and the residence of the landscape architect Lawrence Halprin at Kent Woodlands, completed three years later, are models of what could be accomplished in deriving the greatest benefit and the least discomfort from the

Residence of Clarence Wyle, Ojai, Calif., 1948 (H. H. Harris)

genial sun of the coast. And the delicacy with which the texture of the wood frames was explored was a constant surprise.

The plan of a house by Wurster, Bernardi and Emmons may be deceptively casual; for all its informality, one of its corridors may open at any moment into a scene of extraordinary elegance. In fact, the most elegant modern interior in the United States may be the living room in the frame house that the firm built at Atherton in 1948 for the paraffin manufacturer R. M. Shainwald. At least the author in his travels has come upon no contemporary setting more luxurious than this black terrazzo floor and these walls of Douglas fir stained to reveal an ecstatic orange. Against this background a later owner, Mrs. Mildred Brock, hung her brilliant collection of Mexican paintings.

But we have only begun to list the works of Wurster, Bernardi and Emmons. In 1954 came the Institute for the Behavioral Sciences at Palo Alto, where the partners contrived redwood offices in perfect harmony with the great trees of the environment. Still later, they were responsible for the Ghirardelli Square Development in San Francisco, a feat of city planning that preserved the older buildings with the patience that was found wanting in Kallman, McKinnell and Knowles's Boston City Hall. Wurster died in 1973, but left a legacy.

You might say that Wurster's fellow Jacobite, Harwell Hamilton Harris, was the most sensitive architect since Frank Lloyd Wright in his use of materials, and you would not be mistaken. You might add that his is an exquisitely architectonic imagination, for no one is more aware than he of the poetry of geometry. But you would not be coming close to the essence of Harris's contribution if you failed to stress the fact that he, more than any other Jacobite, was dedicated to the principle that a house must be designed by an individual for an individual. Only a patient man could set out on the quest that such a pledge involves, but patience was second nature to Harris. As deep a student of the history of modern architecture as he was of the characteristics of his clients, he did not need to be told that there is a vast difference between novelty and originality, and his inspiration has never been that of a conjurer. Indeed, you might say that he has no whims, so firmly was his work founded on the precedents of the California tradition in the twentieth century. Wright has had a profound influence, and so have Maybeck and Greene and Greene, but whatever Harris had admired he has made his own.

A native of California like Wurster, Harris was the son of an architect who practiced in and about Redlands before the First World War. In his youth, while a student at Pomona College and at the Otis Art Institute in Los Angeles, he planned a career as a sculptor, but one glance at the Barnsdall house by Frank Lloyd Wright told him that he could be happy only as an architect. He worked for a time in Neutra's office, and then, in 1934, when thirty-one, started on his own.

Guggenheim Museum, New York City, 1959 (Frank Lloyd Wright)

Central Hall, Guggenheim Museum

On his own meant that he was to argue for progressive regionalism. Not one to admire cities like New Orleans that had grown parochial, he was irritated by what he called the regionalism of restriction but inspired by the regionalism of liberation "in tune with the emerging thought of the time." Here was a regional manifestation that had "significance for the world outside itself." This is what he cherished in Maybeck and Greene and Greene.

Great opportunities have always come to great designers. Harris got his chance in 1941 when Weston Havens, the heir to a considerable real estate fortune in Berkeley, asked him to plan a house on a Berkeley hillside facing the bay, with both the Bay Bridge and the Golden Gate in sight. "The house," as Harris has told us, "does not frame the view; it projects the beholder into it. The view is no mere segment of something seen through a hole. It is instead an extension of the sky, the water, and the hills, below and behind one. The height above the ground, and the lack of visible connection with it, together with the soaring effect produced by the rising ceilings as they move outward, tend invariably to lift the beholder into the sky. It is a sky house more than an earth house."

Harris realized that the Havens house was not intended to advertise the view, but to make it possible for the owner and his friends to enjoy the view to the fullest. The inverted gables of the ceilings do much more than project the beholder into the sky—they fill one with a sense of security in the engineering skill of the architect. And inasmuch as this particular open plan permits an unusual degree of privacy, it may be misleading to refer to the house as "poised in flight." Like all successful solutions of architectural problems, this is a peaceful answer.

Much attention was paid to the inverted gables of the Havens house at the time of its publication in the architectural magazines. Much more might have been paid to the architect's imaginative use of woods, from the redwood sheathing, in and out, to the main staircase of curved plywood. Moreover, the occasional sliding doors and the built-in furniture proved that Harris was as conscious as any Japanese of the wisdom of these conveniences.

Few of Harris's houses have been as big as this. And to date he has not been given a site to compare with the Berkeley hillside. But he has been inspired time and again by clients who demanded less than Weston Havens. This is fortunate indeed, for our tax structure has put an end to superb patronage, and Harris, like all architects, must be judged on his skill in solving the problems of men with middling incomes.

Though Harris has often favored low-pitched roofs and horizontal accents, he has experimented with particular success with high-pitched eaves and gable trellises which catch the enchantment of light and shade from dawn to dusk. One of the subtlest of his creations in this style was the redwood cottage he planned in 1951 in Los Angeles for Ralph

John Foster Dulles Airport, Chantilly, Va., 1963 (Eero Saarinen & Associates)

Interior, TWA Building, Kennedy Airport, New York City, 1962 (Eero Saarinen Associates)

Johnson, whose son was a member of the Walt Disney organization. Confined to a small lot in a thickly settled suburban area, the Johnson house was almost as perfect a solution as the mansion on the Berkeley hilltop.

Identification of house and site was always one of Harris's aims. He was never more successful at this than in the country home at Ojai, dating from 1948, of the Chicago leather executive Clarence Wyle. Here the T-shaped plan commanded an unlimited mountainous view with such ease that the house might have stood at this place since the Spaniards came. The gable trellis over the living-room window was as decorative as it was unaffected.

The creator of the Wyle residence has always been troubled by the fact that most people are willing to put up with inoffensive buildings. Until you have found a building that is every inch alive, and into whose arms you surrender yourself as to a partner in a dance, you have yet to discover architecture, he claims.

The inheritance of Wurster and Harris may be claimed by no one, but Charles Willard Moore, a native of Benton Harbor, Michigan, has staged one commanding appearance after another in California in recent years. Like Wurster and Harris, Moore has never been enchanted by the International Style of the Veblenites. "I don't think it's a very useful, interesting, meaningful, worthwhile description of what's going on," he argues. "It's very like the prepared statement of a politician. It's very important to spend a lot of time preparing a statement, as the Bauhaus did preparing a building. But I am also interested in what the politician really thinks." For him, Maybeck is a more arresting figure. "With a lot of just nutty details, like Gothic tracery upside down, Maybeck was really a kind of declaration of independence. He said that the rules which might obtain elsewhere didn't really obtain in California."

On graduation from the University of Michigan architectural school, Moore went on to Princeton for further study, and then worked for a time in the offices of Mario Corbett and other San Francisco architects. For many years he was chairman of the School of Architecture at Yale. He learned to design houses much as Shaw did plays: Shaw professed never to know the ending of a play he was beginning. In this free spirit, Moore conceived in 1969, when he was forty-two, the Paul M. Klotz house at Westerley, Rhode Island, a frame dwelling that may be forever waiting for the last act. Moore's greatest achievement, however, has been the vast Sea Ranch subdivision on the coast north of San Francisco, sponsored by the Oceanic Investors of Hawaii. This was begun in 1965, and with high hopes that the frame condominia and private houses would slip as easily into the environment as the best of McKim, Mead and White had eighty years before. They were meant to weather casually, these dwellings, and Moore himself was casual at the drafting board: now and then a house might have been inspired by an hour or two practicing block lettering.

Residence of P. M. Klotz, Westerley, R.I., 1969 (Charles W. Moore)

Fireplace, residence of P. M. Klotz

And Condominium Number One might pass for a barn, but a barn dreamed of by an artist. Not that care was not taken at Sea Ranch. The landscaping was ideal: the roadways allowed automobiles to vanish from sight.

TRAVELERS TOWARD TOMORROW

Most modern architects, like most architects in the past, are travelers toward tomorrow, hoping for greater recognition once they are dead and gone. But if there is any lesson in the tale of taste, it is that the taste of tomorrow is not ours to command. As the French philosopher Henri Bergson put it, only an extraordinarily lucky man could hope to point out, in what goes on around us, what will be most interesting for the historian in days to come. When such a historian comes to consider our own day, he will be looking for the explanation of his own time, and especially of what is newest about his own time. This newness is something of which we can have no idea, for it is nothing less than creation itself.

The more we understand the nature of time, the French philosopher was convinced, the closer we shall come to understanding that duration means invention, the creation of forms and the continuous elaboration of the absolutely new. Whatever may be the judgment of succeeding generations on the architects of our age—and the judgment is bound to vary from decade to decade—the author likes to believe that more than one designer mentioned in this chapter will be praised for having thought of time in these terms.

Condominium #1, Sea Ranch, Calif., 1965 (Moore, Lyndon, Turnbull & Whitaker)

Sources for Photographs and Line Cuts

All photographs not otherwise credited are the work of the author.

The originals of William Bingham's town house and of that of Robert Morris may be found in William Birch's *City of Philadelphia*, Springdale, 1800. Those of William Bingham's country house and that of William Crammond may be found in William Birch's *The Country Seats of the United States of North America*, Springdale, 1808. The sketch of the Bank of Pennsylvania is by Latrobe. The sketch of "Glen Ellen" is by Davis. The view of the Tremont House is taken from the frontispiece of *A Description of the Tremont House*, Boston, 1830. The interior of the Bell house is from the May, 1886, issue of the *Century Magazine*.

The plan of Stratford, like that of Mount Airy, is reproduced from Thomas T. Waterman's *The Mansions of Virginia*, courtesy of the University of North Carolina Press. That of Gore Place is taken from the Collectaguide Folder to the house, courtesy Gore Place. That of "Glen Ellen" is drawn especially for this book by Miss Betty Ezequelle. That of the Osborne house, as well as that of the Breese house, is reproduced from *A Monograph of the Work of McKim, Mead & White*, courtesy of the Architectural Book Publishing Company. The plan of the Kaufmann house is reproduced, courtesy of the Museum of Modern Art, from *A New House on Bear Run, Pennsylvania*; it has been redrawn for this book by the Manhattan Drafting Company. That of the Havens house, reproduced courtesy *The Architectural Forum* from their September, 1943, issue, has been redrawn for this book by Miss Betty Ezequelle, who also drew the sketch of Flemish and English bond. The plan and elevation of "Tryon's Palace" is by the architect John Hawks. The doorway

290

by Minard Lafever is reproduced from his *Beauties of Modern Architecture,* plate 25, New York, 1835, the Beatty Collection, New York Historical Society. The sketch of the Oelrichs salon is from the McKim, Mead & White Collection, New York Historical Society.

The plan of the Willitts house is from Henry Russell Hitchcock's *In the Nature of Materials,* plate 147, courtesy Duell, Sloan & Pearce. It has been redrawn for this book by James Bachleda. The plan of the Shainwald house, from *House Beautiful,* November, 1950, has been redrawn by the Manhattan Drafting Company.

A Selected Bibliography

PHOTOGRAPHIC RECORDS

Andrews, Wayne, *Architecture in America,* New York, 1960 (New and revised edition, New York, 1977).

——, *Architecture in Chicago and Mid-America,* New York, 1968.

——, *Architecture in Michigan,* Detroit, 1967.

——, *Architecture in New England,* Brattleboro, 1973.

——, *Architecture in New York,* New York, 1969.

Chamberlain, Samuel, *Historic Boston in Four Seasons,* New York, 1938.

——, *Historic Salem in Four Seasons,* New York, 1938.

——, *Nantucket: A Camera Impression,* New York, 1939.

——, *Old Marblehead: A Camera Impression,* New York, 1940.

——, *Portsmouth, New Hampshire: A Camera Impression,* New York, 1940.

Greiff, Constance, M., ed., *Lost America: From the Atlantic to the Mississippi,* Princeton, 1971.

——, ed., *Lost America: From the Mississippi to the Pacific,* Princeton, 1972.

Laughlin, Clarence J., *Ghosts Along the Mississippi,* New York, 1948.

Lincoln, Fay S., *Charleston: Photographic Studies,* New York, 1946.

Pratt, Dorothy, and Pratt, Richard, *A Guide to Early American Homes North,* New York, 1956.

——, *A Guide to Early American Homes South,* New York, 1956.

Pratt, Richard, *A Treasury of Early American Homes,* New York, 1949.

——, and Pratt, Dorothy, *Second Treasury of Early American Homes,* New York, 1954.

Silver, Nathan, *Lost New York,* Boston, 1967.

BIBLIOGRAPHIES

Hitchcock, Henry Russell, *American Architectural Books*, Middletown, 1939.

Roos, Frank J., Jr., *Writings on Early American Architecture*, Columbus, 1943.

Wall, Alexander J., *Books on Architecture Printed in America 1775–1830*, Cambridge, 1925.

GENERAL REFERENCE

Cahill, Holger, and Barr, Alfred H., eds., *Art in America*, New York, 1934.

Condit, Carl W., *American Building Art 19th Century*, New York, 1960.

———, *American Building Art, 20th Century*, New York, 1961.

Da Costa, Beverly, et al., *Historic Houses of America Open to the Public*, New York, 1971.

Hamlin, Talbot F., *The American Spirit in Architecture*, New Haven, 1926.

Jordy, William H., *American Buildings and Their Architects*, vols. 3, 4, New York, 1972.

Kimball, Fiske, *American Architecture*, Indianapolis, 1928.

Kouwenhoven, John A., *Made in America: The Arts in Modern Civilization*, New York, 1948.

Lynes, Russell, *The Tastemakers*, New York, 1954.

Pierson, William H., Jr., *American Buildings and Their Architects*, vol. 1, New York, 1970.

Schuyler, Montgomery, *American Architecture and Other Writings*, 2 vols., Cambridge, 1961.

CHAPTERS ONE AND TWO: THE SOUTHERN TRIUMPH— THE NORTHERN STRUGGLE

THE HISTORIC BACKGROUND

Adams, Abigail, *Letters of Mrs. Adams*, edited by Charles F. Adams, Boston, 1848.

———, *New Letters of Abigail Adams*, edited by Stewart Mitchell, Boston, 1947.

Adams, James T., *The Founding of New England*, Boston, 1921.

———, *Revolutionary New England*, Boston, 1923.

Adams, John, *Correspondence of John Adams and Thomas Jefferson 1812–1826*, edited by Paul Wilstach, Indianapolis, 1925.

———, *Familiar Letters of John Adams and his wife Abigail Adams during the Revolution*, edited by Charles F. Adams, New York, 1876.

————, *Statesman and Friend: Correspondence of John Adams with Benjamin Waterhouse 1784–1822*, edited by Worthington C. Ford, Boston, 1927.

————, *Warren-Adams Letters*, edited by Worthington C. Ford, 2 vols., Boston, 1917–25.

————, *Works*, edited by Charles F. Adams, 10 vols., Boston, 1850–56.

Allan, Herbert S., *John Hancock: Patriot in Purple*, New York, 1948.

Andrews, Charles M., *The Beginnings of Connecticut*, New Haven, 1934.

————, *The Rise and Fall of the New Haven Colony*, New Haven, 1936.

Balch, Thomas W., *The Philadelphia Assemblies*, Philadelphia, 1916.

Baxter, William T., *The House of Hancock*, Cambridge, 1945.

Beardsley, E. Edwards, *Life and Times of William Samuel Johnson*, New York, 1876.

Belknap, Jeremy, *History of New Hampshire*, 3 vols., Boston, 1791–92.

Beverley, Robert, *The History and Present State of Virginia*, edited by Louis B. Wright, Chapel Hill, 1947.

Birket, James, *Some Cursory Remarks made by James Birket in his voyage to North America, 1750–51*, New Haven, 1916.

Bowes, Frederick P., *The Culture of Early Charleston*, Chapel Hill, 1942.

Bradford, William, *Of Plymouth Plantation*, edited by Samuel E. Morison, New York, 1952.

Breck, Samuel, *Recollections*, Philadelphia, 1877.

Brewster, Charles W., *Rambles about Portsmouth*, 2 vols., Portsmouth, 1859–69.

Bridenbaugh, Carl, *Cities in the Wilderness*, New York, 1938.

————, *The Colonial Craftsman*, New York, 1950.

————, *Myths and Realities: Societies of the Colonial South*, Baton Rouge, 1952.

————, *Seat of Empire: The Political Role of 18th Century Williamsburg*, Williamsburg, 1950.

————, and Bridenbaugh, Jessica, *Rebels and Gentlemen, Philadelphia in the Age of Franklin*, New York, 1942.

Brissot de Warville, Jacques-Pierre, *New Travels in the United States of America*, 2 vols., London, 1797.

Brown, Margaret L., "Mr. and Mrs. William Bingham of Philadelphia," *Pennsylvania Magazine of History and Biography*, July, 1937.

Bruce, Philip A., *Economic History of Virginia in the 17th Century*, 2 vols., New York, 1895.

————, *Institutional History of Virginia in the 17th Century*, 2 vols., New York, 1910.

————, *Social Life of Virginia in the 17th Century*, Richmond, 1907.

Burnaby, Andrew, *Burnaby's Travels*, edited by Rufus R. Wilson, New York, 1904.

Byrd, William, *The Writings of Colonel William Byrd*, edited by John S. Bassett, New York, 1901.

Carter, Robert, *The Letters of Robert Carter 1720–1727,* edited by Louis B. Wright, San Marino, 1940.

Chastellux, Marquis de, *Voyages dans l'Amérique Septentrionale dans les Années 1780, 1781 et 1782,* 2 vols., Paris, 1786.

Crèvecoeur, J. Hector St. John, *Letters from an American Farmer,* New York, 1926.

Crofut, Florence S. M., *Guide to the History and Historic Sites of Connecticut,* 2 vols., New Haven, 1937.

Danckaerts, Caspar, *Journal of Caspar Danckaerts, 1679–1680,* edited by Bartlett B. James and J. Franklin Jameson, New York, 1913.

Dodson, Leonidas, *Alexander Spotswood,* Philadelphia, 1932.

Drayton, John, *Letters Written During a Tour Through the Northern and Eastern States of America,* Charleston, 1794.

———, *A View of South Carolina,* Charleston, 1802.

Edwards, Jonathan, *The Works of President Edwards,* edited by Sereno E. Dwight, 10 vols., New York, 1930.

Eisenhard, Luther P., ed., *Historic Philadelphia from the Founding Until the Early 19th Century,* Philadelphia, 1953.

Fisher, Sydney G., *The True William Penn,* Philadelphia, 1900.

Fiske, John, *Old Virginia and Her Neighbors,* 2 vols., Boston, 1897.

Fithian, Philip V., *Journal and Letters,* Princeton, 1900.

Force, Peter, *Tracts and Other Papers,* 4 vols., Washington, 1843–46.

Fox, Dixon R., *Yankees and Yorkers,* New York, 1940.

Franklin, Benjamin, *The Writings of Benjamin Franklin,* edited by Albert H. Smyth, 10 vols., New York, 1907.

Gray, Lewis C., *History of Agriculture in the Southern United States to 1860,* 2 vols., Washington, 1933.

Griswold, Rufus W., *The Republican Court,* New York, 1864.

Hall, Clayton C., ed., *Narratives of Early Maryland,* New York, 1910.

Hamilton, Alexander, *Gentleman's Progress: The Itinerarium of Dr. Alexander Hamilton 1744,* edited by Carl Bridenbaugh, Chapel Hill, 1948.

Hamor, Ralph, *A True Discourse of the Present State of Virginia,* Albany, 1860.

Hartwell, Henry, et al., *The Present State of Virginia,* edited by Hunter D. Farish, Williamsburg, 1940.

Hedges, James B., *The Browns of Providence Plantation: Colonial Years,* Cambridge, 1952.

Hendrick, Burton J., *The Lees of Virginia,* Boston, 1935.

Hill, Helen, *George Mason: Constitutionalist,* Cambridge, 1938.

Hosmer, James K., *The Life of Thomas Hutchinson,* Boston, 1896.

Howe, Mark A. De Wolfe, *Bristol,* Cambridge, 1930.

Hutchinson, Thomas, *The History of the Colony and Province of Massachusetts Bay,* edited by Lawrence S. Mayo, 3 vols., Cambridge, 1936.

Izard, Ralph, *The Correspondence of Mr. Ralph Izard of South Carolina*, edited by Anne I. Deas, New York, 1844.

Jameson, J. Franklin, ed., *Narratives of New Netherland*, New York, 1909.

Johnson, Edward, *Wonder-Working Providence*, edited by J. Franklin Jameson, New York, 1910.

Jones, Hugh, *The Present State of Virginia*, New York, 1865.

Kimball, Gertrude S., *Providence in Colonial Times*, Boston, 1912.

Knight, Sarah K., *The Journal of Madam Knight*, edited by George P. Winship, New York, 1935.

Lamb, Martha J., *History of the City of New York*, 3 vols., New York, 1921.

La Rochefoucault-Liancourt, Duc de, *Voyage dans les Etats-Unis d'Amérique fait en 1795, 96 et 97*, 8 vols., Paris, 1798–99.

McCrady, Edward, *The History of South Carolina under the Royal Government 1719–1776*, New York, 1899.

———, *The History of South Carolina in the Revolution 1775–1780*, New York, 1901.

———, *The History of South Carolina in the Revolution 1780–1783*, New York, 1902.

Mason, George C., *Annals of Trinity Church*, Newport, 1890.

Mather, Cotton, *Magnalia Christi Americana*, 2 vols., Hartford, 1853.

Mayo, Lawrence S., *John Langdon*, Concord, 1937.

———, *John Wentworth*, Cambridge, 1921.

Meade, William, *Old Churches, Ministers and Families of Virginia*, 2 vols., Philadelphia, 1861.

Miller, Perry, *The New England Mind: From Colony to Province*, Cambridge, 1953.

———, *The New England Mind: The 17th Century*, New York, 1939.

Morgan, John, *Journal of Dr. John Morgan 1764*, Philadelphia, 1907.

Morison, Samuel E., *The Puritan Pronaos*, New York, 1936.

———, *Three Centuries of Harvard*, Cambridge, 1946.

Morton, Louis, *Robert Carter of Nomini Hall*, Williamsburg, 1941.

Myers, Albert C., ed., *Narratives of Early Pennsylvania, West New Jersey and Delaware*, New York, 1912.

Quincy, Josiah, Jr., "Journal 1773," *Proceedings*, Massachusetts Historical Society, vol. 49, June, 1916.

———, "London Journal, 1774–1775," *Proceedings*, Massachusetts Historical Society, vol. 50, June, 1917.

Ravenel, Harriott Horry, *Charleston: The Place and the People*, New York, 1906.

———, *Eliza Pinckney*, New York, 1896.

Rogers, Mary Cochrane, *Glimpses of an Old Social Capital*, Boston, 1923.

Salley, Alexander S., ed., *Narratives of Early Carolina*, New York, 1911.

Sewall, Samuel, *Samuel Sewall's Diary,* edited by Mark Van Doren, New York, 1927.

Smith, John, *The Works of Captain John Smith,* edited by Edward Arber, 2 vols., London, 1884.

Stevens, Maud Lyman, *A History of the Vernon House,* Newport, 1915.

Stiles, Ezra, *The Literary Diary of Ezra Stiles,* edited by Franklin B. Dexter, 3 vols., New York, 1901.

Tilghman, Oswald, *History of Talbot County, Maryland,* 2 vols., Baltimore, 1915.

Tolles, Frederick B., *Meeting House and Counting House,* Chapel Hill, 1948.

Tyler, Lyon G., ed., *Narratives of Early Virginia,* New York, 1907.

Van Rensselaer, Marianna G., *History of the City of New York in the 17th Century,* 2 vols., New York, 1909.

Wallace, David D., *The Life of Henry Laurens,* New York, 1915.

Wansey, Henry, *The Journal of an Excursion to the United States of North America in the summer of 1794,* Salisbury, 1796.

Weeden, William B., *Early Rhode Island: A Social History of the People,* New York, 1910.

——, *Economic and Social History of New England,* 2 vols., Boston, 1890.

Wertenbaker, Thomas J., *Patrician and Plebeian in Virginia,* Charlottesville, 1910.

——, *The Planters of Colonial Virginia,* Princeton, 1922.

——, *Torchbearer of the Revolution,* Princeton, 1940.

——, *Virginia under the Stuarts,* Princeton, 1914.

Weston, Plowden C. J., ed., *Documents Connected with the History of South Carolina,* London, 1856.

Winsor, Justin, ed., *The Memorial History of Boston,* 4 vols., Boston, 1880–81.

Winthrop, John, *The History of New England from 1630–1649,* edited by James Savage, 2 vols., Boston, 1853.

Woodmason, Charles, *The Carolina Background on the Eve of the Revolution, the Journal and Other Writings of Charles Woodmason,* edited by Richard J. Hooker, Chapel Hill, 1953.

Wright, Louis B., *The Atlantic Frontier,* New York, 1947.

——, *The First Gentlemen of Virginia,* San Marino, 1940.

ARCHITECTURAL HISTORY

Andrews, Wayne, "The World of William Sprats," *Country Life,* March 8, 1973.

Armes, Ethel M., *Stratford Hall: The Great House of the Lees,* Richmond, 1936.

Bailey, Rosalie F., *Pre-Revolutionary Dutch Houses and Families in Northern New Jersey and Southern New York,* New York, 1936.

Beirne, Rosamond R., and Scarff, John H., *William Buckland,* Baltimore, 1958.

Bridenbaugh, Carl *Peter Harrison, First American Architect,* Chapel Hill, 1949.

Briggs, Martin S., *The Homes of the Pilgrim Fathers in England and America*, New York, 1932.

Brock, Henry I., *Colonial Churches in Virginia*, Richmond,, 1930.

Congdon, Herbert W., *Old Vermont Houses*, Brattleboro, 1940.

Cordingley, W. W., "Shirley Place," *Old-Time New England*, October, 1921.

Downing, Antoinette F., *Early Homes of Rhode Island*, Richmond, 1937.

———, and Scully, Vincent, Jr., *The Architectural Heritage of Newport, Rhode Island*, Cambridge, 1952.

Eberlein, Harold D., *The Architecture of Colonial America*, Boston, 1915.

———, and Hubbard, Cortlandt V. D., *Portrait of a Colonial City: Philadelphia 1670–1838*, Philadelphia, 1939.

Foote, Henry W., *John Smibert: Painter*, Cambridge, 1950.

Forman, Henry C., *The Architecture of the Old South*, Cambridge, 1948.

Fuller, George S. T., "The History of the Royall House and Its Occupants," *Medford Historical Register*, March, 1926.

Garvan, Anthony N. B., *Architecture and Town Planning in Colonial Connecticut*, New Haven, 1951.

Glenn, Thomas A., *Some Colonial Mansions*, Philadelphia, 1898.

Howells, John M., *The Architectural Heritage of the Merrimack*, New York, 1941.

———, *The Architectural Heritage of the Piscataqua*, New York, 1937.

———, *Lost Examples of Colonial Architecture*, New York, 1931.

Isham, Norman M., *Trinity Church in Newport, Rhode Island*, Boston, 1936.

———, and Brown, Albert F., *Early Connecticut Houses*, Providence, 1900.

———, and Brown, Albert F., *Early Rhode Island Houses*, Providence, 1895.

Kelly, J. Frederick, *Architectural Guide for Connecticut*, New Haven, 1935.

———, *Early Connecticut Meeting Houses*, 2 vols., New York, 1948.

———, *The Early Domestic Architecture of Connecticut*, New Haven, 1924.

Kimball, Fiske, *Domestic Architecture of the American Colonies and of the Early Republic*, New York, 1922.

———, and Carraway, Gertrude S., "Tryon's Palace," *New-York Historical Society Quarterly*, January, 1940.

Lancaster, Robert A., *Historic Virginia Homes and Churches*, Philadelphia, 1915.

Leiding, Harriet K., *Historic Houses of South Carolina*, Philadelphia, 1921.

Morrison, Hugh S., *Early American Architecture*, New York, 1952.

Newcomb, Rexford G., *The Old Mission Churches and Historic Houses of California*, Philadelphia, 1925.

———, *Spanish Colonial Architecture in the United States*, New York, 1937.

Place, Charles A., "From Meeting House to Church in New England," *Old-Time New England*, October, 1922, January, April, and July, 1923.

Ravenel, Beatrice S. J., *Architects of Charleston*, Charleston, 1945.

"The Restoration of Colonial Willimsburg," *Architectural Record*, December, 1935.

Reynolds, Helen W., *Dutch Houses in the Hudson Valley Before 1776*, New York, 1929.

Rogers, Meyric R., *American Interior Design*, New York, 1947.

Sale, Edith T., *Interiors of Virginia Houses of Colonial Times*, Richmond, 1927.

————, *Manors of Virginia in Colonial Times*, Philadelphia, 1909.

Shelton, William H., *The Jumel Mansion*, Boston, 1916.

Shurtleff, Harold R., *The Log Cabin Myth*, Cambridge, 1939.

Smith, Robert C., "John Notman's Nassau Hall," *Princeton University Library Chronicle*, Spring, 1953.

Stoney, Samuel G., *Plantations of the Carolina Low Country*, Charleston, 1938.

Sweeney, John A. H., *Grandeur on the Appoquinimink*, Newark, Del., 1959.

Tatum, George B., *Philadelphia Georgian*, Middletown, 1976.

Tilghman, J. Donnell, "Bill for the Construction of Chase House," *Maryland Historical Magazine*, March, 1938.

————, "Wye House," *Maryland Historical Magazine*, June, 1953.

Trowbridge, Bertha M., ed., *Old Houses of Connecticut*, New Haven, 1923.

Warren, William L., "William Sprats and His Civil and Ecclesiastical Architecture in New England," *Old-Time New England*, January and April, 1954.

Waterman, Thomas T., *The Dwellings of Colonial America*, Chapel Hill, 1950.

————, *The Early Architecture of North Carolina*, Chapel Hill, 1941.

————, and Barrows, John A., *Domestic Colonial Architecture of Tidewater Virginia*, New York, 1932.

Watkins, Walter W., "Hancock House, Boston," *Old-Time New England*, July, 1926.

Westcott, Thompson, *The Historic Mansions and Buildings of Philadelphia*, Philadelphia, 1877.

Wise, Herbert C., and Beidleman, H. Ferdinand, *Colonial Architecture for Those About to Build*, Philadelphia, 1913.

CHAPTER THREE: THE FEDERAL PERIOD

Asher Benjamin, 1773–1845

Benjamin, Asher, *The Builder's Assistant*, Greenfield, 1800.

————, *The Country Builder's Assistant*, Boston, 1798.

————, *The Practice of Architecture*, Boston, 1833.

————, *The Rudiments of Architecture*, Boston, 1820.

Booth, Vincent R. "Restoration of the Old First Church of Bennington, Vermont," *Old-Time New England*, January, 1940.

Thompson, Florence H., "More About Asher Benjamin," *Journal of the Society of Architectural Historians,* October, 1954.

NOTE: In the Gallatin Collection of the New-York Historical Society is Benjamin's historically important letter of August 5, 1802, addressed to Gideon Granger.

CHARLES BULFINCH, 1763–1844

Bulfinch, Ellen S., *The Life and Letters of Charles Bulfinch,* Boston, 1896.

Kirker, Harold, *The Architecture of Charles Bulfinch,* Cambridge, 1969.

———, and Kirker, James, *Bulfinch's Boston,* New York, 1964.

Morison, Samuel E., *The Life and Letters of Harrison Gray Otis,* 2 vols., Cambridge, 1913.

Place, Charles A., *Charles Bulfinch: Architect and Citizen,* Boston, 1925.

Wick, Peter A., "Gore Place," *Antiques,* December, 1976.

MAXIMILIAN GODEFROY, FL. 1806–1824

Alexander, Robert L., *The Architecture of Maximilian Godefroy,* Baltimore, 1974.

Davison, Carolina V., "Maximilian Godefroy," *Maryland Historical Magazine,* September, 1934.

———, "Maximilian and Eliza Godefroy," *Maryland Historical Magazine,* March, 1934.

Hoyt, William D., "Eliza Godefroy," *Maryland Historical Magazine,* March, 1941.

GEORGE HADFIELD, c. 1764–1826

Bullock, Helen D., *My Head and My Heart,* New York, 1945.

Cunningham, H. F., "The Old City Hall of Washington, D.C.," *Architectural Record,* March, 1915.

Elliot, Jonathan, *Historical Sketches of the Ten Miles Square,* Washington, 1830.

Townsend, George A., *Washington Outside and Inside,* Hartford, 1873.

Trumbull, John, *The Autobiography of Colonel John Trumbull,* edited by Theodore Sizer, New Haven, 1953.

ETIENNE-SULPICE HALLET, FL. 1789–1796

Bennett, Wells I., "Stephen Hallet," *Journal of the American Institute of Architects,* July-October, 1916.

JAMES HOBAN, c. 1762–1831

Kimball, Fiske, "The Genesis of the White House," *Century Magazine,* February, 1918.

PHILIP HOOKER, 1766–1836

Root, Edward W., *Philip Hooker,* New York, 1929.

WILLIAM JAY, FL. 1817–1824

Arts Committee of the Junior League, *Guide to Savannah,* Savannah, 1947.

Jay, Reverend William, *The Autobiography of the Reverend William Jay,* New York, 1855.

THOMAS JEFFERSON, 1743–1826

Adams, William Howard, ed., *The Eye of Jefferson,* Washington, 1976.

Bruce, Philip A., *History of the University of Virginia,* 5 vols., New York, 1920–22.

Frary, Ihna T., *Thomas Jefferson, Architect and Builder,* Richmond, 1931.

Guinness, Desmond, et al., *Thomas Jefferson Architect,* New York, 1973.

Jefferson, Thomas, *Papers of, Correspondence,* 60 vols., Princeton, 1950–71.

Kimball, Fiske, "The Building of Bremo," *Virginia Magazine of History and Biography,* January, 1949.

———,*Thomas Jefferson, Architect,* Boston, 1916.

———, *Thomas Jefferson and the First Monument of the Classic Revival in America,* Harrisburg, 1915.

Kimball, Marie G., *Jefferson: The Road to Glory,* New York, 1943.

———, *Jefferson: The Scene of Europe,* New York, 1950.

———, *Jefferson: War and Peace,* New York, 1947.

Randall, Henry S., *Life of Thomas Jefferson,* 3 vols., New York, 1858.

BENJAMIN HENRY LATROBE, 1764–1820

Brown, Glenn, *History of the United States Capital,* 2 vols., Washington, 1900–1903.

Bryan, Wilhemus B., *A History of the National Capital,* 2 vols., New York, 1914–16.

Documentary History of the Construction of the United States Capitol Building and Grounds, 58th Congress, 2nd Session, House Report 646, Washington, 1904.

Hamlin, Talbot F., *Benjamin Henry Latrobe,* New York, 1955.

Kimball, Fiske, "Some Architectural Designs of Benjamin Henry Latrobe," *Library of Congress Quarterly Journal,* May, 1946.

———, "The Bank of Pennsylvania," *Architectural Record,* August, 1918.

———, "Latrobe's Designs for the Cathedral of Baltimore," *Architectural Record,* December, 1917, January, 1918.

———, and Bennett, Wells I., "The Competition for the Federal Buildings," *Journal of the American Institute of Architects,* January-December, 1919.

Latrobe, Benjamin H., "Anniversary Oration Pronounced Before the Society of Artists," Supplement to *The Port Folio,* 1811.

———, *Impressions Respecting New Orleans,* edited by Samuel Wilson, Jr., New York, 1951.

———, *The Journal of Latrobe,* New York, 1905.

Latrobe, John H. B., "Construction of the Public Buildings in Washington, D.C.", *Maryland Historical Magazine,* September, 1909.

Rusk, William S., *William Thornton, Benjamin H. Latrobe, Thomas U. Walter and the Classical Influence in Their Works,* unpublished Ph.D., Johns Hopkins, 1933.

PIERRE-CHARLES L'ENFANT, 1754–1825

Bryan, Wilhemus B., "Something About L'Enfant and His Personal Affairs," *Records* of the Columbia Historical Society, vol. 2, 1899.

Dix, Morgan, *A History of the Parish of Trinity Church,* 4 vols., New York, 1898–1906.

"The French Fête in Philadelphia," *Pennsylvania Magazine of History and Biography,* July, 1897.

Kimball, Fiske, "Origin of the Plan of Wishington, D.C.," *Architectural Review,* September, 1918.

Kite, Elizabeth S., *L'Enfant and Washington,* Baltimore, 1929.

L'Enfant, Pierre-Charles, "L'Enfant's Memorials" and "L'Enfant's Reports to President Washington," *Records* of the Columbia Historical Society, vol. 2, 1899.

Morgan, James D., "Major Pierre-Charles L'Enfant," *Records* of the Columbia Historical Society, vol. 2, 1899.

Morris, Gouverneur, *The Diary and Letters of Gouverneur Morris,* 2 vols., New York, 1888.

Oberholzer, Ellis P., *Robert Morris,* New York, 1903.

Simpson, Sarah H. J., "The Federal Procession in the City of New York," *New-York Historical Society Quarterly,* July, 1925.

JOHN McCOMB, 1763–1853

Demarest, William H. S., *A History of Rutgers College,* New Brunswick, 1924.

Wilde, Edward S., "The New York City Hall," *Century Magazine,* April, 1884.

NOTE: The notebooks, drawings, etc., of McComb are in the possession of the New-York Historical Society.

SAMUEL McINTIRE, 1757–1811

Bentley, William, *The Diary of William Bentley,* 4 vols., Salem, 1905–14.

Kimball, Fiske, *Mr. Samuel McIntire, Carver, The Architect of Salem,* Portland, 1940.

Morison, Samuel E., *The Maritime History of Massachusetts,* Boston, 1921.

ROBERT MILLS, 1781–1855

Gallagher, H. M. Pierce, *Robert Mills,* New York, 1935.

Hoyt, William D., Jr., "Robert Mills and the Washington Monument in Baltimore," *Maryland Historical Magazine,* June, 1939.

Joseph-Jacques Ramée, 1764–1822

Hislop, Codman, Larrabee, Harold A., "Joseph-Jaques Ramée and the Building of North and South College," *Union College Alumni Monthly*, February, 1937.

Larrabee, Harold A., "How Ramée Came to Schenectady," *Union College Alumni Monthly*, February, 1937.

Réau, Louis, *L'Art Français aux Etats-Unis*, Paris, 1926.

Tunnard, Christopher, "Joseph-Jacques Ramée," *Union Worthies*, No. 19, 1964.

William Thornton, 1759–1828

Brown, Glenn, "Dr. William Thornton, Architect," *Architectural Record*, July–September, 1896.

Clark, Allen C., "Doctor and Mrs. William Thornton," *Records* of the Columbia Historical Society, vol. 18, 1915.

Tayloe, Benjamin O., *In Memorian Benjamin Ogle Tayloe*, Washington, 1872.

CHAPTER FOUR: THE ROMANTIC ERA

The Social and Historical Background

Alger, William R., *Life of Edwin Forrest*, 2 vols., Philadelphia, 1877.

Arthur, Stanley C., and De Kernion, George C. H., *Old Families of Louisiana*, New Orleans, 1931.

Boynton, Henry W., *James Fenimore Cooper*, New York, 1831.

Clinton, De Witt, *A Discourse Delivered Before the American Academy of Fine Arts*, New York, 1816.

Cole, Thomas, "Sicilian Scenery and Antiquities," *Knickerbocker Review*, February and March, 1844.

Cooper, James F., *Home as Found*, New York, 1860.

———, *Notions of the Americans*, 2 vols., Philadelphia, 1836.

Dickens, Charles, *American Notes*, New York, 1898.

Ellet, Elizabeth F., *The Queens of American Society*, New York, 1867.

Fuess, Claude M., *Daniel Webster*, 2 vols., Boston, 1930.

Hone, Philip, *The Diary of Philip Hone*, edited by Allan Nevins, New York, 1936.

Irving, Pierre M., *Life and Letters of Washington Irving*, 4 vols., New York, 1862–64.

July, Robert W., *The Essential New Yorker: Gulian Crommelin* Verplanck, Durham, 1951.

Noble, Louis L., *The Course of Empire*, New York, 1853.

Pickering, Henry, *The Ruins of Paestum*, Salem, 1822.

Quinn, Arthur H., *Edgar Allan Poe*, New York, 1941.

Richardson, E. P., *Washington Allston*, Chicago, 1948.

Tocqueville, Alexis de, *De la Démocratie en Amérique*, 2 vols., Paris, 1951.

Trollope, Frances, *Domestic Manners of the Americans*, New York, 1949.

Trumbull, John, *Address Before the Directors of the American Academy of Fine Arts*, New York, 1833.

Van Rensselaer, Emily D., *Recollections of Presqu'Ile*, typescript, New-York Historical Society, 1895.

Verplanck, Gulian C., *Discourses and Addresses*, New York, 1833.

Willis, Nathaniel P., *The Prose Works of N. P. Willis*, Philadelphia, 1849.

GENERAL SURVEYS

Andrews, Wayne, *American Gothic: Its Origins, Its Trials, Its Triumphs*, New York, 1975.

Dunlap, William, *A History of the Rise and Progress of the Arts of Design in the United States*, 3 vols., Boston, 1918.

Hamlin, Talbot F., *Greek Revival Architecture in America*, New York, 1944.

Lancaster, Clay, "Oriental Forms in American Architecture," *Art Bulletin*, September, 1947.

Loth, Calder, and Sadler, Julius T., *The Only Proper Style, Boston*, 1975.

Meeks, Carroll L. V., "Romanesque Before Richardson in the United States," *Art Bulletin*, March, 1953.

Stanton, Phoebe B., *The Gothic Revival and American Church Architecture*, Baltimore, 1698.

Tuthill, Louisa C., *History of Architecture from the Earliest Times*, Philadelphia, 1848.

REGIONAL STUDIES

Alexander, Drury B., *Texas Homes of the Nineteenth Century*, Austin, 1968.

Burnham, Alan, ed., *New York Landmarks*, Middletown, 1963.

Burnstone, Howard, *The Galveston That Was*, New York, 1966.

Cochran, Gifford A., *Grandeur in Tennessee*, New York, 1946.

Conover, Jewel Helen, *19th Century Houses in Western New York*, Albany, 1966.

Coolidge, John P., *Mill and Mansion*, New York, 1942.

Curtis, Nathaniel C., *New Orleans: Its Old Houses, Shops and Public Buildings*, Philadelphia, 1933.

Dickson, Harold F., *A Hundred Pennsylvania Buildings*, State College, 1954.

Ferry, W. Hawkins, *The Buildings of Detroit*, Detroit, 1968.

Greiff, Constance M., et al., *Princeton Architecture*, Princeton, 1967.

Hammond, Ralph C., *Ante-Bellum Mansions of Alabama*, New York, 1951.

Hitchcock, Henry Russell, *Rhode Island Architecture*, Providence, 1939.

Howland, Richard H., and Spencer, Eleanor P., *Architecture of Baltimore*, Baltimore, 1953.

Jackson, Joseph, *Early Philadelphia Architects and Engineers*, Philadelphia, 1923.

Jacobson, Hugh N., *A Guide to the Architecture of Washington, D.C.*, New York, 1966.

Julien, Carl, and Milling, Chapman J., *Beneath So Kind a Sky*, Columbia, 1947.

Kilham, Walter H., *Boston After Bulfinch*, Cambridge, 1946.

Kirker, Harold, *California's Architectural Frontier*, San Marino, 1960.

Koeper, Frederick, *Illinois Architecture*, Chicago, 1968.

Lancaster, Clay, *Ante-Bellum Houses of the Blue Grass*, Lexington, 1961.

———, *Back Streets and Pine Trees*, Lexington, 1956.

———, "Three Gothic Revival Houses in Lexington," *American Collector*, December, 1948.

Lockwood, Charles, *Bricks and Brownstone*, New York, 1972.

Newcomb, Rexford G., *Architecture in Old Kentucky*, Urbana, 1953.

———, *Architecture of the Old Northwest Territory*, Chicago, 1950.

Nichols, Frederick D., *The Architecture of Georgia*, Savannah, 1976.

———, *The Early Architecture of Georgia*, Chapel Hill, 1957.

Peat, Wilbur D., *Indiana Houses of the 19th Century*, Indianapolis, 1962.

Sawyer, Elizabeth M., et al., *The Old in New Atlanta*, Atlanta, 1976.

Smith, J. Frazer, *White Pillars*, New York, 1941.

Stutz, Charles Morse, *The Architectural Heritage of Early Western Pennsylvania*, Pittsburgh, 1966.

Tatum, George B., *Penn's Great Town*, Philadelphia, 1961.

Van Trump, James D., and Ziegler, Arthur, Jr., *Landmark Architecture of Allegheny County, Pennsylvania*, Pittsburgh, 1967.

White, Theophilus B., ed., *Philadelphia Architecture in the 19th Century*, Philadelphia, 1953.

CAST IRON AND OTHER UNROMANTIC ANSWERS

Bogardus, James, *Cast Iron Buildings: Their Construction and Advantages*, New York, 1856.

Field, Walker, "A Re-examination of the Invention of the Balloon Frame," *Journal of the American Society of Architectural Historians*, October, 1942.

The First Hundred Years, Otis Elevator Co., New York, 1953.

Gayle, Margot, 1921, *Cast-Iron Architecture in New York City*, New York, 1974.

Greenough, Horatio, *Form and Function*, Remarks on Art by Horatio Greenough, edited by Harold A. Small, Berkeley, 1947.

Petersen, L. A., *Elisha Graves Otis*, Newcomen Society, New York, 1945.

Weisman, Winston, "Commercial Palaces of New York," *Art Bulletin*, December, 1954.

HENRY AUSTIN, 1804–1891

Meeks, Carroll L. V., "Henry Austin and the Italian Villa," *Art Bulletin*, June, 1948.

JAMES HARRISON DAKIN, 1806–1852

Scully, Arthur, Jr., *James Dakin, Architect*, Baton Rouge, 1973.

ALEXANDER JACKSON DAVIS, 1803–1892

Andrews, Wayne, "Alexander Jackson Davis," *Architectural Review*, May, 1951.

———, "America's Gothic Hour," *Town & Country*, November, 1947.

Couper, William, *One Hundred Years at V.M.I.*, 4 vols., Richmond, 1939.

Davis, Alexander J., *Rural Residences*, New York, 1837.

Delafield, John R., "Montgomery Place," *Yearbook*, Dutchess Co. Historical Society, 1929.

Donnell, Edna, "A. J. Davis and the Gothic Revival," *Metropolitan Museum Studies*, vol. 5, Part 2, 1936.

Kimball, Le Roy E., "The Old University Building and the Society's Years on Washington Square," *New-York Historical Society Quarterly*, July, 1948.

Lathers, Richard, *Reminiscences of Richard Lathers*, New York, 1907.

Newton, Roger H., *Town & Davis: Architects* New York, 1942.

Pierson, David L., *History of the Oranges to 1921*, 4 vols., New York, 1922.

Sigourney, Lydia H., "Residence of Ithiel Town, Esq.," *Ladies Companion*, January, 1839.

Stephens, Ann S., *Fashion and Famine*, New York, 1854.

Vose, Reuben, *Reuben Vose's Wealth of the World Displayed*, New York, 1859.

Winthrop, Theodore, *Cecil Dreeme*, New York, 1861.

NOTE: The diaries, sketches, letters, etc. of Davis may be consulted at Avery Library, Columbia University, at the New York Public Library, at the New-York Historical Society, and at the Metropolitan Museum.

ANDREW JACKSON DOWNING, 1815–1852

Bremer, Frederika, *America of the Fifties: Letters of Frederika Bremer*, edited by Adolph B. Benson, New York, 1924.

Carmer, Carl, *The Hudson*, New York, 1939.

Downing, Andrew J., *The Architecture of Country Houses*, New York, 1858.

———, *Cottage Residences*, New York, 1847.

———, *Rural Essays*, New York, 1853.

———, *A Treatise on the Theory and Practice of Landscape Gardening*, New York, 1860.

Vaux, Calvert, *Villas and Cottages*, New York, 1857.

Wightwick, George, *Hints to Young Architects* . . . with additional notes by A. J. Downing, New York, 1847.

LEOPOLD EIDLITZ, 1823–1908

Schuyler, Montgomery, "A Great American Architect: Leopold Eidlitz," *Architectural Record*, September, 1908.

———, "The Work of Leopold Eidlitz," *Architectural Record*, October and November, 1908.

ORSON SQUIRE FOWLER, 1809–1887

Creese, Walter L., "Fowler and the Domestic Octagon," *Art Bulletin*, June, 1946.

Fowler, Orson S., *A Home for All*, New York, 1854.

Ver Noy, Amy P., "Fowler's Folly and Its Builder," *Yearbook*, Dutchess Co. Historical Society, 1948.

JAMES GALLIER, 1798–1868

Gallier, James, *Autobiography of James Gallier*, Paris, 1864.

JOHN HAVILAND, 1792–1852

Crawford, William, *Report on the Penitentiaries of the United States*, London, 1834.

Demetz, Frédéric-Auguste, and Blouet, Guillaume, *Rapports sur les Pénitenciers des Etats-Unis*, Paris, 1837.

Haviland, John, *A Communication to the County Commissioners*, Philadelphia, 1849.

Teeters, Negley K., "The Early Days of the Eastern State Penitentiary," *Pennsylvania History*, October, 1949.

A View and Description of the Eastern Penitentiary of Philadelphia, Philadelphia, 1830.

MINARD LAFEVER, 1798–1854

Brown, Roscoe C. E., *Church of the Holy Trinity*, New York, 1922.

Lafever, Minard, *The Architectural Instructor*, New York, 1856.

———, *The Beauties of Modern Architecture*, New York, 1835.

———, *The Modern Builders' Guide*, New York, 1853.

Landy, Jacob, *The Architecture of Minard Lafever*, New York, 1970.

DETLEF LIENAU, 1818–1897

Kramer, Ellen W., "Detlef Lienau," *Journal of the Society of Architectural Historians*, March, 1955.

JOHN NOTMAN, 1810–1865

Smith, Robert C., *John Notman and the Atheneun Building*, Philadelphia, 1951.

FREDERICK LAW OLMSTED, 1822–1903

Mitchell, Broadus, *Frederick Law Olmsted*, Baltimore, 1924.

Nevins, Allan, *The Evening Post*, New York, 1922.

Olmsted, Frederick L., *A Journey to the Seaboard Slave States*, 2 vols., New York, 1924.

Olmsted, Frederick L., Jr., and Kimball, Theodora, *Frederick Law Olmsted*, 2 vols., New York, 1922–28.

Roper, Laura W., *FLO: A Biography of F. L. Olmsted*, Baltimore, 1974.

Stevenson, Elizabeth, *Park Maker, A Life of Frederick Law Olmsted*, New York, 1977.

Van Rensselaer, Marianna G., "Frederick Law Olmsted," *Century Magazine*, October, 1893.

JAMES RENWICK, JR., 1818–1895

McKenna, Rosalie T., "James Renwick, Jr. and the Second Empire Style in the United States," *Magazine of Art,* March, 1951.

Owen, Robert Dale, *Hints on Public Architecture,* New York, 1849.

Stewart, William R., *Grace Church and Old New York,* New York, 1924.

ISAIAH ROGERS, 1800–1869

Eliot, W. H., *A Description of Tremont House,* Boston, 1830.

Williamson, Jefferson, *The American Hotel,* New York, 1930.

SAMUEL SLOAN, 1815–1884

Sloan, Samuel, *The Model Architect,* 2 vols., Philadelphia, 1852.

WILLIAM STRICKLAND, 1788–1854

Gilchrist, Agnes A., *William Strickland: Architect and Engineer,* Philadelphia, 1950.

Obituary Notice, *Proceedings,* American Philosophical Society, 1859, pp. 28–32.

Strickland, William, *Reports on Canals, Railways, Roads and Other Subjects,* Philadelphia, 1826.

RICHARD UPJOHN, 1802–1878

Upjohn, Everard M., *Richard Upjohn, Architect and Churchman,* New York, 1939.

Upjohn, Richard, *Upjohn's Rural Architecture,* New York, 1852.

THOMAS USTICK WALTER, 1804–1887

Bates, William N., "Nicholas Biddle's Journey to Greece in 1806," *Proceedings,* Numismatic & Antiquarian Society of Philadelphia, 1916–19.

Biddle, Edward, "Girard College," *Proceedings,* Numismatic & Antiquarian Society of Philadelphia, 1916–19.

Newcomb, Rexford G., "Thomas U. Walter," *The Architect,* August, 1928.

Walter, Thomas U., *Two Hundred Designs for Cottages and Villas, etc.,* Philadelphia, 1846.

SOLOMON WILLARD, 1783–1861

Wheildon, William W., *Memoir of Solomon Willard,* Boston, 1865.

CHAPTER FIVE: THE AGE OF ELEGANCE

THE SOCIAL, ARCHITECTURAL, AND HISTORICAL BACKGROUND

Adams, Henry, *Henry Adams and His Friends,* A Collection of His Unpublished Letters, compiled by Harold D. Cater, Boston, 1947.

——, *The Education of Henry Adams,* Boston, 1918.

Allen, Frederick L., *The Big Change,* New York, 1952.

Oakes Ames: A Memoir, Cambridge, 1884.

Andrews, Wayne, *The Vanderbilt Legend,* New York, 1941.

Balsan, Consuelo V., *The Glitter and the Gold,* New York, 1952.

Bourget, Paul, *Outre Mer: Impressions of America,* London, 1895.

Bunting, Bainbridge, *Houses of Boston's Back Bay,* Cambridge, 1967.

Castellane, Boni de, *Comment j'ai découvert l'Amérique,* Paris, 1924.

Clews, Henry, *Fifty Years in Wall Street,* New York, 1908.

Codman, Florence, *The Clever Young Boston Architect,* Augusta, 1970.

Cook, Clarence C., *The House Beautiful,* New York, 1878.

Cram, Ralph Adams, *My Life in Architecture,* Boston, 1936.

De Wolfe, Elsie, *The House in Good Taste,* New York, 1913.

Downey, Fairfax, *Portrait of an Era as Drawn by Charles Dana Gibson,* New York, 1936.

Doyle, Mary Virginia, "John Calvin Stevens in Pursuit of Art," unpublished master's essay, Brown University, 1957.

Eastlake, Charles L., *Hints on Household Taste,* Boston, 1876.

France, Jean R., et al., *A Rediscovery: Harvey Ellis, Artist and Architect,* Rochester, 1973.

James, Henry, *The American Scene,* New York, 1946.

———, *An International Episode,* New York, 1920.

———, *The Letters of Henry James,* edited by Percy Lubbock, 2 vols., New York, 1920.

Koch, Robert, ed., *Artistic America: Tiffany Glass and Art Nouveau Samuel Bing,* Cambridge, 1970.

McAllister, Ward, *Society As I Have Found It,* New York, 1890.

Maher, James T., *The Twilight of Splendor,* Boston, 1975.

Martin, Edward S., *The Life of Joseph Hodges Choate,* 2 vols., New York, 1920.

O'Gorman, James F., et al., eds., *The Architecture of Frank Furness,* Philadelphia, 1973.

Olwell, Carol, et al., *A Gift to the Street,* San Francisco, 1976.

Riis, Jacob, *How the Other Half Lives,* New York, 1890.

Roosevelt, Theodore, *An Autobiography,* New York, 1913.

Spencer, Herbert, *Social Statics,* New York, 1892.

Trollope, Anthony, *North America,* New York, 1951.

Van Brunt, Henry, *Architecture and Society: Selected Essays of Henry Van Brunt,* edited by William A. Coles, Cambridge, 1969.

Wecter, Dixon, *The Saga of American Society,* New York, 1937.

Wharton, Edith, *A Backward Glance,* New York, 1934.

———, *The House of Mirth,* New York, 1936.

———, and Codman, Ogden, *The Decoration of Houses,* New York, 1902.

Zaitzevski, Cynthia, *The Architecture of W. R. Emerson,* Cambridge, 1969.

The World of Henry Hobson Richardson, 1838–1886

Artistic Country Seats, 5 vols., New York, 1886.

Artistic Houses, 2 vols., New York, 1883–84.

Hitchcock, Henry Russell, *The Architecture of H. H. Richardson and His Times,* New York, 1936.

Richardson, H. H., *A Description of Trinity Church,* Boston, n.d.

Sturgis, Russell, et al., *Homes in City and Country,* New York, 1893.

Van Rensselaer, Marianna G., *Henry Hobson and His Works,* Boston, 1888.

————, "Recent American Architecture," *Century Magazine,* May, July, August, 1884, January, 1885, and February, March, May, and June, 1886.

McKim, Mead & White: Charles Follen McKim, 1847–1909; William Rutherford Mead, 1846–1928; and Stanford White, 1853–1906

Andrews, Wayne, "McKim, Mead & White: Their Mark Remains," *New York Times Magazine,* January 7, 1951.

————, *Mr. Morgan and His Architect,* New York, 1957.

————, "New York's Own Architects," *New-York Historical Society Quarterly,* January, 1951.

Baldwin, Charles C., *Stanford White,* New York, 1931.

Benjamin, S. G. W., "Steam Yachting in America," *Century Magazine,* August, 1882.

Blomfield, Sir Reginald, *Richard Norman Shaw,* London, 1940.

Chapman, John Jay, "McKim, Mead and White," *Vanity Fair,* September, 1919.

Granger, Alfred H., *Charles Follen McKim,* Boston, 1913.

Low, Will H., *A Chronicle of Friendships,* New York, 1908.

A Monograph on the Work of McKim, Mead & White, 4 vols., New York, 1925.

Moore, Charles, *Charles Follen McKim,* Boston, 1929.

Reilly, C. H., *McKim, Mead & White,* London, 1924.

St. Gaudens, Augustus, *The Reminiscences of Augustus St. Gaudens,* 2 vols., New York, 1913.

Scudder, Janet, *Modeling My Life,* New York, 1925.

Scully, Vincent J., Jr., *The Shingle Style: Architectural Theory and Design From Richardson to the Origins of Wright,* New Haven, 1955.

Sturgis, Russell, "The Works of McKim, Mead & White," *Architectural Record,* May, 1895.

White, Lawrence G., *Sketches and Designs by Stanford White,* New York, 1920.

Wight, Peter B., "Reminiscences of Russell Sturgis," *Architectural Record,* August, 1909.

Note: The archives of McKim, Mead & White may be consulted at the New-York Historical Society.

Richard Morris Hunt, 1827–1895

Burnham, Alan, "The New York Architecture of Richard Morris Hunt," *Journal of the Society of Architectural Historians,* May, 1952.

Schuyler, Montgomery, "The Works of the Late Richard Morris Hunt," *Architectural Record,* October–December, 1896.

Van Brunt, Henry, *Richard Morris Hunt: A Memorial Address,* Washington, 1896.

Van Pelt, J. V., *A Monograph of the W. K. Vanderbilt House,* New York, 1925.

GEORGE BROWNE POST, 1837–1913

Sturgis, Russell, "A Review of the Work of George B. Post," *Architectural Record,* June, 1898.

WILLIAM APPLETON POTTER, 1842–1909

Schuyler, Montgomery, "The Work of William Appleton Potter," *Architectural Record,* September, 1909.

BRUCE PRICE, 1845–1903

Sturgis, Russell, "The Works of Bruce Price," *Architectural Record,* June, 1899.

WILLIAM HALSEY WOOD, 1855–1897

Wood, Florence, *Memories of William Halsey Wood,* Philadelphia, 1938.
NOTE: His notebooks, sketches, etc. are now in the possession of the New-York Historical Society.

ERNEST FLAGG, 1857–1947

"The Works of Ernest Flagg," *Architectural Record,* April, 1902.

HORACE TRUMBAUER, 1868–1938

"A New Influence in the Architecture of Philadelphia," *Architectural Record,* February, 1904.
See also the sketch of Trumbauer by Wayne Andrews in the *Dictionary of American Biography.*

CARRÈRE & HASTINGS: JOHN MERVEN CARRÈRE, 1858–1911; AND THOMAS HASTINGS, 1860–1929

Gray, David, *Thomas Hastings, Architect,* Boston, 1933.
Hastings, Thomas, et al., *Six Lectures on Architecture,* Chicago, 1917.
Hotel Ponce de León, St. Augustine, n.d.
"The work of Messrs. Carrère & Hastings," *Architectural Record,* January, 1910.

CHARLES ADAMS PLATT, 1861–1933

Cortissoz, Royal, *Monograph of the Work of Charles A. Platt,* New York, 1913.
Croly, Herbert, "The Architectural Work of Charles A. Platt," *Architectural Record,* March, 1904.
Platt, Charles A., *Italian Gardens,* New York, 1894.

CHAPTER SIX: THE CHICAGO STORY

THE MIDWESTERN BACKGROUND

Andrews, Wayne, *Battle for Chicago*, New York, 1946.

Eaton, Leonard K., *Landscape Architect in America*, Chicago, 1964.

Fuller, Henry B., *The Chevalier of Penieri Vani*, New York, 1890.

————, *The Cliff Dwellers*, New York, 1893.

————, *Under the Skylights*, New York, 1901.

————, *With the Procession*, New York, 1895.

Herrick, Robert, *Memoirs of an American Citizen*, New York, 1905.

Lewis, Sinclair, *Main Street*, New York, 1920.

Norris, Frank, *The Pit*, New York, 1934.

JOHN WELLBORN ROOT, 1850–1891

Hoffmann, Donald, *The Architecture of John Wellborn Root*, Baltimore, 1973.

————, ed., *The Meanings of Architecture: Buildings and Writings by John W. Root*, New York, 1967.

Monroe, Harriet, *John Wellborn Root*, Boston, 1896.

DANIEL HUDSON BURNHAM, 1846–1912

Hines, Thomas S., *Burnham of Chicago*, New York, 1974.

Moore, Charles, *Daniel H. Burnham*, 2 vols., Boston, 1921.

THE EVOLUTION OF THE SKYSCRAPER AND OF AMERICAN ARCHITECTURE

Bragdon, Claude, "Harvey Ellis," *Architectural Review*, December, 1908.

Christison, Muriel B., "How Buffington Staked His Claim," *Art Bulletin*, March, 1944.

Condit, Carl W., *The Rise of the Skyscraper*, Chicago, 1952.

Early Modern Architecture, Museum of Modern Art, New York, 1940.

Eaton, Leonard K., *American Architecture Comes of Age*, Cambridge, 1972.

Raymond M. Hood, New York, 1931.

Morrison, Hugh S., "Buffington and the Invention of the Skyscraper," *Art Bulletin*, March, 1944.

Schuyler, Montgomery, "The Skyscraper Up to Date," *Architectural Record*, January–March, 1899.

Starrett, William A., *Skyscrapers and the Men Who Build Them*, New York, 1928.

Steinman, David B., *The Builders of the Bridge*, New York, 1945.

Swales, Francis S., "Harvey Ellis," *Pencil Points*, July, 1924.

Tallmadge, Thomas E., *Architecture in Old Chicago*, Chicago, 1941.

Tselos, Dimitri, "The Enigma of Buffington's Skyscraper," *Art Bulletin*, March 1944.

Upjohn, Everard M., "Buffington and the Skyscraper," *Art Bulletin*, March, 1935.

Weisman, Winston, "New York and the Problem of the First Skyscraper," *Journal of the Society of Architectural Historians*, March, 1953.

————, "Slab Buildings," *Architectural Review*, February, 1952.

————, "Towards a New Environment," *Architectural Review*, December, 1950.

Whitaker, Charles H., ed., *Bertram Grosvenor Goodhue: Architect and Master of Many Arts*, New York, 1925.

THE WORLD'S FAIR OF 1893

Schuyler, Montgomery, "Last Words About the World's Fair," *Architectural Record*, December, 1893.

Tunnard, Christopher, *The City of Man*, New York, 1953.

LOUIS HENRI SULLIVAN, 1856–1924

Adler, Dankmar, "The Chicago Auditorium," *Architectural Record*, June, 1892.

Connel, Willard, *Louis Sullivan: A Biography*, New York, 1971.

Hope, Henry R., "Louis Sullivan's Architectural Ornament," *Magazine of Art*, March, 1947.

Morrison, Hugh S., *Louis Sullivan*, New York, 1935.

Schuyler, Montgomery, "A Critique of the Works of Adler & Sullivan, D. H. Burnham & Co., and Henry Ives Cobb," *Architectural Record*, 1896.

Sullivan, Louis H., *The Autobiography of an Idea*, New York, 1949.

————, *Democracy*, Detroit, 1961.

————, *Kindergarten Chats*, New York, 1947.

————, *A System of Architectural Ornament*, New York, 1924.

THE CHICAGO SCHOOL

Birrell, James, *Walter Burley Griffin, Architect*, Saint Lucia, 1964.

Brooks, H. Allen, *The Prairie School*, Toronto, 1972.

Gebhard, David, *Architecture of Purcell and Elmslie*, Palos Park, 1974.

————, et al., *Architecture of Minnesota*, Minneapolis, 1977.

Johnson, Donald Leslie, *The Architecture of Walter Burley Griffin*, South Melbourne, 1977.

Peisch, Mark L., *The Chicago School of Architecture*, New York, 1964.

The complete file of *The Prairie School Review*, 1964–, is essential.

THE WORLD OF FRANK LLOYD WRIGHT, 1867–1959

Andrews, Wayne, "Looking at the Latest of Frank Lloyd Wright," *Perspectives USA*, Summer, 1953.

Clark, Robert J., *Arts and Crafts Movement in America 1876–1916*, Princeton, 1972.

Drexler, Arthur, ed., *The Drawings of Frank Lloyd Wright*, New York, 1962.

Eaton, Leonard K., *Two Chicago Architects and Their Clients: Frank Lloyd Wright and Howard Van Doren Shaw*, Cambridge, 1969.

Farr, Finis, *Frank Lloyd Wright,* New York, 1961.

Gannett, William C., *The House Beautiful,* Park Forest, 1963.

Hitchcock, Henry Russell, *In the Nature of Materials 1887–1941: The Buildings of Frank Lloyd Wright,* New York, 1942.

Manson, Grant C., *Frank Lloyd Wright to 1910,* New York, 1958.

Sergeant, John, *Frank Lloyd Wright's Usonian Houses,* New York, 1976.

Shay, Felix, *Elbert Hubbard of East Aurora,* New York, 1926.

Storrer, William A., *Architecture of Frank Lloyd Wright,* New York, 1974.

Tselos, Dimitri, "Exotic Influences in the Work of Frank Lloyd Wright," *Magazine of Art,* April, 1953.

Twombly, Robert, *Frank Lloyd Wright: An Interpretive Biography,* New York, 1973.

Wijderveld, H. T., ed., *The Work of Frank Lloyd Wright,* New York, 1962.

Wright, John Lloyd, *My Father Who Is on Earth,* New York, 1946.

Wright, Frank Lloyd, *An Autobiography,* New York, 1932.

————, *Drawings for a Living Architecture,* New York, 1959.

————, *Frank Lloyd Wright on Architecture,* edited by Frederick Gutheim, New York, 1941.

————, *The Future of Architecture,* New York, 1953.

————, *Genius and the Mobocracy,* New York, 1949.

————, *The Living City,* New York, 1958.

————, *The Natural House,* New York, 1954.

————, *A New House on Bear Run, Pennsylvania, by Frank Lloyd Wright,* New York, 1938.

————, *The Story of the Tower,* New York, 1956.

————, *Taliesin Drawings,* New York, 1952.

————, *A Testament,* New York, 1931.

CHAPTER SEVEN: MODERN TIMES

MODERN TIMES

Banham, Reyner, *Theory and Design in the First Machine Age,* New York, 1960.

Behrendt, Walter C., *Modern Building: Its Nature, Problems and Forms,* New York, 1937.

Blake, Peter, *The Master Builders,* New York, 1960.

Cook, John W., et al., eds., *Conversations with Architects,* New York, 1973.

Cram, Ralph Adams, *My Life in Architecture,* Boston, 1936.

Creese, Walter L., *The Legacy of Raymond Unwin: A Human Pattern for Planning,* Cambridge, 1967.

————, *The Search for Environment: The Garden City Before and After,* New Haven, 1966.

Eaton, Leonard K., *American Architecture Comes of Age,* Cambridge, 1972.

Giedion, Sigfried, *Space, Time and Architecture,* Cambridge, 1947.

Hitchcock, Henry Russell, *Architecture: 19th and 20th Centuries,* Baltimore, 1958.

———, *Modern Architecture: Romanticism and Reintegration,* New York, 1929.

———, and Drexler, Arthur, *Built in USA: Post War Architecture,* New York, 1952.

———, and Johnson, Philip C., *The International Style: Architecture Since 1922,* New York, 1932.

Jones, Cranston, *Architecture Today and Tomorrow,* New York, 1961.

Kulka, H., *Adolf Loos,* Vienna, 1931.

Loos, Adolf, *Trotzdem,* Vienna, 1931.

Lurçat, André, *Architecture,* Paris, 1929.

Mock, Elizabeth, ed., *Built in USA—Since 1932,* New York, 1945.

Mumford, Lewis, ed., *Roots of Contemporary American Architecture,* New York, 1952.

Pevsner, Sir Nikolaus, *Pioneers of Modern Design,* New York, 1949.

Richards, J. M., *An Introduction to Modern Architecture,* Harmondsworth, 1940.

Robinson, Cervin, et al., *Skyscraper Style: Art Design New York,* New York. 1975.

Scully, Vincent, Jr., *American Architecture and Urbanism,* New York, 1969.

Soleri, Paolo, *The City in the Image of Man,* Cambridge, 1969.

———, *The Sketchbooks of Paolo Soleri,* Cambridge, 1971.

Venturi, Robert, *Complexity and Contradiction in Architecture,* New York, 1966.

———, et al., *Learning from Las Vegas,* Cambridge, 1972.

Zevi, Bruno, *Storia dell'Architettura Moderna,* n.p., 1953.

THE THOUGHT OF WILLIAM JAMES

James, William, *Essays in Radical Empiricism,* New York, 1912.

———, *Human Immortality: Two Supposed Objections to the Doctrine,* Boston, 1898.

———, *The Letters of William James,* edited by his son Henry James, 2 vols., Boston, 1920.

———, *The Meaning of Truth,* New York, 1925.

———, *Memories and Studies,* New York, 1911.

———, *A Pluralistic Universe,* New York, 1909.

———, *Pragmatism: A New Name for Some Old Ways of Thinking,* New York, 1907.

———, *The Varieties of Religious Experience,* New York, 1936.

———, *On Vital Reserves,* New York, 1922.

———, *The Will to Believe,* New York, 1897.

Morris, Lloyd, *William James,* New York, 1950.

Perry, Ralph B., *The Thought and Character of William James,* 2 vols., Boston, 1935.

The Thought of Thorstein Veblen

Dorfman, Joseph, *Thorstein Veblen and His America,* New York, 1934.

Riesman, David, *Thorstein Veblen,* New York, 1953.

Veblen, Thorstein, *Absentee Ownership and Business Enterprise in Recent Times,* New York, 1923.

———, *The Engineers and the Price System,* New York, 1921.

———, *Essays in Our Changing Order,* New York, 1934.

———, *The Higher Learning in America,* New York, 1918.

———, *Imperial Germany and the Industrial Revolution,* New York, 1915.

———, *The Instinct of Workmanship,* New York, 1914.

———, *The Place of Science in Modern Civilization,* New York, 1919.

———, *The Theory of Business Enterprise,* New York, 1935.

———, *The Theory of the Leisure Class,* New York, 1934.

California: Promise and Performance

Aidala, Thomas, and Bruce, Curt, *The Great Houses of San Francisco,* New York, 1974.

Baird, Joseph A., Jr., *Times' Wondrous Changes,* San Francisco, 1962.

Gallion, Arthur B., *A Guide to Contemporary Architecture in Southern California,* Los Angeles, 1951.

Gebhard, David, et al., *A Guide to Architecture in San Francisco and Northern California,* Santa Barbara, 1973.

———, *A Guide to Architecture in Southern California,* Los Angeles, 1964.

———, *Kem Weber and the Moderne,* Santa Barbara, 1969.

———, *Lloyd Wright,* Santa Barbara, Los Angeles, 1972.

———, *Los Angeles in the 1930s,* Santa Barbara, 1976.

Kirker, Harold, *California's Architectural Frontier,* San Marino, 1960.

McCoy, Esther, *Five California Architects,* New York, 1960.

Olmsted, Roger, et al., *Here Today: San Francisco's Architectural Heritage,* San Francisco, 1968.

Woodbridge, Sally, et al., *Bay Area Houses,* New York, 1976.

Marcel Breuer, 1902–

Blake, Peter, *Marcel Breuer,* New York, 1949.

Le Corbusier (Charles-Edouard Jeanneret-Gris), 1887–1965

Jeanneret-Gris, Charles-Edouard, *Une Maison—un Palais,* Paris, 1928.

———, *Oeuvre Complète,* 5 vols., Zurich, 1946–53.

———, *Précisions sur l'Etat Présent de l'Architecture et de l'Urbanisme,* Paris, 1930.

————, *Quand les Cathédrales étaient blanches,* Paris, 1937.

————,*Vers une Architecture,* Paris, 1923.

CHARLES SUMNER GREENE, 1868–1957, AND HENRY MATHER GREENE, 1870?–1954

Bangs, Jean M., "Greene and Greene," *Architectural Forum,* October, 1948.

————, "Prophet Without Honor," *House Beautiful,* May, 1950.

Current, William R., and Current, Karen, *Greene and Greene: Architects in the Residential Style,* Fort Worth, 1974.

Makinson, Randall L., *A Guide to the Work of Greene and Greene,* Salt Lake City, 1974.

"New Appreciation of Greene and Greene," *Architectural Record,* March, 1949.

Strand, Janaan, *A Greene and Greene Guide,* Pasadena, 1974.

WALTER GROPIUS, 1883–1969

Bayer, Herbert, et al., eds., *Bauhaus 1919–28,* New York, 1938.

Giedion, Sigfried, *Walter Gropius Work and Teamwork,* New York, 1954.

Gropius, Walter, *The New Architecture and the Bauhaus,* New York, 1937.

————, *Scope of Total Architecture,* New York, 1955.

Wingler, Hans, ed., *Das Bauhaus,* Bramsche, 1962.

HARWELL HAMILTON HARRIS, 1903–

Harris, Harwell H., *A Collection of His Writings and Buildings,* Raleigh, 1965.

————, "How a House Can Enrich the Life Within," *House Beautiful,* May, 1953.

PHILIP C. JOHNSON, 1906–

Hitchcock, Henry Russell, *Philip Johnson, 1949–65,* New York, 1966.

ALBERT KAHN, 1869–1942

Ferry, W. Hawkins, ed., *The Legacy of Albert Kahn,* Detroit, 1970.

Nelson, George, *The Industrial Architecture of Albert Kahn,* New York, 1939.

LOUIS I. KAHN, 1901–1974

Giurgola, Romaldo, and Mehta, Jaimini, *Louis I. Kahn,* Boulder, 1975.

Scully, Vincent, Jr., *Louis I. Kahn,* New York, 1962.

BERNARD R. MAYBECK, 1862–1957

Bangs, Jean M., "Bernard Ralph Maybeck, Architect, Comes Into His Own," *Architectural Record,* January, 1948.

Cardwell, Kenneth H., *Bernard Maybeck,* Santa Barbara, 1977.

Maybeck, Bernard R., "Selections from the Writings of This Year's Gold Medalist," *Journal of the American Institute of Architects,* May, 1951.

LUDWIG MIËS VAN DER ROHE, 1886–1969

Johnson, Philip C., *Miës van der Rohe,* New York, 1953.

Mizner, Addison, 1872–1933

Johnston, Alva, "The Palm Beach Architect," *The New Yorker*, November 22 and 29, December 6 and 13, 1952.

Orr, Christina, *Addison Mizner, Architect of Dreams and Realities*, Palm Beach, 1977.

Tarbell, Ida M., *The Florida Architecture of Addison Mizner*, New York, 1928.

Moore, Charles Willard, 1925–

Bloomer, Kent, and Moore, Charles W., *Body, Memory and Architecture*, New Haven, 1977.

Moore, Charles W., et al., *The Place of Houses*, New York, 1974.

Richard J. Neutra, 1892–1970

Boesiger, W., ed., *Richard Neutra: Buildings and Projects*, Zurich, 1951.

McCoy, Esther, *Richard Neutra*, New York, 1960.

Neutra, Richard J., *Amerika*, Vienna, 1930.

———, *Life and Human Habitat*, New York, 1956.

———, *Mystery and Realities of the Site*, Scarsdale, 1951.

———, *Survival Through Design*, New York, 1954.

———, *Wie Baut Amerika?* Stuttgart, 1927.

Paul M. Rudolph, 1919–

Moholy-Nagy, Sybil, *The Architecture of Paul Rudolph*, New York, 1970.

Eero Saarinen, 1910–1961

Saarinen, Aline, ed., *Eero Saarinen on His Work*, New Haven, 1962.

Temko, Allan, *Eero Saarinen*, New York, 1962.

Eliel Saarinen, 1873–1950

Booth, Henry S., ed., *The Saarinen Door*, Bloomfield Hills, 1963.

Christ-Janer, Albert, *Eliel Saarinen*, Chicago, 1948.

Rivard, Nancy, "Eliel Saarinen in America," unpublished master's thesis, Wayne State University, 1973.

See also the sketch of Eliel Saarinen by Wayne Andrews in the *Dictionary of American Biography*.

Rudolph M. Schindler, 1890–1953

Gebhard, David, *Schindler*, New York, 1971.

Schindler, Rudolph M., *Collected Papers*, mimeographed, n.d., in the library of The New-York Historical Society.

William Wilson Wurster, 1895–1973

McCoy, Esther, "William Wilson Wurster," *Arts and Architecture*, July, 1964.

Wurster, William W., "Architectural Education," *Journal of the American Institute of Architects,* January, 1948.

———, "The Architectural Life," *Architectural Record,* January, 1951.

———, "The Outdoors in Residential Design," *Architectural Forum,* September, 1949.

———, "San Francisco Bay Portfolio," *Magazine of Art,* December, 1944.

Index

There are separate headings for banks, capitols (including state houses), churches, college buildings (including schools), court houses, city halls, hospitals, and prisons.

Other Books by the Author

Pride of the South: A Social History of Southern Architecture (to be published early 1979)

Architecture in America, Revised Edition, 1977

American Gothic, 1975

Architecture in New England, 1973

Siegfried's Curse: The German Journey from Nietzsche to Hesse, 1972

Architecture in New York, 1969

Architecture in Chicago and Mid-America, 1968

Architecture in Michigan, 1967

Germaine: A Portrait of Madame de Staël, 1963

Best Short Stories of Edith Wharton (Editor), 1958

Who Has Been Tampering with These Pianos? (under the pseudonym of Montagu O'Reilly), 1948

Battle for Chicago, 1946

The Vanderbilt Legend, 1941